New Studies on Lex Regia

Studies in Early Modern European Culture
Studi sulla cultura europea della prima età moderna

Vol. 5

Edited by
Paolo L. Bernardini & Laura Orsi

PETER LANG
Bern · Berlin · Bruxelles · Frankfurt am Main · New York · Oxford · Wien

Fabrizio Lomonaco

New Studies on Lex Regia

Right, Philology and Fides Historica in Holland Between the 17th and 18th Centuries

PETER LANG
Bern · Berlin · Bruxelles · Frankfurt am Main · New York · Oxford · Wien

Bibliographic information published by Die Deutsche Nationalbibliothek
Die Deutsche Nationalbibliothek lists this publication in the Deutsche Nationalbibliografie; detailed bibliographic data is available on the Internet at ‹http://dnb.d-nb.de›.

British Library and Library of Congress Cataloguing-in-Publication Data:
A catalogue record for this book is available from The British Library.

Library of Congress Cataloging-in-Publication Data

Lomonaco, Fabrizio.
New studies on lex regia : right, philology, and fides historica in Holland between the 17th and 18th centuries / Fabrizio Lomonaco.
p. cm. – (Studies in early modern european culture, ISSN 1661-0555 = Studi sulla cultura europea della prima età moderna ; v. 5)
Includes bibliographical references (p.) and index.
ISBN 978-3-0343-0543-3
1. Lex de imperio Vespasiani. 2. Executive power–Rome. 3. Roman law–Influence. 4. Law–Netherlands–Roman influences. 5. Law–Netherlands–History–18th century. 6. Law–Netherlands–History–17th century. I. Title.
KJA245.L66 2011
349.49209'032–dc22

2011009918

This publication uses of a contribution of the MIUR (cofinanced project PRIN 2008) and of the University of the Studies in Naples Federico II, Dept. of Philosophy "A. Aliotta".

Cover illustration: *old books*, from iStockphoto.com © by Gilmanshin.

ISSN 1661-0555
ISBN 978-3-0343-0543-3

Hochfeldstrasse 32, CH-3012 Bern, Switzerland
info@peterlang.com, www.peterlang.com, www.peterlang.net

Printed in Switzerland

To my mother, *Clara Fallace*,
with deep gratitude
for all that her lively and smart presence
she gifted me with

Contents

Acknowledgements

In the years of study devoted to this research I have incurred several debts of acknowledgement. In the first place towards the Directors of the Asser Instituut (The Hague), the Bibliothèque Nationale (Paris), the Cambridge University Library, the Fryske Akademy (Leeuwarden), the 'Gerard Noodt' Instituut (Nijmegen), the Grotiana Foundation and the Koninklijke Bibliotheek (The Hague), the Archivi di Stato of Florence, the Biblioteche Nazionali of Florence, Naples and Venice, the University Libraries of Amsterdam, Genoa, Leyden, Munich, Naples and Utrecht, the Ecole Française, of the Biblioteca Vallicelliana and the Dutch Institute of Rome, the Institutes of Art and Culture in Forli, the Italian Institute for Historical Studies of Naples. All without exception but with extreme courtesy and helpfulness responded to my continuous requests for information and documents.

To Professors G.C.J.J. van den Bergh di Nijmegen, S.E.W. Bugter of the "Gymnasium Bernrode" (Heeswijk-Dinther), P. Dibon of the Ecole Pratique des Hautes Etudes (Paris), A.C. 't Hart of the Rijksuniversiteit (Leyden), J.H. Meter of La Sapienza University (Rome) and Stolte jr. of the Rijksuniversiteit (Groningen), experts of Netherlands culture, I am indebted for their kind suggestions and essential bibliographical indications.

Heartfelt thanks are extended to Professors Raffaele Ajello, Fiorella De Michelis Pintacuda, Giuseppe Giarrizzo and Maurizio Torrini for reading the typescript and for giving me invaluable advice regarding method and content.

I would like to thank Leon Pompa for his useful comment on the first version of this work and for correcting the English of the text.

A special debt of gratitude is to be bestowed on my friends Professors Giuseppe Cacciatore, Enrico Nuzzo and Gianni Paganini who have followed and encouraged the research developments with their kind patience, constantly providing me with their invaluable support.

My studies owe an even greater debt to the constant and affectionate guidance of my magister Professor Fulvio Tessitore for his lessons intellectually rigorous-albeit liberal in their genesis and development, than I am able herein to express.

It seems to me right, besides being deeply felt, that I have chosen to renew the dedication made eighteen years ago to my mother who, over the years, I have had the privilege of watching grow old with dignity, with her unchanging capacity to love and to suffer solely through love.

F. L.

Naples, 16 March 2010

Preface

In the essays in this volume, Fabrizio Lomonaco continues to present the results of his immaculate and highly sensitive research into the thought of a series of comparatively neglected late eighteenth century Dutch thinkers, some of the earlier parts of which were published in his *Tolleranza e libertà di coscienza* (Naples, 1999). The questions with which these thinkers were concerned centred round producing a historical methodology and canons of critical interpretation adequate to understanding and benefiting from the nature and authority of the traditions of sovereignty contained within and transmitted by the great texts of Roman law. The enormous political and religious uncertainties that followed the problems faced in Britain by the Stuarts and in Holland by the absolutist House of Orange, raised questions about the legitimacy and limits of claims to sovereignty in general, to which the political theories of Grotius, Pufendorf, Hobbes, Locke and many others offered different solutions, legitimising different kinds of arrangements. In this situation the problem of how to interpret and assess the value of the heritage of Roman law became acute. The four Dutch thinkers with whom Lomonaco is primarily concerned here, Gronovius, Perizonius, Ulrik Huber and Gerard Noodt, were all in their way disciples of Grotius but, because of Grotius's great fame, they have generally been regarded as `pale imitations' of the great philosopher of natural right. But, as Lomonaco shows, even if their work never achieved the fame of their great master, each was, in his own way, particularly given the different problems with which he had to contend, a considerable thinker.

Although Vico does not figure as a direct and important influence on these thinkers, though there are many affinities between him and them, Lomonaco commences by mentioning one of those ironies with which history often presents us, and, if I may add, one of those misfortunes which attended almost every aspect of Vico's life. It is well known that it is to Croce that we owe the beginnings of the modern growth of interest in Vico. But Croce's Vico was an early idealist, thus finding his historical place in a line of eschatological philosophers of history leading to Hegel and Marx, a kind of philosophy of history which has now lost its appeal, leading to Vico's comparative neglect. But, having aroused interest in Vico among Italian scholars, many aspects of Croce's interpretation have now come to be criticised by those first inspired by it, to the extent that Vico's interests in critical philology, historical methodology, and the correct interpretation of Roman law, have come to be seen as central to his concerns and to place him, together with the relatively obscure thinkers and sources he cites, in a different historical tradition, that with which the present studies are concerned and which Niebuhr did so much to develop.

As Lomonaco shows in masterly detail, the cultural and historical context in which Grotius's followers found themselves had already changed. There was little agreement among scholars as to how to interpret the great texts of Roman law upon which Grotius had laboured, while Cartesian scepticism had led to parallel developments in historical Pyrrhonism. The *Lex Regia De Imperio Vespasiani*, with which Lomonaco's scholars were concerned, serves as an important exemplar of the way in which philological research, interpretation of the nature of Roman law and the political conclusions to be drawn from them, came together. On the one hand, there were those who claimed that there had never been such a law, despite the discovery of part of a bronze plaque which appeared to refer to it. Then, of those who accepted that there had been such a law, some claimed that it revealed that the powers therein ascribed to Vespasian were powers that devolved upon all emperors by right of the legitimacy of the sovereignty that Roman law conferred of itself on all legally installed emperors. Then, again, there were others who argued that these powers did not devolve upon the emperors in virtue of the authority of Roman law alone but powers that needed to be conferred upon each new emperor upon the occasion of his instalment, thus shifting the basis of the legitimacy of these powers back to the people who temporarily conferred them.

To Gronovius belongs the honour of clarifying this confusing situation. A much travelled and widely admired scholar, he realised that jurisprudential issues such as these could not be resolved on the basis of hypotheses alone and that any acceptable result must relate jurisprudential interpretation to historical fact. Hence the need for a critical historical methodology, involving a sophisticated philology, based on miniscule knowledge of the texts and their histories, and psychological assessments of the motives of their producers and, later, their glossators. How he thus brought jurisprudential interpretation and historical fact to bear upon each other and the conclusions he reached on the substantial point at issue, I leave the reader to discover in detail.

Ulrik Huber was another thinker with a grounding in rhetoric, judicial and political study, who wanted to bring order and certainty into the interpretation of the whole corpus of judicial disciplines, the authority of which, based on the assumption that the Holy Roman Empire had had a continuous career throughout the Middle Ages, was threatened by the discovery of new French and German texts. Like Gronovius, he saw the importance of connecting juridical interpretation with historical fact. The *Lex Regia* was again an important test case since the Pyrrhonist, Martin Schoockius, had published a work denouncing it as a figment invented by Tribonianus to justify Justinian's power and was prepared to cast similar doubt on almost all the other rights protected in the Digest. But by using reputable historical sources – in particular, Suetonius, Dio Cassius and Tacitus –

Huber was able to show that the *Lex* was an authentic Roman document, attesting to the fact that the prerogatives of the emperors were based upon a tradition going back to Augustus, but limiting their sovereignty to actions laid down in law. In all this, Huber remained dose to Grotius's conception of natural rights, but alter the Treaty of Westphalia had thrown the whole question of the basis and limits of sovereignty into confusion he found himself, though no philosopher, drawn into the debate how best, and on what basis, to preserve Grotius's natural rights within society. Here he diverged from Grotius and sided with Hobbes, particularly on the point that every strict right implied a power of coercion, executable ultimately by force. If the sovereign's right is the power to make people obey him, then it cannot be transmittable by him to the people since he would lack the power to do so. But Huber modified this harsh doctrine by limiting the sovereign's power to that of protecting the people, since, again, the sovereign would lack the power to enforce upon the people actions contrary to their protection. It is not difficult to see here what Huber had gained from his study of Roman law.

Huber's approach to historical fact was further developed by another learned philologist, Perizonius, even though he disagreed with Huber's conditioned absolutism and argued for a more democratic system. But Perizonius's main contribution to the debate over historical fact was to seek to find a secure basis for the certainty of historical facts, singular though they be, that could aspire, in their specific field of enquiry, to standards of rigour thought to be achieved in Cartesian thought, facts to which of course, Cartesian method was not applicable. Rejecting mere acceptance of former histories and, similarly, the sweeping rejection of all histories, as found in many works by La Mothe le Vayer, he sought a half way house between blind faith and sweeping scepticism, by basing the reliability of historical belief on probability or verisimilitude. Bayle was, of course, a major background figure to these complicated debates between sceptics and libertines on the one hand and these humanist historians on the other. But Bayle's sceptical position, Perizonius argued, depended on a demand for standards of proof in areas where they could not be reached and, as such, they could not serve to justify a wholesale refusal to assess critically even such potentially tendentious sources as, for example, the memoires of Popes. The probability of each potential historical fact had to be assessed in its own right, by methods proper to the matter in question.

Lomonaco's fourth author is the even less well known Gerard Noodt, whose interests were more strongly in the political issues at stake. Influenced first by Pufendorf and then by Locke, he moved from an absolutist to a consensual view of the foundations of sovereignty. In support of this he reverted to the authority of Roman law and to the *Lex Regia* in particular, which, he claimed, was a periodical law, proposed to each emperor once and once only, and conferring upon him powers that other emperors had gathered along the way. So the emperor's sovereignty was limited by a specific deed and not by some general law of sovereignty. A particularity could not be grounds for a general principal. This meant that Noodt had to dispute Grotius's reading of the *Lex* which, supported by an appeal to the evidence of the reputable Dio Cassius, Grotius had used to provide a historical basis with which to argue for the absolute autonomy of sovereignty. Noodt refuted this interpretation by critica) use of a much wider range of sources, including Ulpian and beyond. For Noodt, the people, then, were the possessors of sovereignty, thus retaining the right to oppose tyrants who used their conferred powers for their own ends rather than for safeguarding those of the people. This represented an important turning point in the development of jusnaturalism. For in ancient jusnaturalism laws were imposed differently on different orders of men but now in modern natural right theory, it appeared as the right of all men to be respected in their individuality.

Lomonaco's superb studies raise an important further question, which he touches on without elaboration. One can see, within the confines of this work, that major questions about political sovereignty were raised by these highly skilled Dutch scholars, utilising older traditions as a source for reflection on current problems and reaching conclusions of continuing relevance. But why, then, with the partial exception of some of the historically important giants in these fields, did their work come to be neglected until Niebuhr made its rediscovery so important? The answer to which Lomonaco points lies in the further irony that the Dutch thinkers were so concerned with the methodological problems involved in our entitlement to have confidence in particular historical facts against the claims of historical Pyrrhonism, that, though their victory over historical Pyrrhonism made possible the 'philosophical' histories of the Enlightenment, those of Vico, Gibbon, Montesquieu and others up to Winckelmann, the focus of interest had then turned to broader cultural themes, such as art, religion and custom, to which the precise philological labours and interests required to defeat historical Pyrrhonism seemed irrelevant. How this should have occurred, and given the range of his historical and analytical abilities, is something we can hope to learn from Lomonaco's continuing researches in this area.

Leon Pompa

Introduction

The studies brought together in this volume represent but a first part of the research the present writer has either already got under way or has planned to complete with regard to certain thematic 'areas' that are crucial for the historical and philosophical culture of Europe between the seventeenth and eighteenth centuries. In this paper the critical analysis of this culture takes place within the Dutch juridical and philosophical setting, which is but seldom ever examined by traditional and even less so by Italian historiography for reasons well known: at the beginning of the 20th century interest in the seventeenth-eighteenth century world was so markedly affected by the great Vico-centred debate that numerous study profiles were influenced by its outcomes.

Croce's well-known picture of Vico as being "né più né meno che il secolo decimonono in germe" had finished up by setting his work both against and outside his own century. The more positively the claim for the solitary genius of the author of the *New Science* was established among historians and philosophers, the more diminished and paler appeared his interlocutors, both direct and indirect ones alike. European culture, which in its essential features appeared abstractedly rationalistic between the 17th and 18th centuries had erred either in not recognizing itself in Vico or in not attempting to appreciate his doctrine. Nowadays no one could fail to recognize the biased character of this interpretation enveloped as it is in too rarefied an atmosphere and incapable of grasping the complexity of historic-cultural phenomena both in and around Vico. The same may be said with regard to that historicist 'realism' the neo-idealistic school relates to. The latter both desired to and succeeded in bestowing a new dignity on historical studies, as well as a new sense of criticism on Viconian studies, which had been lost sight of by the earlier abstract generalizations of positivist analysis. In reducing philosophy to a theory of historical judgment to a methodological instance of historiography, and inspired by Vico's uniting philosophy with philology, Croce had postulated uniting philosophy with historiography which did not differ in method but only in content. And not only: in distinguishing *res gestae* from *historia rerum gestarum* and by ascribing importance to the history of historiography that aimed at clarifying and articulating that distinction, he transmitted to historical studies – as has been rightly observed – the discovery of the great critical experience of modern philology, understood in the Viconian sense as the new science of history[1].

The outcome of this critico-methodological re-appraisal at the historiographical level was presently to lay down the premises for revising judgment on Vico, almost without intending to do so. Following in the wake of Croce and with investigations both overtly and indirectly proposed and encouraged by the author of *La Filosofia di G.B. Vico,* distinguished scholars including Gentile, Nicolini, Corsano, Cortese, De Ruggiero and Fubini set about studying the philosopher's "biography" in detail, that is to say they began to observe Vico in his own day, in se and per se, examining all his personal features as well as his cultural and political milieu, thereby either toning down or fully, yet unconsciously going so far beyond Croce's interpretation, as has been perceptively observed, that "l'erudizione di Nicolini implica, senza volerlo, la smentita di quanto è tenacemente di Spaventa nelle proposte critiche della storiografia idealistica"[2]. Hence, later expert criticism, and more so Italian criticism, has not made *tabula rasa* of the neo-idealistic interpretation, but rather by taking account of the results achieved, has resumed the discussion

1 CANTIMORI (1966) 1971, pp. 406–409.
2 PIOVANI 1969 [1990], p. 73.

on the sources and the European cultural climate prior to and contemporary with Vico with appropriate documentation, yet at the same time has been extremely careful not to attempt theoretical syntheses, but rather to elaborate philologically-guided analyses by focusing on a comprehensive picture of Italian and European history, as well as on relationships that may be traced from the ideas that were circulating at that time. Nor has this objective meant putting forward any claim for historiography as a mere accumulation of data with no control over the pre-established selection and investigation criteria. Such is a misinterpretation that has in fact risked distorting Vico's highly varied and complex thought profile and its achievement forever. It is also useful to observe that the rightful task of re-assessing Vico's *solitude* has been got underway and developed with critical caution so as not to fall in the opposite error to the one just indicated, namely that of equating modern seventeenth-eighteenth century philosophy with Vico's. The crucial need to rectify traditional interpretation by emphasizing the close associations linking the Neapolitan philosopher with his times must not become a pretext for original and highly attractive, yet equally contrived comparisons. Setting Vico free from the historiographical framework that candidates him as Kant's and Hegel's predecessor does not mean enveloping him in yet another equally suffocating set project that aspires to derive the genesis of the culture of his day from various aspects of his reflections. To do so Vico would lose his most original and intransigent physiognomy that he was to regain when ceasing to be romantic, only to founder in the vast sea of the seventeenth-eighteenth-century world. Rather, the problem is to measure the differences, to regulate interpretation methods that are badly controlled in a critical sense. Thus Viconian studies of the last few decades initially aspired to be principally historico-philological prior to being "philosophical". With all the debts to Croce and his school's commitment duly acknowledged, this dimension may nowadays be considered sufficiently well met by the more authoritative expressions of what has been defined as the "new course" of Viconian studies, implemented and promoted in 1968 by the initiatives introduced to celebrate the third centenary from the philosopher's birth. With the problems and concerns that had fired the neo-idealistic formulae now solved, investigations were carried out which by encouraging contacts also among different cultural experiences have contributed towards establishing further historical and erudite forms of knowledge by transforming obsolete exegetic approaches into fundamental values and theses. What was introduced by such a radical re-appraisal with all the critico-philological difficulties and questions it implied is a Vico translated immediately and indirectly into the history of his own times, a Vico introduced through the culture that went before him, with motives and interests that were subsequently re-elaborated, and indeed transformed by his powerful philosophical genius.

Research aimed more seriously at showing that the significance and extent of such hermeneutic innovation has been biased towards the problems relating to the erudition and antiquarian studies of the Viconian age. Issues introduced and for the most part discussed by the well-known useful contributions made by Arnaldo Momigliano[3], who by establishing the characteristics and limitations of the philosopher's knowledge of antiquity in the light of the differences encountered between central-northern Italian culture and those of the south, has helped to reveal certain invaluable testimonies that are able to document Vico's contemporaries' main interests and, indirectly his own complex originality, thereby stimulating further enquiry and study. Indeed this examination sufficed to shed further light on many obscure areas and identify analogies and new relation-

3 See MOMIGLIANO (1965) 1980, pp. 191–210 and MOMIGLIANO (1966) 1984, pp. 204–229.

ships, and prevent traditional hypotheses and texts from being simply proposed anew. Thus, the study of 'Pre-Vicoism' and Vico's early years has become the starting point for further investigations into European historico-philosophical activity between the seventeenth and eighteenth centuries. What went before Vico has helped for example, to gain a better insight into Grotius, his fourth "auttore", who has already received highly-focused attention but who still merits even further examination. Explicit confirmation of this are the basic works of 'pre-Vicoism' scholars, including De Giovanni, Badaloni, Mastellone and Comparato who have clearly pointed out the significance and extent of the contribution that might be made to the formation of Viconian thought through contacts with Grotian ideas that were rife throughout late 17th century Naples. Badaloni's *Introduzione a G. B. Vico* is thus also an introduction to "filosofia civile napoletana" which, being a product of "filosofia della natura", served its apprenticeship under Ugo Grotius's natural law whose humanism made the Neapolitan philosopher side "con coloro che credono possibile nella pacifica Napoli, strappare almeno sul piano della cultura quelle libertà che Batavi ed Angli alleati della Spagna, avevano già messo in atto, e che viceré spagnoli, avendo compreso la situazione, non disdegnavano di limitatamente favorire"[4].

Within this thematic perspective also feature the origins of Vico's interests developed by Giuseppe Giarrizzo, a leading expert in historico-historiographic culture between the seventeenth and eighteenth centuries and in problems regarding historical method posed and addressed by antiquity studies and Pyrrhonist criticism. In an extensive 1968 study devoted to *Vico's Politics,* which is one of the more representative works of the "new course" of Viconian studies, the Sicilian historian with

4 BADALONI 1961, pp. 227, 310; on this pages see the critic position of FASSÒ 1971, pp. 28ff.

his precise demonstrative rigour documented the thesis he asserted of the considerable political proposal of Vico's reflection which contrasts sharply with the Crociano-Nicolinian arguments on Vico's political indifference, and all of which was coherently contained within the pacific linear process of his theoretical development culminating in the 1744 *New Science*. This in contrast, follows a line of forward development only from the *Inaugural Orations* up to the *Universal Right* , until the " 'crisi' del 1723, che inaugura con la *Scienza Nuova Prima* (1725) uno spostamento significativo nella valutazione dell'apporto umano al processo storico e iscrive entro una diversa cornice. I risultati delle precedenti esperienze pratiche e intellettuali, con la conseguenza (sempre più vistosa nella *Scienza Nuova Seconda*) di cancellare taluni degli originari significati, per assumerne altri, forse meno incisive e pertinenti". In a word, those which in the 1744 edition would have been in keeping with the trend of "trasferire la grande scoperta del 'diritto universale delle genti' da presupposto e sostegno di una politica riformatrice a fondamento conservatore di una 'pratica' " no longer called on to favour the "sorgere delle nazioni" but to prevent or contain their fall[5]. And yet the significance of this interpretation does not arise from a simple contrast between theses (non-solitary political Vico versus solitary Vico, the non-political philosopher), in that it comes about and is articulated in the light of a general re-appraisal of the Italian and European historico-juridical situation between the seventeenth and eighteenth centuries, wherein Vico, the historico-philosopher rather than the philospher of history, takes part in a direct and an indirect dialogue, thanks indeed to his political proposal, a clear indication of the radical historicity of his meditation on the great problems of modern Neapolitan and European society. And in this new interpretation perspective, the relationship between the philosopher and his sources, as well as

5 GIARRIZZO (1968) 1981, pp. 55–56.

with his Dutch ones, came to be presented in decidedly non-traditional terms. For this Giarrizzo purposefully drew up a list of still-open questions – still awaiting their full development – emphasizing the need to re-examine the entire problem regarding *Universal Right*:

> Il [...] debito a Grozio e al dialogo Grozio-Gronovio è immenso [...]. Più grave è la responsabilità culturale della tesi balorda del 'superamento' vichiano del Grozio, che ha indotto a cancellare anni cruciali della biografia intellettuale del Vico, e che ha falsificato i dati della sua stessa *Autobiografra,* e del *Diritto Universale* ha fatto una prima, imperfetta redazione della *Scienza Nuova,* invece dell'esito imponente di un travaglio intellettuale complesso che attende ancora il suo storico. Si tenti la ricostruzione, che può esser tentata, del commento a Grozio; si esamini la struttura dei tre scritti, e soprattutto si studino le relazioni particolarmente complesse tra il *De Constantia* e il *De Uno.* E' un impegno di ricerca tremendo, ma per esso passa il nuovo corso degli studi vichiani[6].

In more recent years the need for an integral "historicization" of Vico – for an interpretation which may prove valid enough to set him in the cultural reality of his day – has been attempted with increasing success by philosophical and historiographic investigations. Yet one must be fully aware of the fact that one is responding to the need to explode the ancient myth of Vico's isolation by reconstructing in adequate terms "dall'interno la storia della mente del filosofo", yet without having established extrinsic connections and relationships or those pure coincidental ones between this history and the general one of the culture of his day[7]. Thus tracing Vico's thought to the European history of his time does not mean simply continuing to single out direct and indirect sources. It is also concerns investigating the origins and meanings of those sources, of having a clearer understanding of the background to certain solutions,

6 GIARRIZZO (1968) 1981, pp. 98–99. See LOMONACO 1992–1993.
7 GALASSO 1982–1983, p. 204.

and relating these to precise historical intrigues, episodes and historico-cultural situations. In this perspective the urbane polemics that also developed between Berlin and Aarsleff[8] on the Neapolitan philosopher's "originality" have proved fruitful as well as those between Garin and Rossi regarding *Vico's contemporaries*, with findings and suggestions being put forward especially in the Italian setting through a concern for emphasizing with greater documentary skill both the sources as well as the complex and varied spheres of influence on Viconian thought, beyond their apparent, external similarities. It is the advanced problem which is the real problem not only of the partial and most original use that Vico has made of his sources but also that of his methods – that hitherto have not yet been adequately identified and studied – of the diffusion of these very sources that may be retraced, but not exclusively so, in the books he read or in direct quotations. If the list of the authors quoted directly by Vico can prevent one from attributing to him interpretations simply on the basis of vaguely perceptible analogies, then a catalogue built up exclusively on the *name index* of his works provides an approximate library. In a complex world such as Naples was between the 17th and 18th centuries account must also be kept of the ora1 tradition or simply the manuscript and clandestine one, as well as of the frequent debates and academic writings, and of the most mediocre works and the numerous learned *journals* then in circulation, in addition to the great private epistolary *commercium*, all of which are vehicles which often come up with surprising and unexpected information[9].

Rather than simply becoming sterile in its new generic declarations of principle the "new course" of studies has also duly revealed the validity of comparisons and confrontations regard-

8 See BERLIN 1976; AARSLEFF 1981 and BERLIN 1981.

9 GARIN 1981 with reference to P. ROSSI 1999, pp. 275 ff. On this theme see LOMONACO 1984–1985, pp. 395, 408–409; 1987–1988, pp. 371–372.

ing method. If the proposed 'precursors' and all the arbitrary transpositions of theses and problems have appeared but slightly productive, the comparisons between thinkers and their like problems or even identical ones have in contrast proved to be more stimulating, provided they have been set in the light of rigorous critical limits and documentable influences. The original varied diffusion of a theme or sensitivity throughout differing cultural environments has allowed one to achieve highly relevant results which have considerably changed the image of European historico-philosophical culture between the seventeenth and eighteenth centuries. For the new awareness and critico-methodological experiences in contemporary Viconian historiography change has also proved significant, by opening up perspectives that allow one to re-examine many common areas and extend traditional horizons of inquiry into fields almost unknown. Thus a new interest in Italy was brought about for the activity of history and for Dutch philosophy of the seventeenth-eighteenth centuries also through Vico himself and through a modified interpretation of his radically new reflection. Besides the leading personalities of culture – from Grotius to Bayle, from Spinoza to Le Clerc – examined in their potential relationships with the author of the *New Science*[10], other figures and other critical sensitivities have taken on greater consistency, knowledge of whom thicken the plot of the patrimony handed down to Vico's world, albeit within recognized and recognizable limits. In this regard it is useful to bear in mind the fundamental and well-known works of Santo Mazzarino, also for the relevant and direct contributions they make to the study perspective favoured in the following pages. In an original 1971 essay, the in-depth analysis of the Viconian relationship between "custodia degli

10 A new interest in Italy was brought about Dutch philosophy of the seventeenth-eighteenth centuries also through MASTELLONE 1983; MASTELLONE 1985 and CONTI 1983; 1984; 1987, pp. 145–163.

ordini" and "custodia delle leggi" to understand the history of the *orders* in ancient Roman society, proposed highlighting interesting analogies found with the Dutch historians Perizonius and van Bynkershoek on the themes of Roman 'archaism', especially on morality and legislation of *spolia optima* and *patria potestas*, with reference to the problem of the origins of the "ordine equestre". In this context Vico who "è, quanto alla genesi del suo pensiero, uomo del Settecento", is located between Godefroy and Gibbon. A historian of ancient Rome and philosopher of the recurring *cycles* and returning "barbarie" able to relate the annal-writing tradition to systematic histories of law and thus still herald the 19th century was now Niebuhr, the great master of philological historiography and no longer Hegel or Italian neo-idealism[11]. To support and further this interpretation a contribution might then be made by the text of a brief but highly stimulating conference held in Utrecht in 1979 on *Vico, Holland and Modern Conceptions of History*. For the novelty and characteristics of the "new course" of studies themselves, a discussion on Vico and the Dutch of the seventeenth-eighteenth century could not be generic. In the full fascinating picture of the *decline and fall of the ancient world of classical historical thought* always under the critical control of the historian, Vico's image was effectively related to his *traits* at the time of the great modern European juridical-philosophical culture and in particular of the Dutch culture, bringing one's attention back to the central relationship between Roman and natural law in the light of the important discussion on the significance of *patria potestas.* Hence the attention paid to Gronovius' and Huber's theses and to those of Noodt's and Bynkershoek's compared with those of Grotius' and Hobbes' which had considered the concept of *patria potestas* as opposed to *status naturae,* the one for its tyrannical character, the other in

11 MAZZARINO 1971, pp. 11 and note, 20, 27 and note, 40 and note, 56, 84, 78.

that it considered *matris potestas* original and in keeping with nature[12]. The close tie between Vico's reflections on the ethico-political history of ancient Rome and the discussions and interests of seventeenth-eighteenth century Dutch historians and jurists developed and integrated traditional knowledge, in full accord with the critical exigencies already advanced by "pre-Vicoism studies", through research into Grotius and civil philosophy in Viconian Naples. It was in fact a question not only of indicating direct or indirect analogies, but of signalling a thematic coincidence that implied a common task, thus worthy of being verified and documented in its true dimensions and circulation also within the Naples setting, contributing to identifying the sources and real limits of Vico's meditation on ancient history, particularly on Roman history. Yet this investigation held back from expounding a thesis of a Vico in continuous direct dialogue with contemporary Dutch thought. The search for signs of continuity between phases of Viconian speculation and the work of the Dutch, that were culturally distant both in time and space has not provided any solutions, nor has there been any attempt to find a solution through a sort of hunt for its predecessor as though of some feasible use. In fact, the limits of these possible parallels have not been overlooked through recognizing the particular originality of Vico's conception of a linear course of history, at the same time, cyclic, capable of spreading the dynamics of historical development and defining universalizing laws, without however, denying the specificity and individuality of the historical fact. The myth of *isolation* has not been replaced by the equally inadequate one of a mere dependence on the simple repetitiveness of problems not pertaining to Vico. Applied to ancient Roman history, his *geometric* method of historic development leads to new propositions for the meaning of the proposed *origins* and *fall of nations*, and more advanced

12 MAZZARINO 1979, pp. 360–361.

proposals on the criticisms of a Perizonius on the historiographical traditions of ancient Rome:

> The common interest in the problem of the *patria potestas* of both Vico and the Dutch scholars is of importance for the history of historiography, well beyond the discussion on an individual topic of the Roman family law. We have already seen that the theme was one that affected, in essence, the whole conception of the roman ethical (and therefore political) history; and, more generally, the whole conception of mankind's historical development [...]. What is Vichian, however, is the insistence on that 'geometric method', which led to idea of a linear development. To be sure, it is a linear development, within a cycle itself completely closed[13].

The problems outlined, the perspectives identified and the proposals that have been advanced thus represent the real novelty of the "new course" of Viconian studies, and introduce a decisive turning point, namely that of proceeding further to examine the problems, perspectives and proposals from close range, with and without direct reference to Vico. And it is in this setting that the present work is located wherein other clarifications, including those regarding methodology are nevertheless first set out in order to focus light on the context and its significances point by point. Although mention is made of historians, philologists, scholars and jurists who were certainly known to the author of the *New Science* but not always explicitly referred to by him, the pages which follow are neither the outcome of any research into Vico nor to any lesser extent the result of an investigation into his Dutch "precursors", through concern with guaranteeing him a birthright or a critically-matured basis for the theses discussed. Nor has the study sought to present a comprehensive outline of modern Netherlands culture, relative ancient Roman-law study sources or the thinkers examined. Rather, the aim has been to explore, also by sifting through the

13 MAZZARINO 1979, pp. 359, 367.

most widespread learned reviews, certain meritorious points of Dutch reflection on antiquity between the seventeenth and eighteenth century, and particularly on the role that the image of Rome has assumed in the construction of a certain politico-cultural model. Although the specific topic of interest has been held constant throughout, the research has not failed to emphasize – albeit only partly so – the contributions made by reflection on the knowledge of classical historical thought which is exceptionally rich, complex and also materially differentiated on which it will still be necessary to make constant progress within realistically-limited historico-historiographic parameters, also following the well-known relevant works by Huizinga and Geyl, and by Venturi, as well as following the reformed undertaking of Anglo-Saxon historiography ranging from Wilson to Kossmann and from Haley to Price[14].

At this juncture the case of the dispute on the *Lex Regia de Imperio Vespasiani* proves to be relevant hereto, that is to say the inscription reproducing the final part of an act approved by the people and by the Roman Senate between 69 and 70 A.D. legitimizing the *potestates* granted to Vespasian on the occasion of his ascendancy to the throne. Destined to involve the attention of some of the greatest Dutch representatives from the philological and historico-juridical school, this debate – wrongly neglected by historians of historiography and philosophical culture, more especially by Italian ones – was not merely some scholarly exercise in literary-rhetorical *regulae* dictated by the *ars historica,* by the Ciceronian *opus maxime oratorium,* nor was it the privileged *locus* of application of traditional motives and lexes of Aristotelian political classical-humanist language. Certainly, in part it was also all this. Yet the history of the *lex,* inasmuch as the stoma of the irresistible political progress of the *princeps,* as factor determining the equilibrium of *ius publicum,* represented an important occa-

14 See here Chap. 2. 3, notes.

sion for Dutch culture at the end of the seventeenth century for reflection on the origins of modern absolutism, and on the reasons for the conflict between *auctoritas* and *libertas.* In other words it was a historically-defined *locus*, useful during the years proving most uncertain for the fate of the Seven United Provinces of the Netherlands for initiating a comprehensive investigation into the effective juridical-political mechanisms of civil and religious society, in the light of the experiences developing in the European political culture of the late seventeenth century. Following the anti-Spanish struggle, delicate contrasts were opened up in 1672, when the assassination of John de Witt, Grand Pensionnaire of Holland and *leader* of the 'Regents' party, had marked the end of the flourishing twenty-year republican period (1653–1672) and the restoration of the Stadtolderat of William III of Orange, supported by the nobility, by the poorest peasant classes and by the most intransigent orthodox Calvinists against the threatening invasion attempts of Louis XIV, stemmed once and for all only by the Peace of Nijmegen of 1678. With faith in the revolution now quashed for ever, the internal crises necessitated re-defining the principles of juridical science as well as the jurist's competencies, and theorizing new relationships between *jurisprudence* and *power,* to be subjected to the primacy of *politics* by clearly posing the question of the survival of the republican government against the limits that the international context imposed[15]. In this historico-political situation Grotius becomes a fundamentally important point of theoretical and ideological reference for such a task, an authoritative guide both for guaranteeing as well as enhancing the complex processes of transition from *provincia* to *respublica* that had come about. Yet his writings on the *Lex Regia* that take pride of place herein also show the impossibility – and this is one of the underlying themes of the analysis here attempted – of identifying late-

15 Cf. VISENTIN 1998.

seventeenth century Dutch historico-political reflection as a unit block distinguished by the dominant personality of the jurist of Delft. Gronovius and Perizonius' philological-scholastic commitment, and Huber's historico-juridical interests reveal not only autonomous articulations regarding problems but also a full awareness of their objectives even when they are compared critically with the theses of the *De iure belli ac pacis* in order to define, through essential historico-philological comparisons, the characteristics of and limits to the definitions of *summa potestas,* of *obligatio ex consensu* (Gronovius and Perizonius) or of the *ius potestatum circa sacra* (Huber). Yet when Grotius' disciples in criticism break with their master's theses and show the relevant consequences of this rupture at the historico-historiographical level of organization, they arrive at the common paradoxical assertion of a Grotian interpretation model for an extreme formulation of anti-Grotian reflections. In setting out different solutions for the theme of the origin of *potestas* and for the relative problem of the definition of the concept of *status naturae,* of the *origin* and *nature* of the *contracts,* they agree on the need to reconcile jurisprudence with history, and the science of law with the science of history, and also to formulate a new *topic* of jurisprudence in terms and contents different from those of a humanistic-renaissance making. They act more especially within a reflection prompted by the realistic physiognomy of human nature, and its historical *nature*, and arrive at an interesting re-examination of the traditional concept of *Reason of State,* making use of Suetonius and Cassius Dio, Tacitus and Machiavelli, permeated into Aristotelian ethico-political paradigms and into the well-tried motives of Stoic origin that are widespread throughout the Dutch culture of an Erasmian and Calvinist tradition. Yet the approach to traditional historico-political literature, far from meaning a passive acceptance of the great classical models, and especially so for Huber, did not even imply adhering to the precepts of ancient pedagogy on the *arcana imperii* and the myth of the good or bad *Reason of*

State, but rather was concerned with obtaining only general policy *instructions* and *admonitions* from ancient and modern history. The responses guaranteed by conventional "precepts" to the problems regarding the origin and limits of sovereign power now appeared completely inadequate and obsolete. The modern juridical theories searched for more satisfactory ones for the queries posed by *scientia iuris* that was modified in methods and contents. They searched for *a science of law* capable of referring to "laws" and "principles" of *universal and natural right geometrically ordered,* and of being compared with the *new science,* and setting itself as the basis and order of the State in accordance with a doctrinal approach that had found expression in the juridical subject matter of the "philosophia novantiqua", established in Europe since the time Pufendorf had published his *Elementorum iurisprudentiae universalis libri II* in 1660, following the Peace of Westphalia (1648) and the great debates on *Public Law* in the German Empire. With circumspect critical sensitivity, the picture of the theoretical-historiographical reference of Dutch historians and jurists, including more especially Huber, becomes complicated on several fronts when comparing Grotius' theses with and against those of Bodin and Althusius, as well as Hobbes and Spinoza, in the utilization of a model, namely that of the "praetorian" law which invited reflection, in keeping with and in dispute with Perizonius, on the modern problem of the relationship between 'civil equity' and 'natural equity', as opposed to the ancient *Ratio politica de Statu,* a *new* and *just* need for *Ratio Status,* that arose as *aequitas civilis* on the old basis of 'natural equity' and referred to in the order of history. In such a changed theoretical-doctrinal context, destined to be fully developed only by Vico's later political proposal, the other side of the coin of the ancient Reason of State, historical Pyrrhonism which had deliberately spared historico-juridical studies in an obstinate rejection of a possible truth in history, does not appear to have any reason for being.

However, the significance of Dutch seventeenth-eighteenth century reflection on the *Lex Regia* cannot be examined only in reference to historico-political motivations but also (and this is yet another of the interpretative proposals supporting this research) in the light of the various complex discussions developed on the fringe of Descartes' philosophy and Dutch Cartesianism at the end of the seventeenth century. Examination of the polemic regarding the value of the *fides historica* has here, in fact, taken its initiative from Gronovius' interventions to add to Perizonius' theses as a symbolic moment and, in a certain sense, as a conclusive one, wherein it is shown that among the main reasons inspiring the *querelle* the leading philosophical one regards the *certainty* of history, the definition, that is to say, of its value and limits, and the conditions which make knowledge of it possible: the latter being a motive critically-reproposed by recent philosophical historiography following the re-appraisal of Hazard's well-known theses who was convinced that Cartesianism, Libertinism and Jansenism work together to deny any sense and value to historical knowledge, but in fact bring about the "collapse" of the historical knowledge of Greece and Rome[16].

In the Netherlands where Descartes lived between 1629 and 1649, the anti-Cartesian polemic, activated by Gomar and the Aristotelian Voetius and Steuart both within and outside the Universities of Leyden and Utrecht, ended by passing progressively into second level, to die out mid-century and share the same fate as every other stance of intolerance or dogmatism. In fact, to reconstruct a new discourse on *certainty* invited the decidedly productive function of methodical doubt also at the praxis level. Going beyond the ancient *arcana iuris of the traditional politico-social order*, elaborated on the foundations of Roman law of late-medieval and humanistic juridical science, and examining the facts disputed with all interpretations absolutizing the con-

16 HAZARD (1935) 1968 [2007], pp. 55–60.

tents of historico-juridical discourse meant upsetting the foundations of the ancient regime and its very concept of truth which not even Grotius' iusnaturalism appeared to be capable of dislodging once and for all. Essentially, it meant invalidating the mechanisms of the formation of the *consensus gentium* as a source of certain truth by restoring the value of *probabilitas* within a completely new empirical perspective, as opposed to the original Aristotelian one that had represented the most valid support of late-scholastic probabilism, and above all in the settings and courses of philological criticism and erudition in which the practice of a new methodology was taking root with Cartesian culture. As in scientific investigation, so also in critico-erudite production all that was not a clear and distinct phenomenon was rejected, with the 'document' assuming the same force as the experimental fact and the 'verification' of the facts founded on precise empirical procedures. The 'philology' of learned scholars such as Gronovius and Perizonius distinguishes and analyzes the content of the *Corpus Iuris* with the same will to understand through experimenting which animates the transforming action of the 'new science'; it teaches that there is not a given order in which to refer all the different realities of human history as it observes that every reality whether ancient or modern desires to be and must be explained *iuxta propria principia,* that is to say according to its own *forms* which are shown not to be a regulating *ratio* but are respectful of the relationship and movement among things investigated, a reason for which in order to be really human, man's reason must be able to be defined as *historical.* Thus, against this complicated backcloth, the strong anti-dogmatic charge of erudition and antiquity commitment expressed a total rejection of the modern myth of truth, as reality out of time, above and beyond history, affirmed by the theoretical modules belonging to dogmatic Cartesianism of a mainly Malebranchian tone in which much Netherlands culture of the late-seventeenth century had been taking shape. However, that such Cartesianesim was the most conspicuous but not the only component of this culture comes about from the extreme variety of interests and from the willingness of the so-called Netherlands 'Cartesians' to take account of only certain motives of Descartes' philosophy. Also in this context, therefore, the new is juxtapositioned with the old; the modern with the ancient is in certain ways old. However, a rigidly Cartesian approach would have led to the complete dissolution of the principles of classical political philosophy, of its very analysis and discourse procedures still widespread in historiography.

The theoretical contribution made by Cartesianism became essential first in Gronovius' interests and then in Perizonius, as already in Bayle and Le Clerc, but a Cartesianism essentially reduced to providing methodological indications that can be made use of in historical knowledge, in view, that is to say, of factual, and not necessarily mathematical, *evidence*. The same evidence that Arnauld, Nicole and Huet in the wake of Gassendi had already prompted with autonomous elaborations and aims by changing the perspective of orthodox Cartesianism of a Malebranchian matrix from within, and by acknowledging both validity and autonomy even to the moral *non-mathematical certainties* that are to be traced in sacred and profane history. Hence, the research already apparent in Gronovius and then later even matured beyond their marked divergences in Perinzonius' "moderate" criticism and in Le Clerc's "philosophical" criticism of a Lockian matrix, midway between scepticism and traditional apologetics constructed on new rules (the criterion of *probability,* the use of *common sense* and *reasonableness* in distinguishing between *true* and *false*) and empirical instruments against abstract conceptual superimpositioning and apodeictic demonstrations of the *ratio philosophandi.*

From the examination of ancient and modern historiography on Rome, from the reservations and doubts advanced regarding the historico-juridical tradition (from Cluver to Bochart, and from Jacob Gronovius to Dodwell) and regarding the *Lex Regia* in particular (from Connan to Estienne up to Bodin, Gentili and Schoockius), Gronovius just as Huber and later Perizonius, apart from their very bitter contrasts (above all those between Huber and Perizonius), did not reach radically-differentiated, uncertain or approximate critical positions. Re-problematizing the relationships between philology and history and the methodological patrimony of the constructive critical work of Bayle and Le Clerc, they developed a desire to guarantee a certain epistemological consistency to historical knowledge, an attitude of trust in the possibility of reaching results somehow certain, albeit limited, of a new 'logic' of historical knowing, that was less abstract and more empirical, founded on the rules and methods of the new *critique,* to safeguard the *fides historica* and react sufficiently well against the opposite, yet substantially equivalent risk of the dogmatic acceptance of all the testimonies and of the radical, corrosive destructive action of historic Pyrrhonism of Cartesian origin: a non-absolute scepticism which from the failure of that *fides* derived the impossibility of knowing history, still considered as a rhetorical expression of ever uncertain and contradictory testimonies as they are regulated by the passions and prejudices of men, and not in accordance with criteria of *certainty* and *accuracy*, valid for the sole constructions of scientific reason. The maturing of critical experiences in interpreting the *Lex Regia,* that is to say a non-literary source, is new and not only from the methodological point of view in the fact that in the Dutch seventeenth-eighteenth culture the relevant element born of a certain receptivity of antiquary work helps to re-propose the complex problem of the value and limits at the historico-historiographic level, or the specificity of historic knowledge. For Gronovius, Perizonius and Le Clerc as well as for Locke the basic question is the meaning to be ascribed to the techniques and methods of historiography, and in particular to tradition as a possible verifiable source of knowledge. The study of the documented *fact* obliges one to reject every abstract conceptual superimposition to confer a marked historical importance to erudite, antiquarian work which, as an essential component of theoretical-historiographical discourse becomes the sign or look-out post for a new possible relationship between tradition and criticism and between philology and the 'new science' of history.

Yet in this context, erudite research, prevalently nurtured by historico-juridical investigation could not of itself constitute an effective 'locus' of contrast against critical action of post-Cartesian Pyrrhonism. Tormented by doubt, the history of erudites and philologists ceased to be an interpretation of human projects, anticipated and guided by the traditional providential plan, to become an *exact* and *certain* narration of *particular* facts, witnessed by *reliable* documents. In order to reject the conclusions of erudition and historical Pyrrhonism that unconsciously yet paradoxically converge, committed to resolving a problem, namely that of the *sense* and *aim* of human history, that is equally insoluble in the setting of orthodox Cartesianism just as it is in that of 'informed' Cartesianism directed, that is to say, towards the exigencies of the modern critical-philological method, it will be necessary to wait for more mature historiographical enlightenment, destined with and without Vico to elaborate an original combination of 'philosophical history' and antiquary method of erudition and philosophy, of *reason* and *history*. From this viewpoint, even in the eighteenth-century Dutch culture the Roman tradition with its myths will continue to attract the attention of jurists and philologists, beyond the trends often tending towards motives for an immediate academic polemic or towards obsolete rhetorical repetition.

In 1699 the problem of the interpretation of the *Lex Regia* was to reappear in the *Dissertatio de iure summi imperii et lege regia,* composed by the jurist Gerard Noodt on the occasion of the closure of his Rectorship at the Academy of Leyden[17]. Certain decisive passages of this small-scale work bear witness to the presence of ancient and modern authors already explicitly utilized by Gronovius and Huber as in the case of Tacitus (whose expressions, taken from *Hist.,* I, 1, introduce the writing) and Livy, Dio and Suetonius, utilized by Lipsius and Grotius. Noodt referred to these authors in the setting of a reflection which, starting out from the analysis of the relationship between *prince* and *subjects* and originally rejoining the tradition of humanistic jurisprudence, would have reproposed and gone further into the theme of *auctoritas* and *obligatio ex consensu* with theoretical and historiographic vigour, all in the light of the contemporary politico-religious debate on the self-regulating capacity of human reason in the world which now needed to change rather than continue to investigate insignificant details, in the *exactness* of particulars exalted by erudite 17th century *Historica*[18].

Having reached this point, our discussion must now come to an end so as not to go beyond the time limits imposed on this study by touching on issues that represent the origins of eighteenth century reflection on the *Lex Regia.* Reflection which apart from Noodt's dissertation already mentioned and reviewed with interest and special mental acuity by Le Clerc[19] (the same who in signalling out a noteworthy study of the young Brenkman in 1712, Noodt's pupil had emphasized its importance for the original comment on the "lese majesty" contained in the *Digesto*)[20] matured in the subsequent intervention of Gronovius'son, Jacob, *magister humanarum litterarum* at Pisa (1673–1674)

17 NOODT 1724, I, pp. 623–633.

18 VAN DEN BERGH 1988.

19 Cf. *BIBLIOTHÈQUE CHOISIE* 1705, VII, pp. 228–255 and 1707, XII, pp. 420–423.

20 Cf. *BIBLIOTHÈQUE CHOISIE* 1712, XXIV, pp. 334–350. See STOLTE 1981, pp. 12–13.

and author of a *Honoraria Dissertatio de lege regia* (1712)[21]. Here, on abandoning for good the classical description of the *intrigues* of *power* of the ancient Reasons of State, one arrived at a new, changed historical and historiographical synthesis of late-Republican Roman and Imperial politico-constitutional reality, and at a re-examination of the origins of sovereignty and the *princeps-populus* relationship in the fully modern awareness of the indissoluble bond between law and philosophy, and between philology and history.

F. L.

21 GRONOVIUS 1712. On this Gronovius see FABRONI 1791–1795 [1971], vol. III, pp. 662–665.

For Beginning: Philology, Right and History

The title which I have chosen for my new introduction, I must confess, risks promising more than it can deliver. And although I am not so conceited as to think that my research exhausts the complexity and vastness of the subject in question, neither am I that keen on general and abstract treatises which result in generic repetitions of empty and abstract intellectual phrases. In fact, my present task is actually very limited and certainly does not aspire to be a premature (if not conceited) recapitulation of studies already completed or in progress. No less risky would be the *sic et simpliciter* adoption of that famous *Contributo alla critica di me stesso* (Croce), but I intend to use it all the same as the guiding motif for this paper, because it seems to me that a handy and "home-made" formula of *self-representation* is more suitable for expressing that systematization which study requires. Anyway, that is what I promised myself and it is as important as public corroboration.

"Writing about oneself" generally involves all the risks of idealizing rationalization, and often proposes solutions to issues which are actually far from being resolved. It will therefore not be a rhetorical stratagem or a vainglorious word-game if I proceed by going backwards and forwards over the studies of the last 20 years in order to find those clarifications which are the result of a reflection-in-progress upon my readings, including reading I have done specifically for this new introduction.

Obviously, all research is based on the scientific experiences of the person who proposes it, but it also develops from those human relationships that contribute to the generation of questions and points of reflection (which obviously have to be subsequently interpreted and transformed) and to the creation of a shared cultural environment. The thoughts that follow and which I wish to share here with my friends and colleagues, originate both in the philosophical school to which I belong, and in the human and intellectual relationships which I have been lucky enough to have had (without exaggeration, a lifetime of genuine good fortune), and even from the physical locations in which I happened to work.

May 2008 is a date that reflects a consistent element in my aforementioned good fortune, since it coincides with our mentor Fulvio Tessitore's 43th anniversary of university teaching (46rd, if you include the three courses of lessons he conducted as a professor *incaricato*). It is worth recalling that it was his wish – even more than that of his own mentors – that this school of philosophy should achieve public recognition – long before any other personal gratification – a wish pursued exclusively through the legitimate projection of "daily work", as he likes to call it, and a task he has performed with total dedication. The cultural education and *ethos* of many of the students and scholars of my generation have been strongly influenced by the "professor", with his stern calls for a serious and continuous commitment to study, and his more light-hearted appeals to investigate what he defines as distant and diverse "positive knowledge". We may not have answered these calls (at least in my own case), but we cannot forget them, such was and still is the charm of the man who proposes but does not impose, driven as always by human and "professional" duty to persuade his interlocutor to make up his or her own mind.

Calmly, and without undue exaggeration, I wish to recall that the sources of my studies are closely linked to the name of my master. Following my B.A. thesis on *Religione, natura e storia in Herder* in 1981, which I discussed with him, I was asked to embark on a search which, without rejecting the university background, would lead me into new research perspectives with rather fewer links to the formal "scholastic" pattern. This was the first and extremely tough test of my independent and responsible commitment to the profession whose task was to train the man first and then the volunteer scholar on probation. In the early 1980s, my professor of History of Philosophy and History of Political Doctrines at "Federico II" University was updating and reorganizing his main philosophical writings – most of which I knew already – on the authors and ideas of nineteenth and twentieth century Italian historiography (from De Sanctis to Villari and Comparetti; from Amari to Caetani; from Croce to Levi della Vida; from Fausto and Nicola Nicolini to Rosselli; from Carlo Antoni to Bianchi Bandinelli and Piovani). However, as I read them again in the volume of *Filosofia e Storiografia* for the publishing house Morano in 1985, these writings gained new meaning for me. This time my commitment as an informed reader had grown, aware as I was of the novelty of philosophical reflections which would broaden my interest in questions of historical method, about which I knew only too little.

The volume in question presented a profile of its author's extensive research program which investigated the historiographical questions and methodological issues associated with historical study with the aim of grasping the meaning and value of historicism, "considerato come una delle espressioni determinanti della filosofia contemporanea", which shares – as a critical analysis of reality – the modern sense of philology as *historical science* and *understanding* of what has happened in its historical reality. A philology-philosophy opposed, therefore, to philologism which represents an excess of technicism and a corruption of the true philological method, which is based on a recognition of the *individuality* of experience and *otherness* of the past in the different stages of human history, between *perspectivism* and *possibil-*

ity, between the *exceeding* and the *facticity* of becoming[1]. These were the problematic passages I had already clearly perceived and on which I worked in an effort to advance a basic premise of the studies to follow: *understanding* as a way to access the reality of the human subject, to legitimate – far from the illusions of false immediacies – the importance of philosophical historiography and, with that, the historicity of philosophizing which leads us to rigorously pursue the possible meanings and different motivations of the "truth" of a "doctrine". Which presupposes a convinced and consistently pursued repudiation of human history as rational knowledge of a reality that is material, eternal and immutable, of history as metaphysics and "philosophical history" (Hegel), indifferent to the *understanding* of historians-philologists, because it lives within the process of self-awareness of the spirit, the sole reality of a reason which is rationality, confined within the *apriori* and the absolute of a safe and optimistic development leading to endless improvement.

I don't believe I distort the reconstruction of my youthful studies too much when I see in these argumentations – the result of an instructive encounter with the brilliant "esami di coscienza storiografica" of Eugenio Garin and Pietro Piovani – the spur which led me to select Vichian subjects and problems of interest in the name of that "concreteness" which also recalls Croce in theorizing – as is well known – the synthesis of *history* and *philosophy*, inspired precisely by Vico's unity of philosophy and philology, by awareness of the *certain* and knowledge of the *truth*. The Italian neo-idealism, indeed, although also inclined towards the dissemination of a "neo-spaventismo storiografico" and a decided antipositivism (which is unfair when compared to so much learned positivistic historical research), had wanted and knew how to restore to historical studies, even those about

1 TESSITORE 1985, pp. 7, 10, then also in TESSITORE (1987) 1988, p. 105.

Vico, a new sense of philology and scholarship that was missing from previous, abstract generalizations[2].

Faithful to the teachings of Croce and, in particular, to the fundamental integration between problems of history of historiography and the "evocazione del fatto singolo", dominated by the "bisogno di una esatta comprensione"[3], I came across the work of Arnaldo Momigliano who, from the early nineteen-seventies to the nineteen-eighties, "revisited" historicism (1974), questioning, among other things, the *regole del gioco nello studio della storia antica* (1974) and *retorica della storia* (1981). In these studies, collected in the copious volume *Sui fondamenti della storia antica* (1984), I was greatly struck by the emphasis he placed on the need to recognize the historical imprint of every working method or hypothesis[4]. Far from the hollow abstractions of pure methodology, which risk reducing history to useless "rhetoric", even the reflection on *Historicism revisited* starts from an acknowledgement of a "process of selection, explanation and evaluation" of documents and facts, complicated by the mutable

2 "Non c'è storia filologica e storia non filologica: la storia o è filologica o non è. Non c'è scienza storica là dove il metodo filologico, che è il metodo della storiografia, non è seguito" (cf. PIOVANI 1966, pp. 48–49, but also pp. 53–54ff.).

3 MOMIGLIANO (1936) 1984, pp. 128–129. In a letter (Oxford, 9 September 1946) to Croce Momigliano observed: "Metodo astratto al di fuori della concreta ricerca è naturalmente escluso per me come per Lei" (see DIONISOTTI 1989, p. 57). And the thesis of "unità della ricerca storiografica e della ricerca storica" is confirmed in 1987, in observing that "storia della storiografia di per sé, senza esame di problemi storici definiti nelle loro fonti originali; e storia, sia di eventi sia di strutture [...], senza una precisa consapevolezza delle scaturigini della propria ricerca non mi hanno mai attratto" (MOMIGLIANO 1987, p. 8).

4 A reference to Croce is in the *Preface* to a work of 1984 when Momigliano mentions his lesson that "la storia della storiografia aiuti a definire, affrontare e risolvere i singoli problemi storici", lesson to which Momigliano is "rimasto fedele con senso di gratitudine" (MOMIGLIANO 1984, VIII). Cf. GABBA, 1995, pp. 401–402.

experience of the subject who is selecting them. If the freedom of the latter is always possible in the sphere of method and of choice, it nevertheless remains conditioned by the documentation they happen to read and interpret. Therefore, confronted by the irreconcilable contradictions of a historicism that implies "a danger of relativism", despite the *fides historica* of a "patriarch" such as the German historian Leopold von Ranke, in Momigliano "the historian will worry less about his own inevitable situation in history than about the historical situation of his evidence, previous historians included"[5]. And yet, favouring "techniques" in the work of the historian has not produced a cult of neutral and sterile philologism. On the contrary, there is definite confidence of being able to define the conditions in which *truth* can be ascertained and to confer, upon every abstract conceptual supposition, a particular depth on philological work as the essential component of historiographical discourse, a sign of the relationship between tradition and criticism, between *knowledge* of the past and *science* of history. All of which goes against "philosophical history" and "costruzioni a priori come lo hegelismo" in their aversion to philology, and which is therefore situated "al centro della resistenza contro la storia a priori di marca filosofica o teologica"[6].

Although it may make constant reference to events, it is, nevertheless, the judgement over the reliability of the source material which allows a legitimate reconstruction of the past which, far from presenting itself immediately to the historian, is, in every case, the result of a process of critical analysis of the related evidence. It is therefore crucial to establish the validity of a method of verifying the reliability of the historical documentation used, not so much as a pragmatic-empirical support for this

5 MOMIGLIANO (1974) 1980, pp. 24, 25, 30. On this theme cf. DIAZ 1988, pp. 343–346.

6 MOMIGLIANO (1958) 1984, p. 83.

or that conception of it but as a focal point for the "regole del gioco nello studio della storia", as related, in 1974, to the ancient world. The historian must know the sources he uses, because control over an event is not achieved by extrapolating the fact from the source, but by examining it within itself and its degree of certainty in a specific historical-cultural space. "Ciascun documento è il prodotto di una situazione specifica e ci dice qualcosa sulla medesima. [...] Lo scopo dello storico è di riconoscere la situazione specifica che permette di collocare il documento nel suo esatto contesto di spazio e tempo". However, he should not be interested in the sources in themselves and for themselves but as evidence of fact within the context of the source which hands it down. We must therefore abstract the documents from the positivistic fetishism which identifies them with facts and make it clear that the historian is not an interpreter of sources but of those realities of a past life that is evidenced by the sources:

> Tutto il lavoro dello storico è su fonti. [...] E tuttavia lo storico non è un interprete di fonti, pur interpretandole. E' un interprete di quella realtà di cui le fonti sono i segni indicativi o frammenti. [...] Egli trova il significato del testo e dell'oggetto che ha davanti a sé perché lo capisce come se appartenesse ancora a quella situazione passata a cui di fatto appartenne. Lo storico trasferisce ciò che sopravvive nel mondo che non sopravvive. E' questa capacità di interpretare il documento come se non fosse documento, ma episodio reale di vita passata, che da ultimo fa lo storico. [...] Lo storico capisce uomini e istituzioni, idee, fedi, emozioni, bisogni di individui che non esistono più. Capisce tutto ciò perché i documenti che davanti a sé, debitamente interpretati, si presentano come situazioni reali.

If histories as opposed to novels must be true and not founded on invented facts, the competent historian is someone who knows how to discover the *truth* that lies beneath the weight of his sources, even at the cost of discovering the "possibilità di falsificazione [...] propagandistica o ideologica [...], essa stessa oggetto di storia". Although during his research he may find a problem he considers his *own*, the historian must never forget what the event he selected represented before he became involved. If the *truth* of history lives in the present through its related documents, its interpreters must "inventare tecniche per la scoperta della falsificazione. Queste tecniche si fondano essenzialmente su una sempre migliore conoscenza degli oggetti autentici"[7] .

However, my initial focus in my studies of Vico also owes much to a famous essay written in 1950 on *Ancient History and the Antiquarian*. In it the central idea of reclaiming antiquarian "techniques" in order to identify the *true* origin of tradition and to counter the pitfalls of post-Cartesian *Pyrrhonism* in studies of Ancient Rome (from La Mothe le Vayer to Bayle, Huet to Hardouin, Fréret to De Beaufort), was based on the aforementioned capacity of antiquarians to focus particular attention on the distinction between "original and derivate authorities". The aim of this research was to recall, within the structure of historical research into the ancient world, the analysis of both the literary and the non-literary tradition (archaeology and palaeography, numismatics and epigraphy), the subject of increasing attention in the "conflict" between scholarship and philosophy in the sixteenth and seventeenth centuries up until the revolutionary "combination of philosophic history with the antiquarians' method of research" in Winckelman and Gibbon, through to the eighteenth century, when "was no longer any justification for making a distinction between antiquarian and historical studies"[8]. However, attention on the antiquarian method as an accepted position in research introduced doubts and uncertainties about that a priori and ideal synthesis of investigation and inter-

7 MOMIGLIANO (1974) 1984, pp. 481, 484–485, 479, 482. Cf. BERTI 1988, pp. 310–311.

8 MOMIGLIANO (1950) 1955, pp. 68, 95ff., 100, 69.

pretation in historiography which had sustained Momigliano in his youthful espousal of the Crocian doctrine, later rendered problematic by a brilliant paper in 1955 on *Il linguaggio e la tecnica dello storico*[9]. In the 1950 essay, the reference to the modern synthesis between philosophy and scholarship, embodied in the work of the philosopher-historian Gibbon, brought to fruition a central thesis in the youthful and brilliant work of 1936 (on *La formazione della moderna storiografia sull'impero romano*) about the fundamental contribution of jurists of the fifteenth and sixteenth centuries to the historical-scholarship method, to contrast Pyrrhonistic scepticism with "l'approfondimento della contrapposizione tra diritto naturale e diritto positive" which had "aveva messi all'avanguardia della coscienza delle variazioni storiche: ricercatori di fatti e capaci di intendere il fatto non giuridico come motivo del fatto giuridico"[10]. Under threat from Pyrrhonism, and predominantly fuelled by legal research, history ceased to be an interpretation of human designs, traditionally planned and guided from on high, to become a *precise* and *certain* narrative of specific facts, evidenced by trustworthy and indisputable documentation. As well as complicating the language of the historian, the polemic tide was destined to enrich the theoretical dimension, forcing it to reformulate the complex relation-

9 "E' vero – observes Momigliano – che i fatti non possono considerarsi sufficientemente accertati se non quando sono soddisfacentemente interpretati, ma è anche vero che un fatto soddisfacentemente interpretato può scoprirsi inesistente [...]. La regola tradizionale di stabilire prima i fatti non è sempre applicabile, ma l'opposta asserzione che ogni conoscenza storica è *illico et immediate* sintesi di accertamento e interpretazione di fatti non corrisponde all'esperienza. La sintesi è l'*ideale* a cui tende lo storico, ma talvolta fra assodamento e interpretazione intercorrono dei decenni, e talaltra la scoperta di una soddisfacente interpretazione può essere seguita dalla scoperta che il fatto è inesistente" (MOMIGLIANO [1955] 1960, p. 372). On this theme cf. SASSO 1985, pp. 215–216 (cf. also pp. 213–214).

10 MOMIGLIANO (1936) 1984, p. 103.

ship between *truth* and *certainty*. From this point of view, Pyrrhonism and scholarship appeared to have converged in their final conjunction of a conception of history that deals *de singularibus*.

Thus, philology and law emerged as the two great core themes of my historical-historiographical interest, which were furthered by another work of great antiquity. I refer to the inaugural lecture given at the first international congress of the Italian Society of Legal History in 1963. Dealing with the *Conseguenze del rinnovamento della storia dei diritti antichi*, Momigliano started by addressing the complicated subject of the relationship between legal history and general history. In a gently teasing tone, he began by saying that it was right to celebrate the "fine della storia del diritto come branca autonoma della ricerca storica", indirectly denouncing the (now inadmissible) positivistic defence that legal technique has a "specificity" of value, a defence maintained up until the end of the eighteenth century, when the distinction between the history of historians and the history of lawyers became functional to the "nozione settecentesca di storia della civiltà"[11]. This notion invites us to understand the law not only as a set of standards and obligations, but also as the discipline of a society to which it is bound by a constitutive relationship. To find in the law the reality of the world that it regulates means to identify *ius* from the point of view of the history of culture, and to recognize in it the not insignificant role played by Roman jurisprudence.

The force of Momigliano's "Consequences" directly fuelled my own research on one of the most emblematic documents in the history of Ancient Roman law: the inscription of the *Lex regia de imperio Vespasiani*, in which the new fact from both the methodological and non-methodological point of view was the

11 MOMIGLIANO (1964) 1984, p. 185. The historiographical implications are discussed by AJELLO 1976, pp. 3–5.

interpretation of a non-literary source which, arising from a particular receptiveness of the ancient work, contributed to the reposing of the complex philosophical problem of history and of its degrees of certainty, of the limits and conditions that make knowledge of it possible and which define its epistemological autonomy. The study of documented *fact* obliges us to reject all abstract conceptual superposition, to ascribe significant historical weight to scholarly and ancient work which becomes the sign of a new relationship between the heredity of ancient philology and historical method. All in the light of the renewed interest in ancient history, albeit scarcely well informed or approached with any lucidity and in all its developments at Leiden by "un gruppo di professionisti della filologia e dell'antiquaria, spesso trasmettenti la professione nell'interno della famiglia, molto efficienti come regolari provveditori di edizioni critiche di classici per tutta Europa"[12]. This proposition is a fine web of relations and information that relates to the very specific political, religious and cultural reality of a modern Holland which, after Lipsian extremism, inherited from Vossius and from Graevius (inclined to contrast Seneca and Tacitus to Livy and Cicero as models of classicality), had undergone the grafting of Calvinism, been purged of the Armenian "heresy" on the day after the synod of Dordrecht (1618) and nourished by the post-Erasmus humanistic tradition of Scaligero and Grotius, Saumaise and Casaubon through the stoic themes of classical literature[13].

In complicated discussions on *fides historica*, developed at the margins of the philosophy of Descartes and Dutch Cartesianism at the end of the sixteenth century (from Gronovius a Perizonius, from Huber to Noodt), the practice of a new methodology began to be established. In it a confident attitude began to grow towards the reliability of history, in the possibility of guar-

12 Momigliano (1958) 1984, p. 79.
13 Cf. Den Boer 1979 and Barfoot et al. 1992.

anteeing the ascertainment of facts and of preserving the rules of *critique* from the *impasse* created by the sceptical, acritical and a priori negation of all certainty, the result of ascribing to the modern myth of an intellectual truth, specific to the theoretical premises of dogmatic Cartesianism in which Dutch culture of the later sixteenth century was prone to take refuge. However, the fact that the philosophy of *cogito* might be only the most eye-catching, although not the exclusive component of this culture, results from the extremely wide variety of interests of the so-called "Cartesian" Dutch scholars and from their tendency to accept only some of the arguments of Descartes' work. To the works of Gronovius first and Perizonius later, as previously with those of Bayle, Le Clerc and Noodt, the contribution offered by a certain Cartesianism appeared essential, one that was able to provide methodological directions that could be used in historical knowledge, with a view, namely, to factual, though not necessarily mathematical *evidence*.

The substance of the new structure (and this is one of the leading threads of the analysis I embarked on) lay not in a return to the classics or in a transformation of the subjects of historical research, but in a different approach to the questions, addressed in the light of the new and complex intertwining of law, ancient scholarship and politics. The *Lex de imperio Vespasiani* represents a dominant show of strength on the part of the *princeps* as the determining factor in the equilibrium and organization of the *ius publicum*. *Lex* becomes, in other words, a 'place' that is historically defined and a useful starting point from which to embark on a complex investigation into the effective legal and political mechanisms of Dutch civil and religious society following the twenty years of Republican prosperity (1653–1672) and the restoration of the Statholder William III of Orange with the support of the nobility, the poorer agricultural classes and the more intransigent elements of orthodox Calvinism in the face of threats of invasion by Louis XIV, which were finally contained by the Treaty of Nijmegen in 1678. With revolutionary confidence shattered, internal crises forced them to redefine the principles of jurisprudence and what the duties of the lawyer really are, and gave rise to new theories about the relationship between *jurisprudence* and *power*, and a recognition of the primacy of *politics*. This clear-sightedly called into question the survival of the republican government in the face of the limits imposed by the international political balance of power. With monitored critical sensitivity, the table of reference of Dutch historians and jurists becomes complicated in further directions, interpreting (Huber) the theories of Grotius for and against those of Bodin and Althusius, of Hobbes and Spinoza, by using the model of "praetorian" law which invites one, in harmony and in dissension with Perizonius, to reflect on the wholly modern question of the relationship between "civil equity" and "natural equity", to oppose to the ancient *ratio politica de Statu* a diverse, new and just demand for *ratio*, a sort of *aequitas civilis* grafted on to the old trunk of "natural equity" and with its roots in the order of history. In this theoretical-doctrinal context, which will be developed right to the very end solely by the "politics" of Vico presented below, the other face of the ancient Reason of State, "historical Pyrrhonism" and its aim of invalidating the causal link between events and their movements, no longer have any reason to exist.

In studying these topics I have benefited from the most recent critical literature on Vico which, also for professional reasons, I began to read in the mid-nineteen-eighties when I was a researcher at the Consiglio Nazionale delle Ricerche, attached to the "Centro di Studi Vichiani", that great department of study and research so wished for by Pietro Piovani at the end of the nineteen-seventies and directed for more than thirty years by Fulvio Tessitore. From a complicated assortment of readings and investigations, surveys and research papers there emerged an initial possible direction, thanks above all to the Vichian writings of Giuseppe Giarrizzo, which I read and re-read in the collection (not by chance published in Naples) of 1981 on *Vico, la politica e la storia*. I do not believe that I exaggerate when I say that they transformed the way we think about the history of philosophical and historiographical culture of seventeenth-century Naples and Europe in the light of the relationship between *cultura illuministica e mondo settecentesco* (as described in a youthful essay of 1956), a fundamental thematic juncture, this, sustained by youthful historicism, and yet also a meditation upon problems that are more diverse than the Crocian question and important for investigating the intertwining of the "storia degli intellettuali meridionali" with "storiografia vichiana", which appeared as a "rischio obbligato", imposed by that "stessa tradizione meridionale" on the "storico della cultura" and elected to be run deliberately, choosing "quel particolare punto di vista come osservatorio privilegiato per una 'storia totale' ". This changes the way in which we understand philosophical research "che 'sta sotto', e dà unità e senso, allo specifico lavoro filologico e antiquario", as we read in the beautifully written introduction to the volume, with sensitivity to the debt of gratitude owed to Momigliano "per i temi e la direzione stessa del [mio] discorso" and to Piovani for having involved him in developing the " 'nuovo corso' di studi vichiani nel [suo] prestigioso napoletano *Centro*"[14]. And there is research, that of Giarrizzo, all of it consistently dominated by the complex and fertile theory of the "sostanziale 'politicità' della riflessione vichiana". The latter arises from a complex rethinking of Italian and European historical and legal reality of the sixteenth and seventeenth centuries, in which the Neapolitan philosopher/historian is preferred to the philosopher of history, participates in a dialogue both direct and indirect, thanks to that very "politicity", the unmistakable sign of the constitutive historicity of his meditation on the great issues of modern Neapolitan and European society: the question of

14 GIARRIZZO 1981, p. 7. Cf. also GIARRIZZO (1956) 1981, pp. 241–264.

feudality and the "lotta vittoriosa che l'individualismo agrario viene conducendo nel Sei e Settecento in Europa e nel Mezzogiorno napoletano, contro i *communia* e le consuetudini contadine"[15]. On that subject, the history of culture that had favoured the discourse of Italian and European history as a place of a complex intersection between "il potere e il condizionamento sociale"[16], encountered the scholar of the ancient world and the classical philologist, impatient with absolute historicism and ethical-political history, because formed by the school of "storicismo degli storici"[17], a definition attributed to his mentor, that great classical scholar from Catania, Santo Mazzarino, a historian who lived during the last days of the ancient world and the late Roman Empire, the *Decadenzidee* of ancient and modern history. In that perspective, the relationship between Vico and his sources, including the Dutch ones, began to be advanced in terms that were distinctly far from historiographical tradition.

The topics thus identified and the research perspectives that emerged convinced me of the usefulness of pounding the same beat that linked Giarrizzo to the author of the *Pensiero storico classico*, connected separately to Vico and his world through *chronicling* and *law*. Having widened the field of investigation, it was as though a wall had suddenly collapsed, revealing a panoramic view so wide as to provoke a feeling of vertigo. After Grotius and Gronovius, a new critical consistency was adopted in annotated ancient and modern publications, authors and texts of scholarly philology and historical-philosophical culture, a presence which once established rendered the web of Vichian heredity much finer. Mazzarino's search for traces of Neapolitan philosophy in the works of the Dutch scholars (from Perizonius to Bynkershoek), separated by time and space, was not resolved

15 GIARRIZZO 1981, pp. 107, 55–56. On this Author see TESSITORE 1983.

16 So TESSITORE 1999, XII.

17 GIARRIZZO 2002, pp. 275–292.

nor did it try to resolve itself in any kind of hunt for predecessors of dubious utility[18]. Nor did it neglect the limits of these possibilities when confronted with the recognition, in the original Vichian concept, of an interest in defining universal laws of how history comes into being without in any way denying the individuality of events, far from the humanistic *imitatio* and all rationalistic and legal-naturalistic abstractions. For all that, Vico is a man of the seventeenth century, set between Godefroy and Gibbon, two authors admired by both Mazzarino and Momigliano (who preferred Gibbon), although clearly different for reasons of theory and history of historiography. In the historian of the ancient *Fra Oriente e Occidente*, there is a prevailing sensitivity to the subject of the *crisis* of the Roman empire in its relationship of 'conversion' with the "impero cristiano"[19]. A relationship which is also favoured in indirect polemic with Momigliano, who had used this 'conversion' to denounce the failure of modern historiography to realize its own basic objective (the unity of the history of the Empire and the history of the Church, as asserted by Mazzarino) and to express, in this case also, the indefeasible requirement for specific and rigorous control of sources in a history of historiography, in awareness of the "dilemma" between *truth* and *falsehood*, which is "essenziale per ogni attività storiografica"[20]. Not without reason, in Mazzarino admiration for Gibbon is preceded by a eulogy to Godefroy and his *Com-*

18 MAZZARINO 1971, pp. 20, 40, 56, 84, 92; MAZZARINO 1979, pp. 360–361.

19 MAZZARINO 1954, p. 8.

20 So Momigliano on Mazzarino, judged without historical method, "rabdomantico, 'profetico' interprete del passato condizionato dalle sue opinioni politiche, dalla fede religiosa, da caratteristiche etniche e infine, ma non esclusivamente, dalla situazione sociale" (MOMIGLIANO [1967] 1969, pp. 61, 74). Already in review of *Fra Oriente e Occidente* was explicit the dissent about a "metodo (che) non va: esso eredita dal Vico le bizzarrie della tradizione combinatoria, non l'austerità del pensare" (MOMIGLIANO [1948] 1969, p. 582). On this review and dissent see GABBA 1995, pp. 413–415.

mentarius (1665) on the *Codex Theodosianus* for the contribution it makes to our knowledge of the inner workings of the legislation and administrative life of the late Empire, inescapable reasons for documenting and interpreting the theory of the "enorme precocità" of the historiography of the Empire in comparison to that of the Republic[21]. And it is with Godefroy that Vico receives and in his own way transforms traditional themes of the history of Ancient Rome, denying the authenticity of Heraclitus's letter VIII (reported by Godefroy in *Fontes quatuor iuris civilis* [1653]), and thereby disproving the foreign origin of the decemvirate legislation for that highly original historical identification of Ancient Roman *heroism*, in antithesis to the *humanitas* of more advanced ages, in order to avoid the errors of the "*Giureconsulti della Giurisprudenza Ultima*" who were determined to "estimare le cose de 'tempi primi non conosciuti da quelle de' loro tempi ultimi"[22]. Exercised on the critical and methodological level, there is a need to distinguish, in Roman legislation, between those elements that belong to ancient law and those that were introduced in modern times. It is this historical sensitivity which guides Vico in his analysis of the whole body of laws, related by tradition to a single official legislative act. It documents the most complex and obscure fragment of the XII Tablets *(FORTI SANATE NEXO SOLUTO IDEM SIREMPSE JOUS ESTO)*, a place that confirmed and applied that fundamental *law* of Vichian philology-philosophy that states "di non disprezzar punto le *Volgari Tradizioni*; ma d'investigarne il *vero*, che loro diede motivo di pubblicamente nascere, e conservarsi, e di spiare le cagioni,

21 So in MAZZARINO 1954, pp. 14–16, 24, 61.

22 VICO (1725) [1979] 1990, t. II, pp. 1028–1029; VICO (1744) 1990, T. I, p. 900. On the opposition of " 'eroismo' romano d'età aristocratica arcaica alla umanità romana di età più avanzata" and the foundation of "una concezione rettilinea della storia romana, che ebbe gran parte nella formazione della critica moderna sulla tradizione intorno alla storia arcaica romana" see MAZZARINO 1975, p. 7.

onde poi ci sono venute ricoverte di *falso*". Whence, therefore, the careful re-reading of the ancient source (Festo), rediscovered in Godefroy and related not to the "Socj Latini" but to the *foreigners* at home, to the "*plebi* delle *Repubbliche Eroiche*"[23]. For all that, the XII Tablets, shorn of any trace of hidden or philosophical wisdom, become the place in which there converge all those Roman laws that sanction the right of liberty in the *civitas* albeit in decidedly different and by no means comparable times. From here, the progressive superimposition of new rules upon old laws and the contradictions between barbaric measures and civilized legislative acts that no "pareggiatore" has ever managed to reconcile, just as no grammarian has ever managed to explain the distance between the "*selvaggi*, e *fieri*", customs described in the *Iliad*, and those "tanti, e sì *dilicati*" told of in the *Odyssey*. In may in fact be explained by the Vichian interpretation of history, which theorizes about a *rectilinear* evolution, differentiated within its own times, but always constant within the compass of each *cycle*. To support this model of development means to emphasize, with the exemplary greatness and longevity of Rome in its proceeding by "giusti passi", the "continua fatiga del metodo geometrico", already applied in *De uno* and reprised in *Scienza Nuova 1744*[24]. In history, besides all the endless possible varia-

23 VICO (1730–1731) 2004, pp. 527, 528. To the "Origini ragionate degli *Ospiti Eroici*" is related the explanation of "*Forti Sanate*" which is "il *subbjetto di tutta quella contesa*" for the "*dominio certo de' campi*" (VICO [1744] 1990, t. I, pp. 738, 717–718). Vico mentions GODEFROY 1653, p. 139.

24 VICO (1744) 1990, T. I, pp. 820, 953; VICO (1725–1728) 1990, T. I, p. 18. See MAZZARINO 1979, pp. 366–369. In a letter to N. Concina Vico observes: "A' Sostenitori della Favola delle XII Tavole venute di Grecia sarà facilmente infrenato il furore col solamente replicar loro, che rovescino i Principj della Scienza Nuova, e ne incolpino il metodo, con cui sta condotta; perché il risentirsi delle sorprendenti conchiusioni è di cervelli ottuse, che sentono il grosso delle cose, e deboli per tenere la continua fatiga del metodo geometrico; col quale innumerali verità escono maravigliose in mattematica, le quali pur sono per quella via di-

tions, there is also an original or spontaneous conformity between the ideas and institutions of all peoples, because "*Idee uniformi* nate appo *intieri popoli* tra essoloro *non conosciuti*, debbon'avere un *motivo comune di vero*". That is the great *criterion* in the *common sense* of the human race, taught to nations by divine *providence* without the need for "*umano provvedimento*"[25]. History, which is *eternal* because ever present to man at every moment of his becoming and *ideal* because it does not coincide with reality, cannot be translated in classical terms of religious *metaphysics*. It is, first and foremost, a necessary *structure* for bringing the apparent, chaotic weave of *events* into *order* and for regulating the actions of men, a long way from those tendencies or inclinations which can lead to the decadence of civilization. To save the identity of nations, far from an empty and dispersive singularity, it needs to converge in a common and constant process of civilization to which every experience of thought and legal life has to conform. To insist, on the other hand, that it is possible to "transmit" any production of *ius* means admitting an extrinsic view of the law, and negates that historicity which the *constancy* of its development effectively shows. Applied to ancient Roman history, the *apriori* geometric method of historical development leads to new ideas on the meaning of the origins and fall of "nazioni", ideas that are far more advanced than the criticisms of a Perizonius of the historiographical traditions of ancient *civitas*. The historian of royal and republican Rome, the Vico of Mazzarino, philosopher of recurring cycles and barbarians of the

---

mostrate" (VICO to Concina [1736] 1992, p. 184). On Vico and Concina see LOMONACO 2005, pp. 20–25.

25 VICO (1730–1731) 2004, p. 527 and VICO (1744) 1990, T. I, p. 499. "Questo sarà uno de'perpetui *lavori*, che si farà in *questi Libri*, in dimostrare, che 'l *Diritto Natural delle Genti nacque privatamente appo i popoli*, senza sapere nulla gli uni degli altri; e che poi con l'occasioni di *guerre*, *ambasciarie*, *allianze*, *commerzj si riconobbe comune a tutto il Gener'Umano*" (VICO [1744] 1990, t. I, pp. 499–500).

"inumanissima umanità", knew how to link the "annalistica" tradition to the "sistematica storica" of law. He presaged not the philosophy of Hegel, but rather the historical-philological method of Niebuhr, that great master of "philological historiography" and architect of the delicate transition from the scholarly to the scientific phase of the historiography of ancient Rome that has made it possible to reconstruct it from criticism of the sources[26]. These theories meant repudiating the neo-idealistic image of the solitary and isolated philosopher, because precursor of true Crocian "historicism", an image that Mazzarino had no hesitation in defining as an "erroneous presupposition"[27]. And this historicism defined the "sistematico" and the "formale", extending with this latter adjective the qualification adopted by Omodeo (for the criticized unrealistic activism of the followers of Gentile) to the more Hegelian than Hegel theory of *Aesthetics* in the preference for "philosophical history" and its inexorable dialectic-categorical progression towards "original" and "philological" history, to that identification, in early Croce, of history and art as moments of intuition on the part of the individual. The author of that famous memoir of 1893 was the only one that "avrebbe potuto essere compreso dai Greci", in contrast to the "Croce definitivo, dalla *Logica* in poi, sino alla morte"[28]. It is precisely by excluding the *philological* from the neo-idealistic system that modern Romanists can rediscover the true meaning of Vico's legacy, to which they owe the creation of a new method which instead of valuing the "inversione dell'iter genetico nell'iter ermenuetico"[29], sets store by the consciousness of the positive search for "analogie" between events and institu-

26 MAZZARINO 1971, pp. 34, 46.

27 MAZZARINO 1979, p. 356.

28 MAZZARINO 1964, pp. 70, 75–76 and also MAZZARINO 1960, p. 398. On the theme cf. TESSITORE (1990) 2000, pp. 221–223, then also – with many printing errors – TESSITORE 2003, pp. 60–63.

29 So BETTI 1957, p. 52.

tions. For Mazzarino, this is equivalent to establishing, with Vico and after Vico, the possibility of moving between *historicism* and *sociology*, a formula that corrects, and stands on its head, that great comment by Carlo Antoni that he could detect in the transition from "dallo storicismo alla sociologia" a degenerative descent from one discipline to another, incapable of understanding that the "il confronto tra istituti di età e luoghi diversi non esclude la loro storicizzazione, anzi la fonda"[30]. This involves capturing not simply a reversal of technical formulae or questions, internal to the academic establishment of historians, but an innovation in the paradigms of the study of the ancient world and the history of modern culture that reveals another distance from the historiography of the Crocian neo-idealistic matrix. This is borne out in experiences and discussions between historians of Roman law such as Arangio Ruiz and Pietro De Francisci, which are quite incomprehensible without the idealistic experience, or rather stimulated by the "necessario (l') *interdit* crociano" but significantly active in the field of legal historiography, in favour of the "l'avvicinamento sempre maggiore fra storiografia del diritto e problematica della storia sociale"[31]. And to that judgement we can add the later writings of Mazzarino in 1966 on two "storico e dogmatico" moments in the research into classical societies which "coesistono [...] sin dai secoli XVI e XVII: da un lato studio dei *facinora Triboniani* e tentativi di storiografia giuridica, dall'altro *specimen moderni usus Pandectarum*"[32].

The developments in my research on philosophy, law and history, with particular reference to the legal philosophy/philology of Gianvincenzo Gravina, intended modestly to take up the issue only raised by Mazzarino who, in the closing statement to his essay, recalled "la sua (del Gravina) trattazione

30 MAZZARINO 1971, p. 20.

31 MAZZARINO 1964, pp. 88, 83.

32 MAZZARINO 1966, p. 69 and note.

della *lex de imperio Vespasiani*", considering its "vicende dell'interpretazione […] tra le più istruttive per il nostro tema […]; in realtà (almeno a mio giudizio) l'idea della *lex de imperio* ha una sua storia, che diversifica il bronzo vespasianeo della Sala del Fauno dalla *lex de imperio* teorizzata da Ulpiano"[33]. The critical re-examination of this *lex* – itself not literary either, since it is again taken from a fragment of *tabula* preserved in Campidoglio – is evidence of an effort at historical understanding of the "inganni" of Tribonian. However, the reality of the legal datum should not be confused with the empiricity of the single fact, since it is clearly related to that element of the *universal* that resides in every accomplished legal action, intent on overcoming its own singularity and strengthening its own existence. This need is sustained in the *Origines iuris civilis* (1708) by collaborating with the Cartesian method, which adds a necessary rational systematization to the legal material. This chimes with the unity and metaphysical value of Gravinian *mens*, in tune with the aspiration of Southern European philosophical-historical culture of his time to present itself as *system*, in a theoretical perspective shared by Doria and even by Vico[34]. Related to the *system* of human *mens*, the principle of law is a reflection of that universal order consistent with all legal *experience* in the *form* of history. Having elevated knowledge of the law to a formal concept, Gravina is able to observe different legal experiences, dominated by special interests and yet operating in a "connection" to which every action must be related. In order for jurisprudence to present itself as *scientia* and deal effectively with the emergence of new deficiencies in the current system, it must transcend the literal interpretation of laws and arrange their contents in a strictly rational and unitary order, free from dogmatic presuppositions. Gravina

33 *Ibid.*

34 Cf. NUZZO (1985) 1987–1988, p. 66 and on Gravina see LOMONACO 2004, XI–LXII and 2006, pp. 53–102.

is persuaded by Platonic/Neoplatonic Cartesianism that in order to understand historical systems of *ius* it is essential to develop a universal model drawn from human reason. Only thus can meditation on the *nature* of law become research into its *origins*, in the dual sense of an ideal origin, related to the absolute principle (of divine *mens*), and of historical origin, with the aim of understanding the meaning of *ratio* in the manifestations of its becoming. An examination of the legal world from its origins supports the conclusions of theoretical research, which reveal that law is the means through which man recognizes in history the action of *lex* divina, which although operating differently throughout the ages, constantly grants him the possibility to pursue ethical and rational finalities. And yet, this recognition is still sustained by traditional values, by the Platonic/Neoplatonic concept of the relationship between the idea of *order* and that of *time,* both etched on a horizon which is both *rational* and *civil*, a concept in harmony with the Ciceronian ideal of knowledge as "consensus et concertus doctrinarum" and re-proposed by humanistic culture. But this, assisted by the Platonic interpretation, does not allow us to get right to the heart of the historical origin of universal laws, and therefore to discover the ideal principle of law, its validity and certain foundation, hidden and captured *in* time. If law is considered to be that place in which man's conscience-reason reveals its own identity and ceases to hide behind superficial facts and contingencies, Gravinian thought has problems moving from the ancient to the modern in its search for a connection between *ratio* and *auctoritas*, *system* and *history*, in its attempt, basically, to merge the study of the *genesis* of *ius civile* with research into its rational basis and thereby weld together historical knowledge and scientific and legal knowledge. It attempts to reconstruct the progress of *nations* as *ordo*, whose laws testify to the application of a principle of *uniformity* between the *civil* universe and *natural* necessity. In the *Origines*, to explain the causes of the periodic corruption of the life of individuals and their institutions, there is an analysis of human *natura*, condemned by its *cupiditates* to a condition of repeated dissatisfaction. An analysis which is worthy of emphasis, since it shows how the complicated unravelling of that ambiguous *nature* is reconciled with the anticipated integration of historical world and natural legality, describing man's development in a *cyclical* sense in a continuous alternation of *progression* and *regression*, corresponding to the inevitable and periodic corruption of forms of government, to the transition from princedom to aristocracy, from aristocracy, through oligarchy, to democracy and back to princedom again[35]. Convinced of the recurring, contradictory presence of good and evil, of virtue and vice in the world, Gravina is not interested in transferring the discredited belief in a golden age from the origins of time to the end of history, because he does not wish to restore credence to the idea of a presumed progressive improvement without a solution of continuity and, therefore, conflicting with his model of a natural *cycle* applied to human history for and against Bodin[36]. The virtue-corruption polarity, identifiable in the predominantly cyclical progression of becoming, turns the *fall* into a necessary, endogenous and more or less unavoidable event of history, which is periodically restored to its initial state of evolution. A return, however, which cannot be associated with any predetermined and consistent date, i.e. with that principle of natural law which, in this context also, renders the Gravinian concept of *decadence* forever irreconcilable with that of Vico, whose *recourse*, and ex-

35 GRAVINA (1708) 1756, t. I, Book I, Chap. 20, p. 122a, but also p. 121b. On the *scientia iuris* in the age of Gravina – "a metà strada fra storia e sistema, tra *ratio* e *auctoritas*", settled on the "elaborazioni tanto più sorde alle richieste della vita giudiziaria, quanto più culturalmente raffinate e complesse" – cf. AJELLO 1976, p. 119.

36 GRAVINA (1708) 1756, I, Book II, Chap. 19, p. 121a–b; Book III, Chapp. XI–XII, XVII, pp. 226a–231b, 236b–237b. See LOMONACO 2004, LVI–LVII.

treme remedy, includes the notion of *possibility* and excludes all mere *repetition*[37]. And it is precisely in the light of the *Decadenzidee* that, in Mazzarino, we see opposition growing to the idea of perfection (in the Enlightenment, idealistic and positivistic sense), a perfection deprived of "posto in un sistema di assoluto storicismo" as against the "storicismo degli storici" which, even in the analysis of the *Aspetti sociali del quarto secolo* (1951), is already committed to Ranke. This is the German historian sacrificed by idealistic and neo-idealistic *philosophical history*, the author of a *universal history*, convinced like Hegel and Croce that "ogni epoca è vicina a Dio" although for that very reason disposed to support, without Hegel and without Croce, the "positività" of history, to consider it as a series of experiences of the *positive* and the *negative*, as "necessari momenti di un necessario rapporto dialettico"[38]. *Decadence* is not the negation but the reflection of forms of life in human history in a perennial variation of situations and "organic" and social, "natural" and political limits. Mazzarino's 1964 essay highlighted another important reason for *Decadenzidee*, coinciding with the "significato centrale del tema 'rivoluzione' nell'ambito dello storicismo ottocentesco", evoked with direct reference to the work of Niebuhr, that great historian of the *customs* of the Roman people, as recorded in his interpretation of the *consulate*, and ascribed to a "esigenza sociale" for the long phase of transition *from monarchy to republican state*[39]. In these pages, the topic is related explicitly to his great early work of 1945, to a phase (1935–1948) of deliberate anticlassicism, expressed in brilliant studies of Ancient Rome by a conviction that the criterion of "continuity" as used in the interpretation of history is but one dimension which, if allowed to become absolute, risks destroying the value of human actions

37 MAZZARINO 1979, pp. 369–370.
38 MAZZARINO 1951, pp. 22, 23. Cf. TESSITORE (1996) 1997, pp. 39–40.
39 MAZZARINO 1964, p. 83 and note.

and their unfailing novelty of significance, albeit of a negative kind. An *exemplum* of this is the acknowledged presence, in the Italian-Etruscan states of the mid-sixth century BC, of the confluence of different institutional realities and corresponding social and political organizations, all oriented towards the republican collegial magistrature in various forms and related experiences, and all emblematic expressions of an irregular evolution that cannot be assimilated in the presumed rectilinear development of Roman history and its constitution:

> Il passaggio dalla monarchia alla magistratura collegiale [...] è, nel processo generale, [...] qualcosa che lascia sentire un comune travaglio e un interesse culturale comune. Questo "qualcosa" è proprio nel "modo" del processo: non avvenuto d'un tratto, con "salti" e iati inesplicabili; ma per conquiste progressive, anche se, naturalmente, accompagnate da crisi e scosse più o meno violente[40].

Not immune to the fascination of Altheim's vitalistic "evolutionism", perceived through Meyer, the study of classical antiquity forces Mazzarino to eject the concept of historical evolution that "non fa salti" (as theorized by romanticism and by positivism) and to acknowledge continuity and discontinuity in history as the formation of two series of concrete facts that follow and intertwine with one another in a web of successive experiences, thereby creating the actual fabric of social and political becoming, which is crushed in shifting times of unstable crisis and unforeseeable refoundations. Having read Ortega y Gasset and Bergson, the latter opposed to the "fede hegeliana nella perenne razionalità del reale", Mazzarino sees *crisis* as the generator of the new, constitutionally open to life, according to the theory and practice of the "criticism" of science; what this "parve insegnare ai filosofi, la filosofia dell'azione volle insegnare agli storici: lo 'slancio vitale' parve inesplicabile senza

40 MAZZARINO [1945], pp. 117–118.

questo anelito al nuovo e all' 'epoca' che un'altra ne sostituisce, e in certo modo distrugge. Anche la storia, come la natura, procederebbe per salti". He documents Ancient Rome in the age of the legislative decemvirate and the military tribune with the "equiparazione degli ordini" and the resistance of the "curie" and the "centurie". It is here, in fact, that are rooted the bases of a perspective that knows how to accommodate crisis within a new context of decipherability and constructibility of history, always mediated, inevitably dyadic and conflicting: "In Roma confluivano, a un tempo, evoluzione e rivoluzione. Questo fu veramente il 'miracolo' romano. Questo è anche un insegnamento per noi. La storia non è storia di distruzioni che non ricostruiscano, di conservazioni che non rinnovino. Come lo stato romano, essa ha due volti: la rivoluzione e la continuità; l'eterno rinnovarsi e l'eterno durare". *Philosophy of action* and dialectics of *crisis* and *conservation* lie at the heart of a lecture on *from monarchy to the republic state*, of a reflection on the origins of ancient Roman 'democracy' which, given in the immediate Italian post-war period, also contains a political appeal to the middle classes to make themselves the ruling classes:

> C'è, ancora, un'altra caratteristica e quasi insegnamento (non ci scandalizzi la parola) in questa formazione progressiva della repubblica romana. La fondazione della repubblica fu opera soprattutto degli opliti, vale a dire dei plebei abbienti; ma le sue conquiste sarebbero andate perdute, senza le secessioni di tutta la plebe – compresi i non abbienti – nel corso del 5° secolo. Vale a dire: solo perché i plebei abbienti si fecero esponenti di tutta la plebeità, i *classici* anche degli *infra classem*, solo per questo la «rivoluzione politica» del 6° secolo non rimase vana, e la repubblica si consolidò per un lungo tempo. Oggi non ci son più né *classici* né *infra classem*; e la parola "plebe" ha tutt'altro senso, e le distinzioni di classe uno "stile" infinitamente diverso dal romano. Ma anche noi possiamo dire che la funzione del "terzo stato" (romanamente dei *classici* od opliti) è priva di senso e di contenuto, se esso non diviene altresì educatore e guida e suscitatore del "quarto stato". Ogni grande organismo statale ubbidisce a una esigenza e (anche qui non ci scandalizziamo della pa-

rola) a una legge: le classi superiori non possono vivere all'infuori dei fermenti storici elaborati dalle inferiori. A questa "legge" ha ubbidito anche Roma[41].

The first three chapters of the study which follows were first published as Volume 19 of the new series of "Studi Vichiani" (founded by Pietro Piovani and Fulvio Tessitore) for the Guida publishing house in Naples in 1990. However, had this research not been reviewed by some prestigious Italian and foreign reviewers, it would have had only a limited distribution.

Apart from the important presentations of Giuseppe Cacciatore ("Il Mattino" of 18 June 1991) and Ernesto Paolozzi ("Il Giornale di Napoli" of 20 July 1991) and the critically documented papers by Fiorella De Michelis Pintacuda (in "Bollettino del Centro di studi vichiani", 1991) and Carlo Colombero (in "Filosofia oggi", 1993), it is worth mentioning the detailed reviews of Hans W. Blom (in "Geschiedenis van de Wijsbegeerte in Nederland", 1993), M. van Gelderen (in "Bijdragen tot de Geschiedenis", 1993) and Gustavo Costa (in "New Vico Studies" del 1993). The latter, in particular, has offered the reader of Anglo-American philosophy a powerful synthesis of the contents and perspectives of my research. As he observed: "Probably Lomonaco's chief merit is in the fact that he demonstrates the positive influence Cartesianism had in historical research [...]. Lomonaco points out that, along the dogmatic branch of Cartesianism, based on mathematical and metahistorical principles, there was another, more flexible kind of Cartesian philoso-

41 MAZZARINO [1945], 92, pp. 224–225, but also p. 124. See LORAUX 1998, pp. 187–198 (with particular reference to *Oriente e Occidente* and to *Il pensiero storico classico*). On the work of 1945 see GIARRIZZO (1992) 1995, pp. 199–200, 246–247. Altheim's work is present in opposition against Mazzarino for that "continuo dare per certo quello che certo non è, e, assai spesso, nemmeno probabile", for that "costante confusione tra ciò che è interpretazione spiritualmente ricca di una situazione storica con ciò che è invece artificiale drammatizzazione" (*ivi*, p. 581).

phy, which rested on moral certitudes, derived from sacred and profane history. The intellectual activities of authors such as Gronovius and Perizonius, as well as those of Bayle and Le Clerc, were grounded in Descartes' thought [...]. In this way, the Dutch antiquarians established the polarity between philosophy and philology – a polarity essential in Vico's *New Science*". I have quoted this passage because over the years I have not only frequently revisited the subjects and leading figures of XVIth and XVIIth centuries. Dutch culture (as attested by the published and non-published pages included in Chapters IV and V of this paper), I have also carried out an in-depth investigation into that "essential polarity" that I have cultivated under the guidance of my mentor, Fulvio Tessitore, and which is central to Vico's philosohy.

CHAPTER I

Johannes Fredericus Gronovius: Philologist and Historian

When announcing the death of Johannes Fredericus Gronovius (28th December 1671) to Falconet on the 22nd January 1672, Guy Patin observed: "Je viens d'apprendre du jeune van der Linden que Monsieur Gronovius est mort a Leiden. Il restoit presque tout seul du nombre des [Savants] d'Hollande. Il n'est plus, dans ce pais-là, de gens faits comme Joseph Scaliger, Baudius, Heinsius, Salmasius et Grotius"[1].

Numbered amongst the greatest scholars of his age, the Professor of Eloquence and History at the *Athenaeum Illustre* of Deventer since 1642[2] is still awaiting the historian to make a close analysis of his thoughts and works against the background of the cultural, political and religious events of one of the most complex and tormented periods of Dutch and European history during the central decades of the 17th century. He was a most clear-sighted interpreter of this period, taking part with incisive critical vigour in the debate that gave birth to modern reflection on ancient history, amid a vast circulation of ideas which finds in his own collection of letters one of the most significant testimonies of all the seventeenth century[3].

1 PATIN 1846, cit. by COHEN 1921, p. 221.
2 Cf. VAN SLEE 1916.
3 DIBON et al. 1974; DIBON and WAQUET 1984.

A Journey to Italy

What the scholarly journey into Italy during the 17th century – the rightly styled "age of observation"[4] – may have represented for Europe's men of learning is now common knowledge following Hazard and Pintard's classic investigations. The traveller's main objective is to gain knowledge of classical, humanistic and ancient Italy through sources and manuscript documents: Clüver's *Italia antiqua*, the homeland of art and literature, lived and re-lived in the historical-critical study of *ruins*, bringing the motive of sentiment close to the immediate interest of archaeology and learning[5], while the matured cultural incentives of diaries, memoirs and above all of private correspondence contribute considerably towards enlightening their experiences. It is common knowledge that between the 15th and 17th centuries private epistolary correspondence assumed most wide-ranging relevance as well as being adopted with considerable frequency, since the typical expressive form of the letter proves most suitable for a fairly widespread genre of pamphlet-writing brought about through learned disputes, requests for book and library information, and for intellectual communication in general. The letter, which is a tangible expression of scientific collaboration, becomes an effective instrument for promoting literary, scientific and scholarly news, and for exchanging favors, as well as for collating manuscripts, consulting and copying original codices, thereby also revealing the extent of interest stimulated by contemporary investigations and publications. In several cases, the *epistola* provides evidence for a particularly complex phase in a critical edition of a text, that is often even exposed to bitter and

4 See on this WILSON 1968, pp. 119 ff. and ALPERS (1983) 1984; cf. also DE SETA 1982, pp. 125–263.

5 Cf. DIBON 1964.

long-drawn out controversies among experts. Thus it even goes so far as to offer critico-philological discussion on the texts it examines, as well as all the concerns of research, the realistic level of transformation of learned knowledge, knowledge that is not, nor can any longer be mere solitary contemplation, but rather the outcome of a common commitment in public or private institutions, in a dialogue that knows no national boundaries[6].

This is the case of Johannes Fredericus Gronovius who never wrote a text about his journey in Italy for public circulation, but rather committed his personal recollections of this experience to his private correspondence, which for the range of the interests shown and for the Author's singular capacity for intuition and analysis reveals certain decisive stages in his cultural formation. Before an almost total lack of studies, Gronovius' letters, for the most part conserved in the vaults of the university libraries of Munich and Leyden, certainly cannot be said to have attracted the interest or even the mere curiosity of modern historians. And yet it is a fundamental work – just as Dibon's meritorious research over the past few years has shown it to be – centred essentially on philological-literary questions, filled with note references, articles and objects that for the most part still require integrating and commenting on in their more significant aspects. It is in fact a complete document, hitherto not having proved easy to consult whose plethora of news items, information and references not only makes possible a first awareness of Gronovius' important role and prestigious activity with a complete picture of arguments and details, but also providing interesting information about that very rich network of relationships and friendships that the indefatigable Dutch philologist had created with men of letters, historians, philologists and scholars

6 DIBON 1976, 1978 and 1986, pp. 73–88.

of the European *Respublica Litteraria* of his day[7]. These relationships, occurring at their basic inceptions and verified through the very data they offer, may prove most useful for popularizing a lively image of Gronovius, quite the opposite to that narrow-minded image of a mediator of information and relationships between the Italian world of culture and the mid-seventeenth century Dutch European one. In utilizing the epistolary material available it is in fact possible to infer how much he shared in common with Italian culture, and to emphasize the importance his presence has assumed for this culture, from behind which there clearly emerges the myth of Erasmian Holland, the ideal model of cultural organization with its universities, academies and publishing houses[8]. Also Gronovius'*Album amicorum* helps to reconstruct the significance and trend of his relationships with Italy which, albeit assembling only the autographs of the scholars and the men of letters he encountered in the cities he visited, is nevertheless, following his collection of letters, an inevitable source that is able to shed light on the meaning of certain references and notes that are difficult to interpret for confirming or rejecting projects and research trends[9].

On leaving Hellevoetsluis[10] on the 29th April 1639, and after visiting England and then France passing through Bordeaux, Toulouse, Béziers and Marseille, Gronovius reached Italy in the autumn of the following year. His journey copied the typical scheme of the traditional itinerary not so far different from the aspiration of Rennaissance origin, to visit the classical land, the

7 For a complete information about this documentation see DIBON et al.1974 but also HULSHOFF POL 1961 and BUZAS 1972, pp. 108f. The characteristics of modern *Respublica Literaria* are discussed now in BOTS-WAQUET (1997) 2005.

8 DIBON 1975, p. 32 but see also HACKMANN (1975) 1979, pp. 107–130 and SCHAMA (1987) 1988, pp. 3ff.

9 *Album amicorum* 1634.

10 GRONOVIUS to Rivet 1639, p. 51.

sancta mater studiorum. Decided on by the caprice of the two young patricians of Amsterdam, Laurens and Steven Gerard whom Gronovius accompanied as tutor, the *iter italicum* is also indirectly favoured by the Dutch philologist whose "consensi tandem ut qui frustra repugnarem", expressed to Rivet in 1641[11], is tacit consent to the undertaking, yet disapproved of by the two Gerard boys' uncle, Louis de Geer, and not only for economic reasons[12].

His early historico-philological education, his literary and juridical studies, everything in Gronovius fired his love for Italy and 'Italian culture'. In 1640, the year when his sojourn in Italy began, he was by no means unknown to the citizens of the *Respublica Litteraria.* In 1637 he had published a first critical edition of Statius' *Silvae*, much appreciated by Saumaise[13]. The following year he gave Isaac Casaubon's correspondence for publication, a work which initially edited by Rivet, had procured for him the privilege of enjoying personal contacts with the greatest scholars of the day, from Grotius to the Dupuy brothers, and from Sau-

11 GRONOVIUS to Rivet 1641, pp. 142–143: "Ac etsi consilium nostrum esset flectere iter per Arausionem, Avenionem et Delfinatum Genevam, tamen nescio quomodo invasit aliquis instinctus inopinus comitum meorum animos ut in Italiaim transfretare desiderarent. Qui quidem nullos passus est frenos postquam ibidem consobrinum suum ex Helvetiis eodem ivisse acceperunt".

12 DE GEER to Gronovius 1640, p. 9: "Je n'improuve pas vostre voyage d'Italie, pourvu que mes neveux se contiennent en modestie et crainte du Seigneur! Car ce sont lieux [glissants] pour la jeunesse". See, after PINTARD (1943) 1983, GIDDEY 1960, pp. 183ff. and STONE (1965) 1972², pp. 757–767.

13 GRONOVIUS 1637 and SALMASIUS to Gronovius 1637, p. 245: "Cum dixero a multis annis in hac academia non prodiisse opus, in quo limatissiini iudicii et eruditionis consummatae plura vestigia iinpressa appareant, veras ac tuas tibi laudes reddidero, non adscitas nec fucatas".

maise to Daniel Heinsius[14]. And it is precisely to the latter that in April 1639 Rivet summoned the young philologist who prepared to undertake the *grand tour* in Europe, with a letter of recommendation with universal tones, addressed in fact to "lectoribus omnibus amicis et notis", and such as to summon "omnes quibus notus sum et qui mihi bene volunt" to favour the pupil "omnibus bonis et doctis clarissimus, tam eruditionis quam probitatis nomine, mihi certe inter primos qui eius opera sum usus in evulgandis τοῦ μαχαρίτου. Isaaci Causoboni Epistolis in quo labore bonam operam navavit"[15]. Still in 1639 the *Observationes* were published by Gronovius, an important collection of critico-philological reflections favourably received by Grotius[16] who, at the time of his exile in Hamburg (1633) had set his young pupil on the path towards historico-literary studies, then recommending him at the beginning of 1638 in France to the Dupuy brothers[17].

By undertaking the journey in Italy at an adult age Gronovius was at his mental and cultural peak to profit therefrom, and

14 Cf. CASAUBONUS 1638. See on this relation SAUMASIUS to Dupuy 1638, p. 32: "Le Sieur Gronovius que vous pouvez [connaître] par l'édition des Epistres de Casaubon s'en allant en France, je n'ai pas voulu le laisser aller sans l'accompagner de mes lettres pour le recommander à mes amis encore qu'il porte avec soi sa recommandation. Il est assez [connu] en ce [pays] par les marques de son esprit et de sa doctrine, les livres qu'il a publiés comme ces miscellanea et ce qu'il a fait sur les Sylves de Statius". Cf. BOTS 1994, pp. 145–155.

15 RIVET to Gronovius 1639, p. 42.

16 GRONOVIUS 1639 and GROTIUS to Gronovius 1639, pp. 192–193: "Tantae sunt suavitatis, Gronovi doctissime, Observationes tuae, ut semel in manus sumptas, [quamquam] in multis negotiis, deponere nunquam potuerim. Sunt omnia plena emendationibus ingeniosis, explicationibus pereruditis".

17 GRONOVIUS to Grotius 1638, p. 160: "Insigne amoris indicium postremae tuae, a.d. XIV Kal. Mart. datae mihi praebuerunt, quae comitate tua puteanis fratribus commendatum me nuntiabant".

to be able to desire legitimately "hanc peregrinationem quanto possum bellissimo χύχλω absolvere"[18]. In November 1640, after crossing through Genoa, Pisa and Leghorn he reached Florence where he stayed for about two months until mid-January 1641. Among his correspondence his references to his stay in Florence prove particularly interesting, representing an important stage – together with that of Pisa and Siena – on his journey to Rome and Venice[19]. From their very beginnings the contacts he made with the environment of scholars fomented with ideas and interests. In the letter dated 8th April 1641 written to Rivet the Dutch philologist he makes a point of recalling the meetings held with Doni "et literarum et musices peritissimum ac Bannii [J.A. Ban] amicum, magnum item Galilaeum et P. Victorium. [Pietro Vettori II]"[20] . In Florence and in all the other cities he visited, Gronovius – just as Sarrau emphasised to Rivet in 1641 – "n'est pas amusé à des choses de néant"[21], but approached the greatest representatives of Italian literary life, desirous of being able to have access to their libraries and their private archives. Of these contacts we have several direct significant testimonies. Particularly relevant is the contact with the grand-ducal court who, being informed about the research activated by the illustrious visitor, actively and openly encouraged developments by introducing him to the consultancy of the collections and manuscripts of its library. Traces of these fruitful relationships will be visible not only in the correspondence but also in the printed works of his maturity. In a small-scale work dated 1668, dedicated in fact to the Granduke Cosimo III, *Allocutio ad serenissimum principem Cosmum, magnum Etruriae principem,* Gronovius emphasizes the essential contributions offered to his critical editions of

18 GRONOVIUS to Heinsius 1641, p. 148.

19 On the "Grand Tour" see BATES 1911, p. 96.

20 GRONOVIUS to Rivet 1641, p. 143 and GRONOVIUS to Heinsius 1641, p. 147.

21 SARRAU to Rivet 1641, p. 30.

the works of Livy and Seneca by the research initiated among the Granduke's precious collections, observing:

> Hic ego si de me meisque ludicriis aliquid infulciam, vereor ne putidiusculus habear. Etsi hoc malo, quam ingratus videri reticendo, quid privatim vobis debeam. Ego igitur quam parum in hoc genere valeam, et optime scio, et libenter agnosco, sed (ut modestissime dicam) plus centum T. Livii Historiarum et L. Annaei Senecae Tragoediarum loca, quae nemo antehac ne doctissimorum quidem intelligebat, nunc ope Medicéa sine offensione leguntur[22].

Attracted into our country (Italy) by his interests in archaeology and antiquity, by the importance of the new critico-philological studies, Gronovius with all-consuming curiosity assembles both facts and testimonies of ancient and modern historical culture, introducing into the most subtle disquisitions the positive spirit of the researcher, and critic for whom the experimental datum has an objective and evidential, albeit primary, value with regard to every consideration of a theoretical order. Behind Gronovius, behind his authors is all the travail of European erudition of the sixteenth-seventeenth century, witnessed at Leyden by Scaligero's work, later carried on and enlarged upon by that of Vossius, Daniel Heinsius and Grotius whose humanistic impulse *thesauri, recueils,* erudite compilations and, above all, new critical editions of the classics represent the outcome of a collective work through which scholars of different cultures and faiths search for the *truth*: a truth which tends less and less to be defined by the criteria of absolute transcendent certainty.

However, in the Florence of the Medici of the mid-seventeenth century, admired as the home of *libertas,* the spread of culture had appeared to him also marked by a mortifying logic of cautions, far too cautious to blunt every compromising

22 GRONOVIUS 1668, p. 10.

point in the cultural debate, in accordance with a strategy which in the long term would have caused several ambiguities and uncertainties to transpire. And this environment must have soon disappointed him if at the beginning of 1641, in the above-mentioned letter dated 8th April of that very same year written from Venice to Rivet, he proposed moving to Rome[23]. An initial cause of very bitter disappointment was doubtlessly presented by the open and covert obstacles set by the Florentine librarians against his desire to consult the manuscripts of the Laurentian library:

> Duobus libellis supplicibus Magno duci oblatis, postquam integras tres septimanas omne indignitatum genus quod qui ad magnatum portas ambitionis alicuius gratia excubant ferre coguntur, ad secretarii ianuam tulissem, non potui impetrare ut scribere mihi in bibliotheca illa etiam sub custodis oculis liceret. Nam movere inde librum ac domum portare, quod per totam Galliam licet, sub poena excommunicationis prohibitum est. Id adeo accidit mihi, quia omnes isti bibliothecae praefecti fungi sunt ac fatui, omnisque eruditionis imperitissimi quidam clerici, caetera Itali hoc est suspicaces et nimis cauti qui quid ego vellem ne intelligere quidem poterant, credentes aut libros magicos aut arcana status me scrutari[24].

23 GRONOVIUS to Rivet 1641, pp. 144ff. Cf. DIAZ 1976, pp. 465–545. On Vossius' life and work, Rademaker's essay apart, see WICKENDEN 1993, especially pp. 80–123ff.

24 GRONOVIUS to Rivet 1641, p. 143 and GRONOVIUS to Heinsius 1641, pp. 147–148: "Scito, mi Heinsi, hic longe abundantiores esse quam uspiam vidi, literarum thesauros, sed homines difficillimos quos, nisi longo tempore et magno usu, delinire non possis. Ex uno disce omnes; Florentiae duobus libellis supplicibus magno duci oblatis, postquam tres integras hebdomades ad primi secretarii ianuam (non enim admissionem ad illos fraterculos gigantum petere licet sed exspectandum est donec ipsi e thalamis statis horis procedant) quotidie mane ac vesperi excubando, omne genus indignitatum pertulissem, non impetrare potui ut in bibliotheca medicaea ad D. Laurentii aedem scribere mihi aut notare liceret. Pro magno beneficio datum est, ut legere in ea possem, cum clerico cla-

Thus his stay in Florence revealed the features and the tones of a symbolic contrast between the image of classical Italy and the contemporary one, resulting in fact, not only as home of the arts and letters but also the place for the 'tyranny' of librarians, of unbearable vulgarity, where superstition, ignorance and stupidity reigned supreme. Protagonist of such an experience is an honest disenchanted spirit that assessed what it has directly seen and recorded so far removed from common places and preconceived ideas. In short, it is a truer Gronovius with that special need of his to examine only through his own eyes, and to judge for himself.

For such an intellectual temperament as his, his sojourn in Rome must have assumed special importance. Rome is above all the ancient city whose history he knows, whose testimonies he venerates and whose language he speaks. He approached Rome in awe and with the trembling soul of the scholar and classicist who admires the spectacle offered by antiquity, magnificent and yet disturbing, since in addition to the aesthetic emotion of wonder, he feels an almost physical fear in the presence of the awe-inspiring remains of ancient grandeur[25]. Thus there emerges from Gronovius' correspondence not only the portrait of a city at the forefront of erudition and information exchange, but also

vigero vacaret. At olim publice patuit cuivis. Nisi ego artificio quodam et Philippi Macedonis ἑλεπόλει (nosti dictum eius de asino onusto) mihi subvenissem, tantis opibus Tantalus interfuissem". On this theme see also GRONOVIUS to Dupuy 1641, p. 167 and GRONOVIUS to Heinsius 1645, p. 163.

25 GRONOVIUS to Rivet 1641, p. 144: "Citius itaque destinato Romam pereximus. Nusquam narrare sustinui tibi quae communia cum vulgo peregrinantium mihi evenerunt; sed hic, etsi ex tantis monumentis nihil pene restet, idque quod superat corrumpatur in dies, tamen nec spectando oculi nec recondendo spectata ac memorando mens mihi satisfecit. Saepe pertentare animum ac membra sacer horror cogitantis quantorum heroum olim nutricem terram tererem, saepe lacrimae in oculis, quos in cineres totius mundi trophaea abiissent, recordantis".

that of a certain gravitational centre – in years of fierce censorious opposition against the doctrines of the *new science* – at the cardinals' palaces and the curia of Urban VIII where the Dutch scholar was certainly known[26]. Deliberately therefore in the letter already quoted to Rivet dated April 1641 did he (Gronovius) stress the oppressive act of excommunication in Rome that was exercised simply for the loan of a book, and likewise recording the event in the *Index* of the Casaubon's *Epistolae* he edited and published personally in 1638: "Nec mihi nocuit quicquam, quod decimo fere post adventum meum die Casauboni Epistolae pillacio ad Pasquini statuam publice adfixo prohiberentur. Holstenius serio negavit mihi suo id factum consilio, sed culpam in quendam Puteanorum fratrem monachum contulit"[27]. Also in the letter to Doni dated 7th August 1641, even without making explicit reference to the actual influence exerted by the Roman censure, he observed, with regard to the restrictions imposed on the editing, that "verum est, quod suspicabar, esse ibi quaedam, quae in istis orbs difficulter poterunt publicari"[28]. Not every-

26 RICHTER to Gronovius 1642, p. 240: "Nolebam praeterea ideo ad te scribere, quia inscius eram locorum hoc vel illo tempore haereres, dum nunc cum Belgis, nunc Britannis, nunc cum Gallis vitam transigebas; Praesertim quum te, post Galliam peragratam, etiam Italiam perlustrasse inaudiverim; atque ita quidem, ut Romae etiam Summo Pontifici non ignotus bene vixeris; licet Casauboni Epistolae (thesaurus ingens, pro cuius publicatione orbem literatorum in aere tuo habeas) ut liber haereticus, Vulcano ibi traditus dicatur [...]". On this see MOLLERUS 1759, III, p. 265.

27 GRONOVIUS to Rivet 1641, p. 144. See also GRONOVIUS to Heinsius 1641, pp. 148–149. On *Casauboni Epistolae* in the *Indice dei libri proibiti* cf. DIBON 1981, pp. 61–62.

28 GRONOVIUS to Doni 1641, p. 163. See ROTONDÒ (1973) 1982, pp. 1397–1492. On the hostile attitude towards Roma see GUEZ DE BALZAC to Gronovius 1641, pp. 447–448: "[...] C'est donc vostre séjour en Italie que j'approuve extrémement, et le désir que vous avez eu de [connaître] et de considérer le plus raisonnable peuple du monde. Mais pourquoy ne parlez-vous point de Rome, aussi bien que de Venise?

thing appears to Gronovius to have been censured, however. In Rome even his critico-philological culture proves to have been considerably enhanced by the consultation and study of some important manuscripts, despite the constant difficulties of gaining access to the Vatican and Farnese libraries[29]. However, he did not limit his interests simply to ancient Classical texts: from a letter dated August 1656 written to Clément we learn that in Rome he copied the manuscript of Comnena's *Alexiades* the edition of which was then taken from him by the Jesuit Poussines: "Narro tibi me Romae partim mea, partim multo auro redempta manu descripsisse Alexiades Annae Comnenae, et quia mendosum erat exemplar, cum florentino, ob hanc ipsam causam, in eam urbem quam iam videram, reversum contulisse. Fecit idem postea otiosius Lucas Holstenius, ex cuius codice meum exemplum paraveram et si edere vellem, illum iam emendatiorem be-

N'estimez-vous que les neveux d'Antenor, et contez-vous pour rien les [enfants] d'Enée? Il me semble que le père Strada méritoit bien autant de curiosité de vostre part, que le père Fulgentio, et que vous ne déviez point mespriser le légitime héritier, ou plustost le vray esprit de Tacite, pour courir après l'ombre et les restes de Frà Paolo. Vous ne me dites pas un seul mot de la cour des princes Barberins. Il est certain [néanmoins], que toute sorte de vertu est la bien-venuë en cette cour, vint-elle de Hambourg, et de delà l'Elbe. Les muses sont logées dans le palais [...]. Et peut-estre que si vous aviez escrit *ad Romam,* l'élégie que vous avez escrite *ad Venetias,* ce bon Pape qui [sait] faire des vers, vous eust respondu, au lieu que le Doge n'a pas [su] le faire".

29 GRONOVIUS to Rivet 1641, p. 144: "Vaticana horis illis quibus patet uti liberrime potui, sed quia longissime distabat inde habitatio nostra et tot incidebant palatio (non enim omnes urbi) festi dies, ut raro pateret, vix bis aut ter in ea sum moraturus [...]". See also GRONOVIUS to Heinsius 1641, p. 148: "Romae Farnesianae celeberrimae quondam aditus muro obseptus est ne cuiquam eius usus concedatur. Aliae durissimas semper et adversas praecipue festinantibus habent leges. Non tamen omnino vacuis rnanibus redimus; adeo improbitas laboris mei omnes difficultates vicit".

nigne obtulit"[30]. And these signs alone suffice to emphasise the Author's thinking as critic and philologist accustomed to reading and collating documents and manuscripts for verifying historical truth. Already in a letter to Nicolaas Heinsius dated 1637, after making a balance of the most modern critical studies ("Ubi sunt illi Heinsii, Grotii, Dousae, Meursii, Scriverii, Putschii", he identified and their *vera dignitas*

> non in mutatione literae aut syllabae, ut calumniantur, sed in cognitione linguarum, antiquorum rituum, historiarum, praeceptorurn sapientiae consistit. Haec cum coniuncta sunt, et lectio diligensque labor ingenio et iudicio non destituitur, existit inde praeclarum illud egregium, posse de unoquoque scriptorum veterum, non quod audieris ab alio, sed quod senseris, iudicium ferre, genium uniuscuiusque penetrare, mentem et oeconomiam abditam saepe et in recessu conditam eruere, phrasin agnoscere, locos corruptos restituere, quae verae critices munera sunt, et erant olim apex literarum[31].

And this is likewise witnessed by the dialogue in Rome, the papal city and at one and the same time the city of disbelief, with Gabriel Naudé, the celebrated librarian of Cardinal Mazzarino, exemplary witness to that complex and variegated cultural phenomenon which is 17th century Libertine thought, on whose horizon, as has been rightly noted "l'erudizione è divenuta uno strumento critico che non si limita a conquistare una nuova dimensione dell'antico (riscoprendo e rivalutando autori coperti da secolare silenzio o condanna: Epicuro, Lucrezio, Sesto Empirico) ma che, attraverso la scelta e la giustapposizione di testi sapientemente scelti, mette in crisi un pacificato mondo di valo-

30 GRONOVIUS to Clément 1656, p. 681.
31 GRONOVIUS to Heinsius 1637, p. 16. On critico-philological Gronovius' activity see HALL 1913, pp. 119–120 and KENNEY 1974, pp. 58, 70.

ri"[32]. In a letter to Naudé no less, dated 28th April 1641, the Dutch philologist intervened directly in the fundamental problems of translating and editing the classics, showing the need for an adequate apparatus of notes for every edition that aspires to be truly critical. And with specific reference to the texts of Livy and Seneca, he showed the need to order the annotations into an adequate logical sequence, thus emphasizing the useful competence performed by the dissertations of history and law in upholding the more significant observations:

> Consilium tuum de meditatis in S. et L. est sane probum et minus occupato et longaevum sibi otium spondenti omnino sequendum, nec ego nisi in minima parte a te dissentio. [...] quam si rationem tenere in Seneca vellem, liber exiret maior quam Delrii miscellanea, et in annos multos representationem curae meae haberem comprendinandam. Hoc vero gratificari vobis possum ut librorum Livii ordinem in meis sequar: aut ubi materia suppetit, ad unam principalem varias adiungam alias observationes, utque ita ex capite velut rivulos deducam [...]. Et sic me incepisse agnosces ex primis capitibus miscellarum; sed cum id maturam quoque poscat meditationem, angusto autem spatio temporis tum includerer, milleque occupationes et caput et circa salirem latus, anxie de hoc comtu operis laborare desii, et contentus singulis auctoribus singulas dedicare sectiones, de ipsarum ordine aut cognatione sollicitudinem insuper habui[33].

From a methodological – but not only methodological – viewpoint, this need revealed for a historico-critical attitude towards the newly edited classical texts is of great importance. On the changed cultural front of mid-seventeenth century, the traditional humanistic deference towards the past and the exegetic authority that had been established proved to be conditioned by certain new interests that became the instrument for further ac-

32 GREGORY 1979, p. 18. On "gusto dell'ironia e della duplicità" cf. – in addition of PINTARD (1943) 1983, I, pp. 109ff. – BIANCHI 1988, pp. 17–18.

33 GRONOVIUS to Naudé 1641, pp. 150–152.

tion and reflection. Within the Gronovian perspective, the work of the scholar acquired marked historical importance which, as an essential component of historic and historiographic discourse, remained the sign for a new highly original elaboration of the *fides historica.* The cult of *memoirs* no longer burnt itself out in a fruitless return to the ancient past in the collection of ancient relics nor in a slavish imitation, but tended to become the life blood for the new civilization, albeit always constructed in the awareness of what had been inherited from the past. No longer a mine of examples or an accumulation of useless data, the past itself presented itself to the eyes of the historian as an autonomous organism with its own traditions and laws of development. Far from adopting uncertain and provisional critico-philological stances, Gronovius now developed an attitude of trust towards the trustworthiness of history, and towards the possibility of defining the conditions of verifying historical facts, directed towards protecting the rules of *critique* realistically, and safeguarding the *fides historica,* thus reacting against the *impasse* provoked by the affirmation of alleged mathematical-type *evidence*, and by the sceptical negation of every *certainty*. In short, what supports such a tendency to go beyond approximative critical modules is the desire to guarantee a certain assurance to the historical fact examined, to discredit absolute scepticism as being both *a priori* and uncritical, by attributing a more realistic and definite significance to historical research, and by breaking away from the modern myth of a mental truth that was peculiar to the theoretical and historiographical forms and schemes of dogmatic Cartesianism wherein much Dutch culture of the late seventeenth century had taken refuge[34].

34 On this theme after SIEGENBEEK 1829–1832 and MOLHUYSEN 1913–1924 see COHEN 1921, pp. 535–668; THIJSSEN-SCHOUTE 1950 and THIJSSEN-SCHOUTE 1954, pp. 52ff., 462ff., 538ff.; DIBON 1954. For an up-to-date information see GORI 1972, pp. 7–63, BERTELLI 1973, pp. 312ff. and BORGHERO 1983.

Nor did the Dutch philologist limit himself to researching per se and gathering information and documents in solitude in that he also fulfilled that same office for others. In the eyes of the scholars residing in Italy he represented a sure and trustworthy informant, to whom it was possible to turn in order to obtain information and advice, as is shown by the fact that Lucas Holstenius constantly avails himself of his works and judgement, his fellow countryman and pupil of Vossius and Daniel Heinsius resident in Leyden between the years 1616 and 1622, before settling in Rome in 1627 as librarian to Cardinal Barberini. Holstenius is tireless in asking for explanations, clarifications and interpretations of texts, and in communicating the findings of his investigations. In particular, he does not fail to impart to his friend Gronovius the need to collate in Florence "Procli vitam a Marino scriptam"[35]. For the particular quality of its contents, for the vastness and variety of the arguments treated, the Gronovius-Holstenius correspondence covers an important chapter in identifying the developments of Gronovius' cultural experience in Italy. Praised for his collection of letters with the expressions *noster, popularis meus, incomparabilis noster,* the future *praefectus* of the Vatican, not only facilitated the research of his learned philologist friend in Rome by introducing him to the Barberini library, but also recommended him to his friends in Florence, Padua and Venice[36].

Finally, his encountering and first reading of Leone Allacci's work also dates back to his time in Rome. The scholar and theologian of' Greek origin, guardian of the Vatican from 1661 on

35 HOLSTENIUS to Gronovius 1641, p. 88. "Mitto literas aliquot ad amicos, quos praecipuos habeo Florentiae, Venetiis, Patavii non quod tu hederae istius illicio egeas, sed ut hoc quoque officii genere affectum meum tibi tester". On the relationship between Gronovius and Holstenius see MIRTO 1999, pp. 29, 30, 87, 88, 94ff., 196–198.

36 GRONOVIUS to Naudé 1641, p. 141 but also GRONOVIUS to Rivet 1641, p. 144; GRONOVIUS to Heinsius 1641, p. 147.

the demise of Holstenius[37], enjoyed at the same time as the latter direct noteworthy relationships with the Dutch philologist, without failing, as Manacorda rightly pointed out to project his image and work onto the Italian cultural panorama and more especially that of Venice by instructing Aprosio among others on the characteristics and developments of his critico-philological and historico-erudite studies[38]. And it is precisely from Venice in the previously-mentioned letter dated 8th April 1641 while giving an account of the highlights of his *iter italicum*, that Gronovius confided to Rivet the real opportunities that the Roman environment of learning had procured for him:

> Hic omnia mihi reddidit faciliora popularis mei L. Holstenii, viri profecto eruditione maximi, humanitas. Patronus eius, illustrissimus cardinalis Franciscus, honorem mihi habuit ingentem; bibliothecam suam aperuit et cum in ea morari vellem, cubiculum assignavit, libros etiam quos desiderarem in conductum meum ferre permisit [...]. Gilbertus etiam Naudaeus gallus sui cardinalis de Balneo benignissime supellectilem librariam mihi et obtulit et frui ea concessit: potuissemque apud plures eodem gaudere beneficio si diutius manere ibi potuissem[39].

At the end of the month of March 1641, having ruled out the possibility of staying in Rome any longer, his decision to set out for Florence, Bologna and Padua, with Venice as his final destination, that had come to him as divine inspiration, had been strongly favoured by del Naudé's concern. The latter had, in fact, obtained a letter of recommendation in Gronovius' favour from Contarini, the Venetian ambassador at Rome, a letter

37 *Album amicorum* 1641, 174. Cf. MUSTI 1960, pp. 467–471.

38 MANACORDA 1901–1902 and 1902–1903, p. 247.

39 GRONOVIUS to Rivet 1641, p. 144. In the correspondence with Heinsius Gronovius observes: "[...] Nam extra ordinem istum nominare debeo magnum cardinalem Franciscum de quo iactantius quaedam scribere possem, vera tamen, si id moris esset mihi" (GRONOVIUS to Heinsius 1641, p. 147).

which, destined for the procurator Giovanni Nani, would have been delivered to the learned Dutchman by Liceti in Bologna[40].

Interesting and of considerable relevance are the pages that Gronovius' correspondence devotes to his stay in Padua, and to the small yet active group of scholars gravitating around the University, referring above all to Rhodius, Scioppius, Sohier, Ferrari, to Vizzani and Vesling. Padua, the mid-seventeenth-century stronghold of Averroism of unorthodox Aristotelism, characterised by the university teaching of Cremonini and Liceti, is the city that keenly participates in European scepticism, for which the contemporary Libertine culture incurs great debts; it is what Pintard has effectively defined as "a seminary of disbelief", bent on conciliating Peripateticism and Christianity in recognition of the political necessity of a 'hypocritical' equilibrium between philosophy and religion, between Aristotelism and Christianity[41]. In this setting Gronovius' experiences and interests were utilized, beyond the pure and simple exigencies of bibliographical information, to discuss specific problems of textual criticism and commentary on classical manuscripts, as well as on recent studies in the course of preparation. Particularly interesting at Padua is the relationship of scientific collaboration established with Joannes Rhodius, the Danish medical doctor and antiquary who permitted the Dutch philologist to consult an important rare manuscript of Statius' *Silvae* he possessed, then utilized by the Gronovian edition of the Latin poet's work. Direct testimony of this is in the letter sent from Venice to the Danish scholar on the 30th April 1641: "[...] Silvae tuae ms. multum mihi profuerunt. Inveni aliquot coniecturas meas confirmatas quod

40 NAUDÉ to Gronovius 1641. On this theme cf. also GRONOVIUS to Naudé 1641, pp. 140, 150; GRONOVIUS to Heinsius 1641, p. 147 and 1645, p. 164.

41 GRONOVIUS to Heinsius 1641, p. 147; GRONOVIUS to Rhodius 1641, p. 154 and *Albun amicorum* 1641, p. 174. Cf. – after PINTARD (1943) 1983, pp. 106–109 – SPINI (1950) 1983, pp. 149ff.

non parvum nostris laboribus est solatium: inveni et materiam aliquot novarum observationum"[42].

Besides Padua, the historico-cultural motivation of his *iter italicum* found renewed strength and energy also in Venice where his philological-erudite interests were to become stimulated and enlightened in their analytical reasoning. Gronovius certainly remained in Venice as guest of the Dutch merchant Egidio Wachtman until Ascension Day 1641, as shown by the letters sent to Rivet and Nicolaas Heinsius[43] at that time. An ancient republican institution, staunch opponent of Spanish prepotency in Italy and anti-Protestant repression, the lagoon city stirs his fantasy, and stimulates his historico-historiographic knowledge. Compared with Sparta, Athens and Rome, Venice is a modern *locus*, but already a classical one for reflection on themes still central to the historico-political debate on the various forms of government, on their nature and history, and on the *myth* of their stable duration[44]. The Venetian scholars and men of letters considered Gronovius, Grotius' pupil, not only as the champion of free scientific research, the bibliomaniac whose only concern was to guarantee and enhance scholastic information and the circulation of ideas and writings among the citizens of the literary republic, but also, and more especially, as the humanist who succeeded in uniting a most refined taste in criticism with learning, by decking his works out with innovative critical annotations and comments. He gives an apt description of this image as well as some details regarding his arrival in Venice. The *Biblioteca Aprosiana,* a most interesting basic critical catalogue of the

42 GRONOVIUS to Rhodius 1641, p. 153.
43 GRONOVIUS to Rivet 1641, p. 145 and GRONOVIUS to Heinsius 1641, p. 148.
44 On this *myth* in addition to the classical pages of Fink and Gaeta, Chabod and Sestan see BURKE (1947) 1988; HAITSMA MULIER 1980 and NUZZO 1982, pp. 199–222.

works published in Italy in the 17th century, and still largely unpublished, specifying:

> Era non molto prima capitato in Venetia venuto di Roma con lettere del Commendatore, ed abbate *Cassiano* del *Pozzo,* e del gran *Leone Allacci,* dirette a Don *Iacopo Filippo Tomasini* padovano de' *Canonici Secolari di S. Giorgio in Alga,* l'eruditissimo *Giovanni Friderico Gronovio,* col quale hebbe occasione di trattare per tutto quel tempo, che si trattenne in quella città, havendogli prestati molti libri, servendolo anche in occasioni di confrontare *Manilio* con un ms. della bibliotheca di *S. Antonio* de' Canonici Regolari Scopettini [...]. Con questa occasione fece un segnalato favore al *Tomasini,* cavando per lui l'Indice di tutti i libri di quella, e posto per primo nelle *Biblioteche Venete* mss. [...]. Ad alcuni non mancò di fare qualche notarella. Cosi nel leggio 9 a p. 14. *Panegyrici, Plinii, Latini Pacati* etc. in memb. *Codex satis correctus, et consentiens in bonis lectionibus cum codicibus livineii.* Nel XVI. pag. 16. *Manilii Astronomica F.M. Codex antiquus optimae notae et quo post Gemblacensem Scaligeri non potest inveniri melior. Habet omnes fere bonas lectiones a Scaligero notatas.* In piccioli leggii nel muro dalla parte settentrionale. *D. Augustinus* de Trinitate. *Eleganter cum miniaturis.* lvi pag. 19. *Maniilii Astronomicon. Liber rarus antiquo charactere.* F. M.[45]

The close relationships with Gronovius during his Venetian stay obviously succeeded in involving him with the main literary and cultural events of the first half of the 17th century. In fact to that period dates back the first meaningful contact with the renowned scholar and patron of the arts Giovan Francesco Loredano whose historical works the Dutch philologist had doubtlessly read as can be deduced from a letter from the Venetian nobleman in reply to the eulogy expressed to him: "Mi loda VS. per gentilezza, ed io la ringratio per debito [...]. E' ben vero che studiando V.5. Seneca ha voluto forse farmi conoscere, che *frigida laus est vituperatio;* e per questo s'è lasciata trasportare ne gli eccessi, lodando Ia mia Historia per non dannarla affatto; Comunque si sia io aggradisco ogni sua espressione, e la prego comandarmi, che vederà quanto io stimi la sua gran virtù, e qual capita-

45 Aprosio 1673, pp. 140–141.

le io faccia del suo amore"[46]. Behind the rhetorical and sentimental emphasis of epistolary conventions were also detected testimonies which from the historico-historiographical viewpoint were significant of the interest aroused by Gronovius' presence in Italy. It was through Loredano in fact, that the Dutch scholar entered into direct relationship with the members of the Venetian Academy of the "Incogniti", founded by the Venetian historian in 1630[47]. Eight of the eleven autographs collected in Venice and reported by Grovinius'*Album amicorum* come from members of this academy[48] which welcomed the erudite Dutchman, devoting to him a brief, but significant bibliographical note in the volume dedicated to *Le Glorie degli Incogniti* (1647) and reproducing the image under which were appended the following lines, as a reminder of his critico-philological activity on Latin poetry:

STATIUS a stando dictus,
nisi fulciat illum. RIDICA,
dum coepit iam titubare, cadet.

In inaugurating the interesting chapter on Gronovius and his works' fortune in Italy and duly providing some information about the philologist's interests and studies as a youth, the bibliographical source emphasised with critical clarity the strong link which through the personality within him led towards uniting law studies with those of ancient law, that is to say jurisprudence with antiquity: "[...] Ma restato finalmente Gio. Federico in braccio alla propria volontà, e vedutosi destinato alla Corte, et al

46 LOREDANO to Gronovius 1648, I, pp. 62–63.

47 In a letter to Rivet 1641, p. 162, GRONOVIUS annotates: "L'Académie des Incognux qui m'ont kit l'honneur de me recevoir en leur très noble compagnie". On this Academy cf. CICOGNA 1847, pp. 364, 558 and MAYLENDER (1926–1930) 1976, III, pp. 205–206.

48 Cf. DIBON and WAQUET 1984, pp. 174–175.

governo della republica, conosciuto, che per ben'intendere i principii delle leggi gli faceva mestiere della notitia dell'antichità, si diede con sommo fervore a rivoltar gli autori greci, e latini"[49].

Without upsetting the traditional canons of literary creation, reflection of the academic "Incogniti" assumed a moderately libertine tone in many innovative cases of special interest in seventeenth-century Italian culture. Indeed, despite the critical adhesion towards, and methodological caution of Cremonini's respected philosophy, the admiration of the "Incogniti" behind the veil of prolix descriptions and fictional conventions, turned towards motives and authors who were certainly on the fringes of the Catholic Counter Reformation, such as Marino with his *Adone* for poetry, and Boccaccio with his *Decameron* for prose, accompanied by Aretino, by definition as an example of cynism and dissoluteness, and Boccalini with his well-known *Ragguagli di Parnaso,* persecuted by the *Index* and the Spanish authorities[50]. In reference to this context, Gronovius' letters leave no doubts about the presence and the direct utilization of the Dutch philologist's work in mid-17th century erudite Venetian culture. Consequently, Gronovius is the privileged reference point of an interesting moment in the long and bitter dispute on Marinism, concentrating on the expressive and stylistic artificiality of the *Adone* and on its presumed "immorality", the reason for the latter being the condemnation imposed by the Congregation of the *Index* in 1627. An efficacious work by the already-mentioned Aprosio *L'occhiale stritolato di Scipio Glareano* [Angelico Aprosio's pseudonym], *per risposta al Signor Cavalier Tommaso Stigliani* (1641) profits from use of the authority and prestige of the Dutch philologist and of his rigorous critico-philological principles. Herein

49 *Le glorie degli Incogniti* 1647, pp. 236, 238. On Statius see also a significant bibliographical note in APROSIO 1673, pp. 149–150. On Gronovius to Loredano 1641 see *Appendix* to LOMONACO 1987, pp. 527–529.

50 Cf. SPINI (1950) 1983, pp. 154ff.; SPINI et al. 1980, pp. 117–124 and BERTELLI et al. 1986, IV, 2, pp. 565–598.

the erudite collector and bibliophile of Ligurian origin, being also a member of the academy of the "Incogniti", examines and defends the first three cantos of the *Adone* from the critical and philological viewpoint, in dispute with the antiMarinist Stigliani, author of the *L'occhiale,* published in 1627, after Marino's death. On pages 199 and 200 of the small-work, Aprosio, justifying the procedures of the "invenzione" of the "linguaggio metaforico" confirmed by Marinian poetry, far different from the metaphorical procedures and schemes of sixteenth-century literary Aristotelism, observes: "Il Sig. Gio: Federico Gronovio, il quale alla modestia, e gentilezza inarrivabile ha congiunta profondissima eruditione, e degna degli Encomi di Daniele Heinsio, di Niccolò suo figliuolo, di Giovanni Isacio Pontano, di Tommaso Graswinckelio, di Vincenzo Fabritio, e di Pietro Strateno, che si leggono nella sua Diatriba sopra le selve di Statio stampata in Haga da Theodoro Maire il 1637. in 8. mostrarà quanta ragione habbia l'opponitore". And then taking his cue from a passage from Book 2 of the "dottissime Osservazioni sopra diversi scrittori stampate in Leida da Isaaco Cómelino, 1639, in 8. cap. 19", Aprosio claims "di haver mostrato a questo gentilissimo Signore, della cui amicitia grandemente mi pregio, che ho letto i suoi libri, e che m'hanno servito per rispondere allo Stigliani, il quale non vuole, che si faccia trapasso da parole, a cose"[51] In confirmation of this meeting of motives and positions, with Aprosio's work being concluded, by deliberately publishing Gronovius' *Elegia de vindiciis Adonidos Mariniani datis a Scipione Glareano contra Thomam Stilianum,* however then referred to by the already quoted *Biblioteca aprosiana,* as comment on the activity carried out by the erudite Dutchman in the lagoon city[52]. Thus from the contact with erudition, Gronovian Italian philology was prompted to a cer-

51 APROSIO 1641, pp. 199–200 and APROSIO 1673, p. 141. On Aprosio cf. ASOR ROSA 1961, pp. 650–653.

52 APROSIO 1641, p. 2. The same *Elegia* is published also in SPINI to Aprosio 1670: cf. LOMONACO 1987, pp. 531–533.

tain type of historical interpretation in which a humanistic culture was enriched by modern instances. The relevance obtained from these is significantly recorded by Aprosio's interesting letters that bear witness to some important letters of the Dutch scholar's participation in the research and study of manuscripts, books and critical texts utilized by contemporary erudite literature. A symbolical document of such collaboration regarding themes and problems of criticism and philology is the letter dated 17th January 1642, written by Aprosio to Gronovius. Here information and considerations of a philological character, experiences and personal memoirs are continually mixed together not without having effectively enlightened new critical contributions made by the thoughts and works of Gronovius to seventeenth-century Italian learning: "Sto copiando il V E R A T R 0 in risposta all' 0 C C H I A L E, e stimo che si stamperà l'estate che viene. In esso pure mi ricordarò del mio Sig.r Gronovio: sicome me ne ricordo hora nelle Note all'Arte degli amanti dell'Ill.mo Sig.r Pietro Michiele, che al presente si stampano". The letter then continues by underlining next to the most recent Aprosian studies, the main orientations of the modern Italian culture of learning, its relevant and original critico-philological exigencies which through Gronovius' effective mediation tend to compare with the experiences of the men of "letterati d'Hollanda"[53].

From Geneva where he was staying in the summer of 1641 for more than two weeks, Gronovius traced from the entire work carried out in Italy a brief but keen and enthusiastic critical balance. And in a letter dated 8th August 1641, written to the Swiss Paganino Gaudenzio (whom he knew personally at Pisa in 1640, where the historian of Rome and of Tacitus in particular, had taught *belle lettres* at the University since 1628)[54] stressed the

53 APROSIO to Gronovius 1642: see LOMONACO 1987, p. 521.

54 Cf. *Album amicorum* 1640, p. 173. On Gaudenzio see COSTA 1984.

value of the amendments that he could now introduce on the basis of the materials gathered and the sources consulted in Italy, for a new critical edition of the writings of Statius and Livy:

> Ex plurimis mss. Titi Livii codicibus, quos immenso labore atque taedio exhausto in italicis diversis urbibus contuli, habeo ultra ducentos locos emendatiores in quibus doctissimi viri Glareanus, Sigonius, Lipsius aliique haeserunt. Nec Statium interim insuper habui, Silvis praesertim aliquot mss. repertis, a quo quia recentior sum, et textum ad manum habeo idemque auctor tuam olim curam meritus est, ut facile et sine studio iudicare possis unum atque alterum locum hic expendendum proponam [...][55].

Thus an experience rich in nuances and contrasts, of lights and shades, that Gronovius has lived in mid-seventeenth century Italy. And such a picture cannot be denied by the account, albeit positive, that the Dutch scholar gave of his *iter italicum* in the letters written on his return journey to Amsterdam (which occurred in January 1642), intending to emphasize the extraordinarily rich variety of the journey[56] and the nostalgia his departure from Venice had so evoked in him as to make him compose the elegy "ad inclitas Venetias"[57]. Yet all this did not prevent him from becoming bitterly aware of the falling trend in the book market, the limits and obligations which in the Venetian city had impeded him in the letters of recommendation already mentioned, obtained from the Venetian ambassador in Rome, in order to render the Marciana library accessible to him: "[...] In Marciam non nisi fugitivo oculo penetravi; quin sum e-roque inde exclusissimus. Ille ad quem missas a te mihi tradiderat Licetus, per aliquot dies pedibus remisque quaesitus, tandem

55 GRONOVIUS to Gaudenzio 1641, p. 165.

56 GRONOVIUS to Heinsius 1642, pp. 169–170.

57 GRONOVIUS to Rivet 1641, pp. 160–162. The *Elegia* is already in GRONOVIUS to Loredano 1641, p. 162 but without the line dedicated to "Incogniti": see LOMONACO 1987, pp. 527–529.

praesente Thomasino in domo publica obvius mihi fuit"[58]. Nor must the tones of this consideration give any surprise. Here too a well-established trend of the epoch is activated and vigorously so in attributing to Italy and to the Italians certain well-defined faults, to introduce *myth* into their discussion, against which the greatest scholars, Gronovius' contemporaries, had occasion to write at times and in similar modalities. During the years 1640 and 1641 at the time of the latter's sojourn in Italy, the myth of the peninsula had fallen for good. As early as 1636 Peiresc noted bitterly that "non vedonsi hormai da alquanti anni uscir opere di consideratione in Venetia ne in l'altre città d'Italia, come prima [...]. Restino estinte le lettere in Roma ancor quando il mondo intero stava in grande aspettazione del contrario"[59]. Gronovius' correspondence is also full of the classical accusations whereof Italians and Italy of the middle of the 17th century were wont to be made target. Promoting his own ideas through his writings and in private conversations, and availing himself of the authority of a direct, articulated intellectual experience, the Dutch philologist also contributed towards propagating among the learned and particularly among the Dutch a typical image of Italy, a country superb for art and nature, but now condemned to an inexorable decline, despite the considerable energies that still survived, as the cultural production was now experiencing a phase of monotonous sterility. In December 1645 he advised Nicolaas Heinsius when about to leave for Italy: "Caeterum editorum librorum bibliotheculam tecum portes oportet: adeo ne vulgarissimi quidem illic venales"[60]. In such a situation outlined as above, the first prize for culture remains with France. Ad-

58 GRONOVIUS to Naudé 1641, p. 150. On the book-market in the Venetian city see – after PINTARD (1943) 1983, I, pp. 83ff. – ULVIONI 1975.

59 DE PEIRESC to Barberini 1636, p. 90.

60 GRONOVIUS to Heinsius 1645, p. 164. On this theme cf. MAUGAIN 1909, pp. 93–109 and KENNEY 1974, pp. 92–93ff.

mired by Gronovius Italy is and still remains basically the one which mirrors "gallicam facilitatem et humanitatem". Thus, Naudé, to seal many advantageous favours bestowed on his Dutch friend, deserved the worthy eulogy: "Et in te uno me Galliam in Italia reperisse"[61]. And so likewise Nicolaas Heinsius, recalling the invaluable help received from Doni in Florence, defined him "ad gallicam comitatem et elegantiam prorsus factum"[62]. In this regard, it is also useful to note that it is precisely through Heinsius that the bond between Gronovius and Italy continued to exist to the point of being able to indicate the Author of the *Observatione* significant fortune in seventeenth-eighteenth century Italian culture, and more especially Neapolitan. Interesting in this respect are the contents of the letter written to Daniel Heinsius' son, a celebrated Leyden humanist, to his close friend Gronovius on the 4th May 1644, some days after his arrival in Naples, to express to him the admiration which following the sad spectacle of ancient Rome, the city of Naples had woken in him, devoted from the origins to the cult of erudition and fine arts: "Ego vero nunc post romanas illas antiquitates perlustratas funestissimi spectaculi pertaesus Neapolim admiror, in qua nihil requiras merito praeter eruditionem et elegantiorum literarum cultum, ad quas tamen civitatem hanc a natura factam credas"[63].

In 1647, with Gronovius' Italian journey now being over some six years, the history of the fortune of his thought and his works in the peninsula ideally opened up. And it was Naples that a most relevant chapter of this history deals with, since Gronovius' interests that developed during his *iter italicum* had encountered most impressive cultural themes and problems in

61 GRONOVIUS to Rivet 1641, p. 143 and GRONOVIUS to Naudé 1641, p. 149.

62 HEINSIUS to Dupuy 1646, p. 4.

63 HEINSIUS to Gronovius 1647, p. 180. On Heinsius and Gronovius' Italian journey see MASTELLONE 1963.

the late 17th-century Neapolitan republic of letters, the critico-philological work of the Dutch scholar acquiring noteworthy value as a historiographic model meriting further examination. To mediate among Neapolitan culture and its greatest expressions, including also foreign ones in the intellectual life of the epoch is, as is commonly known, the fundamental experience, the powerful culture, and the critical sensitivity of Antonio Magliabechi[64]. The Florentine librarian had certainly read the *Oratio de lege regia* (1671), Gronovius' last work, published posthumously in 1678 by his son Laurentius Theodoor and sent to Florence by his other son, Jacobus, on 14th June 1678[65], as well as the *Allocutio ad serenissimun principem Cosmum, magnum Etruriae principem* (1668) mentioned earlier which appeared on the second "shelf" of the Florentine *Biblioteca volante* (1677) of Cinelli Calvoli among the works belonging to the granduke's library, had been defined by Magliabechi in a letter to Panciatichi as just ordinary and with several shortcomings from the stylistic viewpoint:

> II peggio è, che anche l'allocuzione del Gronovio è cosa non solo ordinaria, ma vi sono molti errori [...]. Lo stile è odiosissimo all'usanza dell'altre cose del Gronovio, che, come ella meglio di me sa, è veramente eruditissimo; ma circa allo stile, ec. In oltre, come ho detto, vi sono de' solennissimi errori [...]. Si vede, che ha trascritto di qua, e di là, senza saper niente con fondamento. Molte altre cose simili potrei accennarle, che per brevità tralascio, come anche circa alla lingua, e VS. Illustrissima ben vede ne' due versi, che ho copiati, quel *salaria,* che molto ben so, che è di Plinio, ma ad ogni modo, ec. Altrove si loda da se stesso estremamente[66].

64 G. Valletta "stando sempre più desideroso di notizia de' libri per accrescere la [mia] libraria", is interessed to have "il *Seneca tragico* del Gronovio, ancorché si abbia molti e di molti glossatori" (VALLETTA to Magliabechi 1681, II, p. 1052 and 1682, p. 1059). For the reconstruction of this context see LOMONACO 1987, LOMONACO 1990 and also MIRTO 1994.

65 GRONOVIUS to Magliabechi 1678 I, pp. 458–459. On this Gronovius cf. MASTELLONE 1975, p. 51 and espec. TOTARO 1999.

66 MAGLIABECHI to Panciatichi [sine anno]. Cf. CINELLI CALVOLI 1734–1747, III, p. 81.

The Myth of Rome in the "Oratio de Lege Regia"

Despite what Magliabechi believed, the complicated approach to problems my research favours suggests that I should dwell with special attention focused on Gronovius' last studies and especially on his *Oratio de lege regia,* delivered on the 8th February 1671 (on conclusion of the Author's second and last Rectorship held at the Academy of Leyden), published posthumously in 1678 by his son Laurentius Theodorus and later translated into French by Barbeyrac and published in 1714[67]. In this writing it is possible to trace interests and motives which, on account of his historico-critical intellect and rigour, were destined to become a precious testimony of changed historiographic attitudes towards ancient Rome. They were either faintly sketched out or already fully developed at Leyden by "un gruppo di professionisti della filologia e dell'antiquaria, spesso trasmettenti la professione nell'interno della famiglia, molto efficienti come regolari provveditori di edizioni critiche di classici per tutta Europa"[68]. And this transpires not only from their clear legacy as an important rhetorico-erudite tradition but also from within this group, from an attempt at historico-historiographic analysis closer than may be believed to the political religious and cultural reality of Leyden in the late seventeenth century, when, following Lipsian extremism inherited from Vossius and Graevius and aimed at setting Seneca and Tacitus against Livy and Cicero as models of

67 GRONOVIUS 1678, in BARBEYRAC 1731, then in LOMONACO 1988.

68 MOMIGLIANO (1958) 1984, p. 79. On this theme after SIEGENBEEK 1829–1832 and SCHOTEL 1875, MOLHUYSEN 1913–1924 and COHEN 1921, see DIBON 1954 and DE MICHELIS PINTACUDA 1967, pp. 31–61. For an up-to-date information cf. LUNSINGH SCHEURLEER and POSTHUMUS MEYJES 1975, pp. 161–172 and 467–479; FEENSTRA and WAAL 1975, pp. 15–44; FEENSTRA 1979, I, pp. 331–349; and FRIJHOFF 1981, pp. 341–377.

classicism, Calvinism, now purged of Arminian heresy on the morrow of the synod of Dodrecht (1618) continued to be grafted into the post-Erasmian humanist tradition of Scaligero and Grotius, of Saumaise and Casaubon, through the Stoic motives of classical literature. All this was when the conflict was resolved which had involved orthodox Calvinism of Gomar, and especially the Aristoteleian academic dogmatism of Voetius at Utrecht and his pupils Steuart and Schoockius at Groningen, in dispute with the emerging Cartesian philosophers, ranging from Heyden to Regius, and from Van Hooghelande to Heereboord[69].

By no means a jurist or politician by profession, Gronovius, Daniel Heinsius' successor at Leyden as "ordinarius graecae linguae et graecarum historiarum" from 1658 onwards, was by vocation, mental habit and cultural formation essentially a philologist and historian[70], yet quite capable of combining philological

69 PAQUOT 1768, t. II, pp. 429–430: "Cette méthode infectoit presque toutes les Académies de l'Allemagne. On y avoit abandonné Cicéron, pour imiter le stile coupé, et pointilleux de *Juste-Lipse.* Ce grand homme [...] ainsi dans la crainte de se confondre avec la foule, il emprunta le langage décrié de Sénèque et de Tacite, qu'il déconseilloit lui-même aux autres. Cette témèrité lui réussit, grâces à sa profonde érudition; mais un peuple de démi-[savants], qui voulurent le copier, tombèrent dans la pédanterie la plus burlesque. L'Allemagne fut bientôt remplie de ces singes. On y courut de toute part après les pointes et les *concetti* [...]". On "General Crisis of the 17th century" see ASTON ed. 1968, VII–VIII, pp. 1–4, 135–161, 229–264 and AHSMANN-FEENSTRA 1984.

70 *Album studiosorum Academiae Lugduno-Batavae* 1875, XLIII; SIEGENBEEK 1829–1832, I, pp. 176ff, 190, 223; II, pp. 19–21, 135–136, 280 and MOLHUYSEN 1913–1924, III, pp. 4–5, 14–23. And so Grotius' reviewer observed: "Ni la Théologie, ni le Droit Naturel et des Gens n'avoient fait son étude, et s'il s'y trompe, assez souvent, il faut compenser cela, par les bons services qu'il a rendus aux Auteurs Latins, qu'il a publiés, par les remarques Critiques, qu'il a imprimées à part, et par son Ouvrage *de Pecunia Vetere,* qui est un excellent Livre" (*BIBLIOTHÈQUE ANCIENNE ET MODERNE* 1720, XIII, pp. 159–160).

with juridical studies, works of political-religious interest with editions of the Greek and Latin classics, and antiquarian research into diplomas and numismatics with historical-juridical investigations[71].

Grotius and Vossius' disciple was thus led towards observing the juridical history of ancient Rome more especially through his critico-philological studies, through his interest in assembling law in its genesis and development, that is to say from its historical point of view. As a professional philologist he examined the history of Rome through his exceptional inexhaustable aptitude for history and philology, retracing the end of the republic and the beginning of the imperial power no longer as history in the form of a rhetorical-type account, but as an essay in the form of a critical reconstruction of the past, assisted by documentary, literary, epigraphical and archaeological data, and thus verifying the findings of traditional historiographical practice on ancient Roman law. In the modern history of interpreting the *Lex Regia*, his intervention deserves special attention for being among the first to bestow on the theme a specific treatment which was completely different from the isolated historical, philological and literary observations that the followers of the so-called school cult of Cuiacio and Fabro had expressed on the argument, treating it only indirectly in the setting of a more general historico-critical study of Justinian's *Corpus Iuris*[72]. The essence of Gronovius' new system of interpretation is not to be found in his use of the classics, nor in the change in contents or objectives of historical research, but in a different approach to problems, in another type of interpretation of traditional themes, and in a series of new study methods. The theme of

71 GRONOVIUS (1643) 1656; GRONOVIUS (1661) 1664. In addition to the pages of MOLLERUS 1759, III, pp. 273–274, 275 cf. BUGTER 1980, pp. 1–56 and LOMONACO 1987, pp. 531–533.

72 HEINECCIUS (1735) 1771, pp. 27–49. On the theme cf. PALAZZINI FINETTI 1953, II, pp. 67–442 and MAFFEI (1956) 1972, pp. 60–65.

Roman history is no longer treated from its origins, but from Caesar and the *crisis* of the republic. The aesthetic appeal of all antiquity, the enthusiastic admiration of the great past gives place to the selective historico-critical study of a brief period of time, one that more resembles the present, that finishes by limiting almost everything to the pages which describe the constitution of the empire from the death of Caesar. What remains of Roman history proves interesting only inasmuch as it depends on the content of those pages.

Gronovius was attracted towards reflecting on the *Lex Regia* principally by the eminently political spirit which animated his main historiographical model, namely Tacitus, the "Aristotele del nuovo metodo storico-politico" preferred to Livy by three 17th century historians[73]. In effect, when one speaks of Tacitus and 'Tacitism' much caution is recommended in the use of the terms that always refer to precise meanings which the texts in circulation began to take on. At Leyden, starting from the beginning of 1600 relevant from the critico-philological viewpoint is the interpretation of Tacitus *(Ann.,* VII–XII and *Hist.,* I–V) through the *Leidensis B.P.L. (Bibliotheca Publica Latina) 16 B* manuscript, one of the 31 fifteenth-century examples, considered to be derived from the "Mediceo II" *(Laurentianus 68.2)* codex composed at Monte Cassino between 1038 and 1058. The Lipsian edition gives considerable support to this interpretation, being supplied with Grotius' notes (written at the end of 1617), first appearing at Leyden in 1640 and subsequently re-published in Amsterdam in 1672, together with Gronovius' postille and notes[74].

73 TOFFANIN 1972, p. 213. Background for this context can be found in CORNELISSEN 1938; DROETTO 1968, pp. 101–151 and ETTER 1966.

74 GRONOVIUS 1678. On this manuscript see – after MENDELL 1957, pp. 307ff and 369ff. – KOESTERMAN 1960; SABBADINI 1971, pp. 183–194 and BUGTER 1980, pp. 65ff, 231ff.

From an explicit reference to the first Book of the *Annales*, the Leyden philologist sets out to formulate his *Oratio* and consider "artes et rationes, quibus reipublicae orbem convertit, atque a libertate ac consulatu ad principatum deflexit C. Iulius Caesar Octavianus Augustus". A most refined humanist, Gronovius also praises Tacitus for his style. Yet more than on any other argument his great admiration for the ancient historian invites discussion on the inadequate modern interpretations of the *Lex Regia*. Thus, 'Tacitism' becomes foremost an expression for Gronovius' critico-philological rigorism and his polemic with the immature historical method of the 16th and 17th centuries. The polemical tone and the critical perspective that support the initial moments of his reflection rule out the fact that the Author wishes to follow only the stereotyped lines of classic-style neo-academic deference in treating "haec quaestio nobilissimae subtilitatis, civilium peritis et antiquitatis amatoribus diu multumque versata et iactata"[75]. The humanistic-academic component is certainly present in the *Oratio*; yet, the specifically cultural assumption and the use of classical models in the reconstruction of ancient history do not remain separate from the need to try and achieve critico-methodological clarification and promulgation, since, in the strongly critical approach of Gronovian thought, erudition is not a vain ornament or abstract motive for intellectual pride, but rather a guarantee of a scientific approach towards a discipline, namely philology, which aims at setting itself at the head of the needs and duties of the present, by giving *body* to motives, as well as cultural and political interests with historical *figures*.

The first part of the *Oratio* is a critical survey of the most significant results reached by sixteenth-seventeenth century juridical philology. It is a synthetic but very clear-sighted appraisal originating and maturing within a historico-philological perspec-

75 GRONOVIUS 1678, pp. 18–19. Cf. LESUISSE 1961, pp. 157–165.

tive, with immediate direct contact with the factual data to be analyzed and interpreted. For Gronovius it becomes most urgent to control the models of humanistic jurisprudence through the direct study of the events documented by the *lex* in question, by rigorously distinguishing what has definite historical value and thus projecting to historians, and to antiquarians themselves a different terrain of confrontation and discussion. Gronovius singles out the significance and value of some methodological and hermeneutical implications present in the previous interventions on the theme regarding the problem of *certainty* in historical knowledge. By indirectly contesting Coras and Balduinus' intepretations[76] who, on the basis of passages treated by the *Digesto* (XI, 8, 2) and the *Institutiones* (I, 2, 6*)*, had assimilated the *Lex Regia* into other laws established by the ancient kings, concerning, for example, the supplication of a pregnant woman and paternal power, the Dutch scholar emphasizes that unlike the laws made by the kings ("a regibus"), the *Lex Regia* refers directly to the kings ("de regibus"), to their power and their very authority. Nor is there any point in rejecting the authenticity of such an interpretation, an illegitimate and contrived attempt from the critico-philological viewpoint that Hotman made to single out the origin of the *lex* in question in Livy's account (XXXIV, 6, 7)[77]. For Gronovius it is likewise necessary to reject the sceptical theses of certain modern interpreters who had gone so far as to claim that this law had never been made nor ever even proposed, being in substance a pure illusion, a political stratagem expressly invented to favour the ruling princes, and give tone to their tyranny. Such for example, was Connan's, Estienne's and more so Schoockius' view, scholars who on the basis of similar suppositions already formulated against the *Lex Salica,* which

76 CORASIUS 1598, Book V, Chap. 8, pp. 347–350; BALDUINUS (1545) 1728, pp. 11ff.

77 GRONOVIUS 1678, pp. 22–23. In this context cf. HOTMAN 1567, pp. 20–21 and HOTMAN 1599–1600. Cf. CARCOPINO 1937.

excluded women from the crown of France, Ulpianus or Tribonianus had claimed as authors of such deceit, adulators of Alexander Severus and Justinian: "Horum, inquam, cum omnium nemo legis regiae mentionem fecerit, quidam eo sunt progressi, ut illam unquam promulgatam, nedum iussam et acceptam, inficias irent, dicerentque id nomen inane sine corpore ac specie fuisse, merumque [...], pro rerum potentibus mendacium, et praetextum atque obtentum pingendae colore pulchro et excusatius exercendae tyrannidis, patremque eius suspicarentur hi Ulpianum, alii Tribonianum, qui Severo Alexandro aut Flavio Justiniano hanc scilicet adulationem tulerint expensam"[78].

In the Leyden philologist's opinion, the thesis explicitly referring to Manuzio, Cuiacio, Hotman and Van Giffen[79] is likewise to be rejected, who, through utilizing a famous passage of Tacitus (*Ann.,* III, 26), believed they were able to identify the *Lex Regia* with that norm which had authorized Romulus, in accordance with the simplicity of ancient times, to govern in full autonomy of his judgement; a norm, later abrogated with the expulsion of the Tarquins and reproposed at the time of Augustus at a time when the good of the peace required that sovereign power be conceded to one man alone. Nor is there any better critical reception for the opinion, judged unfounded and 'far fetched', of those who, taking their cue from Ciceronian testimonies (cfr. spec. *De legg.,* III, 3*),* referred the *Royal Law* to the *Twelve Tables,* basing their interpretation on the modification presumed to have occurred in the Augustan age, of a non-existing decemviral law[80]. A further significant polemical indication oc-

78 GRONOVIUS 1678, pp. 24–25. Cf. CONNANUS 1553, Book I, Chap. 16, pp. 68–74; ESTIENNE 1600, Book III, Chap. 4, pp. 123–132; SCHOOCKIUS 1661, edited by LOMONACO 1990, pp. 243–314.

79 MANUTIUS 1557, pp. IIIff.; CUIACIUS 1556, pp. 8–10 and GIPHANIUS 1611, pp. 20–22.

80 GRONOVIUS 1678, pp. 26–28: "Plurirni ad ipsa Palilia et natales urbis regrediuntur, *Legem Regiam* non aliam rati, quam quae Romulo pro veteri

curred with regard to the interpretation attributable to Broëus, and before whom to Muret, who availing himself of Cicero's suggestions *(Oratio de lege agraria contra Rullum,* XIX, 2 and *De legg.,* I, 15) claimed they were able once again to find the origins of the *Lex Regia* in the legislative provisions proposed by Valerius Flaccus, that aimed at ratifying everything that Sulla had done in the civil war, whereof he had proved to be a most cruel victor; provisions subsequently modified, in the person of Julius Caesar, when he was nominated dictator for life and, after him, in the person of Augustus and the other emperors[81]. Others claim to assert with certainty that the *Lex Regia* was voted in 730 during Augustus' tenth consulate. Yet others claim that the pri-

---

simplicitate, ut libitum, imperitandi copiam fecit; eam posterius exactis ob Tarquiniorum superbiam regibus cum caeteris eorundem placitis refixam, abolitam, intermortuam, postquam ad unum omnia conferri pacis interfuit, quasi ab inferis excitatam et renatam, postliminio in possessionem suam redidisse. Sic Manutius, Cuiacius, Hotomannus, Gifanius, ingentia nornina. Duodocim [Duodecim] tabulas nonnulli trecentis post annis eam dedicasse et priores introduxisse opinantur, atque interpolatione levi tributum uni, quod illic duobus assignabatur, hoc modo: *Regio imperio duo sunto, hique praeeundo, iudicando, consu/endo, praetores, iudices, consules appellantur.* Sed haec lex M. Tullii Ciceronis est platonico more legislationis imaginem in ficta ad instar romanae et condenda republica adumbrantis; non decemvirorum sine persona, ut poterant, agentium, quod ille simulabat; neque in Campo Martio, sub Quirinali, ad Tiberim, tribus ordinibus classicorum civium, sed in luco Arpinati, sub quercu Mariana, ad Fibrenum amnem, Q. Tullio Cicerone et T. Pomponio Attico uti rogas, dicentibus perlata est".

81 GRONOVIUS 1678, p. 28: "Ecce autem, qui ad Sullanam dominationem descendant et interregem proditum L. Valerium Flaccum inculcent, ferendo, ut rata essent, quaecumque L. Cornelius Sulla belli civilis victor cruentissimus egisset, isque, quem vellet, civium indicta causa impune occideret, *Regiae Legis* initium Romae fecisse; quae in C. Iulio Caesare, cum dictator perpetuus diceretur, deinde in Augusto et caeteris, qui imperatores perpetui creabantur, instaurata sit". Cf. BROEUS 1622, pp. 42–43; MURETUS 1744, pp. 24–26.

vileges attested by the lex regia voted in favour of Augustus passed implicitly to the emperors of the Julio-Claudian house, to be later explicitly confirmed in favour of Vespasian, thus protecting his rather humble origins with less hatred and violence[82]. Historically unfounded, according to Gronovius, is also the interpretation – referring back to Clapmarius – which denies the existence of a royal law before Vespasian or, at the most claims that it was solicited or extorted by force. With such criticism is finally associated the one addressed to those who, like Gentili, despairing of discovering the real origin of this law, express great regret in recalling a similar ordinance considering it so cancelled out by time that today there remains only the name: "Aliis ante Vespasianum legem regiam nullam fuisse; vel si fuerit, aut emendicatam aut vi extortam. Alii denique totum negotium desperantes splendide miserantur Leges et Senatusconsulta de stillicidiis, aquaeductibus, aleatoribus et fullonibus et huiusmodi minutis de rebus non obruisse oblivionem vetustatis; qua lege imperium orbis terrarum ac possessio humani generis ad unum pervenerit, praeter nomen nihil sciri". Contemporary scholars lacked an adequate knowledge of history and the awareness that historical experience is the matrix of juridical ideas, their reconstructions

82 GRONOVIUS 1678, pp. 28–30: "Nec defuit sub specie maioris accusationis audacia praecise definiens et hoc foetu nobilem reddens annum [a.] U.C. XXX et DCC, consulatum Augusti X, quum senatus in acta eius iurare coeperit eumque omni legum necessitate solverit. [...] Rursum alii probabile censuerunt ab Augusto immissum et subornatum, qui huiusmodi quid ad populum ferret; inque id pnivilegium, nemine factum mutante aut in disquisitionem revocante, et posteros eius successisse, post exstinctam stirpem postque Galbae, Othonis, Vitelii arma, in Vespasiano renovatum, quo mediocri ortus loco ad eandem magnitudinem auspicatius et non tantummodo per arma procederet. Ne hac quidem fini steterunt sed visum aliis maiestatem reipublicae, quum Caesar Iulius primum, mox Octavius Augustus, populo metu eripuerint, eam demum Vespasiano lege regia esse collatam". Cf. DE AMAYA 1667, Book I, Chap. 1, p. 428.

proving insufficient from the historico-historiographical viewpoint, articulated, in fact, through default of method, blindly, without order or principle. All this prompted facing the theme in question *ex novo*, in order to redefine historically "originem et auctoritatem partis in omni iuris corpore vel uberrimae ac fulgentissimae [...]"[83].

In implementing a rigorous critical framework for the problems associated with the interpretation of the *Lex Regia,* the Leyden philologist begins with a historico-linguistic analysis to emphasise what it particularly and specifically indicates, thus avoiding a vagueness which has often provoked considerable confusion of heterogeneous elements and problems, wrongly found under a single terminology. Late Roman Republican history and events connatural with the very existence of the *Lex Regia,* need to bring together the meaning of the expressions *re, regio, regno,* in the modifications of which the transition from republic to principate is emblematically reflected. Particularly efficacious for identifying the possible significance of the *Lex* in question is the highlighting of the early Roman aversion for the epoch and mentality of kings, arrived at through an in-depth study on the internal "evidence" of the literary texts, still faithful in method and contents to the narration of the traditional historians and more especially of Appian (*De bell. civil,* II) and Livy (VI, 19 ff.; XXVII, 19), of Cicero (*Oratio de lege agraria contra Rullum,* I, 5 e 8; II, 6; *Oratio Pro P. Sulla,* 7; *De divinatione,* II, 54; *Epist. ad Att,* I, 16) and Florus (III, 14 e 16), of Tacitus (*Ann.,* VI, 1; *Hist.,* II, 70), Juvenal (*Sat.,* XI, 8) and Plutarch (*Vitae Caesar.,* I). First and foremost it is expedient to consider "alterum incredibilis invidia, infamia, odium, detestatio, quae inoleverat, *regis,* et *regni* et *regii* cuiusvis in homine romano: alterum summa et antiquissima cura principum, ut quod habebant actitabantque, praes-

83 GRONOVIUS 1678, pp. 30, 23. See CLAPMARIUS (1605) 1624, Book II, Chap.15, pp. 64–65 and GENTILI (1600) 1763–1769, t.V, pp. 279–294.

tigias quasdam oculis vulgi faciendo celarent et habere atque activare ne viderentur"[84]. For this consideration Gronovius goes so far as to affirm that Justinian's interpretation of the *Lex,* based on the model of the Ulpian fragment (*libro primo Institutionum*, in *Dig.*, 1, 4, 1 *pr.*) is historically illegitimate, as it is not possible to claim that this particular law was given a name that would have stirred the memory back to a time that is odious for the Roman people to which the emperors always tried to avoid making any allusion in following the example of Caesar:

> Hos igitur eo ingenio praeditos tantisque agentes artibus, tali tamque exoso regium nomen tempore, commisisse, ut aliquid, quod de illorum dignitate ferretur, *regium* proclamaretur, atque in eo imperatorem populum uni sese addixisse et obnoxium fecisse, et omne suum atque in se ius iudiciumque transdidisse et velut sequestro posuisse, insolentissime ac superbissime iactaretur, quasi libertatem prostratam palam pedibus calcarent aut catenatam ante currum ducerent: non aio docto, sed tantum sano et consipienti cui potest probari?[85]

However, the *Lex Regia,* on the basis of which the Roman people would have conferred *omne suum imperium a potestatem* on the emperor, is not pure invention, since it can certainly be established that despite the aversion nurtured for the name ("rem exstitisse sine nomine [...] cum maxime nascebatur, insinuabat, obrepebat; non semel et confertim, non uno ictu atque impetu, sed paullatim, morando, per intervalla [...]"). An illuminating example of such political pratice is provided by Caesar's ascendancy to the title of consul, dictator and finally tribune of the people, as the perpetuity assumed by this last office represents a great advance towards the *royal law,* which without ever appearing in explicit or formal and immediate terms, has on various occasions revealed itself, according to significant modalities, as documenting the historico-juridical character of customs and

84 GRONOVIUS 1678, p. 32.
85 GRONOVIUS 1678, pp. 44–45. On the theme see WYDUCKEL 1979.

laws of different times[86]. Clarification and development of this interpretation comes about in recalling Augustan power and the politico-constitutional events decisive for the affirmation of the principate. Augustus appears to Gronovius as a "hypocrite", a cunning and insolent simulator who as a very great politician, pretended to want to restore the republic to Rome, but who in contrast only strengthened his own personal power. It is no wonder that his first concern was that of the apparent restoration of the Republican orders and of the ancient *libertas* with his decisive wish to renounce the odious title of triumvir and Head of State for the effective power over the traditional magistracies by assuming only the office of consul, thereby seemingly avoiding imposing on the people subversive politico-constitutional solutions to republican legality:

> Quid modestius illo, *deposito triumviri nomine consulem se ferens ad tuendam plebem tribunicio iure contentum?* Quantus ostentator civilitatis, qui longa magis et speciosa quam fida oratione ipse principatum sibi abrogavit, et arma, provincias, vectigalia, leges et iudicia senatui restituit [...]. Iustum

86 GRONOVIUS 1678, pp. 45–49: "Hoc, quod iam mihi planum faciendum est, quamvis utramque paginam historiae istorum temporum faciat, et obvium sit, neminem tamen ad hoc usque, quod sciam, advertit. Itaque semper quaesitus Osiris, semper clamatus Hylas, neque usquam inventi; dum enim exspectant et circumferunt oculos, sic ubi occurrat uno versiculo et contingenti scriptura traditum; Velitis, iubeatis, quirites, ut sit lex regia et populi omnis in se suosque potestas ab ipso ad Caesarem transferatur; eandem prorsus rem plus centum versibus sparsam et obtutum nusquam fugientem videre non potuerunt. Ut si quis Mercurii acervo conspecto anxius sciscitetur, quis mortalium, quanto sarraco vel plaustro, quo die in eum locum tantam molem lapidum convexerit; qui omnino non convecti, sed coniecti sint et quidem longo tempore ac manihus mille praetereuntium [...] Praeterea congesserunt ei consulatus continuos in quinquennium, dictaturam non semestrem sed annuam, tribuniciam potestatem per omne vitae spatium. Quantus hic ad *legem regiam* gradus fuerit, ex hoc postremo vel solo cognoscitur, quod *summi fastigii* vocabulum Tacitus praedicat".

volumen exiret, si conquirerem omnia, quae ille, quum parte nulla imminueret quaesitam semel potentiam, fecit et comparavit, a mirifice iniminuisse [imminuisse], ac submisisse, quibusdam etiam prudentibus iudicaretur.

He pretends not to realise that his *imperium* was substantially different from any magistratual *imperium* and that the same *tribunicia potestas* to which he traced back his own constitutional power was far greater, adding thereto the special faculty of doing *quaecumque ex usu rei publicae esse censebit,* of disposing, that is to say, of the property and the very life of the citizen, making laws, declaring war and promoting peace, forming alliances and electing magistrates, giving orders to everyone and to the Senate itself *(ius agendi cum patribus),* and above all of being exonerated from the observance of numerous laws and plebiscites[87].

In this context of argumentation the cultural influences of Gronovius' hermeneutics are numerous and complex. With Tacitus *(Ann.,* I, *2* e 9), Plutarch *(Vit. Caesar.,* I) and more especially Suetonius (*Vit. Aug.,* 7, 52, 53*)* Cassius Dio's *Roman History* is set as a basic model for the study on the genesis of the Roman Empire. It depended in fact on the 'utilitarian' interpretation of the ancient historian, on his utilization of 'sophisticated' culture in an interpretation scheme taken from Thucydides' thought and problematically associated with the Stoic conception of Panaetius and Posidonius some important choices on the terrain of historiographical organization, to such an extent that his influence was more than a simple transmission of non-critical motives and interpretation schemes. Significant, however, is the fact that Gronovius may feel narrator of a particular event – the ascendancy of Augustus to the title of father of the fatherland and master of the laws – for which Dio (LI–LIV) is the main source, but which is, at the same time, a source that may be rectified: "Lepidum: est autem memoratu, qua fabrica legum omnia impe-

87 GRONOVIUS 1678, pp. 38, 41, 54ff.

dimenta perfregerit, eisque solutus sit Augustus, si vera scribit hanc in rem Dio, quod tamen habet non parum dubitationis"[88]. Dione's critical interpretation, arrived at through the important exegetic mediation of Isaac Casaubon's *Comment* on Suetonius is highly relevant for identifying certain decisive episodes in the historical genesis of the *Lex Regia* and for the problematic periodization of Roman history, a periodization that in Gronovius, however not only relies on the often deceptive Dionian chronology, but also on a definitive ethico-political reasoning:

> O ludibria! Quantum est in rebus inane? Qui sine scrupulo totum invito et senatu et populo imperium rapuerat ac digito temperabat, is, homo timidus scilicet, virginali verecundia non audet obfirmare sese, ut tribubus de suo ipsorum minam vel quadringentos sestertios nummos adspergat, quasi depeculaturus aerarium et legi cinciae fraudem facturus, nisi senatus frontem eius tam infirmam perfricuisset [...]. Nunc interrogo conscientiam vestram, satin haec regia? Et plus quam regia? Etiamsi tum, quum fierent, legis regiae mentio atque usurpatio religiosissime vitaretur; satin populus et imperium et libertatem suam principi sic gratificabatur; etsi verborum talium apertam et dilucidam orationem refugerent, et illi simpliciter ac sine figura se dedisse, hi accepisse tam improbum donum diffiterentur[89].

From the historiographical pratice viewpoint, albeit adopting biographical schemes of narration in this interpretation context for his intent to remain faithful to traditional literary sources and in order for there to persist in him a moralistic-pragmatical vision that forces him to express judgements on the life and character of the emperors, the main protagonists in his description of Roman history, the Leyden philologist succeeds in making significant contributions to the revision of the traditional narrative scheme. By limiting and also orientating the same biographical episodes to the essential portrait, to particular edifying

88 GRONOVIUS 1678, p. 60. See GABBA 1955.

89 GRONOVIUS 1678, pp. 60–62 and GRONOVIUS (1672) 1703.

motives for at least two typical places of classical historiographical production – the proverbs and the anecdotes – Gronovius thereby introduces drastic reductions. This tendency to go beyond the constitutional modules of biographical practice backed by the new centrality of the historical fact, to be investigated in its inflexible individual reality, which is manifested in the current social and political situation. In this changed historico-historiographical orientation traditional humanistic deference towards the past and authority is conditioned by certain new interests, and becomes instrumental for highly topical action and reflection[90]. For its origin and nature Rome offers Gronovius an image of an exceptionally stable and organized human society, proving to be the example he preferred, since – in sharp contrast to Cluverius' opinion[91] – it is the least uncertain and best preserved one. By utilizing traditional Roman history critically, the disciple of Scaligero and Saumaise, rather than accepting it passively, practiced interpretation choices that were by no means rhetorical which placed references to contemporary political problems in a historiographical setting, through the allusive force of certain postille and comments which were anything but politically neutral. Thus, the purely doctrinal character of the *Oratio,* the typically humanistic assumption of referring to the myth of Rome in historical reflection proved functional for the need to investigate the contrasts of contemporary civil life and in particular the characteristics and the significance of the actual sovereign power in relevant assonance with certain incidents and historiographical experiences that developed during the cultural debate of the time.

In such a complicated setting, Gronovius is especially close to Grotius for the common scientific matrix, for a direct know-

90 On the theme BERTELLI 1962, pp. 169ff. and BERTELLI 1973, pp. 301ff.

91 Cf. SCHÖFFER (1968) 1975, pp. 78–101 and COSTA 1977, pp. 200ff and 357.

ledge of the works of the historian and jurist of Delft. However, it is useful to see in Grotius, especially in Grotius the historian and philologist, the enthusiastic admirer of Gronovius' *Observationes*[92], not only the greatest model of his critico-philological culture, but also those aspects in which the master's lesson was assimilated by his young pupil. Sensitive to motives dominating the politico-cultural debate of that time, Grotius in the *De Iure Belli ac Pacis* takes his cue from the constitutional events of the ancient world, to intervene in the problem of *auctoritas,* in the character and limits of sovereign power in certain decisive thematic places, significantly commented on by Gronovius' important notes, which, written in 1663 and appearing posthumously in the 1680 edition, are still awaiting their historian, following the restrictive judgement which they received from Barbeyrac at the beginning of the 18th century[93]. In Chapter 3 of the 1st Book of Grotius' work, where dealing with the "Belli partitio in publicum et privatum" and the "Summi imperii explication", the *summa potestas* is defined as that "cuius actus alterius iuri non

92 GRONOVIUS (1639) 1662.

93 GROTIUS 1680. On this edition cf. TER MEULEN et al. 1950, pp. 236–237. Cf. BARBEYRAC 1724, p. XIV: "Si ce Savant eût été aussi versé dans les matières de pur raisonnement, et dans les principes de la Science dont il s'agit, qu'il étoit habile dans la Critique et dans l'étude de l'Antiquité, on pouvoit tout attendre de lui. Mat [...] la plupart des Notes de GRONOVIUS sont assez inutiles, puis qu'elles ne font qu'exprimer le sens de l'Auteur en d'autres termes, qui ne sont pas toujours plus clairs, ou qu'elles ne peuvent servir tout au plus qu'à ceux qui sont novices dans l'intelligence de la Langue *Latine* [...]. Dans le peu d'endroits où cet Interprète traite des choses mêmes, il donne à gauche presque toujours, faute d'avoir assez médité les matières; ce qui fait aussi que, tout habile Critique qu'il étoit, il se méprend assez souvent dans l'explication des termes et de la pensée de son Auteur. Bien plus: on le voit broncher quelquefois, en fait de choses purement d'Erudition, d'une manière à [paraître] tout autre, si on en jugeoit, par-là, que ce qu'il étoit effectivement en ce genre d'Etude [...]".

subsunt, ita ut alterius voluntatis humanae arbitrio irriti possint redid". And if it distinguishes the *subiectum* into *commune* (which is the *civitas, coetus perfectus)* and into *proprium* which "est persona una pluresve, pro cuiusque gentis legibus ac moribus": in a word, the Sovereign. To the problem arising from such definitions of principle, whether it is lawful for a people to alienate its own liberty from the sovereign, Grotius answers in the affirmative, rejecting "eorum opinio, qui ubique et sine exceptione summam potestatem esse volunt populi, ita ut ei reges quoties imperio suo male utuntur et coërcere et punire liceat". In integrating this thesis, Grotius then makes reference to Roman Law to observe that if the laws of the ancient Hebrews and those of the Romans allow every man to make himself the slave of whomever he wishes to, then why could a free people not submit itself to one or two peoples, transferring to them entirely the right to govern it, without reserving any part for itself?[94] Finally taking his cue from Aristotle's (*Politics,* III, 4) Philostratus' (*Vit Apollonii,* VII, 3) and Livy's (XLII, *5*), considerations according to which there are still peoples of such a nature that know how better to obey than to command, makes explicit recourse to

94 GROTIUS 1680, pp. 50ff., 59, 60–61: "Alterius cum dico, ipsum excludo qui summa potestate utitur; cui voluntatem mutare licet, ut et successorem, qui eodem iure utitur, ac proinde eandem habet potestatem, non aliam. [...] Licet homini cuique se in privatam servitutem cui velit addicere, ut et ex lege Hebraea et Romana apparet. Quidni ergo populo sui iuris liceat se uni cuipiam, aut pluribus ita addicere, ut regendi sui ius in eum plane transcribat; nulla eius iuris parte retenta? [...] Neque vero non multae exstare possunt causae cur populus ius totum imperandi a se abdicet, aliique tradat, puta quia in periculum vitae adductus alia lege qui se defendat reperire non potest; aut quia inopia pressus aliter habere non potest copiam unde se sustentet [...]. Accidere etiam potest, ut pater familias latifundia possidens neminem alia lege in suas terras habitantem recipere velit; aut ut quis magnam servorum copiam habens eos manumittat sub imperii ferendi et census pendendi le gibus; quae suis exemplis non carent. De servis Germanorum apud Tacitum est [...]".

Roman history, read through the references to Tacitus' texts (*Ann.,* I, 9 and *Hist,* I, 1), Florus' (IV, 3) and Lucan's (*Phars.,* I; IX), going so far, in implicit dispute with Bodin's historiographical theses (*De Republica,* I, 8) that aimed at claiming the exclusively democratic character of the Roman Republic, to such a significant conclusion: "Est et interdum is civitatis status ut videatur nisi sub libero unius imperio salvus esse non posse; quod de Romana, qualis erat Caesaris Augusti aetate, multis prudentibus visum est". From the reasons adopted the consequences can likewise be successfully derived that are relevant for the solution to the problem of the *obligatio ex consensu,* through which the very genesis of the law passes and the conditions of sovereign power are defined. Men often submit themselves, Grotius observes, to the domination of another, but sometimes they have been reduced to such a state despite themselves as is shown by a 'legitimate war': "Iam vero bello iusto, ut ante diximus, sicut acquiri potest dominium privatum, ita et dominium civile, sive ius regendi non aliunde pendens [...]. Quid, quod nulla respublica adeo reperta est popularis, in qua non aliqui aut valde mores aut externi, tum vero et foeminae et adolescentes a deliberationibus publicis arceantur?[95]". Going further into this consideration, the Author of the *De iure belli ac pacis* succeeds in making specific references to late-Republican and Imperial Roman history, observing, with a comment on the famous passage reported by the *Digesto* (1.4.1.) and relating to the *Lex Regia*: "Sic postquam Romani principes imperium vere regium usurpare coeperunt, dicitur populus in eos omne suum imperium et potestatem contulisse, etiam in se, ut interpretatur Theophilus". Here, in addition to a sign that draws one's attention to Theophilus'*Parafrasi Institutiones* (1.2.6.), also for Grotius, just as earlier for Gronovius, the main source is Roman history commented on by Cassius

95 GROTIUS 1680, pp. 61–62. See – after BOOT 1883 – DROETTO 1968, pp. 191–203, 381–385.

Dio, on the basis of whose testimonies (espec. LIII) it is legitimate to support the Roman emperor *"liber est, suique ac legum potens, ut et quod vult faciat, et quod non vult non faciat"* [96].

Thus there are similarities of interests and problems between Grotius and Gronovius, but differences in their politico-cultural design, arrived at through a different use of the same problems in the Gronovian interpretation, that aimed at favouring among the motives of the *iustum-aequum* of natural law (with which the important theme of *consensus* is associated) as well as those of *utilitas-necessitas* which imply a motive of autonomous legitimation, the historico-empirical loci of the argumentations of the *De Iure* always duly, critically verified. In an extensive note (to the *De Iure*, II, 9, 5, 11), for example, in order to refute Grotius' thesis, according to which "electio Imperatoris ad populum pertinebat; et aliquoties a populo per se, aut per Senatum facta est" (a thesis which reaffirmed the claim already stated in the third chapter of the thirteenth paragraph of the previous book: "Contra, Romanum imperium etiam sublata omni senatus et populi potestate per electionem conferebatur"), Gronovius does not hesitate to show historical incongruencies in the facts quoted: the interregnum Grotius speaks about does not come about before, but after Aurelian's death and before the reign of Tacitus, which is sufficient to show that the soldiers had the right to elect the emperor rather than to receive him directly from the Senate. Furthermore, Gronovius observes that what the Author of the *De Iure* calls Albino's Letter is a speech addressed viva voce to the army without any reference to any law of the Senate (Capitolino, *Vit. Albin.*, 13). However, the letter relating to the Gordiani, reported by Capitolino (in *Maximin. duob.*, 15), attests only that the Senate had recognized the two

96 GROTIUS 1680, p. 63. On this theme see VAN EYSINGA 1942–1947 and VAN OVEN 1954, vol. I, pp. 269–287.

Gordiani, already elected in Africa, as affirmed by the same biographer elsewhere (in *Gordiani.,* 11)[97].

This arrangement devised by Gronovius for the historical verification of certain juridical contents is extremely important from the methodological and historiographical viewpoint. In contrast with every dogmatic interpretation absolutizing the contents of historico-juridical discourse, Gronovius' intervention, stimulated by modern criticism (first from Bacon and Cartesius, then from Hobbes and Spinoza, from Pufendorf, Bayle and Locke) against the mechanisms of formation of the *consensus gentium,* aimed at recomposing the discourse on certainty relating to such *consensus,* the negation of which risked invalidating the absolute value of the *ordo* elaborated on the fundamentals of Roman law by late-medieval and humanistic juridical science[98]. Essentially for Gronovius to dwell on Grotius' interpretation of the *summa potestas,* basically inclined to support the reasons of absolutism at the theoretical and historiographical level, meant compromising the necessary, effective historical confirmation, invalidating *consensus* as a source of truth, and with that the very constitutional *fictio* on which the common right and constituted political-social order were founded. With regard to all this the Leyden philologist gave some importance to Grotius' considerations on late-Republican and Imperial Roman history, and to the relative literary sources used, a precise significance historiographically radicated in the juridical voluntarism of sixteenth-century Spanish scholarship[99], a significance intent on exposing

97 GROTIUS 1680, pp. 68, 231 and GRONOVIUS 1680, pp. 102–106. On the *consensus* cf. FAUCCI 1968, pp. 507–510, 542–543 and then LANDUCCI 1972, pp. 23ff.; GREGORY 1979, pp. 38, 56–57; BOBBIO et al. 1979 (1984), pp. 29ff. and VENEZIANI 1982.

98 See AJELLO (1968) 1976, pp. 126–133, 172–174; AJELLO 1985, pp. 916–917.

99 Cf. SUAREZ 1614, III. 2, p. 249: "Ergo intelligi debet constituta per modum pacti, quo populus in principem transtulit potestatem sub on-

the *auctoritas* of sovereign power as *iniuria* if not adequately supported by the consensus of the people, and if exonerated from observing the law, the garantors of stability and the very certainty of sovereign right. In confirmation of this thesis, the reference once again in Gronovius' *Oratio* to the myth of Rome and in particular, to Roman history of the post-Augustan imperial age proved decisive.

The final semblances of the republic, preserved by the cautiousness of Caesar and Augustus disappear with Tiberius, "neque immemor callidi magistri discipulus [...]". The declarations of deference addressed to the Senate, which initially characterize Tiberius' *imperium*, do not in fact remove the suspicion, the painful conviction that Augustus' successor is a hypocrite, a simulator, able to dazzle the world with a false show of humility, ready, immediately on the death of Augustus, to react as Lord, without however openly taking possession of the supreme authority, indeed refusing the title of *dominus* and that of consul, to declare himself, instead, simply senator, prince of citizens and not master of slaves:

> Iam primum qui poene adhuc animam agente Augusto principatum neque corripere neque agere dubitasset, eundem oblatum pertinacissime recusare; cuncta incipere per consules tamquam veteri republica et ambiguus imperandi, procumbentibus denum ad genua patribus concedens; queri sibi onerosam iniungi servitutem ab iis, qui nescirent, quanta bellua esset imperium [...]. Praeterea consulibus adsurgebat, et decedebat via, utque ipsum praeceptorem vinceret, non Consulem se ferebat, sed Senatorem[100].

---

ere, et obligatione gerendi curam reipublicae, et iustitiam administrandi, et princeps tam potestatem, quam conditionem acceptavit, ex quo pacto firma, et stabilis permansit lex regia, seu de regali potestate; non ergo immediate a Deo, sed a populo reges hanc habent potestatem".

100 GRONOVIUS 1678, pp. 41, 43, 42.

Ambition, self-love, and personal interest mortified the remote civil virtues. From the ruins of the ancient constitutional order rose the Roman empire, the image of vices favouring the birth of a policy of conquest. For such an interpretation as this Gronovius calls Tacitus (*Ann.,* I, 7; XII, 5; XV, 34) to solemnly confirm his own interpretative scheme, enhancing his testimonies with observations also taken from Suetonius (*Tib.,* 14, 24, 29, 31) and Martial (*Epigr.,* X, 72, 8–9). It is, in fact, Tacitus who with his presence rooted in the ethico-political paradigms of Aristotle (*Politics,* LII, 9; IV, 5), preserves Roman history from the opportunistic promising of miracles of Livy's exalting historiographical narrations, privileged sources from traditional, even critically-inadequate reflections on Rome of the epoch of kings and the early Republic. From this last viewpoint it is useful to stress how in Gronovius' hermeneutic appproach the traditional is not always literally betrayed. However the same traditional historiographic interpretations and sources work together to activate the critical commitment of re-interpreted Roman history, a history incapable of being converted into universal history, thanks to its being continually measured with the facts of Rome, with its inevitable declines. The myth of ancient Rome, precisely because it was the most idealized political sytem had declined, also represented the place most frequented by the reflection on the problem of decadence in history. However, in Gronovius' modified meditation the great theme of decadence tended to lose the moralistic inspiration of traditional interpretations of Livian origin (centred mostly on the theme of the corruption of customs) at the very moment in which he formally reproduced its fundamental hermeneutic scheme, basing his argumentative nucleus in pre-Gibbon fashion[101] somewhat on the organic recognition of non-external but endogenous causes of decline, al-

101 Background for this theme can be found in GIBBON (1776–1788) 1967, Chap. 3, pp. 61ff.; Chap. 44, pp. 1661ff, 1708.

ternatively also with the historiographic determinism of Polybian origin (the natural evolution of political forms). The fall of the Roman Republic was, in fact, put forward in the 1678 *Oratio* not as a sudden and unexpected event, but as the final act, temporally defined and politically coherent, of a historical process that was to be investigated in its various, specific components. The political change accompanying the republican crisis was slow and gradual, as the emperors knew how great the people's attachment to the ancient institutions was and how strong the value of the republican tradition proved to be: "Pari ambitione absconditum et dissimulatum ibant immodicae potestatis modum et se crevisse de republica nesciri atque in arcanis haberi volebant: adeo ut simplicioribus et incautis minusque tectis aliquando capital fuerit, quod impudentem mimum intelligerent, prodidisse". Thus, the power of the Caesars, at first competing with that of the Senate, gradually finished up by prevailing, without however their leaving anything to conceal it, so as not to let it be seen to its fullest extent, and thus to make it less odious and wielded in safety, without being exposed to envy and treachery[102]. From Tiberius onwards, with the development of the praxis relating to the creation of the *princeps,* those titles and competencies that the first emperors had imperceptibly assumed together with various renewals tended to be attributed openly and on one occasion only, through a senatusconsultum subject to ratification by the comitia. In significant assonance with the interpretative schemes of the *Commentarii* of Saumaise and Casaubon on Roman Imperial history, and in particular with the work of Sparziano on the life of the emperor Hadrian, Gronovius observed:

102 GRONOVIUS 1678, pp. 37–38: "Quare ignota, nisi quod ipsi earn omnibus integumentis occultabant et obscurabant, nec patere, quantum pateret, patiebantur, ut minore cum invidia, sine fascino, sine insidiis ea fruerentur".

> Porro sic primi; non ita contanter successores. Equidem senatus auctoritatem interponebant et illi; at non per tot gradus, articulos, ambages, furtim in arcem erepebant; quippe qui, quae duobus istis vellicatim et saltuatim, prout occasio inciderat, per metum, imagine meritorum, obtigerant, ea semel, uno senatusconsulto coacervata et ingesta in ipso principatus aditu arroganter invaderent. Videres interdum, qui nomen unum alterumve aut omnino aut ad tempus remitterent [...]. Sed iura et potestatem omnem avide statimque induebant; atque etiam quae repudiarent aut proferrent, censeri et deferri sibi laetabantur.

The accumulative conferring of titles becomes an explicit and customary fact, a tacit constitutional praxis in the principate of advanced times, according to what is testified also by Cassius Dio (LVII, LIX, LX), Suetonius (*Tib.*, 26, 67; *Claud.*, 12; *Neron.*, 8), Plutarch (*Vit. Galbae*, I) and above all by Tacitus (*Ann.*, I, 72; XII, 69; *Hist.*, I, 47; II, 55; IV, 3) with regard to Vespasian's ascendancy to power of which the Senate assigned all that was wont to be conferred on the Heads of State[103].

In developing and integrating the narration treated by traditional literary sources, Gronovius utilizes the final content of an inscription of a bronze tablet, "pretiosius, et monumentum antiquitatis unicum", reproducing a fragment of the *Lex Regia* promulgated for Vespasian between 69 and 70 A.D.[104] The content of the constitutive inscription being in fact the key to an adequate interpretation for understanding at the level of historiographical reconstructon "verum [que] exemplum tantae ordinationis et solae reliquiae comitiorum imperii orbis terrarum". It was a question of a decisive moment in the history of the Rornan Empire to investigate with detailed critico-philological ex-

103 GRONOVIUS 1678, pp. 62–63, 65, 295–298. Cf. *Historiae Augustae Scriptores* 1671, pp. 1–220.

104 GRONOVIUS 1678, p. 65. On history of this *Lex* cf. – after DE FRANCISCI 1925 and BARBIERI 1957, pp. 750–758 – MAZZARINO 1972; GIUFFRÈ ed. 1977, pp. 181–184; LUCREZI 1982, pp. 143 ff.; ARCHI 1986, pp. 11–36.

amination, engaged in polemics with those who showing little competence in the knowledge of ancient inscriptions, resolutely denied the existence of a *Lex Regia,* claiming it to be an unreal *monument*, or judged it "cum Vespasiano natam [...], aut, undecumque nasceretur, et quidem si diis placet, tum relatam, ob novitatem gentis et personae, hariolati"[105].

Associated with the proconsular *imperium* and with the *tribunicia potestas,* the *Lex Vespasiani* is a *lex de imperio,* a law regarding the various privileges conferred on the prince by the people, a general and periodical law which is repeated for the election of every emperor, a legal formula of what in the past was only in the praxis and not a legal surrogate of the auctoritas which Vespasian lacked on account of his humble origin. When approaching the testimonies treated by traditional literary sources, those taken from the authors of the *Historia Augusta,* especially from the writings of Capitolino, Sparziano and Lampridio biographers respectively of Macrinus, Didius Severus Jiulianus and Alexander Severus, Gronovius observes:

> Ego vero nullus ambigo, quin a Tiberio usque ad Romulum Augustulum, in occidente imperantium ultimum, translati principatus par foret ingressus in scenam, et mutato Caesare formula prorsus eadem et perscriptione, paucis, si forte, interlitis, idem senatusconsultum repeteretur [...]. Hoc igitur senatusconsultum ex tot velut segmentis et clavis caesareae purpurae consutum, tardeque in unam massam coalescens, deinde translaticium et quovis novo cum principe interpolatum et renovatum [...][106].

105 GRONOVIUS 1678, pp. 65, 70–71. The reference is to SCHOOCKIUS 1668, section III, Chap. 15. On GRONOVIUS (1661) 1664 cf. HEINECCIUS (1726) 1744, II, pp. 81ff.

106 GRONOVIUS 1678, pp. 71, 75–76: "Quod toties in principibus imperium auspicantibus usitatum legimus, id in eodem solemni nunquam intermissum haud timide argumentamur; et, ubi reticetur, non pro non facto, sed pro vulgari nimis et legitimo et omnibus noto transmitti". On *Histo-*

From the formal viewpoint, Gronovius emphasises that the document in question, although designed explicitly as a *lex* and terminating with the formulae typical of the comitial laws is drafted not in the imperative form of the former, but in that of a senatusconsultum which, being transformed into a *lex* drawn up by the comitia, fixed the constitutional chart designed to establish the inherent rights, by the wish of the senators and the people, for the imperial dignity: "Neque offendere nos debet *legem* perhiberi, quod alii *senatusconsultum* commemorant. Nam ipsum illud, quod Vespasiano senatum decresse Tacitus tradit, ter in scripto, quod ea de re factum est, *legis* nomine venit; et postquam comitia translata sunt ad patres, leges quoque ibi ferri oportuit, ac discrimen inter senatusconsulta et leges ex loco et personis suffragia ferentium cessavit [...]". Thus, if it is impossible to claim that the *Lex Regia* may prove compatible with the constitutional praxis of the early emperors, without any trace of it being found in the relative sources, it is not however wrong to think that later, when there was no reason to fear a confrontation between the imperial power and the royal authority, the title attributed to that *lex* was adopted into the current juridical language. Thus, in commenting on the reflections on the theme of Tacitus (*Ann.,* I, 15; III, 60) and Cicero (*De divinatione,* II, 54), of Appian *(De bell. civil., praefatio)* and Cassius Dio (LIII), Gronovius observes:

> Denique *Legem Regiam* dici satis fert, non item *Senatusconsultum Regium,* linguae latiaris consuetudo. Iidem iureconsulti, qüum nimia potestas unius horribile secretum esse desiisset; quum adsuefactus iugo populus romanus libertatis memoriam, speciem, desiderium deposuisset; quum erubesceret nemo Caesarem timere; quum principem omnia, populum nihil posse, non illis periculo, non his dolori et indignationi foret, et neque in principe superbum, nec populo vile atque humile putaretur, iamque scapham scapham appellare liceret; populum principi omne impe-

---

ria Augusta cf. MAZZARINO 1972, II. 2, pp. 278ff.; MOMIGLIANO (1954) 1966, pp. 143–180 and SARTORI 1980.

> rium et potestatem suam concessisse *Lege* illa *Regia* definierunt; quod videlicet rebus factum erat iam tum, quum verbis adhuc parceretur[107].

As heir to, and preserver of humanistic culture, Gronovius went so far as to make the paradoxical affirmation of an anti-humanistic method for an extreme explanation of the humanistic model. By combining historiography with philology, and jurisprudence with history, he showed himself to be aware of the connection between *right,* in its wider meaning, and *power* within a reflection of human psychology, whose categories, becoming inextricably caught up in the concrete physiognomy of human nature, in the solid mobility of its historical *nature* favoured an interesting rediscovery of the concept of Reason of State, in terms more directly Tacitan. However, the close intimacy of the rapport which binds the Dutch interpreter of the *Lex Regia* to the historian of the Roman Empire in what is essential, or in the profoundly critico-philological vocation of his meditation, cannot be understood without the historiographical rule for which the name of Tacitus is made use of in the 17th century both for and against, but in every case always with reference to that of Machiavelli. In partially correcting the moralism of Livian origin with the voluntarism of the political action in the psychological interpretation of absolutism, significant, yet indirect and never explicit hermeneutic suggestions extrapolate the pages of Gronovius from the historical reflection on Rome of the Author of the *Discorsi sopra la prima deca di Tito Livio.* The theme of mystification and deception as instruments for realizing the order and primacy of legality more effectively, the Prince's personal power derives from well-known Machiavellian motives, widely diffused in sixteenth-century political literature and vulgarized by the libertines, strongly marking both the analysis of the conflicts of the "ordini" – in which Machiavelli saw a reason more for the

107 GRONOVIUS 1678, pp. 80–81. On this theme cf. BARBIERI 1957, pp. 750–758 and MAZZARINO 1972.

strength rather than for the decadence of the Roman State – as well as the attention paid to the theme of the "prolungazione degl'imperii", as an autonomous cause of the end of the republic[108]. However, in the Gronovian interpretation Tacitism which as has been recently observed is 'orthodox' and at the same time 'critical'[109], does not simply consist in confounding the principles of Machiavellism under the false pretences of Tacitus, in accordance with a interpretative scheme adopted by almost all the politician-historians of the second half of the sixteenth-century from Jacopo Sertino to Boccalini, and from Justus Lipsius to Canonieri[110]. Gronovius' Tacitus is a Tacitus aware of the fatal decline of Republican institutions, and of the infinite intrigues characterizing the *arcanum imperii,* being even disposed not only to denouncing them with ruthless bitterness, but to tracing them back and understanding them within the order of history, thus retracing testimonies for a historical justification for the conventional lie of the Reason of State which, on the basis of the theory of power gained by violence, Machiavelli had shown in the crude, empirical and unscrupulous form of current political pratice, taken from the direct control of the classical categories of Aristotelian ethics and traditional religion. In such a complex cultural elaboration, Gronovius' meditation went back to problematic themes and places of classico-humanistic political philosophy of clear Aristotelian influences (the themes of the origin and legitimacy of political action and those relating to the techniques of the formation and conservation of power, of the States and their sovereigns), mediating them with the proven interpretation modules of Stoic origin, widespread in 17th century

108 MACHIAVELLI (1513–1521) 1938, T. II, Book I. 4, pp. 114–116, 422–423 and Book I. 25, p. 169. See – after TOFFANIN 1972 – MEINECKE (1924) 1970, pp. 25ff., 76–78, 120–121, 134–135, 198–199.

109 This is the thesis of BUGTER 1980, VII, pp. 193–200.

110 TOFFANIN 1972, pp. 59ff, 213ff. Cf. also D'ADDIO 1962.

Leyden culture, as Dibon's studies have clearly shown[111]. Thus, Gronovius' Tacitus meets with the other great classical model, so closely linked to the modern way of feeling, namely Lucius Annaeus Seneca (*De ira,* II, *5; De dementia,* 1, *5*) whose extraordinarily widespread diffusion among seventeenth-century Dutch humanistic circles is well known, thanks above all to the lively Erasmian tradition, revived by the writings of Lipsius and Scioppio, Vossius and Daniel Heinsius, and, more generally, thanks to the intensive life restored to Stoicism by Calvinism especially at Leyden[112]. In the philologist's interpretative perspective the description of the *arcana iuris* as *arcana imperii* and as *instrumenta dominationis,* expressed any thing but the full adhesion to an absolutist constitutional scheme. In conclusion of his historiographical reflection, in fact, he did not hesitate, taking his distances indirectly from the theoretical and historiographical motives characterizing the work of its main source, namely Cassius Dio, to contest the relationship established between the representation of Rome's greatness and freedom and the image of an aggressive conquering republic. For Gronovius, in fact, neither the prince's ability nor his strength found the wielding of power, but rather it was the real and sure consensus of individuals through the laws. Even in this decisive case recourse to the Roman experience is recorded, and to the constitutional myth of imperial Rome where "omnium constitutionum ac rescriptorum principalium pondus auctoritasque in re certa, non imaginaria,

111 DIBON 1954, but also NUZZO 1984–1985, pp. 68–69 and NUZZO 1986.

112 On the theme – after DILTHEY (1891–1904) 1927, II, pp. 43–48, 244ff; TROELTSCH (1923) 1960, I, pp. 215ff.; II, pp. 341, 425 – cf. SANDYS 1903–1908, II, p. 306; SPANNEUT 1973; D'ANGERS 1976; ABEL 1978; SIEDSCHLAG 1978; OESTREICH 1982. In this context see also ALPERS (1983) 1984, pp. 1–17, 19–43, 357ff. On Seneca cf. GRONOVIUS 1658–1659 and 1661. For Gronovius' correspondence with Albert Rubens cf. GRONOVIUS 1876–1877.

inque lege, non vi, fundatur"[113]. The maturing of these theses in the interpretation of a non-literary source is the new fact, the relevant element that is born of a certain receptivity of contemporary antiquarian work and which on the realistic ground of historico-histiographical research helps, likewise, to take a stand on the complex problem of redefining the value and limits, or specificity, of historical knowledge, a problem destined to mark the seventeenth-eighteenth century debate on *fides historica.* From examining ancient and modern historiography on the *Lex Regia,* and from entertaining subsequent doubts on the reflection on the historico-juridical tradition, Gronovius does not go so far as to adopt a relativistic position, but rather develops an attitude of trust in the reliability of history, in the possibility of defining conditions for verifying the truth, directed in a realistic way towards safeguarding the rules of the *critique,* towards protecting the *fides historica,* by reacting to the i*mpasse* brought about by the affirmation of a claimed mathematical-type 'evidence' and by the sceptical negation of every form of certainty. The matured desire to guarantee a certain security for historical fact, to discredit scepticism a *priori* and uncritically, by attributing a more empirical and definite meaning to historical research, unassociated with the modern myth of a mental truth, peculiar to the theoretical-historiographical forms and schemes of dogmatic Cartesianism in which much Dutch culture of the second part of the seventeenth century had sought refuge[114].

If the fact, rather than presenting itself immediately, is always the outcome of a complex, articulated process of critico-erudite analysis, and it is the latter to scrutinise the testimonies, to decide on the basis of their validity, on the reliability of the facts handed down, it is certain that the preliminary work of the historian consists no less than in this critical investigation, that is

113 GRONOVIUS 1678, p. 82.
114 Cf. here note 34.

to say, in the analysis of testimonies. Thus the practical control of the historical possibility of an event cannot occur by extrapolating the fact from its source but by examining it from within together with its degree of *certainty*. History must not therefore be concerned with the fact in se and per se but with the testimonies of the fact in the setting of the sources which hand it down. The abstract and pompous schemes of Baroque allegorism, content with the very moralising on "emblems", gave way to the rigorous historico-philological interpretation of the document examined, to the initial certainties of a modern-type critical and constructive philology, although still lacking in experience in its own possibilities and limits. In Gronovius the knowledge of history is thus an indispensable instrument for studying ancient Roman law. Yet in the critical discourse brought about by the *Oratio* not only is there a discussion on the usefulness of historical knowledge for interpreting the juridical texts or applying the historical criterion of literature to particular points, but also, in contrast, on having a comprehensive view of juridical phenomena in history. The reference to the latter is resolved through a correct and proper awareness of the historicity of the law, because it is in this that its genesis and development may be recognised. The central motives of the interpretation system are, in fact, taken from the real circumstances of things, from the effectiveness of their course, from the sense of a realism that is far removed from abstract rationalistic statements. In the complex psychological intepretation of absolutism, activated by an adequate historical perspective for substantial images, Roman imperial power is investigated in pages that scrupulously clarify the role of prodigious events in human affairs with a rigorously critical spirit and receive the violence and deception of the powerful with a shrewd sense of history. The first consequence on the historiographic front is the retrieval of detail and the individual fact in its relevance and dignity. The study of antiquity, as the research of documents, does not accept identifying and exalting a perfect ideal model. Gronovius, therefore, takes his inspiration from the Roman model not to restore it or imitate it, inasmuch as its being the supreme ideal, but to retrace its particular historical characteristics that are to be highlighted in their true concrete reality. For the Leyden philologist Rome is not therefore a conceptual ideal to be admired, but a reality to be examined in its philologically-ascertainable facts beyond all mere aestheticism. Examining the question of the *Lex Regia* in historiographical terms, Gronovius went so far as to single out its *document*, the real historical datum in which to acknowledge the co-existence of elements belonging to different moments in the long, tormented politico-constitutional life of ancient Rome. The study of the individual fact in its authentic reality obliges the Author to avoid any conceptual abstraction, so that the historical *datum* comes to coincide with the real tangible *action* to be critically investigated in its *effectiveness*. For all this, antiquarian work acquired a marked depth which, albeit not always operating as an aware component of theoretical and historiographical discourse, still remained the sign, the indicator of the complex relationship between *fides iuridica* and *fides historica,* between science of law and historico-political interest[115].

115 See MOMIGLIANO (1950) 1955, pp. 75, 78: "Roman history had been written by Livy, Tacitus, Florus, Suetonius, the *Historia Augusta.* There was no reason why it should be written again, because in the main it could be written again [...]. Ancient history was still written as part of universal history (a tradition especially cherished by Protestant universities), but the section on Greece and Rome of a universal history would practically amount to a summary of the ancient sources in the right chronological order – hardly the business of serious students of 'antiquitas'. [...]. The situation changed in the second part of the seventeenth century. [...] Books on Roman and Greek history began to be written which were not subordinated to a scheme of universal history. They are intended either to presenta n account of events for which the evidence was mainly to be found in coins, inscriptions and archeological remains, or to select and order what was most reale in the ancient literary evi-

With his intervention Gronovius confronted most appropriate politico-cultural themes and interests in the scientific debate of the late-seventeenth-century republic of letters, with his 1678 *Oratio* acquiring in fact the value of a historiographic model worthy of close attention and in-depth analysis[116]. Graevius, a Deventer pupil of the same Gronovius had already written to Le Clerc about the Leyden philologist, expert and esteemed editor of Tacitus and Livy, Statius and Seneca, Suetonius and Phaidrus, in a letter dated May 1687 regarding the interpretation of a passage of Pliny[117]. To go deeper into Gronovius' work was at a later stage to be the "Bibliothèque Universelle et Historique", when in 1693 reviewing the second edition of a collection of writings edited by his son Jacob in 1691. Focusing the reader's attention more especially on the excellent Latin text, and admiring his sound erudition and the particular originality of the Author's philological interests, Le Clerc emphasises the centrality of the *De Sestertiis* treatise "qui [paraît] le plus important de tout le Volume, et qui est comme le fondement de tout le reste", immediately revealing its value from a precise observation point: "Mais parce que [...] cette Edition est préférable aux précédentes, par les Additions et par les Remarques de l'Auteur, qu'on y a jointes, il ne sera pas hors de propos de faire [connaître] le mérite de cet Ouvrage, et l'utilité qu'on en peut tirer, pour l'intelligence des anciens Auteurs". The significance of the

dence, or to offer a re-interpretation of the ancient evidence from some moral and political point of view". See also MOMIGLIANO (1961–1962) 1975, pp. 85–92 and MOMIGLIANO 1978, pp. 361–376.

116 *ACTA ERUDITORUM* 1714, X, p. 470. Here Gronovius'Oratio is definied "docta [...], et quae reliquis omnibus qui in eo lapide volvendo hactenus desudarunt, facile palmam praeripiat". On this Journal see LAEVEN 1986. Cf. also *NOUVELLES DE LA RÉPUBLIQUE DE LETTRES* 1707, XL, pp. 217–222 and *BIBLIOTHÈQUE ANCIENNE ET MODERNE* 1714, II, V, 451–454. On Gronovius'*Oratio* cf. FABRICIUS 1728, Book IV, Chap. 9.1, p. 517; *JOURNAL LITTÉRAIRE* 1714, IV, pp. 62–74.

117 GRAEVIUS to J. Le Clerc 1687, p. 472.

small-scale work and its real intrinsic value are not to be identified in the character of a work complete and void of developments but in a significant contribution to the critico-philological analysis of the ancient: "Tout cela est joint en chaque Livre à la discution d'un grand nombre de passages des Anciens, dont on explique le sens, ou l'on le défend contre ceux qui l'ont mal entendu, ou dont on rétablit le texte, contre les fautes des anciens Manuscrits, ou l'on le soutient, contre la hardiesse des Critiques, qui l'ont voulu changer mal-à-propos". Not only does the effective critico-philological method render the edition commendable, but so too does theinteresting reference to the history of Rome. Paying specific attention to the first Book of the treatise under examination, Le Clerc deliberately dwells on the analysis that Gronovius completes into the *sesterzio* and its value depending on the various historical circumstances:

> Pour l'éclaircissement de ce passage, il faut remarquer que le *denier* valut dix Sols, tandis que le *Sol* pesa une livre, c'est a-dire, jusqu'à la première guerre Punique, comme aussi tandis qu'il pesa deux onces, ou la sixième partie de la livre, ce qui dura jusqu'à la dictature de *Maximus Fabius.* Mais lors que la République Romaine fut réduite par la pauvreté, et par les nécessités urgentes dans lesquelles les victoires *d'Annibal* l'avoient jettée, à faire le *Sol* d'une once ou de la douzième partie de la *livre,* on donna au denier seize de ces *Sols,* et le *Sesterce* qui est le quart du *denier* en valut quatre. Quand ensuite le [temps] eut fait perdre la mémoire de la première valeur du denier, on fut en peine de savoir la raison pourquoi le *Sesterce* valoit quatre *Sols,* quoi que selon son étymologie il n'en dût valoir que deux et demi[118].

At the beginning of the 18th century, first the "Bibliothèque Choisie" and later the "Bibliothèque Ancienne et Moderne", housed other reviews and works of the Leyden philologist trans-

118 *Bibliotheque Universelle Et Historique* 1693, I, IX, pp. 207–209, 214–215, 220–221. Cf. Gronovius 1691, Jacob Gronovius 1683 and ALLIX to Le Clerc 1685, p. 282. On this theme cf. Lo-monaco 1990b.

lated and commented on in French by Barbeyrac[119]. But the cultural and political climate, the very themes of historical and theoretical debate had radically changed, as also was changed the sense of the reference to the prestigious seventeenth-century Dutch philologist, on whom instead, my research intends to dwell, in order to try and retrace therein the thematic and problematic horizons of the historiography-philology link that were interwoven with law, politics and philosophy. A further stage of this is Ulrik Huber's historiographical achievement.

119 Review to GRONOVIUS 1703. In *BIBLIOTHÈQUE CHOISIE* 1704, IV, 3, pp. 246–273; GRONOVIUS-LE CLERC [1710] 1735 in *BIBLIOTHÈQUE CHOISIE* 1709, XIX, 3, pp. 184–185; BARBEYRAC 1714, in *BIBLIOTHÈQUE ANCIENNE ET MODERNE* 1714, I, Part II. 5, pp. 451–454; BARBEYRAC 1720, in *BIBLIOTHÈQUE ANCIENNE ET MODERNE* 1720, XIII, Part I. 3, pp. 149–185.

CHAPTER II

Right, Politics and History in Ulrik Huber

"Corpus Iuris" and Criticism of Right

In 1665 Ulrik Huber, now *Professor eloquentiae, historiarum et politices* at Franeker since 1657, was able on the death of Johannes Jacobus Wissenbach to pass from the Faculty of Arts to that of Jurisprudence and aspire to the Chair of *Ius Publicum,* that was later granted to him in 1670[1]. From this new experiences of life and study, the contents and methods of his teaching activity changed radically both in their premises and aims, showing signs of a radical departure from their original reassuring cultural horizons, in the questioning of an entire order of research.

In a *Dialogus de ratione iuris docendi et discendi* of 1684, aware of the dangers of a misuse of learning the Friesian jurist expressed the need to identify more stable and effective criteria for carrying out studies by proposing to follow "hanc docendi iuris viam [...], quae per examen omnium veteris Iurisprudentiae locorum in emendatione textuum depravatorum desinit, ac ita nobis antiquam Artem nitori suo genuino integritatique restituit". A crucial work of correction was required that would shed light on

1 HUBERUS (1665) 1746, I, pp. 101–123 and then in HUBERUS et al. 1793, pp. 145–182. On this work and on Huber' experiences of life and study see VEEN 1976, pp. 35ff. For an understanding of cultural and political context see FOCKEMA ANDREAE et al. 1968; TH. J. MEIJER 1973 and FEENSTRA et al. 1985, pp. 289–304.

the causes of uncertainty and disorder in which the entire *corpus* of juridical disciplines found itself, that was so uncertain in its principles, so confused in its structure, and so far from being able to represent a definite system of knowledge. These reflections were certainly not new and in fact Huber's observations retraced a very ancient *topos,* going back in fact to a Ciceronian polemic with regard to pedantic erudition, a polemic that was later to occupy considerable space in the sixteenth-century discussions on the *ratio* and *ordo studendi,* that converged in certain classical pages of Bodin's *Methodus ad facilem historiarum cognitionem* (1566). However, the historical conditions were new in which the problems of the re-ordering and unifying the re-elaboration of the *scientia iuris,* at the centre of Huber's intervention, were taken up afresh by introducing new trends and directions into the closed circuits of official scientific structures. Such innovations were now capable of influencing established balances and upsetting ancient forms of solid resistance that were still deeply and forcefully entrenched in the traditional organization of studies, defending a meditative yet uncritical 'image' of knowledge that an unchangeable academic praxis forced into pedagogical schemes that proved almost non-functional for the reality of civil life. Polemical points of reference in Huber's writings were the theses of contemporary jurists, including Bockelman's and Crusius' who still being prisoners of *rhetoric* and *eloquence* modules insisted on using *criticism*, by solving the methodological problems within the terms of *ars oratoria*, without showing any interest in the *principles* of jurisprudence: "Ego ita exstimo tibique consentio, Crusi, non esse perfectum Iurisconsultum, qui se veteribus, hoc est, ipsis Pandectis et Principum Constitutionibus per se totisque evolvendis legendisque non dedat; sed nego id esse tentandum, priusquam paratitlaris notitia omnium librorum Iuris antiqui, exprompta memoria iudicioque comprehensa sit"[2].

2 HUBERUS 1684, pp. 8, 18–19, then in *Appendix* to HUBERUS 1688,

Being brought up on *studia humanitatis,* the study of law must in no way be void of a *logic* or of a *method* in learning, the main aim of which is certainly not that of exalting the meaning of a text through the expansion of tiny insignificant particulars that are researched only for mere exhibitionism of hermeneutic acumen. The main methodological error consisted in putting off the central determining problem by claiming to examine the law "critically" without starting out from the precautionary clarification of the very aim and objective of such an examination. Behind the explicit polemical references, the attack made against criticism and humanistic philology directly involved the never-quoted Gerard Noodt and – as Perizonius revealed to his friend Rijckius in 1684 – his *licentia emendandi* [3]. To shed light on the reasons for the polemic, ancient Roman history and the history of its complex juridical organization was then deliberately quoted. In Huber's opinion interest in Roman Law and in *Corpus*

pp. 1–63.

3 HUBERUS 1684, pp. 76–77: "Nisi me vehementer opinio fallit, hac ratione Iurisconsulti officium melius impletur, quam perpetuis finemque contendendi non habentibus emendandi coniecturis. Maxime quando ita coniecturalis illa Crisis exercetur, ut proprias opiniones vestras de iuris controversiis adiuvetis, rationesque adversantium et obstantia legum argumenta refellatis; quod quidem terbio loco animadvertere cupiebam. Nam si toleranda sine manuscriptis est emendandi licentia, duntaxat tam evidens esse debet, ut minus facile refelli quam adstrui et approbari possit. Quod de talibus, quae tuendis opinionibus, in quibus Interpretes discrepant, adhibentur, nullo modo licet adfirmare [...]". Cf. also PERIZONIUS to Rijckius, 1684. In MEIJER 1971, p. 74 and in VAN DEN BERGH 1988, p. 54: "Huber noster scripsit dialogum inter ipsum et Bokelmannum ac Crusium, in quo per latus Crusii petit Notium, et dum in eum incurrit, plus satis iniquum se probat omnibus qui Crisin aliquando exercent, et humaniora profitentur. Titulus est 'de ratione iuris docendi et discendi' ". On Noodt "criticism" see HUBERUS 1700, pp. 5, 123ff. and 541. On the polemic Huber-Noodt about "necessitas emendandi" see – after VAN DER VLUGT 1916 – VAN DEN BERG 1988, pp. 54–55, 113, 141, 147, 165–166, 296–297, 300–304.

Iuris, in particular, are often filtered by an unadmitted sense of precariousness, by a vain trust in *critica,* destined to disintegrate against the lesson of real events, against the very history of the text examined: "Critica male exercita leges ipsas corrumpit et sacrum Iuris corpus violat ac imminuit". Thus, if on the one hand it is not a sacrilege "reprehendere Iustinianum, vel antiquos Iustitiae sacerdotes", as Wissenbach had taught in his *Emblemata Triboniani* (1633)[4], on the other hand is to be considered "alienissimum ab officio boni Interpretis", the bad habit of contemporaries directed towards:

> Hoc affectare gloriamque exinde captare, sicut facere videntur, qui numerum Iuris naevorum tam immaniter augent [...]. Ideoque dedi hoc biennio in publicis lectionibus operam, ut demonstrarem, [pleraque] loca Iuris nostri, quae ut iniqua, inhonesta, falsa, absurda traducuntur, sano sensu intellecta, nihil eiusmodi continere, cuius a claris hominibus insimulantur. E quarum lectionum memoria nescio, an non aliquando censuram Censurae Juris Romani et Anticriticam huius generis incorrupto eruditorum iudicio sim propositurus[5].

In this polemical context, even if the *Corpus Iuris* no longer appeared an inviolable entity of absolute value, so that an *inter-*

4 HUBERUS 1684, p. 73 and WISSENBACH (1633) 1642. On this author – after HEINECCIUS (1735) 1771, pp. 27–49 – see BIONDI 1911, pp. 5–12; ORESTANO (1953) 1987, pp. 81, 234 and PALAZZINI FINETTI 1953, pp. 239–240, 318–326.

5 HUBERUS 1684, pp. 82–83. Cf. also HUBERUS (1678–1690) 1735, II, p. 282 where he shed light on the reasons for the "tumor eloquentiae tribonianeae". "Credibile est, haec verba (in l. 14, C. 5, 12) esse a Triboniano adsuta, ut interpolations non tantum in Pandectis sed etiam in Codice ab illo sunt exercitae" (HUBERUS [1678–1690] 1735, III, p. 165). On this theme cf. ALBERTARIO (1910) 1953, pp. 19–25; ORESTANO (1953) 1987, pp. 81, 171, 187, 600 and PALAZZINI FINETTI 1953, pp. 240–241, 279–280, 329–333, 357–362.

pretation and a "*criticism of criticism*"[6] had nevertheless proved possible, the entity evoked by the term *ius* could represent something larger than what was witnessed by the traditional texts. Juridical *science* not limited to banal precepts, or to an exclusively erudite philology demanded an appropriate reference to *principles* and *ideas* capable of rendering the system of universal laws accessible to historical knowledge, the logical links of the absolute principles of "universal right". Requests for a refoundation were basically founded on a need to react against the void brought about by the crisis which in the 17th century was essentially the crisis of the juridical *datum*, the crisis of validity of the *norm,* and the crisis of the very *Corpus Iuris,* whose juridical and metajuridical authority was founded on the idea of the continuity of the Holy Roman Empire in the Middle Ages. With this continuity now being interrupted, Roman law that was penetrating into Holland from France and more especially from Germany became a rich mine of data and documents, finding favourable conditions for its re-elaboration in its need to unify the multiple and often contrasting forms of jurisdiction which still obstructed the movement towards political unification, launched by the young republic of the Seven Provinces following the war against Philip VI of Spain. Thus there came about what has effectively been called the "concetto di un diritto romano-olandese (*Roomsch-Holandsch Recht*)", appearing among dogmatic studies, tending towards bringing ancient local laws into harmony with Roman law, and the historico-erudite studies which followed the methods of the impoverished French *cultured* school,

6 *Eunomia romana*'s subtitle startes: "Continens examen praecipuorum iuris locorum, secundum Pandectas et Institutiones; quae ut falsa, iniqua, inhonesta, absurda, corrupta, subornata varie traducta secundum veras Iurisprudentiae, Philosophiae civilis, Historiae et Sacrarum literarum rationes, vindicantur, sanantur aut explicita illustrantur, et cum usu temporum conferuntur" (HUBERUS 1700).

that the *natural law* trend was favourably disposed towards encouraging subsequent codification projects'[7].

Topicality of the "Lex Regia": Rationality, History, 'Ratio Status'

A scholar of philology and erudition, Huber always acted in both fields as a jurist and historian sensitive to the problems of a general theory of "public law", and to its *immota principia*[8] which represent the theoretical foundation of Huber's interpretation of the history of Rome as the history of its *law*. Rome offers the professor, accustomed to expressing himself in a Latinate language, and to consulting *Digesto* and *Pandette,* a privileged example of ancient history, as it reveals itself as a documented state organization of society, a model of justice that was actually implemented. Having adopted Wissenbach's authoritative *Disputa-*

7 CALASSO (1951) 1970, pp. 332–333 and CALASSO 1954, pp. 624–625. On the Roman Law in Holland see VAN OVEN 1934–1935, II, pp. 23–55; KOSCHAKER (1958) 1962 and FEENSTRA (1958) 1962, I, pp. 243–268.

8 HUBERUS (1678–1690) 1735, pp. 46, 95. Cf. Le Clerc's opinion in *BIBLIOTHÈQUE UNIVERSELLE ET HISTORIQUE* about Huber's *Dissertationes theologicae VII* [see HUBER 1688b]: "On s'étonnera peut-être que nous ayons mis cet Ouvrage parmi les Livres en droit; mais c'est qu'encore que M. Huber fasse, par un pur effet de son zèle, l'office de catéchiste a Franeker, et qu'il ait déjà composé plusieurs livres sur des matières de théologie, il avouë néanmoins qu'il n'est pas versé dans cette science; *Ab Rev. viris adversantibus nihil aequius accepi, quam quod me Theologiae negant esse peritum; nec enim unquam id prae me tuli*" (*BIBLIOTHÈQUE UNIVERSELLE ET HISTORIQUE* 1717, IX, p. 556).

tiones Iuris Civilis (1648)[9] but for a brief time and for initial teaching purposes, Huber then began to write his *Disputationes* on the main themes of jurisprudence, together with his historico-philological *Digressiones*, but always distinguishing and separating the juridical questions from those belonging to other ambits of discourse[10].

Significant and most symptomatic of his Roman law study interests is the interpretation of the Lex *Regia,* that was to accompany his entire historico-juridical reflection, as well as represent a useful bank of evidence for bringing his historico-erudite investigations into harmony with his theoretical-doctrinal elaborations and the political problems of late seventeenth-century Dutch society.

The *Lex*, already the object of Huber's polemics in the late seventeen-sixties, is treated in full in the *Disputationes iuris fundamentales* of 1688, subsequently re-elaborated in the second and third editions of the *Digressiones Justinianeae* (1688–1696). His main theses rested on the interpretation of an important passage of the *Institutiones* (1, 2, 6: "Sed et quod principi placuit, legis habet vigorem, cum lege regia, quae de imperio eius lata est, populus ei et in eum omne suum imperium et potestatem concessit"), as well as the almost identical one of the *Digesto* (1, 4, 1. *pr.* Ulpianus, *l. 1 Institutionum*): "Quod principi placuit, legis habet vigorem; utpote cum lege regia, quae de imperio eius lata est, populus ei et in eum omne suum imperium et potestatem conferat". Confirmation of these principles also appeared to be offered by *D.* 1, 3, 31 (Ulpianus, *Liber 13 Ad Legem Juliam et Papiam*) that re-formulated the essential contents of the lex: "Princeps legibus solutus est; Augusta tamen licet legibus soluta non est, principes tamen eadem illi privilegia tribuunt, quae ipsi ha-

9 On these *Disputationes* (HUBERUS 1688) cf. FEENSTRA et al. 1985, pp. 293–295.

10 On HUBERUS (1670) 1688 cf. – after FEENSTRA et al. 1985, p. 296 – VEEN 1976 and VEEN 1985.

bent". Starting out from these premises, Huber faced the entire question from its roots through a careful examination of the ancient documents and of relative contemporary historiography, a continuous confrontation with the more significant conlusions of modern juridical philology, from Coras to Connan, and from Gothofredus to Gronovius[11], and even earlier with the theses of Jacques Cujas whose interpretation of *D.* 1, 3, 31 in the *Observationum et emendationum libri XXVIII,* published between 1556 and 1558 contested the value of the general principle of the Ulpian formula and, in keeping with the anti-absolutist character of his political reflection, limited its applicability only to certain specific laws of private law, in particular to the "Lex Julia and Papia Poppaea", two *leges* issued by Augustus in 18 and 9 B.C. in order to regulate testamentary successions. For the rest the *princeps* was held to respect the limits and laws observed by the people, who before the transfer of the *imperium* possessed only a limited power, and would thus not have been able to transfer a different one[12]. Drawing his inspiration from analogous criteria, even

11 HUBERUS (1678–1690) 1735, pp. 38–39, 77–78, 85–86. On Gronovius' *Oratio de lege regia* Huber observed "Praecipua difficultas est in facto rogationis, quam Vir summus Johan. Frideric. Gronovius *in oratione de Lege Regia* non minus quam caeteri, dum Legem ipsam adfirmare videtur, praeterit ac negat; etsi absque rogatione Lex sit apud Veteres Romanos [...] *nihil et non ens.* Non possunt in animum inducere Viri docti, rogationem esse factam, de qua nihil usquam scriptum reperitur. Enimvero nomen eius qui Legem rogaverit, non memorari certum est; de facto rogationis dubitare non potest, qui a senatu populoque Romano nihil potuisse dari cuiquam, nisi per Senatusconsultum et Legem, cogitet" (HUBERUS 1700, p. 43). On the passage of the *Institutiones* (I, 2, 6) cf. VEEN 1987, pp. 107–110.

12 CUIACIUS (1556–1558) 1836, pp. 703–704: "Quod ait Ulpianus, scribens ad legem Iuliam et Papiam, in *l* 18. *D. de legib. Princeps legibus solutus est,* de legibus poenariis Graeci ita interpretantur [...]; ut illud Aeschyli de Iove [...], quia scilicet iudices non habet; Latini de quibuscumque legibus, cum sit ex inscriptione legis ea sententia tantum accipienda de legibus caducariis, Iulia et Papia, quae satis etiam per se odiosae erant [...];

Donellus did not fail to refer to a *restrictiva legibus* interpretation of the *potestas* assigned to the *princeps*[13]. In Huber's view, in contrast, the Ulpian affirmation reflected a more general significance, proving a worthy doctrinal expression of the evolution of ancient Roman history in an absolutist sense. The terminological differences to be encountered between the Ulpian passage (*D.* 1,

qua de caussa veniam legis Voconiae a senatu Augustus petit apud Dionem. Sed et plerisque aliis pnincipes soluti non erant, licet imperii initio non iurassent in leges, et multo minus si iurassent. Quinimmo ut populus ipse suis legibus tenebatur, ita princeps cui et in quem populus omne suum [imperium] contulerat, adeo ut potestas principis et in ipsum principem esset, *l.* 4. *C. de legib.* [...]. Quod igitur *d. l.* 31. et Dio *lib. LIII* dicens, hoc se ex latino sermone transferre; [...] non de omnibus legibus accipiendum est. Et quod Dio Chrysostomus principem esse [...], et Plato [...], et idem fere, Iustinianus in *Novell. CV.* eo tantum pertinet, ut intelligatur, penes principem esse omnem potestatem ferendarum, vel abrogandarum legum, ut Augustinus ait in *epistola* quadam, *imperatorem non esse subiectum legibus, qui habet in potestate alias leges ferre, non temere quidem, sed ex iusta caussa et re publica, atque adeo confirmandi etiam quae non iure facta sunt* [...]". On the general principle of the Ulpian formula in the modern French culture see MOREL 1970 and REBUFFA 1970, who has noticed in the "umanesimo giuridico [...] da un lato una linea, in qualche caso apparentemente slegata da obbiettivi politici, tendente però di fatto a limitare i poteri attribuibili a chi impersonava l'autorità sovrana: rappresentanti di questa linea abbiamo indicato, sia pure differenziati da diversi fini e da diversi strumenti critici e scientifici, Jacques Cujas e François Hotman. Dall'altro lato una linea nella quale l'interpretazione di certe fonti romane viene finalizzata alla dimostrazione di assunti di teoria politica al servizio del potere regio e dello svincolamento il più esteso possibile di questo da altri poteri presenti nell'ambito della monarchia francese: in questa seconda linea si collocano Guillaume Budé e Jean Bodin" (REBUFFA 1972, pp. 121–122 but also – on Cujas – pp. 113–117).

13 DONELLUS (1589–1596) 1762, p. 90. Huber's polemic with Cuiacius, Donellus and Gothofredus is also in *Eunornia rornana,* about the "cardo quaestionis [...], utrum populus in Principem transtulerit ius suum in actu primo, an exercitium sui iuris ei mandaverit. Hac de re, ex sententia Iuris Romani non potest dubitari, tam clara positione, quam est in *1.* 1. *tit. sequ.* de qua mox agendum" (HUBERUS 1700, p. 39).

4, 1, *pr.*) and that of the *Institutiones* (1, 2, 6) already indicated the significant imperial autonomy: if Ulpian's *conferat* in fact shows an *imperium* and a *potestas* conferred from time to time by the *populus,* then the *concessit* of the *Institutiones* ratifies the reality of a command irreversibly transferred *una tantum* to the hands of the *princeps* on whose wish depended the legitimacy of every *lex*: "Posterius, quod Lex certa de Caesarum Imperio sit lata aliis quoque pridem Doctis Viris incredibile visum ac etiamnum multis videtur [...]. Sed cum dicitur *Lex Illa Antiqua* Justiniano, et *lata* Ulpiano satis indicatur Lex certa demonstrari". Thus the content of *D.* 1, 3, 31 did not imply any restriction for the prince who was not restricted by the Lex Julia et Papia Poppaea, since he was exempt from the obligation to respect all the laws of positive right. In the affirmation of the *potestas legibus soluta* the essential character of sovereignty is perfectly well summed up, according to the Friesian jurist. Being arbiter of the laws, the *princeps* is not subordinate to them, since the desire that produces the law and *potestas* cannot be limited in itself: "[...] Qui nulla civili sanctione tenetur, supra illum civile imperium non, adeoque is est [...], absolutae potestatis, subiectus nulli. Et qui nunquam cogi potest, is nec superiorem nec quidem parem habet, ideoque verus Rex est; quae sunt immota principia"[14].

In the general articulation of these themes in no way was the contribution offered by the exegesis of the Glossators and Commentators neglected[15], whose works Huber with his sure and expert mastery had certainly made use of, even if in practice very little of that exegesis had been explicitly translated into his writings. Thus a simple textual comparison could prove misleading from the hermeneutic viewpoint, if it were not ready to ac-

14 HUBERUS (1678–1690) 1735, pp. 39, 40, 46.

15 In addition to the pages of CALASSO (1949, pp. 239, 269–270; CALASSO 1957) see MCILWAIN (1940) 1956, pp. 80ff.; CORTESE (1966) 1982; PIANO MORTARI 1976; WYDUCKEL 1979 and GAUDEMET 1982, I, pp. 1–36.

cept in Huber's work a different *lay out* of the problems examined, and a different *substance* of theirs, bearing typical late-seventeenth-century connotations. In the context examined Huber's considerations did not in fact exclude the examination of a document that for centuries had been object of juridical interpretation, namely the important inscription relating to the *Lex Regia de Imperio Vespasiani* which, reported in a bronze tablet and not *marble*, as the Dutch jurist had erroneously observed, reproduced the final part of an act enacted between 69 and 70 A.D. to itemize and legitimize the *potestates* officially acknowledged to Vespasian on the occasion of his ascendancy to the throne. Here, as in few other loci of the Roman juridical system, law, politics and history are shown to be intimately correlated. The *lex* showed, in fact, that the validity of the prerogatives of the *princeps* was assured by a historical tradition, rooted in Augustus and then renewed for his successors from Tiberius to Claudius, according to acts and formalities nether new nor occasional but belonging to the normal elective praxis activated by the *Populus Romanus* in favour of the *Princeps* to whom normative power is attributed, and consequently the power to be free from certain specific legislative regulations[16]. As participant in the great critical achievement of the end of the seventeenth century – the one which Arnaldo Momigliano has effectively defined as the affirmation of *non-literary* evidence[17] – Huber describes, comments and orders the content of a source of Roman law, by utilizing the relative historiography. With Tacitus and Suetonius, the testimony more frequently consulted and quoted is Cassius Dio's *Roman History* (LI–LIV). From this classical historiographical model Huber's interpretation learned how to limit biographical references to essential and special expository purposes, and to

16 Cf. *supra,* Chap. 1, note 104.

17 MOMIGLIANO (1950) 1955, pp. 67–106; then also in MOMIGLIANO 1984, pp. 3–45.

consider the history of the empire as the history of *facts* far distant from the traditional moralistic paradigm[18]. However, more than for the originality of critico-hermeneutic observations, Huber's real merit, concerned as he was with elaborating a general theory of the State, is to be sought in his commitment to investigating the document from the historical viewpoint, to redefining in more general terms the conditions for ascertaining the facts, so as not to leave space for historical Pyrrhonism, a dangerous affirmation of which he saw in Martinus Schoockius' theses set out in a *De figmento legis regiae Epistola* dated 1661, then converging, with several modifications and integrations in the pages of the *Tractatus De quadruplici lege regia* (1668)[19]. Voet's disciple and Professor at Groningen, drawing inspiration from doubts and reservations already formulated by Connan against the Salic Law, which excluded female descendency from ascending to the crown of France, had denied the existence of every possible *royal law,* as well as the authenticity of the so-called Capitoline fragment reproducing the final part of the text of that law: "Fateor, non quidem, sequi, aliquae Inscriptiones sunt supposititiae; ergo, eiusdem furfuris haberi debet Fragmentum, vulgo pro lege Regia ostentari solitum; haec solummodo adduxeram, atque hoc tempore iterum exhibeo ut constet novum non esse Inscriptionum fidem in dubium vocare. Cum summa vero ratione suspectari hoc Fragmentum, videntur evincere sequentes rationes, iam antea adductae, et quibus nondum diffido [...]". The Roman emperors exercised an *auctoritas* that originally belonged to the people not through a recognized and accepted law, but by usurping that authority and subjugating the people itself. To those who had unreservedly accepted the conviction

18 Cf. *supra*, Chap. 1, note 90

19 SCHOOCKIUS 1661, edited by LOMONACO 1990, pp. 243–314. On Schoockius, "professor logicae et philosophiae practicae" in Groningen – after BOELES 1864, II, pp. 25–27 – cf. COHEN 1921 and then DIBON 1954, pp. 180–190.

whereby through the *Lex Regia* the *princeps* had obtained the complete, definitive tenure of sovereign powers and *maiestas*, Schoockius posed a long series of questions and reservations, going so far as to support conclusively, on the basis of precise historico-critical references, the idea that the *lex* had been invented by Tribonianus only to adulate Justinian's *potestas*, to be subsequently withdrawn and reformulated by Ulpian: "[...] Ex quibus quantum iudicio, fidei, et diligentiae Triboniani et adiutorum ipsius, imo Iustiniani quoque, tribuendum sit, abunde patet. Speciatim in Ulpianum Triboniani scalpellum se exercuit"[20]. Also amid such a scheme of considerations, the corrosive acid of criticism began to fall on the texts of the Justinian compilation. It was a decisive blow that split traditional legislative cohesion, and also through a clever investigation the authority of a *lex* and all the weight of the underlying historico-historiographical tradition. The polemic had, however, the merit of making waves and showing the dangers of arbitrary historico-philological misrepresentations, by advancing a more empirical and rational method of learning, founded on the instruments of real criticism, likely to achieve results to some extent *certain,* albeit *limited.* Schoockius' interpretation, in effect, far from aiming at legitimising absolute scepticism, is very wary of not writing off every historical narration as fantastic, by setting itself the more reasonable aim of liberating it from the fictions fabricated and transmitted by tradition. The Groningen erudite revealed such awareness, when participating in the polemic against Cartesian philosophy that spread among the Netherland culture during the 1640s from Henricus Regius' "materialistic" perspectives and from the accusations of atheism levelled against Leyden by Steuart[21]. In 1652

20 SCHOOCKIUS 1661, pp. 276–277, 305 and CONNANUS 1553.

21 As STEUART SCHOOCKIUS 1643 (in BERTELLI 1973, p. 314 and note) reproposed the confrontation between Descartes and G.C. Vanini, observing that "Nulla iniuria Renato fit cum subtilissimo atheismi patrono Cesare Vanini comparatur, iisdem enim atribus in imperitorum animis

he was directly involved in the polemic on scepticism, that reappeared, not without first making a conscious and significant choice, the objections levelled against the Cartesian *Cogito* by Gassendi's philosophy:

> [...] *Ego cogito; qui cogitat est; igitur ego sum.* At utro vis modo ruina. Nam si priore forma concludas, propositio illa, *Qui cogitat est* praeiudicium est, antecedens illud, quod tu vis statuere iudiciorum optimum. si posteriore, cum Assumptio illa *Qui cogitat est;* iudicium est, quod neque dependet a tua propositione *Ego cogito,* neque sequitur tuam conclusionem, *Ego sum,* ex qua vis omnia iudicia praeter illud *Ego cogito,* dependere. *Hactenus Gassendus,* cui hactenus nemo ex patronis huius argumenti, cum ratione respondere potuit[22].

Here the adhesion to Gassendism implies special critical caution which is basically translated into an acceptance of a general methodological indication regarding the anti-dogmatic value of the traditional notions of *certainty* and *truth:*

> Cum propositio enim dubia, incertaque ea sit, quae ex aequo inter evidentiam, et obscuritatem iacet; quippe cum nihil sit, quod ad assentiendum, magis quam ad dissentiendum, aut contra inclinet, ut circa istam propositionem, *Stellae sunt pares numero;* Oportet sane, ut propositio, quam Mens habet non certam quidem, sed verisimilem, seu probabilem tamen, amplius quid evidentiae, quam obscuritatis obtineat[23].

To avoid the *impasse* brought about by historical scrupulousness and a pre-constituted formulation on the one hand,

---

atheismi thronum erigere laborat". On Schoockius' objections against the Cartesian philosophy – after SERRURIER 1930, Chapp. 3, 4 and THIJSSEN-SCHOUTE 1950, pp. 185–186; THIJSSEN-SCHOUTE 1954, pp. 79, 476–486, 538, 554, 563 and note – cf. KOSSMANN 1960, p. 27 and espec. VERBEEK 1988 and 1992.

22 SCHOOCKIUS 1652, p. 93. On this work cf. – after PAQUOT 1768 – DIBON 1954, p. 187 and BORGHERO 1983, pp. 104–105, 179, 188 and notes.

23 GASSENDI (1658) 1964, p. 104a.

and by a dogmatic approach on the other, a new methodological 'strategy' was required deliberately designed to question the traditional criteria of historiographical investigation. It was, in a word, a matter of penetrating into the heart of the problem, and re-discussing the notions of *fact* and historical *judgement*, and the value and credibility of testimonies in a reconstruction of the possibility, in short, of the *fides historica* to identify instruments appropriate for defining the conditions for and limits of human knowledge.

In the wake of Cocceius (*Ad tit. Pandectarum*) Huber too protested against the ambitious theses of the "impudentissima [...] bestia"[24], as Vossius defined Schoockius in a letter to Saumaise, judging them unacceptable as they were founded on contrived, arbitrary generalizations which introduce and consolidate a real and proper abstract notion of *Lex Regia,* that make them lose their every significance. Schoockius had destroyed the respect due to antiquity, in the name of a perverse *ratio philosophandi* which claimed apodeictic demonstrations where one could manage perfectly well with just the *authority* of the witnesses and a certain degree of *likelihood:* "Proinde, qui Legem Regiam esse latam negare volunt, salva Justiniani auctoritate, in irritum laborant. Necesse enim est, aut extitisse Legem, aut mentitum esse Justinianum; quod Auctor *de figmento legis regiae,* sine ambagibus profitetur. Ideo coacti fuimus in hac disputatione Justiniano non ex corpore iuris, sed incorruptis antiquae Historiae monumentis patrocinari"[25]. To safeguard the authenticity of the *Lex Regia*, a meticulously documented reconstruction of the Roman constitutional events is thus necessary. Yet, Huber's interest went well beyond a simple juridical datum in an attempt to report jurisprudence within the limits of a specific doctrine of the *actions* and elaborate within the changed theoretical-methodological

24 Cited by VAN SLEE 1916, p. 121.
25 HUBERUS 1688, p. 77.

trend a new *topic* of juridical argumentation, an elaboration which through transforming it linked the rhetorical tradition of humanistic jurisprudence with modern research oriented in the direction of an original opening to the field of *experience* and reason. Basically there was the need to set Roman Law within history that the Friesian jurist, in keeping with Grotian teaching, does not hesitate to bring about in the significance of *foundation* and not only of *ornament* of reason, of *principle,* that is to say, and not only of *example*[26]. Indeed Huber reproached modern interpretations that were easy prey to scepticism of a rationalistic origin, for not allowing themselves to be guided by history as a matrix of juridical ideas, and thus for having levelled unfair accusations of interpolation against Tribonianus and Justinian[27].

Against this complicated backcloth, interest in erudition and antiquary research expressed a considerable anti-dogmatic dimension and the rejection of reason as *necessity,* as reality above and beyond time and human history, clashed with that dogmatic Cartesianism in whose schemes the philosophical and above all the theological culture of 17th century Franeker had been forming. In 1687, when dealing with *De concursu rationis et Sacrae Scripturae* Huber reproached his colleagues van der Waeyen and Röell for applying Cartesian methodology to theology, arriving at the conclusion that

> Cartesium laudatis magistrum. Quis hanc visionis mentalis fiduciam ad sacras literas fideique mysteria transferre vos docuit? Illene, qui hoc urtice cavit, ne non satis magnum discrimen inter veritates acquisitas et re-

26 GROTIUS (1680) 1979, pp. 58–59.

27 HUBERUS 1688, pp. 85–86: "[...] Sed ex iis verbis nihil profertur, cur minus singulorum Principum Maiestas ea lege [ornata] et instructa dicatur, quam universorum simul. Tum vero. Iustinianus usum sui saeculi consideravit, quo dudum id exoleverat, in rogatione ad populum vel decreto Senatus identidem capita potestatis Regiae renovarentur; Sed constituto Principe, ipso iure tum competebant, quae olim sanctione expressa conferebantur".

velatas statueretur; neve dubitationum visionumque suarum novitas et invidia rebus sacris applicata intestabilem ac intolerandum Christianis omnibus. philosophiam suam redderet?[28]

Also used for reflecting on the mysteries of the faith and Scriptures, reason acts legitimately in the theological debates and in testament studies by imposing the rational criterion of evidence on areas of investigation that Descartes himself had preferred not to face[29]. However, a more concrete and definite sense of historico-critical research successfully advances in Huber's critical conscience, which, freed from the modern deductive-type method, takes up direct contact again from within the facts, with a different criterion of truth, prompted by the implicit recognition that the more one claims to extend the mathematical-Cartesian method to different areas of investigation, the more one stimulates destructive scepticism which deduces the impossibility of *certain* and *valid* knowledge from the failure of this attempt. Hence also the confusion that persists in the interpretation of ancient Roman Law and which is also revealed in the continuously resurging trend of speaking of the *Lex Regia* as a unitary event, assuming it in general terms, without first defin-

28 HUBERUS 1687, p. 78, mentioned by THIJSSEN-SCHOUTE 1950, p. 251. On this polemic cf. *ACTA ERUDITORUM* 1687, VIII, pp. 405–408 and *BIBLIOTHÈQUE UNIVERSELLE ET HISTORIQUE* 1687, VI, pp. 371–375, 426–435. On Schoockius' polemic against Descartes cf. VEEN 1976, p. 183 and VAN DEN BERGH 1988, pp. 55ff. and 127ff.

29 DESCARTES to Mersenne (1630) 1897, I, p. 153: "Pour la question *an Dei bonitati sit conveniens homines in aeternum damnare,* cela est de Théologie; c'est pourquoy absolument vous me permettrez, s'il vous plaist, de n'en rien dire, non pas que les raisons des libertins en cecy ayent quelque force, car elles me semblent frivoles et ridicules; mais pour ce que je tiens que c'est faire tort aux vérités qui dépendent de la foy, et qui ne peuvent estre prouvées par démonstration naturelle, que de les vouloir affermir par des raisons humaines, et probables seulement [...]. Les 4.5.6.8.9. et derniers points de vôtre lettre sont tous de Théologie, c'est pourquoy je m'en tairay, s'il vous plaist".

ing its relative historico-cultural references. For such an incorrect approach, the expression *Lex Regia* has often assumed significances that go well beyond the relative Roman Law, by embracing and confounding other episodes of the history of Rome in a vision that would like to be unitary in its assumed, declared continuity. Nor does the use of adjectives that at times are made to follow that expression suffice to detract from it what is generic and incorrect. The constitutional transformation which accompanied the crisis of the *respublica* was slow and gradual because the Emperors showed themselves to be aware of the great prestige of the ancient institutions. In fact Augustus' first concern, later shared by his successors, was to reconcile the apparent restoration of the republican orders and the ancient *libertas* with the crucial desire to exercise effective power over traditional magistracies with the aim of imposing on the people solutions declaredly subversive of republican legality:

> Non scribit, datum esse Augusto ius imperii a populo, tempore certo vel iussu expresso; sed eum paulatim insurgendo in se traxisse dominationem, non ex lege Regia, verum praetextu Consulatus et Tribunitiae potestatis, qua contentus fuerit; idque *nullo adversante;* Quae omnia patientiam populi tolerantiamque, non consensum arguere videntur. Quod si regia potestas ei directe data fuisset, quid opus erat, consularem et Tribunitiam affectare potestatem?

Hence the traditional rejection of the term "regius", opposed to by the people who judge the expressions *king* and *tyrant* as synonymous, considering the former much less tolerable than *dictator* or *dominus,* these latter titles being offered to Augustus but immediately and astutely refused by him:

> Nomen *Regiae* legis multo esse recentius ipsa Lege, neque Augusti aut Vespasiani temporibus adhuc fuisse in usu, sed primum sub Antoninis coepisse usurpari. Porro, quia haec et plura ex ea tabula evidenter patent, operae pretium se facturum putavit Auctor *de figm.* L.R. si fidem eius suspectam, imo si falsam et supposititiam esse lectori persuadere

posset. Quod quam feliciter et quibus rationibus praestare satagat, perpendendum est.

The fall of the republic had been only the final act of a complicated historical and political period of agony at the end of which the emperors had become absolute patrons; a fall, in short, presented not as a sudden and unexpected event, but as the outcome of a long process of attrition: "Ergo nihil est certius, quam Augusto caeterisque Caesaribus delatum esse summum et absolutum Reip. Imperium, et cum fieri nequeat, ut integra Maiestas transferatur ac retineatur oportet, populum omni suo lure se abdicasse"[30]. The history of the *Lex* was presented therefore as a real movement not withdrawing into the intimacy of the psychological datum, but operating within the confines of a reflection on 'politics', as expression of a culture that is found at the centre of civil life and in some way outlines its history. In confirmation of the historico-political importance of the question under examination, Schoockius himself, albeit denying the existence of the *Lex,* stressed its *reasons* critically with reference not only to ancient Roman history but also to monarchies in general. In fact, the *Tractatus* of 1668 deliberately closed with a *sectio* with the significant title "De Lege Regia. Quatenus in omnibus imperiis monarchicis occurrit"[31]. Thus, far from terminating in an exclusively literary-rhetorical dimension, the reference to the antique, even in the exemplary form of the myth, conserved the sense of definite episodes and political experiences. In particular, erudition dated back to Roman history where it searched for a response to the numerous questions posed by the rise of the modern European states.

30 HUBERUS 1688, pp. 67, 89, 97.

31 SCHOOCKIUS 1668, pp. 290ff. On the "lex regia" in historico-political culture of the 17th century cf. OGG (1932) 1938 and, with attention to Holland, DURAND 1973, pp. 5ff., 51ff., 106ff., 153ff., 196ff.

Enacted to remedy the crisis of the imperial *auctoritas* after the tragic end of the *domus Augusta* and the *damnatio memoriae* of Nero, the *Lex de Imperio Vespasiani* represents a moment of overbearing advance in the political strength of the *princeps,* as a factor determining the equilibrium and order of the *ius publicum.* It is in fact understood from a correct analysis that the people, originally sovereign, transferred its *potestas,* thus making the constitution of the State possible and giving up every right, as it would prove logically impossible to transfer and at the same time retain *auctoritas,* however limited. Being attributed to the *princeps* the latter no longer depends on the popular *voluntas*, since it serves to countersign the *essence* of sovereignty which for Huber is in a Grotian sense the power of governing in such a way that the actions of the sovereign cannot be altered by the wish of any other person; it is *summa potestas* not subject to anyone, and is absolute power in the State:

> Verum ut Summa Potestas sit integra penes unum, ac idem tamen alii potestati subiiciatur, hoc sine dubio contradictionem involvit. Quidam ex nostris prope idem volunt, cum populum transtulisse Imperium in Principem aiunt cumulative, non privative, ut traderet simul ac retineret ius suum; quasi tu dicas, dedit pariter ac non dedit.

Thus nothing is more certain, Huber concludes, than the fact that the highest and most absolute office of the State, namely sovereignty, was conferred on Augustus and subsequently on the other Caesars: "[...] Legis huius imperialis originem Augusti temporibus adscribendam, non Iulii Caesaris, cuius nulla fit hic mentio; Dein, Legem non pro universis in perpetuum Principibus semel esse latam, verum sub singuliis Imperatoribus repetitam fuisse renovatamque"[32]. In obeying imperial absolutism, the Romans chose the only way of guaranteeing a possibility of civil

32 HUBERUS 1688, pp. 47, 89.

coexistence. The empire had thus to become absolute for its life to go on.

In this interpretation, a principle had been formulated with special theoretical and doctrinal vigour: that of *derogation* of the law, lawful *exception* for the *princeps* in the light of supreme necessity and political purposes relating to the very existence of the State. The *Reason of State* had already been interpreted as exceptional by Gabriel Naudé, one of the most perceptive interpreters of Machiavelli, treating "coups d'Etat" as *extraordinary* infringements of the "common law". For Cardinal Mazzarino's learned librarian Botero's classical definition had not hit the mark, unlike the "plus spéciale, particulière et determine", one of "*excessum iuris communis propter bonum commune*", since with this latter definition a distinction may be made between the rules which contribute to the foundation of the empires and find their raison d'etre in the laws and between those that Clapmarius calls *arcana imperiorum,* that are legalized not by the people's positive or natural legitimate right, but only by the consideration of *public interest,* which often transcends that of private individuals or single groups[33].

33 NAUDÉ (1639) 1958, p. 68: "[...] *La seconde est proprement ce que les François* appellent, *Maximes d'Estat,* et les Italiens, *Ragion di Stato,* quoyque Botero ait compris sous ce terme toutes les trois différences que nous voulons établir, disant, que la *Regione di Stato, è notitia di mezzi atti a fundare, conservare, e ampliare un Dominio,* en quoy il n'a pas si bien rencontré, a mon jugement, que ceux qui la définissent, *excessum iuris communis propter bonum commune,* d'autant que cette dernière définition estant plus spéciale, particulière et déterminée, l'on peut au moyen d'icelle distinguer, entre ces premières règles de la fondation des Empires, lesquelles sont établies sur les loix et conformes à la raison; et ces secondes que Clapmarius appelle mal a propos, *Arcana Imperiorum,* et nous avec plus de raison, *Maximes d'Estat;* puis qu'elles *ne peuvent estre légitimes par* le droit des Gens, civil, ou naturel; mais *seulement par la considération du bien, et de l'utilité publique,* qui passe assez souvent par dessus celles du particulier". On this theme after the classical pages of HAZARD and PINTARD, LENOBLE, FEBVRE

Roman history still proved typical in this regard, and there is a noteworthy episode in the life of the emperor Claudius who being unable through civil law to marry his niece Julia Agrippina, daughter of his brother Germanicus, had recourse to the Reason of State, which was in contrast with the ordinary law[34]. Far from the theoretical-moralistic schemes of Livy's heroico-republican infatuations – an author who on par with Caesar and Pliny the Elder, Seneca and Cicero, Sallust and Suetonius is even held in Huber's reflection as residual of the philological apparatus of humanistic tradition – precise theoretical-historiographical

---

and those of SPINI and GREGORY, BATTISTA and SCHNEIDER, BERTELLI, PAGANINI and CANZIANI, cf. the general studies of COMPARATO 1980, t. IV, pp. 95–164, ZOLI 1989 and now BOEUF 2007.

34 NAUDÉ (1639) 1958, pp. 68–69: "Ainsi voyons nous, que l'Empereur Claudius ne pouvant par les loix de sa patrie, prendre à femme, sa [nièce] charnelle Julia Agrippina fille de Germanicus son frère, il eut recours aux loix d'Estat, pour fonder son évident contradiction aux loix ordinaires, et l'épousa, *ne foemina expertae foecunditatis,* dit Tacite, *integra iuventa, claritudinem Caesarum in aliam domum tnansferret* (lib. 12). C'est à dire, de crainte que cette femme venant à se marier en quelque grande maison, le sang des Césars ne s'étendist en d'autres familles, et ne produisist une multitude de Princes et Princesses, qui auroient eu avec le temps quelque [prétention] à l'Empire, et en suite occasion de troubler le repos public. *Tibère pour cette même raison ne vouloit donner un mary* à *Agrippina* veuve de Germanicus, et mère de celle dont nous venons de parler, bien que elle luy en demandast un avec pleurs et [remontrances], appuyées sur des raisons si puissantes et légitimes, qu'on ne pouvoit luy refuser [sans] commettre une injustice, laquelle néanmoins estoit légitimée par la loy de l'Estat, puis que Tibère n'ignoroit point *quantum ex Republica peteretur* (TAC. lib. 4. *Annal.*), c'est à dire de quelle conséquence ce mariage estoit, et que les [enfants] qui en proviendroient, estant arrière-neveux d'Auguste, la République Romaine tomberoit quelque jour en des grands troubles et [partialités], à cause des divers [prétendants] à la succession de l'Empire". On this theme and on the complex understanding of the context see – after the classical pages of MEINECKE and DE MATTEI – SCHNUR (1963) 1979; THUAU (1966) 2000; SCHNUR 1975, FIRPO 1976; MANDROU 1977 and STOLLEIS 1980.

models were proposed. In the first place, the works of Tacitus, of ordinary consultation and current use through the Lipsian edition of 1607 in Antwerp and several references to contemporary political literature – from the *Politieke Discoursen* (1662) and from the *Politieke Weegschaal* (1662) of the de la Court brothers to the *Bibliotheca iuridica et politica* (1680) of Cornelius van Beughem, – who made constant use of Tacitus' incisive prose, often without having to indicate explicitly the classical source, that is generally known[35].

Huber referred not only to the pages of the ancient historian, that had filtered into Aristoteleian ethico-political paradigms (a new edition of the Graeco-Latin text of the Greek philosopher's *Politics* had appeared in 1660 at Jema edited by Daniel Hems) through Lipsian philology, for stylistic choices, but above all to the persuasive politicity of its narrative[36]. To quote Tacitus as an acceptable doctrinal precedent implies, moreover, the indirect but ineluctable comparison with Machiavelli's never expressly-referred-to theses, that yet became widespread throughout Holland by the Leyden edition of the 1652 *Discorsi.* Yet far from signifying passive acceptance of great models and classical modules for the Friesian jurist the approach to the Tacitistic-Machiavellian tradition did not intend to remain imprisoned by the precepts of the widespread political pedagogy of the *arcana imperii* and the myth of *good* or *bad Reason of State.* Emigrating to the Netherlands from Italy and more especially from Germany, this could not be rejected without abandoning the formal principles of the ancient moral of Aristoteleian tradition for ever, that had converged in the restoration which even before Botero (a Latin edition of whose work on the *Reason of State* had been published in 1666 at Helmstadt), Lipsius had given in the *Politicorum sive Civilis doctrinae libri sex* (1589) of the Stoic and Ma-

35 See DROETTO 1958, pp. 38ff.

36 See here Chap, p. 1, note 73.

chiavelleian tradition, arriving at the definition of a virtuous Christian *prudentia* mixed with "malignity" and "deception". In these theses, in the critico-political fortune of these definitions, Huber would have seen the persistence of an inadequate *Ratio Status* eulogized, interested only in obtaining *instructions* and *admonitions* of a general policy from ancient and modern history, and leaving the juridical significance of the concepts of state and power, of *maiestas* and *potestas*, undefined[37].

Sovereignty and State in the "De Iure Civitatis"

The analysis of these concepts underwent further in-depth examination and development in the pages of a manual *De iure civitatis* to whose composition Huber devoted many long years of his life. The work published in 1672 soon experienced reprints and new editions until 1694, and gained considerable fame for its Author[38]. Huber is not a philosopher and his interests are not philosophical. He was led to the study of *ius civitatis* not by the promptings of speculation but by the practical necessity of a general re-ordering of juridical knowledge and its methodological adherence to the requirements of a profoundly changed society. Nor could it have been otherwise. After the peace of Westphalia (1648), the great debates on *public law* of the

37 LIPSIUS 1589, pp. 22ff. On this theme – after DE MATTEI (1951) 1982–1984, pp. 68–83 – cf. DINI 1983, pp. 13–123, CAPPELLINI et al. 1987. On Lipsius, editor of Tacitus – after TOFFANIN (1933) 1954, pp. 123–129; TOFFANIN 1972 and RUYSSCHAERT 1949 – see OESTREICH 1969 and BONFATTI 1983.

38 HUBERUS (1672) 1708. On the polemical relations with the "machiavellismo" and Lipsius theory cf. KOSSMANN 1975, pp. 497–504, 537–547 and VEEN 1976, pp. 18ff., 88–99, 106–112, 339–349.

German Empire offered the jurists a terrain of reflection now far removed from the purely methodological discussions of the sixteenth century on the *ratio studendi* of the juridical art, proposing themes more suitable for defining their role and their class location in the new social and political realities of the territorial States.

The inclusion of an extensive specific treatment on *maiestas* in the second (1682) and third edition (1694) of the *De iure civitatis,* came about from his direct political experience matured as a member of the Friesian Supreme Court between 1679 and 1682[39]. It was the reflection on the delicate political contrasts developed in Dutch civil life after the anti-Spanish struggle, the response to a new political situation, that which in 1672, with the murder of the Grand Pensionnaire of Holland and *leader* of the "Regents" party Jan de Witt, had marked the end of the twenty-year republican period (1653–1672), and the restoration of the Statolderat (the office of leiutenant and captain of the armed forces which had survived the feudal regime more especially in Huber's Freisia) of William III of Orange against the threatening invasion attempts of Louis XIV later stemmed for good by the Peace of Nijmegen in 1678[40]. Set on the edges of international political life, Franeker had experienced a definite decline in the second half of the 17th century. The same University, devoid of prestigious masters, had now lost its reputation for ever which for a moment it had seemed able to boast of in republican years, when renowned scholars including Wissen-

39 See BOELES 1878–1889 and then VEEN 1976, pp. 1ff.

40 On this historical context – after the classical pages of MOTLEY and BLOK, PIRENNE and GEYL, KOSSMANN and WILSON, HALEY, PRICE and BOOGMAN – cfr. HAITSMA MULIER 1986, t. V. 3, pp. 407–426 and now BERKEL & DE GOEI 2010, pp. 81–177.

bach and Cup had taught there[41]. In general, the cultural debate had progressively deteriorated into a series of continuous counterpositions and polemics, thus destroying every illusion of radical change in the politico-social balance, and also of a transformation in the religious life that would not necessitate the Christian world being torn to pieces. In the altered political situation the most intransigent orthodox Calvinists disposed towards renewing the bitter politico-religious conflict which fifty years earlier had endangered life in the United Provinces by stirring up bitter disputes between Arminians and Gomarists like those supported by Conrad Vorst against Sibrando Lubbert, and by Grotius against Andrea Rivet until the convocation of the Synod of Dordrecht (1618), had now begun to look favourably on the figure of Statolder, who found renewed vigour thanks also to royalist nostalgia of the nobility and of the poorest peasant classes[42]. With confidence in revolution and the hoped for *unity* and *certainty* of the legislative order having now become critical, the convergence of *ordo* and *ratio,* desired by well-known humanistic syntheses, appeared to be assured only by the restoration of unity to the State. Thus it became more pressing to define juridical science and the tasks of the jurist in a different way of understanding, through a different 'ideological' structure of the relationships between jurisprudence – still contested between technique and pedagogy, between *scientia* and *eloquentia* – and power, between *law* and *politics.* For this task, the pages of the *De iure civitatis* referred expressly to the theoretical-historiographic

41 On University of Franeker – after the studies of GEYL and ROORDA, HACKMANN and FRIJHOFF – new documentation is in JENSMA et al. 1985, pp. 11–39, 56–89, 147–160.

42 See the historical context of these disputes in VOET 1663–1676 and ARMINIUS et al. 1684. On this works – after NOBBS and LECLER, KOSSMANN, DE MICHELIS PINTACUDA and FIRPO – see TODESCAN 1983, pp. 1–18 and SIMONUTTI 1984, pp. 7–54.

proposals of Grotius who was eulogized even by the *Praefatio* as founder and harbinger of rightful and just differences:

> Ante duos et viginti annos usu venit, ut Studiosis rudimentum Iuris Publici Universalis, cuius salivam illis moveram, rogantibus, in Academia disputando proponerem; quod ante hac cum Politica mixtum, Grotius, ab illa quidem separandum esse docuit, ea ut viam ratione, quam, in praefatione magni operis, *De iure belli ac pacis,* exposuit. Sed huic divisioni monstravit, ita, quominus ipse eam institueret, fecit usus et materia scriptionis, quam prae manibus habebat[43].

Reference to juridical reasoning as distinct from politics, becomes, in debate with Bodin, the appeal to a science of the *just* capable of being compared with the *new science,* of setting itself as foundation and order of the State, far from the changing vicissitudes of traditional positive legislation. Behind this design however there was not the search for a unique *methodus* of juridical knowledge that had aimed at elaborating the topical-rhetorical schemes first of the 'systematic' humanistic and then of sixteenth-century encyclopedism, going on to theorize the law as a universal on the basis of classical Ciceronian elements received over time. The search to identify fundamental juridical *principles* for a reflection on the State pointed the way to the definitive departure from the old pictures of the *ars politica* conceived in an Aristotelian sense in accordance with the instruments of *dialectic* and *rhetoric,* substantially changed by re-elaborating the admired Lipsian model aimed at restoring its ancient *purity* to *politics.* A departure which is recorded by Huber's lessons on politics that remained significantly unpublished. These were in fact *Dissertationes politicae* (held between the end of the fifties and the beginning of the sixties), modelled on Lipsius' *Politicorum sive Civiles doctrinae libri sex* (1589) in accordance with the suggestions of the

43 HUBERUS (1672) 1708; cf. also the *Oratio qua disseritur* (1684), in HUBERUS 1746, I, pp. 75–87. On this theme cf. VEEN 1976, pp. 28–29, 112, 360–361.

neo-Stoic politics of Böckler, whom Huber met in Strasburg between 1656 and 1657[44].

The aspiration was to define a "common right" valid beyond its restricted geographical-cultural settings and capable of offering a comprehensive interpretation of society activated by the new scientific interests of the modern jurists against the falshood and lies of the old *politicians.* Aspirations and interests that the doctrinal approach to the political problem in Huber was able to find in the juridical subject matter of the *philosophia novantiqua,* established in Europe since Pufendorf had published the *Elementorum iurisprudentiae universalis libri II* in 1660[45], extraneous to the contemporary Dutch political compilations as those of the brothers Johan and Pieter de la Court in whose *Considerations on the State,* not disposing of any scientific method and still less a systematic picture, simply had recourse to experience for establishing with a plethora of arguments and examples such as to which form of government proves to be the best to an observation based on practice[46].

Returning to the *Lex Regia* in the *De iure civitatis* Huber took the cues offered by the constitutional events of the ancient world to go into the principles of the legitimization of sovereignty defined as the absolute supreme power in the State: "Ut summa potestas ipsa legibus a se latis, aliter quam observatione voluntaria, teneatur". For Huber, therefore, absolute power does not signify licence, but the full juridical power of its owner to act freely in the ambit of the positive legislative order, so that his behaviour proves consistent with the *maiestas* of that *imperium*

44 Cf. espec. KOSSMANN 1971, pp. 164–177. Useful informations also in VEEN 1976, pp. 35–87, 284–336.

45 On the *philosophia novantiqua* in the modern Holland cf. DIBON 1954, pp. 157–158 and VEEN 1976, pp. 18–29.

46 DE LA COURT 1662. On this theme cf. DROETTO 1958, pp. 57ff. and HAITSMA MULIER 1986. On the Republicanism in Holland see KOSSMANN 1985, t. I, pp. 453–486.

with which he was invested. If the *summa potestas* is "ipsa civitas", the "voluntas imperantium, civitatis voluntas intelligitur": "Nam cum obligatio, nisi in personam cadere nequeat, et civitates per eos qui potestatem summam habent, *personae fiant,* manifestum est, ius foederis pangendi ad hanc classem, esse referendum". Thus, in § VI of the *lex de imperio* the acknowledgement of the *ius* and *potestas* of the *princeps* of behaving according to his own conviction does not limit itself to claiming that such conviction should comply with the utility of the State, but also makes an appeal also to the *maiestas* "divinarum humanarum publicarum privatarumque rerum". In order to be able to govern a State, the sovereign must reciprocate unconditionally to the commands that are dictated to him in the interest of sovereignty, as is attested not only by the significance of the Roman *Lex Regia* – that following the decline of the Roman empire became a principle of general theory of public law – but also of the Bible that Huber does not hesitate to read, taking his cue from the story of Samuel (1, 8, 9) regarding the history of the people of Israel[47].

For all this articulation of themes and problems, the doctrinal premises of Huber's reflection found a secure basis in the classical pages of Grotius' *De iure*, a work which did not fail to evoke perplexity and strong criticisms of interpretation regarding the consequences of the application of the definition of *summa potestas* to the problems of the legal origins of the imperial dignity of the Holy Roman Empire. The theme, enriched by numerous references to the contemporary political experiences – more especially French – directly attacked the question of the possible legitimacy of universal monarchy, founded on divine law, guaranteed by the appeal to the Pontifex, as supreme impartial judge. In the third edition of the *De iure civitatis* (1694),

47 HUBERUS (1672) 1708, pp. 64, 329, 69, 93 and Book I, sec. II, Chap. 7: "Quo sententia superior confirmatur aut illustratur, ex iure romano et literis sacris" (HUBERUS [1672] 1708, 56–60). On this theme cf. VEEN 1976, pp. 330–331 and VEEN 1985, pp. 369–370.

Huber directly faced the question, by analyzing a section of the *De iure belli ac pacis* (II, 9, § XI) and in particular, a definition of *auctoritas* "notabilem, magis studio in pontificem Romanum, quod nisi plurimum fallor, eius iudicio praestrinxit; quam soliditate collectionis iuridicae vel historicae; qui tamen propter auctoritatem viri et momentum negotii, silentio neutiquam transmittendus videbatur". Having accepted Grotius' thesis whereby the emperor of the Holy Roman Empire acquired the imperial title from the decision taken by the Roman people (in the second half of the 10th century, in Huber's opinion) to accept the Germanic king as their emperor, the Friesian jurist criticized the illegitimate conclusions thereof arrived at to claim that the Pope, as first citizen of Rome, had proclaimed Charlemagne as emperor, also at a later stage reserving the right to approve or reject the imperial choice of the Germanic electors in the name of the Roman people:

> Quod si populus Romanus, aut qui potestatem eius postea nactus est, pontifex, eam facultatem semper revocare potuissent, aut singulis imperatoribus, si displicerent, obsequium negare, fuisset illa quidem absurda et elusoria concessio; praeter quod ipsius Grotii verbis contraria, quae non de singulis, sed de universo iure eligendi concepta sunt; placuisse, uti, quem Germani regem sumsissent, is etiam suus imperator esset; quod ipsum eventus efficaciter demonstravit; siquidem consensus gentium haud aliunde, quam ab hoc instituto, fastigium imperiale Caesareum Germanis proprium fecit[48].

48 HUBERUS (1672) 1708, pp. 346, 343. Cf. GROTIUS 1680, pp. 233–234: "Postea vero diviso Francorum populo in Occidentalem qui Galliam nunc obtinet, et Orientalem qui Germaniam sive Alemaniam tenet (duo Francorum regna vocat Frisingensis) cum populus Francorum orientalis eligendo sibi reges facere coepisset (nam et ad id tempus Francorum regum successio quasi agnatica non tam a iure certo quam a populi suffragiis dependerat) placuit populo Romano, quo certius praesidium haberet, regem non proprium sibi sumere, sed eum quem Germani fecissent; ita tamen ut ius sibi aliquod retineret probandae vel impro-

The backcloth to this politico-religious polemic at that time was the discussion on the *ius potestatum circa sacra*[49]. In Huber's judgement it is the same story as the German empire (albeit not conserving the text of the official act regarding the conferring of the imperial *dignitas*) to deny Grotius' conclusions and to have it believed that on the basis of a "convention" between emperor, Germanic people and Roman people, the latter had irrevocably and unreservedly transferred the right to choose the emperor, renouncing to reserve for itself or for the Pope the power to revoke that right at its discretion: "[...] Si quid unquam eiusmodi, Caesarum alicui impositum, fuerit, id, ut alia nonnulla quibusdam ex iis, indigna maiestate Augusta, leguntur extorta, transitorium fuit, neque in facultatem convaluit, cum semper a Germanis ista Pontificum arrogantia, de iure et de facto refutata fuerit". The king chosen by the Germanic electors becomes Roman emperor *ipso iure* without the special approval of the Roman people or Pontifex. Therefore, Huber observes in conclusion, the papal coronation of the emperor was destined to prove a

bandae electionis, quantum scilicet ea res ad se pertinebat. [...]. Hacc quoque approbatio per Episcopum edici et solemniter testata fieri peculiari coronatione solebat, quare ex electione septem Principum qui Germaniae corpus referunt, qui lectus est ius habet imperandi Germanis secundum eorum mores; ex approbatione vero populi Romani fit idem rex, aut Imperator Romanus, aut, ut historici saepe loquuntur, rex regni Italiae; atque eo titulo sub se habet quaecumque populi Romani fuerunt, neque pactionibus, aut derelicti occupatione, aut victoriae iure in aliorun populorum imperium concesserunt. Unde illud quoque intelligi facile potest, quo iure Episcopus Romanus vacante imperio invcstituras tribuat feudorum imperii Romani, quia scilicet in populo Romano, tali tempore libero, primas obtinet. Solent autem quae sunt corporis alicuius per prlmam personam corporis nomine expediri, ut alibi quoque diximus".

49 SOLARI (1931) 1974, t. I, pp. 65–130, but see also the important essay on Spinoza: SOLARI (1930) 1974, t. I, pp. 131–193. On the theme cf. SINI 1969.

useless ceremony, that was nevertheless abolished by Charles V[50]. The authority to which even the Pope must bow is the authority of the State that through the law becomes the centre both for the unity of culture, the only element of rationalization of a *humanitas* freed from its natural origins, and from the difficult search for new assurances.

Yet when Huber breaks away from Grotius' theses showing himself aware of this disaffection also on the historico-historiographical organization front, one is confronted with a more general theoretical understanding, that is not able to accept without reservation the version of *maiestas* that the jurist of Delft had given by distinguishing with certain reference to Althusius' *Politica* (1603, 1610, 1614) two concepts of sovereignty (*subiectum commune* and *proprium*), both treated as essential and resolved in the opposing rights of people and prince[51]. Hence attention is concentrated on defining a new juridical doctrine of political relationships, and on reformulating the concepts of sovereignty and law to make them into instruments suitable for the needs of the intervention of the "Artisans of Glory"[52] in society far removed from abstract philosophical speculation. This was a project that, by reactivating a debate well under way through long tradition and concluded at the theoretical level by Bodin at the end of the sixteenth-century, was now expressing a new sense of State, finding its immediate model, again a polemi-

50 HUBERUS (1672) 1708, p. 344: "Sed ut hic, et post Carolum V. omnes imperatores illam coronationem neglexerunt, eoque nihilo minus Caesares Romani fuere, quam qui coronae capiendae causa Romam profecti erant; ita clarum est, actum illum coronationis nihil fuisse quam ritum inaugurationis, sine qua ius regium habet integritatem [...], non minus quam si maxima pompa coronatio celebrata fuisset". Cf. VEEN 1976, pp. 28–29, 112 ff., but espec. VEEN 1985, pp. 375–377.

51 GROTIUS 1680, pp. 59–60. On this theme – after the classical pages of GIERKE (1880) 1943 [1974], 139ff. – cf. LOMONACO 1995, pp. 171–201.

52 See RANUM 1980.

cal one, in Hobbes' positions. With guarded sensitivity for nuances, In many ways Huber complicates the conceptual and historiographical picture of reference by integrating Grotius' interpretation categories with those of the English thinker. In the systematic design of *Leviathan* (a Latin edition of which had appeared in 1668), banned by the Dutch authorities along with Spinoza's *Tractatus theologico-politicus* in 1674, the Friesian jurist found the unity and authority of sovereign power expressed as being founded on the important concept of law as *power*. The traditionally used notion of *virtus* was now deliberately replaced by the Aristotelian one of *power,* as it was preferred to refer directly to the passages of the *Nicomachean Ethics,* rather than to the works of Boethius and Thomas Aquinus, although these were very central to medieval meditations on the theme of justice[53]. *Coercion* is an indispensable act for implementing the law. Every strict right (*ius strictum*) implies a faculty of coercing. Perfect alone is the right to coercion, that is to say a right exactable by *force,* based on the conscience of the *obligatio* of each individual to conform with the sovereign law. The entire *right* that the sovereign has to command is found in the *power* which he disposes of to make people obey him: "Obligationis causa maxime est Superior Potestas". The sovereign cannot therefore be delegated by the people with a *mandate,* but he is necessarily an absolute sovereign in his own right and indivisible in the unity of his functions also in democracy: "Forma eius est, foedus omnium cum omnibus, cuius summa in hoc consistit, *ut quae consensu maioris partis statuuntur, ea cunctos obligent.* Idque *in perpetuum,* quia norunt, quo tempore ab imperio communi recesserint, neminem salutis suae fore certum, omniaque pessum reitura, quod eos minime velle manifestum est". Such a doctrinal structure was to nurture the main reasons for the polemic with the supporters of

53 For an up-to-date information see DEL VECCHIO (1946) 1959 and GARIN 1966, p. 432.

popular sovereignty, including Jakob Voorbroek, better known as Perizonius, he too resident at Franeker as Professor of Eloquence and History since 1682 and bitterly censured in the third edition of the *De iure civitatis* (1694), in a specific *sectio* "exhibens dissertationem de imperio, sine vi, a populo sui iuris constituto"[54]. In an important *Oratio* of 1689, discussing *de origine et natura imperii, in primis regii, a libero et sui iuris populo simpliciter delate,* the Leyden philologist had confuted Huber's definition of *summa potestas,* recognising democracy as the only legitimate form of government: "Abhorret et a moribus publicis omnium Civitatum, a quibus Democratia abest, seu in quibus praecipuam Reip. partem sibi non sumit ipse exercendam populus". And this on the basis of the premise that sovereignty could not be considered to be transferred absolutely, but only conceded (through a *mandate*) by the people who, inasmuch as sole legitimate source of *potestas,* could revoke it at any moment: "Rex autem nunquam in mandata sibi a populo Rep. tantundem iuris obtinet, quantum ipse populus, nisi is disertissime id ei concesserit, et clarissimis verbis indubiisque locutionibus suum a se ius prorsus et plane in Regem ilium transtulerit"[55]. The theses rested on a particular interpretation and evaluation of *status naturae.* Completely different from Huber's deeply pessimistic view with regard to the existence and destiny of human nature, a pessimism which became the logical and historical premise for the idea of a State, suffi-

54 HUBERUS (1672) 1708, pp. 2, 41, 346. "[...] Etsi quo minus a *pari,* causa obligationis esse queat, nihil obstar; siquidem consensus, unde sine dubio nascitur obligatio, est inter Pares. Quin etiam prima lex et simplicissima, per quam e statu naturali receditur in Civitatem, et qua placuit, ut maioris partis voluntas sit omnium voluntas, nihil est aliud quam consensus inter pares, et est fons omnis obligationis ac iuris" (HUBERUS [1672] 1708, p. 2).

55 PERIZONIUS (1689) 1746, I, pp. 39, 62. On this *Oratio* cf. KOSSMANN 1960, p. 99 and MEIJER 1971, pp. 76–81. For the polemic against Noodt see VEEN 1976, p. 322 and VEEN 1985, pp. 359–361, but see also VAN DEN BERGH 1988, p. 193.

ciently strong but not a very 'democratic' one, for dominating the passions in man in a Hobbesian sense, Perizonius started out on the contrary from an optimistic and not very complicated idea of man and his history. The *contract* does not oblige one to renounce natural law nor transfer it into the hands of the *princeps,* as Hobbes and Huber thought, but rather to unite and join individual powers together into one *ius commune.* Not *pactum subiectionis* but *pactum societatis,* on the strength of which, as each joins up with the others, he becomes subordinate only to himself, thereby preserving his original liberty[56].

Beyond the confines of a bitter personal and academic quarrel, the Huber-Perizonius polemic was later to develop again around classical themes of political and historiographical reflection, confirming the alternative solutions set out on the theme of the origin of *potestas* by the contestants, as well as their qualitative distance in their politico-ideological orientations. In a col-

56 PERIZONIUS (1689) 1746, p. 43: "Ego enim vero nihil in Naturae statu homini magis proprium reperire possum, quam ut primum quidem se conservare studeat, quanta potest cura ac diligentia; deinde veto, ut alios quoque eiusdem secum generis et naturae participes, tanquam Cognatos sibi et Consanguineos, amore ac benevolentia prosequatur, eorumque convictum et consuetudinem desideret. [...] Certe Ego nihil aliud vobiscum hac oratione egi, neque aliud quicquam spectavi, quam ut ostenderem, Imperium in liberos suique arbitrii populos duxisse primam revera originem et naturam ex Mandato, licet acceperit deinde saepius maiorem aliquam vim ac Ius cx Pacto; atque adeo neutiquam sequi ex ipsa Imperii simpliciter delati natura, ut liceat impune in populum quovis modo grassari, populo autem nequaquam liceat iniquum illud tyrannidis iugum excutere, tanquam si nihil prorsus sibi adversus eum, cui summa cum libertate sui curam et salutem commendaverat, publicaeque rei permiserat tutelam, servaverit iuris, non modo Civilis, sed ne quidem Naturalis, quo licitum ceteroquin unicuique, vim ab alio intentatam, quoquo modo prohibere, avertere, quin et punier" (PERIZONIUS [1689] 1746, p. 65).

lection of writings published by Perizonius in 1690[57] the object of discussion was the interpretation of *praetorium* in a relevant passage of St. Paul (*Philipp.,* I, 13), destined to offer, in Le Clerc's judgement, "beaucoup de choses utiles pour l'intelligence de l'Histoire Romaine, et de quantité de passages des anciens Auteurs Grecs et Latins"[58]. Against the most lively hermeneutic-philological contrasts, was outlined a different interpretation and utilization of a model, that of the magistrate's right, which had accompanied the modern doctrine of *aequitas* right from the earliest comments on humanistic jurisprudence in the *Nicomachean Ethics,* also in the light of important Stoic motives so widely diffused in Ancient Roman sources and common to such a large part of seventeenth-century culture. By *equity* is traditionally meant the justice of a realistic *case*, that justice triggered not by the strict observance of a general abstract law, but by the observation of the very *nature* of the particular case which presents certain specific and definite characteristics in certain circumstances of time and place. Thus, there exist *cases* whose *just* solution, that is to say, in compliance with the law, is not *equitable,* and the equitable solution is not *just*: they are cases considered by jurisprudence in which a right is determined without coercion, a dissociation between *right* and *coercion,* in accordance with the characteristics that belong to an 'exceptional' situation.

In treating *aequitas* as a criterion of proportionality deducible from natural or civil right according to the now classical formulation of Althusius' *Iuris Romani Libri II* (1586)[59], the great theme was set down by Bodin in the well-known fundamental pages of Book VI *de la République.* If equity is a general principle of a right

57 PERIZONIUS 1690. On the relations with Huber see MEIJER 1971, pp. 73–76.

58 *BIBLIOTHÈQUE UNIVERSELLE ET HISTORIQUE* 1699, XVIII, p. 278 and an interesting abstract is in *ACTA ERUDITORUM* 1691, XV, pp. 237–244.

59 ALTHUSIUS (1586) 1592, pp. 1–2. On the *aequitas* in German history of the 16th century see MAZZACANE 1968–1969, pp. 281ff.

or only the correction (by the courts of appeal) of possible errors committed by the lower courts:

> Ainsi disoit-on qu'il falloit accommoder la loy en jugement; mais tout ainsi qu'il est impossible que la reigle retienne son nom, si elle demeure torte comme la reigle Lesbienne; aussi ne peut-il faire que la loy demeure loy, si on s'en joué comme de cire, et que celuy qui doit obéissance aux loix en soit maistre. Il faut donc pour éviter à la fermeté immuable de la reigle de Polyclète, et à la varieté et incertitude de la reigle Lesbienne, forger une troisième reigle, qui ne soit si roide qu'elle ne puisse ployer doucement quand il en sera mestier, et se redresser aussi tost; c'est à dire, qu'il faut suyvre la justice harmonique, et accoller ces quatre poincts ensemble, à savoir Loy, Equité, Excution de la loy, et le devoir du Magistrat, soit en la distribution de la justice, soit au gouvernment de l'estat[60].

The need that reference to the *equitable* and flexible magistrate model achieves for itself then, is that of proceeding towards a rapid "spreading out" of the *droit coutumier* in view of its unification, thus giving assurance to the right throughout the national territory. Behind a similar need was in short a recognizable tendency towards reinforcing absolute power on which a significant light could be cast by comparing with the events which in Budé's sixteenth-century France had led to the recognition of power and functions similar to the attributes and competencies of the *praetorius praefectus* in the figure of the "chancellor". These themes are taken up and redefined by Hobbes, destined to act as a backcloth to the alternative conceptions that Perizonius and Huber had given to *potestas.* That it was not only a question of an academic or erudite polemic was now well understood from the pages of Perizonius' *Dissertatio philologica de origine, significatione et usu vocum praetoris et praetorii,* where, on de-

60 BODIN (1576) 1593 [1986], Book VI, Chap. 6, p. 259: "De la justice distributive, commutative, et harmonique, et quelle proportion il y-a d'icelles à l'estat Royal, Aristocratique et Populaire". On this theme cf. GIARRIZZO (1977) 1981, pp. 163–165.

termining that the laws and power of the king depended on "potestate suae civitatis", the Dutch philologist arrived at the peremptory conclusion that: "[...] Reges illos, quo arbitrio constituerat, eodem et removere potuit, vel singulos, vel in universum et sempiternum omnes, sublata plane Regia reip. [administrandae] potestate; id quod multis sane exemplis ex antiquissima Historia petitis probari posset"[61]. Yet, in keeping with earlier reflections on the origin and *basis* of *auctoritas,* these considerations of Perizonius appear substantially extraneous to the political issues introduced by the magistrate's authority and by the relative right of equity, as moreover Le Clerc had already well perceived, when emphasizing the focal point of Huber's criticisms behind the disclosure of his historico-philological *errores* in the pages of the "Bibliothèque universelle et historique" (1690)[62].

61 PERIZONIUS 1690, p. 4. Background for these argumentations in Bodin's sixteenth-century France can be found in PIANO MORTARI 1977, I, pp. 202–204 and PIANO MORTARI 1978, pp. 3ff. On the *praetorius praefectus* see MOMIGLIANO (1968) 1969, pp. 403–417 and MOMIGLIANO (1969) 1975, I, pp. 293–332.

62 *BIBLIOTHÈQUE UNIVERSELLE ET HISTORIQUE* 1690, XVIII, pp. 279–280: "M. Perizonius réplique à cela que l'on ne doit pas argumenter par l'étymologie contre l'usage, selon l'aveu même de son Adversaire, qui l'a dit formellement. De plus on ne donnoit pas à l'Empereur, dans la ville de Rome, le titre de *Préteur,* d'où vient le mot de *Prétoire,* mais à d'autres Magistrats proprement ainsi nommés; et le *Prétoire,* et le *Palais* signifient aussi constamment des choses différentes. Voilà sur quoi roule toute cette Dispute, que M. Huber a traité, avec assez d'aigreur, selon la coûtume de beaucoup de Critiques". In this context see also the polemic against Huber (PERIZONIUS 1693 and HUBERUS 1693) in *BIBLIOTHÈQUE UNIVERSELLE ET HISTORIQUE* 1699, XXIV, pp. 184–185: "II y a [longtempsj que *M. Perizonius* [...], et M. Huber en sont aux mains [...]. Il est vrai que M. Perizonius ne [paraît] pas si prodigue de termes durs et injurieux, que M. Huber; mais Il semble qu'on les doive pardonner en quelque sorte a ce dernier. Il est bien difficile de ne se pas [mettre] en colère, quand on est accusé d'avoir commis plus de six-[vingts] fautes contre l'Histoire, dans un assez petit Volume, qu'on a

The disturbing crisis caused by the Thirty Years War that consolidated in alternating parallels – influenced by Vico – between the *ius strictum* of the (oligarchical) aristocracies and the *aequum* of imperial jurisprudence, seem to be followed in the way shown by the polemic rejected by Hobbes's polemical refusal to admit equity as a universal *emendatio legis* and not only as an *emendatio iudicii*: if justice "fulfills the law", then equity

> interprets the law, and amends the judgments given upon the same law. Wherein I depart not much from the definition of equity cited in Sir Edward Coke (*I Inst.,* sec. XXI); *viz.* equity is a certain perfect reason, that interpreteth and amendeth the law written; though I construe it a little otherwise than he would have done; for no one can mend a law but he that can make it, and therefore I say it amends non the law, but the judgments only when they are erroneous[63].

From all this we are brought back to the great theme of the relationship between *civil equity* and *natural equity* which Huber was obliged to think about afresh, but not without further in-depth analyses into the meaning of *Ratio Status.*

Neither the precursor of modern "iusnaturalistic constitutionalism" – as Gierke considers him – nor supporter of *tout court absolutism*[64], Huber labours at constructing a doctrine of *auctoritas* in which to be able to make a *humanitas* raised in the life of the State converge, in an attempt to correct and consolidate the ever meditated theories of Bodin and Grotius, and of Hobbes and

---

composé, pour l'enseigner aux autres. Quand on se seroit trompé dans le calcul; et qu'au lieu de six-[vingts], il n'y en auroit que [vingt], ce seroit toûjours beaucoup, et il y a bien peu d'Auteurs, qui après un semblable affront, fussent capables de se modérer". On the polemic see MEIJER 1971, pp. 46–49, 73ff. and VEEN 1967, pp. 10–19, 2–7, 9–17.

63 HOBBES (1666) 1960, p. 123. Cf. GIARRIZZO (1977) 1981, pp. 171–172.

64 In addition to the classical pages of *Das deutsche Genossenschatsrecht* (1913) 1960, pp. 145–146, 155–156, 173–174, 182–184, 340–342, 377–386 see GIERKE (1880) 1943, pp. 222–223 and now VAN DEN BERGH 1988, pp. 204ff.

Spinoza. In this regard he considered the politico-juridical situation that had come about in the Netherlands which in his opinion represented an aristocratic *respublica*, as significantly stressed in the pages of the *De iure popularis, optimatium, et regalis imperii, sine vi, et a sui iuris populo, constituti, ad regenda hominum circa res maximas iudicia, contra periculosissimos errores, Dissertatio* (1689), with numerous comparisons between Venice, Florence and the "*Batavorum* republ. ubi summa potestas est penes *ordines,* hoc est, equites et civitatium rectores, verissima aristocratia"[65].

In a civilization that no longer has anything that was completely unitary or coherent, not even a single church or religion, the wish to rediscover something in common cannot simply be an appeal to lost unity, but an attempt to realize a new *community*, in the respect of everyone's rights, those rights that are constitutive of every man's nature. Thus, for Huber too, the only *strength* of the State, not sufficiently curbed in its power, runs the risk of not guaranteeing the individuals' *basic* rights. On this point the failure of Hobbes' theory refers to the use of the Cartesian method in politics. In the third chapter of the *prima sectio* of Book I of the *De iure civitatis,* "quo ius naturae hobbesianum examinatur", the rigorously deductive procedure of that doctrine is vigorously attacked, since the theorized union between politics and right comes to clash with the ideas of justice and society that are innate in man, which obliges one to stipulate contracts as free acts of human will. If for Althusius Huber questions the principle that the people can in no way alienate the supreme *auctoritas,* yet, contrary to Hobbes he judges the *conditions* to which the State itself is formed as absolutely valid: "At *Hobbes* ex eodem principio colligit, qui imperium simpliciter transtulerunt tantum iuris in imperantes transtulisse, *quantum potuerunt,* ut nihil exeme-

65 HUBERUS (1689) 1746, I, p. 30. Cf. KOSSMANN 1960, pp. 82–103. On Huber's opinion about the aristocratic *respublica* cf. VENTURI 1970, p. 37.

rint […]"[66]. The subjects cannot have waived all their rights unreservedly in favour of the sovereign, since they in any case represent an *unum quid.* After the transfer of the *summa potestas* the people retains a particular *ius personae,* remaining "universitatem iuris capacem, etiam quando sub imperio est"[67]. The claim was not contradictory to the alleged need – with regard to the interpretation of the *lex regia* – that the *translatio imperii* was absolute, and without reserve. Huber, in fact, does not cancel the Grotian axiom "iuris naturae est stare pactis", but basically confirms its categorical nature, specifying that it does not consist of the formal and irrevocable expression of consensus (for which Hobbes too declared that *pacta sunt servanda*), since the *voluntas* that intervenes to show the *measure* of the right realized in a certain context expresses only the hypothetical nature of the contract. The categorical nature of the pact consists, instead, in the

66 HUBERUS (1672) 1708, pp. 10–19, 40. "Adhuc quidem leges naturae, Id est, dictamina rationis satis aequum ab iniquo separabant; Ineratque animis cupiditas societatis, iudiciumque de rebus ad eam necessariis. Sed quia sine ordine certo non poterat confusio evitari, nec commoda universorurn invicem communicari poterant [...]. Necessaria fuit eiusmodi ratio et modus, *per quem omnium voluntas una fieret*" (HUBERUS [1672] 1708, p. 32). On polemic Huber-Hobbes cf. VEEN 1976, pp. 160–201 and MAZZARINO 1979, pp. 360–361. On Hobbes and his precence in Holland of the 17th century see – after KOSSMANN 1960 – SCHONEVELD 1983, Chap. 2.

67 HUBERUS (1672) 1708, pp. 40, 88. "Quod si verum est, nihil causae fuerit, quare ius novum per liberam consensionem cum imperantibus, acquirere nequeat". "Vemm translato imperio, non manet illa potestas major; limite posito, desinit esse potestas, et imperium, sicut fundatum est, unica manet potestas, limite circumscripta. Quem limitem si Rex manifesto egreditur, eatenus non est Rex. Hinc liquet, non esse necesse, ut progrediamur ad eiusmodi potestatem in Republ. infinitam, qualem sibi fingit *Hobbes;* siquidem causa limitans ante et extra formam Reipubl. collocari potest ac debet" (HUBERUS [1672] 1708, pp. 88, 83). On Huber's theory about *universitas* – after GIERKE (1913) 1960, pp. 117–118, 173ff, 182 and notes – cf. VEEN 1982.

absoluteness of the *imperium naturale,* such as the command of reason inculcated in man by nature and by God who is its author, inevitably ordering men to increase the means suitable for the final end of their own conservation. The contract regards only the *clauses* to which the transfer has occurred: with the *iure civili* valid, its objective remains dependent on that of the *ius naturale* on the basis of which it was stipulated[68].

Returning to the themes and issues that had long concerned Bodin to stress the original absolute *potestas* of the *princeps,* before and far from every unlikely *Lex Regia,* not, however, without showing significant variations and concessions about the respect of *justes conventions*[69], Huber points out that limits juridically inviolable in the light of the natural right may be imposed on *maiestas* by the tacit clauses of the basic contracts. The latter impose on the sovereign a "naturalis obligation", with a *potestas coactiva* with the aim of safeguarding, also in the case of the totally unconditional transmission of state power, the inviolable individual rights of personality, propriety, freedom of thought and obedience to divine command, a right of which every man is by nature proprietor: "Ad tacite intellectas leges praeterea, quae *su-*

68 HUBERUS (1672) 1708, pp. 7, 8: "*Summa* Ratio dicitur, id est, prima, perpetua et supra omnia, omnesque regens actiones humanas. *Insite a Natura,* consequenter ab auctore Naturae Deo, quod ut TheoLogi malunt exprimi in ipsa definitione, ita nihil refragamur [...]. Quod ad priorem attinet sententiam obligatio Iuris obstringens animos [...], *vim coactivam* habere quidem debet, at non solam; haec fluere debet ex alia ratione convincens subiectum imperio, quod etiam parere debeat; cuiusmodi nihil est in potentia inresistibii […]". "Ratio, quare conventiones solennes inter regem populumque vel proceres ita possint inire, ut utrimque vim obligandi habeant, atque ut populo, ius inde contra principem acquiratur, pendet ex iis, quae superius disputata sunt" (HUBERUS [1672] 1708, p. 88).

69 BODIN (1576) 1986, pp. 204–205. On this theme cf. MOREL 1970, pp. 545–555 and REBUFFA 1972. For the relations Huber-Bodin see VEEN 1976, pp. 26–28.

pra tacite in omni imperio excepta intelliguntur, referemus sequentia [...]". The "expressae *leges fundamentals*" possess an equally-binding force which marks the limits of the sovereign right in the very act in which they declare its basis, their being not an enactment of *summa potestas,* but rather the juridical premise of its existence; whence it must be concluded that the juridical relationship between subjects and sovereign, although formally sanctioned by the clauses of the *iure civili* contract, has never ceased to be valid *iure naturae:* "Expressae leges fundamentales ut sciamus quae sint, praemittemus; fundamenti verbum id significare, quo tota structura nititur, et quod primo omnium ponitur, ut cuivis *suopte planum est.* Leges igitur fundamentales erunt proprie, *constitutiones, quae in fundando imperio, ante plenam eius translationem stabiliuntur, ut iuxta eas respublica exerceatur*". The contract is, therefore, a necessary condition for the validity of the *pactum,* or life of the State. Thus the contractual clauses that apparently seemed a violation of the pact were in fact, the most guaranteed implementation, as in the necessary respect for the possibility of the existence of the State matured therein. Thus the concept of a *tacit* constitution was elaborated inferable from the essence of the contract and valid not only in the aristocracy and in the monarchy, but also in the pure democracy, where the violation of the constitution by the majority gives place to a "facultas resistendi" of the minority[70]. The right rests on the principle of the possibility of external constriction which must, however, coexist with everyone's liberty, in accordance with the established laws. If the right is liberty, it is liberty limited by the existence of other liberties that all equally have the right to reject acts of non-liberty. And this cannot happen except with coercion itself that is an act of non-liberty carried out also to reject the act of non-liberty of others. Albeit a concept antithetical to that of liberty, whenever coercion arises as a remedy to a situation of non-

70 HUBERUS (1672) 1708, pp. 85, 86, 45.

liberty, it is a condition necessary for the conservation of liberty itself. To my juridical *duty* there corresponds a *right* in others to force me to carry it out. In this way "force" is necessary for justice, since its task is to reject *another* and *unjust* force that prevents its implementation.

All this also allowed one to reach a solution to the debated question regarding the possibility of setting limits on supreme power and thus of winning for individuals and for non-sovereign "minority associations" established rights of participation in the exercise of *potestas.* The sovereign who goes beyond the established limits renders his acts absolutely null and non-compulsory; in violating the natural right he becomes a tyrant, an enemy of the people, he abuses the powers deriving from his *imperium,* and is liable to punishment. The juridical condition of rebellion for the tyrant can only be found in the same law of nature for which absolute obedience is due to the sovereign. The problem of the limits of *summa potestas,* the relative question of the *resistance* of the subjects, are thus not resolved on the basis of the positive right, but on the basis of the natural one, that is to say, after all things considered, on the right to go to war. If it is not juridically possible *iure civili* to induce the State to save itself, one may nevertheless force it to do so *iure belli,* since the norms of natural right that the State must observe for its own protection cannot be claimed by civil right, but only through the right to go to war. Therefore, prompted by Grotius' distinction between legitimacy of war according to *natural right* and legitimacy according to the peoples' *voluntary right*, Huber observed that "superest ad explicationem belli solennis, ut ritum, qui iure gentium in eo requiritur, paucis explicemus. Est autem ille ritus, indictio, sive denunciatio, quam propterea placuit recipi, ut constaret, non privato ausu, sed voluntate utriusque populi aut imperantium geri bellum. Denique, ut si populus eius vel imperantes non sint immediate in culpa, deliberent, utrum velint suam facere litem, an satisfacere laesis"[71]. The significant conclusion of the articulate discourse was that the cause of the war had to be put down to the existence of monarchical states, and of their difference not being subjectable to the judgement of a superior authority: "Rixae autem summarum potestatum facile in bellum, quia cessant inter has iudicia, erumpunt [...]"[72]. In this perspective, the *virtus imperii,* or the *security* of the State – the conservation of which is, for Huber as for Spinoza, the indispensable condition for its absolutism – joins with the *fines reipublicae* called on to protect the interests of subjects, whose sovereign does not have the *right* to impose actions to the contrary, since for Huber just as for Spinoza, he does not have the *power*[73]. Only in a sys-

71 HUBERUS (1672) 1708, Book I, sec. IX, Chap. 2, pp. 314–316 "De tyrannide in exercitio"; 3, pp. 316–320 "De iure resistendi tyrannis in exercitio, vel tyrannice agentibus"; 4, pp. 320–325 "De iure puniendi tyrannos"; sec. X, Chap. 6, "De sanctione legum fundamentalium".

72 HUBERUS (1672) 1708, pp. 730, 734–735; cf. GROTIUS 1680, Book III, Chap. 3.6, p. 495. "Ius Belli [est] duplex, verum et internum, quod rationibus Iustitiae per se consentit, et externum, quod usu et consensu gentium vim iuris accipit [...]. Inductione specierum id approbatum [...]. Quo iure res hostium capiantur [...]. De iure postliminii, tam personarum [...] quam rerum" (HUBERUS [1672] 1708, Book III, sec. IV, Chap. 5.11–12, p. 739). On *ius belli* cf. also HUBERUS 1746, I, pp. 130–137. On this theme see SCOTT 1994, pp. 13–30. Ilari observes that "HUBER è, assieme a BURGUNDIUS (1586–1649), RODENBURG (1618–1688), PAUL VOET (1619–1677) e GIOVANNI VOET (1647–1714, figlio del precedente), uno dei maggiori esponenti della scuola degli statutari olandesi del XVII secolo, i quali sostennero, sulle orme del giurista francese D'ARGENTRÉ (1519–1590), il principio della territorialità del diritto come criterio generale del diritto internazionale privato. La tesi opposta, particolarmente sostenuta dai postglossatori italiani e dal giureconsulto francese DUMOULIN (1500–1566), si fondava sull'interpretazione del diritto romano e tendeva ad allargare Ia cerchia degli statuti personali" (I-LARI 1981, p. 129 but also pp. 101, 128, 146).

73 On the confrontation between Huber and Spinoza cf. HUBERUS (1672) 1708, Book I, sec. I, Chap. 4, pp. 19–22: "De iure naturae a Spinosa exposito, cum aliorum dictis melioribus"; see on this theme KOSSMANN

tem of a right as power does the Hobbesian imperative *pacta sunt servanda* lose that voluntarist categorical nature that prevented Grotian jusnaturalism from resolving the problem of *resistance* against the tyrant, without however, on this account admitting an autonomous right to the subjects to resist, as the monarcomachists claimed who searched for the origin of the State and the justification of the rebellion, the limit of sovereign power, in the wish of the people as expressed by the contract. However, just as for Spinoza likewise for Huber right as power does not preach to the subjects submission to the *Reason of State*, except as far as their impotence to live *sui iuris* goes, which is as far as where their individual *power* proves inferior to that of all the *populus*. We are here at an important turning-point in a long and tormented juridico-political reflection. In this changed theoretical-doctrinal perspective, space could no longer be found for the traditional literature on the *arcana imperii*. The latter, codified at the beginning of the 17th century in Germany by Besold and later by Clapmarius in the *De arcanis rerumpublicarum* (of 1605, but known above all in the Elzevierian edition published in Amsterdam by Giovanni Corvino in 1644)[74], with the purpose of indicating ways and empirical methods and instruments designed to obtain and conserve forms of personal power, had accomplished its task and could leave the scene, since its esoteric and torbid style was being increasingly substituted by the clarity and rationality of natural *geometrically* ordered right. The very objective of the ancient *Reason of State* became the content of the new reflection on the right of the State, on *public right*. It is no longer necessary to investigate the politics of the sovereign and his

---

1960, pp. 86, 96, 101–103. For the differences about "ius naturae" see VEEN 1973 and VEEN 1976, pp. 202–214.

74 Background for this theme can be found in the classical pages of DE MATTEI 1954, pp. 378–384 and then in ARIENZO and BORRELLI 2000–2001; SCATTOLA 2002–2003 and STOLLEIS (1990) 1998. Cf. also CONTI 1997.

rights, but the power of the State, its very activity that is to be regulated so that it does not work to its own disadvantage, and thus the concept of *summa potestas* may be reconciled with the need for a fixed normative order, with the conscience of modern man, prepared for the new reality of the state by his own action, direct testimony of the natural and divine reasons[75].

Against the ancient *ratio politica de Statu* a different *ratio Status* requirement is set out in Huber, the interpreter of Bodin and Hobbes, as well as of Grotius and Spinoza, as the traditional, albeit consolidated, antithesis between *rectio* and *non rectio* Reason of State has at the same time, although inadequately so in form and content, driven towards a *new* and *just* Reason of State, that comes about as *aequitas civilis* on the old root-base of *natural equity*. In the changed theoretical and ideological context of seventeenth-eighteenth-century European culture – destined only to be presented but not fully justified by Huber's meditation, as it in contrast will be in Vico's subsequent political proposal[76] – historic Pyrrhonism, the other face of the old *ratio Status,* no longer has any raison d'être in its obstinate refusal to reach a *possible truth,* even simply through the mediation of the *equitable* fact of the *praetorian* judgement.

75 Cf. RÖD 1970 and STOLLEIS 1981, pp. 611–626; on this latter work see VEEN 1984, pp. 155–159.

76 See GIARRIZZO (1977) 1981, pp. 172–174 and CRIFÒ 1984, pp. 2061–2085.

CHAPTER III

Historical Pyrrhonism and Roman Tradition: Jacobus Perizonius

In reviewing the *Animadversiones Historicae* of Jakob Voorbroek, better known as Accinctus or Perizonius in the "Nouvelles de la République des Lettres" of June 1685, Pierre Bayle explicitly compared his work to the generalized hypercritical Pyrrhonism of the Jesuit Jean Hardouin:

> Nous avons remarqué ailleurs que le Père Hardouin a dit, que son Traité des Médailles [pourrait] être intitulé *l'Errata des Antiquaires*. Nous pourrions dire que cet Ouvrage de M. Perizonius, Professeur en Eloquence et en Histoire à Franeker, mérite d'être appellé *l'Errata des Historiens, et des Critiques;* car c'est un recueil perpétuel de leurs fautes, tant de celles qui avoient été déjà reprises, que de celles dont il a fait lui-même la découverte[1].

In emphasizing the main contributions Perizonius' investigation had bestowed on the scholarly historiographical review of Roman tradition, the Rotterdam philosopher proposed an original interpretation thereof destined to have considerable influence on its future critical success. The work of the professor of eloquence and history – first at Franeker through Noodt's initiative between 1682 and 1692, and later at Leyden from 1693 – did in fact wait long to shake off Bayles' influential but biased

1 NOUVELLES DE LA RÉPUBLIQUE DES LETTRES 1685, in BAYLE (1727–1731) 1965–1982, I, pp. 298a–b.

assessment and to win a niche among the cultural, political and religious achievements of seventeenth-eighteenth century Europe[2].

Scaligero's disciple was led to observe Roman history through the numerous critico-philological interests developed in Eliano's important and successful edition (1701), and through his assiduous studies of Greek and Hebrew resulting in his publication of *Origines babylonicae et aegyptiacae* (1711)[3]. Endowed with limitless learning, Perizonius gives his research a highly original tone by excluding every possible preconceived apology of antiquity therefrom. What attracts him towards antiquity, backed by his primary desire not to misinterpret its significance, is of a basically critico-hermeneutic character. In other words he is bent on examining texts and their interpreters, and not so much to reconstruct a general sense, or a generic and abstract "spirit". Never does the utilization of the classics remain separate from the need for critico-methodological clarification, since erudition in Perizonius' interpretation approach is never a vain decorative ornament or abstract motive for intellectual pride towards a discipline, such as philology, that requires backing from a scientific

2 On Perizonius from Franeker to Leyden cf. MEIJER 1971, pp. 49ff. and 84ff. For the relationship with Noodt see VAN DEN BERGH 1988, pp. 4–45, 119–120, 242–243, 307, 309. On Perizonius'work in the social and cultural context see BOELES 1878–1889, II, pp. 294–300, MOLHUYSEN 1913–1924, IV, pp. 122ff., 188, 190 and JENSMA et al. 1985, pp. 115, 137, 401, 470. On critic-philological attitude – after GERRETZEN 1940 – cf. the important work of ERASMUS 1962, espec. Chapp. 3 and 4, pp. 60ff.

3 PERIZONIUS 1711. Cf. his *Commentarius* to AELIANUS 1701. For the correspondence with Ryckius: *Epistolicae Dissertationes de Ilia, seu de Rhea Silvia.* "Caeterum de Huius appellatione, quae ab Historicis maxime Rhea Silvia, at a Poëtis Ilia potissimum, fuit dicta, multa ante hos XX ferme annos egi per literas cum Viro Eruditissimo, Theod. Ryckio, Decessore meo, et Amico quondam summon" (AELIANUS 1701, p. 461). On the relationship with Ryckius see ERASMUS 1962, pp. 78ff.

viewpoint. From among the contemporary theoretical and methodological redevelopment and updating imposed by the scientific revolution, the Dutch scholar subscribed to the basic need to elaborate a credible picture of new *certainties* that was not in contrast with 'common opinion' and modern historical criticism. That criticism which had opened up to true learning and which in reproposing the problem of the relationships between philology and history had succeeded in bringing about a changed historical depth to antiquary investigation into the nature of literary sources, that was obliged to make a self re-assessment, and to take conscience of its scientific *status* before historic Pyrrhonism that became rampant towards the end of the seventeenth century: a scepticism of non-integral Cartesian origin, concerned with recognising validity only for the constructions of scientific reason and not for history, in that it is always founded on uncertain and ineluctably contradictory evidence, as it is conditioned by human passions and prejudices[4].

An analysis of the late-seventeenth-century debate on the value of the *fides historica* may usefully start from Perizonius' interventions and return thereto as an important moment and in some ways a conclusive one, in which the main informative themes of the *querelle* and those of historiographical research are interwoven with all the relative philological implications welding together with the more general philosophical problem of the *certainty* of history and its *degrees,* that is to say of the definition, value and limits of the specific conditions that make knowledge about it *possible* and that protect its epistemological autonomy.

4 On this theme and with reference to Perizonius cf. SMITSKAMP 1953, p. 48, WATERBOLK 1960 and ERASMUS 1962, p. 71. On historical Pyrrhonism and Libertine Tradition – after BERTELLI's (1955) and POPKIN's (1979) 2008 and 2003 studies – see BORGHERO 1983 and LOMONACO 1990, Chap. 3, pp. 195ff.

The Debate on the "Fides Historica"

In the *Oratio de fide historiarum contra pyrrhonismum historicum,* declaimed at Leyden on the 6th February 1702 on the occasion of his nomination to *Professor Historiae Foederati Belgi* and printed posthumously in 1740, the debate is significantly dictated and enforced by the Author's need to show the advantages of his own historico-philological method in an academic setting whose hostility he rightly supposes, if it is true that as early as 1693 in an age of triumphant Malebranchian-type Cartesianism the great Bossuet had to admit, yet at the same time deplore "[...] cette insatiable avidité de savoir d'histoire"[5], which he felt his contemporaries to be utterly and totally captivated by. In direct opposition to this admission, the *Oratio* deliberately opens with a eulogy of all history, in keeping with a powerful academic interpretation model for which ancient history (and especially Roman history) could be understood as a paradigmatic moment of the contemporary historico-political process:

> Sed longius etiam ab se invicem in contraria secedunt omnia, quum Hi, qui Graecos tantum legunt et Romanos, omnemque Historiarum scientiam intra florentem istarum gentium aetatem contineri volunt, at reli-

5 BOSSUET (1693) 1862–1866, VIII, p. 31. Momigliano observes: "Verso la fine del secolo due avvenimenti strettamente connessi tornano a serrare i rapporti di filologia e storia. L'uno è La crisi del metodo storico, che prende il nome di 'pirronismo storico', una lunga malattia La cui fase acuta è verso il 1700 e per cui gli antiquari sembrano possedere un rimedio nello studio delle fonti documentarie meno aperte al sospetto di menzogna e di falsificazione. L'altro fatto è la discesa in campo di giansenisti e maurini (simpatizzanti con i giansenisti) – e per contrasto, ma meno vigorosamente, dei gesuiti – allo scopo di purificare la tradizione paleocristiana e medievale. In tale atmosfera J. Perizonius inizia la critica della tradizione storica romana (1685) [...]" (MOMIGLIANO [1958] 1984, pp. 79–80).

quas medii et postremi temporis res gestas. Patriae immo [...], non modo ignorant plane, sed neque scire desiderant, immo reiiciunt penitus et explodunt; tum vero Illi, qui e contrario antiqua inscito prorsus negligunt fastidio, neque intelligunt ea, aut intelligere laborant [...]. At quanto rectius facerent utrique, si neque hi aspernarentur antiquiora, neque recentiora illi; si iungerent omnia, ut oportebat, et [qualemcumque] rerum ab Orbe condito ad haec usque tempora seriem, brevi quasi tabella expressam, mandarent memoriae, ac pectore suo penitus conditam teneret.

However, at the forefront is the need to relate back to a tradition of studies, by first reflecting on the critical work of earlier writers in the light of their specific cultural realities, and then on the new instruments of criticism and on the relative methodological approaches elaborated in the wake of the great advances made in knowledge and information by modern investigations. In upholding this perspective, the Author first succeeded in presenting the significance and merit of their efforts as well as the responsibilities of scrupulous historians who strove hard to interpret and emend the texts in order to contribute thereby to *civil wisdom*, unlike others who unscrupulously mortify the authentic sense of the *auctores* by rashly embarking on continuous observations of a political nature:

Multos etenim, qui historias sedulo legunt, videas in verbis Auctorum indagandis, in eruendis obscuris sensibus, in corruptis emendandis, haerere assiduos, nec proferre suas animi meditationes ad unicos et certissimos earum fructus, h.e. ad sapientiae civilis fines [...]. Alios contra, nihil sollicitos de genuino Auctorum sensu et intellectu, neglecta etiam prorsus Reip. istius, cuius evolvunt Annales, sacra et profana, forensi ac militari, disciplina, provolare continuo reperias ad politicas Observationes[6].

6 PERIZONIUS 1702, pp. 4–5, 2–3. On this work see SMITSKAMP 1953, ERASMUS 1962, pp. 74ff. and MEIJER 1971, pp. 53, 143–147. On this point Momigliano observes: "In the eighteenth century nobody had yet any precise notion of the sources of Diodorus or Tacitus. Nor as yet

All this could come about since the radical doubts expressed about the narratives of Livy and Dioniges of Halicarnassus had now undermined traditional historiographical certainties, and finding a welcome even in the specialist sphere of antiquarian studies, when it was now realized that it was impossible to be adequately informed by literary sources distant in time from the epoch of the facts narrated and, moreover, the more doubtful and contradictory, the less corroborated by any further documentation. Thus the classical sources of Roman history proved to be most unreliable and more especially so the Annals of the Popes, even allowing, as a well-known passage from Livy claimed (VI, 1, 2), for a partial survival from the burning of Rome by the Gauls. Such considerations were basically the same as those which at the beginning of the century had already caused the *geographus academicus* of Leyden, Philipp Cluver to doubt early Roman history in epoch-making pages, and which later would have led Samuel Bochart to reject any historical validity to Aeneas' arrival in Italy[7] and Jacob Gronow to express

---

was the personality of the historian himself an object of conspicuous interest, except in a few cases. Also the idea that a tradition is entitled to respect as the mouthpiece of popular beliefs did not command wide attention. As long as these aspects were not carefully considered, it was inevitable that official documents, inscriptions, and coins should appear more reliable than literary evidence merely based on tradition. It was first of all a question of number. Common sense would offer insuperable resistance to the notion that thousands of documents, coins, and inscriptions could be forged as easily as isolated literary texts" (MOMIGLIANO [1950] 1955, p.84).

7 BOCHART (1663, 1668–1681, 1674) 1681. CLUVERIUS 1624, Book III, espec. Chap. 2, pp. 821, 826, 829: "Urbs igitur a quo et quibus temporibus condita sit, item unde id nominis acceperit, numquam satis constitisse, testantur inter alios antiquos auctores maxime Dionysius Halicarnassensis atque Plutarchus [...] nihil certior est primis illis compluribus variisque Graecorum fabulis, auditu absurdissimis ac maxime ridiculis putidisque". For the polemic against this work cf. RYCKIUS 1684,

doubts on the legend of Romulus with Henry Dodwell claiming the non-existence of authentic documents on the Alban kings[8].

Open to the cultural promptings of his own time, Perizonius never indulged in any of their passive reproductions, but rather gave a reasoned critical balance of the outcomes and the methodological implications that had emerged from modern research into antiquity. Intervening in the problem of the interpretation of documents, he primarily pressed for a careful study of the legitimate procedures of investigation. To be condemned are those historians who uncritically accept everything handed down by tradition and whatever is likewise devoid of critical sense, "omnem iam fidem derogant Historiae [...]". The attitude of the latter renders the work of the historian "vanam [...] operam" preventing the spreading and teaching thereof:

> Quid igitur magis tempestivum dari poterat, quam ut Historiam liberare hac occasione ab ista studerem calumnia, quasi omnia eius sint incerta prorsus, neque ullam mereantur fidem. Quo semel recepto, sequitur, nullum ergo ex eius lectione sedula capi posse fructum; vanam quoque nostram esse operam, qui eas publice privatimque illustrare conamur; denique inutilem fuisse etiam omnem illam curam, qua, et hic, et ubivis gentium, cathedrae in Athenaeis habentur constitutae, ex quibus Historiae inter liberales artes vel diligentissime doceantur[9].

These are motives that had found their historiographical application and expression in the 1685 *Animadversiones historicae*, defining the main features of a moderate philological criticism on the sources of the Roman epoch of kings, of those centuries, that is to say, for which the non-critical work of humanistic historiography had given little satisfaction, an easy prey to the now

pp. 395–467: cf. Chapter on "Philippi Cluverii, praecipue Sam. Bocharti argumenta contra Aeneae adventum adducuntur et refutantur".

8 GRONOVIUS 1684 and DODWELL 1701, pp. 675–680. On these works cf. ERASMUS 1962, pp. 78ff. and 106ff.

9 PERIZONIUS 1702 (1992), pp. 11, 12.

rampant seventeenth-century scepticism of rationalistic origin. Considering the precarious documentation, the study of ancient Roman history as the historian's primary task implied a careful reconstruction of all that the ancient writers could narrate or believed they could narrate, the latter being elements of discourse that can be traced back to the general consideration that the aim and task of the historian is always to distinguish the *truth* from the *false*. Aware of the dangers of a non-sensible use of erudition and criticism, Perizonius stressed the need for a methodological analysis of available literary sources in order to identify stable and rational criteria of historical knowledge:

> Nihil tamen nec praecipue huius illorumque, nec communiter omnium Veterum auctoritati per me derogatum volo, ut quibus semper suus honos et suum pretium constabit apud me integrum et incolume. Quin profiteor ultro, plerosque Veterum et maxime Romanorum istius aevi longe maiore, quam nos vulgo, cura ac diligentia in rebus memoriae prodendis versatos[10].

Even prior to the problem – re-echoing Cluver – of the scarsity of historical information handed down to us on account of Rome's burning by the Gauls, Perizonius did not refer to its origin only as an event of war, but also, and more especially so, to endogenous causes, revealing, as a comment on Livy's well-known account (VI, 1), the scarsity of documents published on

10 PERIZONIUS 1685, p. 5. Mazzarino observes: "La storia degli studi umanistici e rinascimentali relativi alla repubblica romana si identifica, *tout court,* con la storia della cultura dell'umanesimo e del rinascimento; non è storia di una problematica (e di un corrispondente atteggiamento critico), ma storia di una *renovatio,* in cui la romanità (e sia pur una romanità rievocata) è anche subietto, piuttosto che solo obietto, di ricerca. In queste condizioni, umanesimo e rinascimento non potevano preparare al seicento quelle premesse per una considerazione storica della repubblica romana" (MAZZARINO [1954], pp. 12, 16, 18–19). These theses are also in MAZZARINO (1959) 1988, pp. 79–94 and MAZZARINO (1953–1954) 1961, II, pp. 587–589.

early Roman history. Applying the demonstration of invalidity towards the plethora of proof of the continuity between the events of ancient Rome and the epoch of early historians, the Dutch philologist observed that the recognition of errors and falsity in the traditional account does not justify denying credibility, but rather confirms the critical rigour of ancient historians also in faithfully reporting popular opinions, yet always distinguishing the true from the false[11]. When Perizonius' attention dwelt on the concept of *analogy* in the study of language, he deliberately concluded by showing not only *ratio,* but also, and more especially, *usus.* In this perspective, considering the important definitions provided by Weller's scholastic grammar (*de Graeca Nova* dated 1635) – later continued by the Daum *(Diatribe)* – as well as by the fundamental works of Sanctius and Vossius whose *Aristarchus* (1635) had in the second part been concerned with "De analogia et anomalia vocarum", Perizonius based himself on Aulus Gellius' classical definition (*Noct. Att.*, II, 25): "At vero quum Analogia significationis nihil sit aliud, quam similitudo quaedam inter significationem secundariam et primitivam, ex qua illa, recta et commoda quadam translatione, sit orta, sequitur Analogiam hanc constitui non posse, nisi prius eruta et probata sit primitiva vocis signification". However "ceterum de Usu in Abusum degenerante per causam animadversae Analogiae, saepius et pluribus egi infra"[12].

11 "Neque tamen res illis temporibus, et circiter gestas, eo solum, quod quae litteris vel per Pontifices, vel per alios publice privatimque mandatae tunc jam essent, in illa Urbis conflagratione maximam partem interierint, *obscuras* dicit Livius, sed vel maxime etiain eo quod paucissima tunc litteris fuerint mandata, hoc est *rarae per eadem tempora fuerint litterae,* quas verissime vocat *unam fidelem custodiam memoriae rerum gestarum*" (PERIZONIUS 1685, p. 180).

12 SANCTIUS 1687, pp. 6, 77. Cf. MEIJER 1971, pp. 136–137. For the mix between *ratio* and *usus* in Perizonius'study on language cf. KRAMER 1828 and GERRETZEN 1940, pp. 71–72.

The basic structure of tradition – backed up by u*sus,* by the presence of the *carmina,* a legitimate source of historical information – does not therefore merit attack, in spite of the many exegetic difficulties that can be found:

> Sed et maxime de antiquissimis Urbis rebus, quia *certam derogabat vetustas fidem, famae* praecipue fuit *standum* posterioribus scriptoribus, ea autem incertis rumoribus, vel obsoletis traditionibus plerumque subnixa, res gestas populi sui vetustate obscuras in maius semper, immo in miraculum usque extollere gestit nonnulla etiam istarum rerum pro veris tradita in Romanis Historiis reperiri, quae praecipua quidem sui parte vera sint, sed tamen adiuncta etiam habeant Poëticis fabulis et miraculis propiora, quam Historicae fidei, et verisimilitudini, nemo, opinor, negabit[13].

One must therefore neither accept everything nor reject everything of historical tradition, nor attempt an integral and blind rehabilitation, nor a radical and equally arbitrary devaluation. The supporters of extreme Pyrrhonism are thus warned that rejecting all history a *priori* is an error contrary to, but basically similar to that committed by those who accept uncritically, since both procedures do not appear to be confirmed by convincing critical argumentations. On the other hand, although doubting the testimonies of the senses has Pyrrho himself not perhaps contradicted himself by continuing to live? Hence there arises the desire to ridicule the modern conjecturalists suspected or accused of subordinating the verification of the facts to biased judgement or, worse still, to abstract hypotheses:

> Sed quando spectata satis est, et elucet undique, bona Auctoris fides, quando eadem aliorum firmatur consensu, quando res ipsa nullam offert nobis iustam satis dubitandi ansam, tum vero, licet forte in una aut altera levissimi momenti particula error quispiam sedere possit, nihil tamen causae est, quo minus fidem illam sequamur, et nostra meditatione dignissimam iudicemus, haud secus ac ipse Pyrrho, sensibus quidem haud

13 PERIZONIUS 1685, p. 184 but also p. 182. On this theme cf. MOMIGLIANO (1957) 1960, pp. 73, 74.

tuto satis credi existimavit, sed tamen eorum consilio et ductu aeque ac alii in agendis rebus quotidie est usus, neque uti desiisset, etiamsi forsan una aut altera itidem in re duces minus fidos ipse eos comperisset[14].

From such hermeneutic premises Perizonius was thus urged to confront François La Mothe le Vayer's contrary theses whose sceptical attitude in comparisons of the past had been emblematically fixed in the pages of the well-known *Du peu de certitude qu'il y a dans l'histoire* (1668). Here through an analysis of traditional narratives the Author had gone so far as to eliminate all possible cognitive scope for history, as well as to condemn it totally from the psychological viewpoint: "[...] Il n'y a point de loix, lorsque la vraie réligion n'y est nullement intéressée, qui obligent à recevoir pour véritable tout ce qui est couché dans l'histoire, s'il y a quelque apparence d'en douter". As the realm of uncertainty and doubt, history presents a structural epistemological weakness rooted in the human impossibility of getting to the *reality* of facts conditioned by the action of passions and biased prejudices. It is very difficult, not to say impossible for a historian to be able to guarantee *truth* to his narrations, since he always comes up against a thousand inevitable, false *relationships* that men's "malice" or "ignorance" consider to be true, never being able to remove the doubt that *love* or *hate*, "interest" or "fear", which no one can escape from, has in fact corrupted his integrity and judgement[15]. Thus there is no *certainty* in anything

14 PERIZONIUS 1702 (1992), p. 34. Cf. also PERIZONIUS (1683) 1740, pp. 585, 586–587: "Etenim (nam et operae pretium est cognoscere, quam ille studiorum rationem et sectam praetulerit) *regia vera via media* semper incedebat inter duas illas extremas, et sibi maxime contrarias, sed pariter gravissimas fundi litterarii calamitates et pestes, odium Novitatis, hoc est ulterioris profectus, et Antiquitatis fastidium" (cited by MEIJER 1971, p. 53).

15 LA MOTHE LE VAYER (1668) 1756–1769, II, p. 331. On the theme – after the classical pages of Pintard – see BORGHERO 1983, pp. 57ff.;

that the most famous historians have hitherto handed down and those who in the future will commit themselves to the same occupation are destined to see their undertaking fail. With the past celebrated only for an ideologico-propagandistic *use* dictated by the exigencies of the present, the most diverse and unforeseeable corruptions and additions have been possible.

The thesis thus found confirmation at the historiographical level, when the Roman historical tradition was judged scarcely reliable, as its *fides,* rooted in the *memoires* of the popes only apparently contrasted with the *lie* for religious obligations, appeared an worn out empty rhetorical artifice. Irremediable contradictions could, for example, be shown in the account handed down by Julius Caesar which according to La Mothe, presents all the characteristics pertaining to the "biased" and "subjective" account of the victor[16]. To the same victor-vanquished scheme complied the interpretation of the Punic Wars. "If the Carthaginians had won" – the French critic emphasised ironically in the *Discours de l'histoire* (1638) – "les circonstances" would have been presented differently by the particular *genie* of every writer who would have done everything possible for the enemies to pass from the part of the wrong. What makes the stories uncertain is the fact that the authors, wishing through biased interest to pay tribute to the persons they are speaking about or render the news they handled more worthy of attention, attribute to them

---

TARANTO 1987, 1988, 1994; AMODIO 2005 and PAGANINI 2008, pp. 61–100.

16 LA MOTHE LE VAYER (1668) 1756–1769, II, pp. 336, 331, 335: "[...] Quoi qu'il en soit, je tiens pour certain [...] que si nous avions des commentaires d'Ambiorix, ou d'Induciomarus, de Vercingétorix, ou de Divitiacus [...] il s'y trouveroit des récits bien [différents] de ceux de César; et que ces vieux Gaulois et [Allemands] donneroient à leurs guerres contre les Romains des jours bien contraires à ceux, où les a fait voir ce premier des Empereurs, quelque avantage que le sort des armes lui ait donné sur eux".

merits that they do not possess and accompany these with noteworthy *circumstances* and events existing only in their *imagination*. Thus in losing its value of truth, *l'histoire* for La Mothe remained a model of *possible* moral actions, ones which did not really exist, and the validity of the historical tradition passing beyond every chronological limit was shown as a patrimony to be used for modern reflection. However, the recognition of its *utility* came about at the price of a complete reduction to a *moral matrix*, to "une très sage maîtresse de la vie humaine", able to make the historian's work only from this viewpoint not to appear "prévenu par intérêt". In historical works, that are not able to describe reality, "la suspension de créance néanmoins, que je pense qu'on y peut raisonnablement apporter, n'empêche pas, qu'elles ne soient d'ailleurs fort probables"[17]. In such a context as this, the Libertine objection basically exposed a strongly psychological charge. In a word it was a matter not only of a gnoseological or historiographical polemic, but above all of a psychological threat which only an in-depth analysis could help to overcome.

All this did not prevent Perizonius from taking part in order to redefine the significance of tradition in a historical sense completely different from a dogmatic and absolutizing interpretation. In his judgement, the sceptical premises of the French critic do not help to proceed with the necessary caution to distinguish the different degrees of probability and certainty of historical knowledge, as they are based on arbitrary generalizations and forced interpretations that go so far as to invalidate even the reliability of Livy's account of the Punic wars:

> Nihil tamen minus Mothius ille Vaiierius de re omnium celeberrima, seu de Punicis Romanorum bellis, iactitare audit; si Carthaginiensium habe-

17 La Mothe le Vayer (1668) 1756–1769, II, pp. 338, 339; La Mothe le Vayer (1638) 1756–1769, I, p. 783. On this point cf. Bianchi 1988 and Amodio 1998, pp. 5–58.

remus Historias, longe aliter nos memorata ab iis deprehensuros praelia, quam a Livio factum, qui suis semper Romanis victorias adscripserit, easque minore militum numero, sola fortitudine Ducum, ac disciplinae suae praestantia partas[18].

To justify his conclusions La Mothe would have had to demonstrate that the testimonies of the facts discussed are highly improbable. Lacking adequate proof, his method is reduced in contrast to the generic and specious affirmation of the impossibility of verifying ancient Roman history directly on the basis of contemporary sources that have now disappeared, thus setting weak conjectures and theoretical constructions against positive verifiable documents. According to Perizonius *histories* of the historians unlike "romances" must be *true* stories and not based on fantasies or inventions.

No better a reception did Bayle's theses in the *Critique général de l'Histoire du Calvinisme* (1682) have, theses which, in keeping with the sceptical and libertine tradition, identified in prejudices and in insuperable human ignorance the main causes of the changes to be found in the field of history, by proposing a solution, thus radically negative regarding the problem of the truth and knowability of testimonies: "En un mot il n'y a point de *Filouterie* plus grande, que celle qui se peut exercer sur les [monuments] Historiques [...]". To know historically does not mean to *really* know the facts that have happened but only to learn the contrary opinions that opposing "parties" have on the same arguments, as is confirmed by the experience of those who have experience of the lawyers' harangues in the lawcourts[19]. To re-

18 PERIZONIUS 1702 (1992), p. 16.

19 BAYLE (1682) 1727–1731 [1965–1982], II, p. 10a, letter I: "Qu'il est facile d'altérer la vérité de l'Histoire". "L'omission d'une circonstance, la supposition d'une autre, que l'on code adroitement en cinq ou six mots; un je ne say quel tour que l'on donne aux choses, changent entièrement la qualité des actions. Cela [paraît] tous les jours dans le Barreau; il n'y a

flect on the traditional account of the past whose testimonies are clearly uncertain, the historian must trust "bon sens" and realize that facts are not neutral but are predetermined by every author according to his own preferences and prejudices. For every document there is the possibility of falsification for propagandistic-ideological purposes, they themselves being the object of investigation, because they reveal the "interests" of those who have instituted and diffused them. Convinced that he could prove that there is always an implicit or explicit purpose in all erudite research, Bayle, with his gaze focused more especially on the controversies between Calvinist historians and Catholic historians of his own day, emphasized the need to discover the reasons for the return to the past, that is to say the recurring connection between what one wishes to obtain and what has already been reached, finding the *conjectures* and *errors* as adequate explanations in the ideological-political choices of the researcher. The best method and the most correct historical judgement were thus born of a constantly pursued critical analysis of all the possible *opinions* to be traced in one and the same tradition, and thus aiming to outline a 'typology' of the historically false, to single out, that is say, the vehicles through which lies and errors are spread. 'Biased' historians drawn into the *sect* of historic Pyrrhonism are, in fact, historians of little worth, however their great number causes them to be opposed to the *authority* of the worthy, thereby complicating everything: "[...] On peut quelque fois pousser la certitude de l'Histoire jusques à quelque détail"; one may, for example, be persuaded of a fact, of a project or of a particular motive when all the 'parties' converge, when something does not cease to be admitted by those for whom it is *shameful*, or also when being 'glorious' for one party, is not contested by the other. To reflect on history means therefore to ve-

point de faits qui entre les mains de deux habiles Avocats appointés contraires, ne prennent des formes toutes différentes".

rify its possible sense, to believe that in examining the concatenation of many facts and considering the character of the protagonists, sifting through all the circumstances and comparing what has been said by the ones and by the others, may clarify many things, reveal many deceptions, and confute many calumnies: "Mais [...] soyez assûré que l'Historien qui a le plus d'esprit, est ordinairement celui dont la cause [paraît] la meilleure, et qu'il est bien malaisé de parvenir jusqu'à l'évidence"[20].

It was this theoretical-methodological uniting perspective – albeit in the awareness of the different positions and sensibilities – the libertine La Mothe le Vayer and the refined Cartesian of the *Critique Générale,* two distinct but contiguous moments of historical Pyrrhonism: the one bound to the rhetorical tradition of the *ars historica,* attentive to the problems of the order and style of the Ciceronian *opus maxime oratorium,* the other characterized by an attempt to reformulate the problems of historical knowledge in terms of Cartesian philosophy and of applying the criterion of methodical doubt and proof also to the historical facts, even respecting the diversity and peculiarity of different disciplinary settings[21].

Perizonius did not fail to expose the hasty inadequate research method of each of them, claiming in general that the ex-

20 BAYLE (1682) 1727–1731 [1965–1982], I, p. 10b; letter II, pp. 11b–12a: "Jusqu'où on peut pousser la certitude de l'Histoire" and letter III, 13a: "Grande partialité des Historiens *modernes*". On Bayle and historical Pyrrhonism – after LACOSTE 1929 and ROBINSON 1931 – cf. BORGHERO 1983, pp. 217ff., BIANCHI 1987, pp. 11–156 and 1988, pp. 50ff. and ZOLI 1989, pp. 51ff.

21 So BORGHERO 1983, pp. 7–8. In his *Dictionnaire* Bayle observes that in La Mothe le Vayer'works "belles pensées [...], on y trouve de solides [raisonnements]" and "l'Esprit et l'Erudition y marchent de compagnie [...] Il ne cherchoit que des [Arguments] de Pyrrhonisme [...] il ne faut pas être aussi décisif qu'on l'est à condamner comme mauvais et déraisonnable, ce qui ne se trouve pas conforme à nos opinions et à nos coutumes" (BAYLE 1740, IV, p. 413b).

istence of false interpreters does not suffice to invalidate the credibility of all the others. Epistemological reservations on the nature and validity of human knowledge have only indirect importance for the historian who works on the assumption that he is able to believe in the reconstruction and comprehension of the facts of the past. He will certainly have to take account of insurmountable gnoseological limits but only to give a rigorous definition to the limits of his investigation. The specific area of his activity remains the information and documents that must be interpreted and properly assembled to understand what really happened. Also in the lawcourt – observes the Dutch philologist in explicit assonance with the example proposed by the Rotterdam philosopher – there is the one who defends lost causes with judicial technicalities, but the honest judge knows how to distinguish them and the historian must operate like him:

> At quanta, Auditores, quanta haec est Iudicii inclementia, quanta iniquitas? [...] Nonne istic, quae vera sunt, negantur saepe perfricta prorsus fronte, aut argutis eluduntur cavillationibus? Quae falsa, asseverantur constanter, aut fallaci illinuntur fuco? [...] Nihilne istic habent, quod curent, quod attendant, nisi quam scite, quam callide, quilibet Advocatus causas orare norit? [...] An vero solis in Historiis aliter se res habet, ut nulla istic cura, opera, iudicio, indagari veritas queat aut inveniri?

The main argumentation is that in many cases historians may be accorded trust as they speak against the interests of the cause that they in fact defend. All antiquity studies – from the juridical to the haraldic, from the archaeological to the numismatic – were participant in real needs which, according to Perizonius, were expressed in an anxious search for a historical method capable of thinking of the past as a gathering of certain knowledges and not as conventional space in which to place phantasms, the utopias of contemporary investigations. Thus to reject the idea of a history apart, written in bad faith, like Maimbourg's, worked only on the facts that are in keeping with the author's interest, modelled at his pleasure on false testimonies replacing the truth with fanciful constructions of the truth. The latter, "*Temporis [...] Filia*", was however destined to emerge from the confrontation of contrasting positions, supported by the principles of legitimate historical methodology, essentially interested in establishing the correct modalities of cnitico-philogical interpretation of available sources:

> Verum tamen manifestum satis censet Auctor Criticae, in Calvinismum Maimburgii scriptae, exstare Pyrrhonismi istius documentum in eo, quod hodie de una eademque re diversarum partium homines plane contraria ferme asseverare videmus [...]; perdi ergo operam, quae Historiis legendis impendatur; nec legere se eas, ut cognoscat atque exploratam habeat rem gestam, sed tantum ut sciat, quid de re gesta quaeque natio, quaeque factio, dixerit[22].

To respond effectively to the sceptical theses, the defence of the comprehensive authenticity of the traditional narrations on primitive Roman history had therefore to be founded exclusively on the *reality* of the documents that had safeguarded them, and that the Ancient Greek and Roman historians, from Livy to Dioniges of Halicarnassus, to Plutarch, had made use of, by consulting testimonies contemporary to the events described, that for us are now inaccessible. The truth of history depends after all on the intellectual integrity of the witnesses that is thus guarantee of their very authority. These issues were neither new nor simple but Perizonius confronts them with special argumentative rigour. To tradition we may also attribute less value, given the distance of the facts narrated and the complexity of the relative testimonies, but we cannot confuse the *less certain* with the *false*. Real criticism does not contend with facts but with *fables*, and is the chief instrument for historical investigation precisely because it allows establishing the reliability of the evidence, whe-

22 PERIZONIUS 1702 (1992), pp. 24–25, 29, 23–24.

reas in doubting every reality Pyrrhonism condemns men to unescapable and everlasting ignorance. Equally significant, even if not so pronounced, is Perizonius' diffidence towards catholic historiography, guilty of having nurtured Pyrrhonism with the *Index* of prohibited books, accepting legends and eulogizing contradictory writers, thus impeding free confrontation between facts and opinions. Exegetic questions could be adequately reformulated on the other hand, only if the conscience of the absolute truth of the biblical text was no longer accepted as insuppressable starting datum. *Patience* and *method* were indispensable for a correct analysis, meaning that critico-philological method was concerned with verifying the intrinsic value of the source examined, its reality and non-contradictoriness with other testimonies and with actual experience:

> Sicuti iudicio in illis est opus limato ad verum a falso discernendum, sic in Historiis quoque non habenda sunt temere omnia, quae traduntur, pro veris, neque omnia pro falsis, aut incertis [...]. Neque enim, quod in Historiis certum ducimus, unius tantum auctoritate volumus subnixum, sed quanto plurimum potest, diversi generis, nationis, sectae, atque ipsa insuper rerum serie et eventu firmatum[23].

For such principles, historical tradition presents all the requisites necessary for being considered *true*. And Perizonius properly defends its practico-pedagogical utility, the continuity of the moral message that he hands down to us, and which however – albeit with autonomous objectives and highly per-

23 PERIZONIUS 1702 (1992), p. 38. "Quid Romana huius temporis Ecclasia? Aliamne habet mentem, aliudne in nos cepit consilium, quando *Prohibitorum,* et, ut ait, *Expurgandorum,* hoc est, Mutilandorum, Librorum Indicem iam nunc formavit, poenamque interminatur suis, qui retinere illos ac legere ausint? Quid enim aliud hoc ipso declarat, nisi quod, si rerum denuo potiatur ubivis, deletura sit penitus, quantum in se est, omnem doctrinae ac religionis nostrae memoriam" (PERIZONIUS 1702 [1992], p. 37).

sonal elaborations – Arnauld, Nicole and Huet in the wake of Gassendi had already emphasised, by reforming the Cartesiano-Malebranchian perspective from within through extending its gnoseological ambit and conferring validity and autonomy even if the non-mathematical *moral certainties*, to be retraced in sacred and profane history, thus rescued from the destructive action of Pyrrhonism[24].

In the judgement of the Dutch scholar, Pyrrhonism was able to ridicule the ancient virtue without making appeal to the poor reliability of handed-down traditions, but also by noting the radical diversity from modern customs. Yet, also the apparently more ambiguous testimonies must not be rejected simply because the conditions of life have changed: the Spartans, the Romans, the Christian martyrs provide illuminating examples of virtue, which nowadays may no longer be proposed, but which once certainly existed:

> Assertor ille Pyrrhonismi, Vir Doctissimus, quem supra designavi, ridet splendide et repudiat sine haesitatione ulla heroicam Veterum quorun-

24 "Les hommes ne sont pas nés pour employer leur temps à mesurer des lignes, à examiner les rapports des angles, à considérer les diverses [mouvements] de la matière. Leur esprit est trop grand, leur vie trop courte, leur temps trop précieux pour l'occuper à de si petits [objets]; mais ils sont obligés d'être justes, équitables, judicieux, [raisonnables], dans tous leurs discours, dans toutes leurs actions et dans toutes les affaires qu'ils manient; et c'est à quoy ils doivent particulièrement s'exercer et se former". The "true reason" therefore assigns to every being the sense that he deserves: "Elle fait douter de celles qui sont douteuses, [rejeter] celles qui sont fausses, et [reconnaître] de bonne foy celles qui sont évidentes, sans s'arrester aux vaines raisons des Pyrrhoniens qui ne détruisent pas l'[assurance] raisonnable que l'on a des choses certaines, non pas mesme dans l'esprit de ceux qui les proposent. Personne ne doute jamais sérieusement s'il y a une terre, un soleil et une lune, ni si le tout est plus grand que sa partie" (ARNAULD-NICOLE 1662, pp. 6–7, 11). Cf. – after BORGHERO 1983, pp. 13ff. and 84ff. – BIANCHI 1987, pp. 120–121.

> dam constantiam, ultro se morti saepe offerentium; censetque, aevi prioris homines, si vitae reciperent hodie usum, demiraturos talia de suo tempore tradi et credi; sed et de nostro hoc saeculo similia post CCC vel CD annos haud dubie narratum iri. Verum oportet sane, nunquam illum satis considerasse, quam diversi sint mores diversorum temporum, diversarumque gentium [...][25].

Every fact is the product of a particular situation that the historian has the duty to respect by setting it in its relative time-and-space context, and critically analyzing the terms he uses, with different meanings in different contexts, for different moments, as well as the events to which these terms apply. Against every form of scepticism Perizonius considered historiographical rethinking necessary for verifying the truth of the facts, so much more necessary when the experience of the historian, his capacity for intuition and evaluation had been under attack from the difficulty of entering into realities different from his own. Thus it was a matter of paying special attention to traditions, to the written and oral materials, in order to bring together the promptings that drove the ancients to write about history and to know the instruments and the modalities adopted. It is possible to single out the *true* origin of every tradition received. The problem thus becomes historiographical and the coincidence of history and historiography finished up by connecting past and present without any solution of continuity. Modern studies on classical antiquity are to be judged and eventually accepted only if the interpretation of the documents utilized proves adequate. In all events research *into* the ancient historiographical tradition is valid in that it locates the text within its specific historico-cultural space. Driven towards critical re-thinking by the promptings of the present, albeit finding a problem *of his own* in that research, the historian must not, however, forget what the event he has analyzed represented before his intervention. If *true*

25 PERIZONIUS 1702 (1992), pp. 39ff.

history lives in the present through documents, its interpreters are not "philosophers" who search for responses to problems of their present by manipulating the past, but more modestly are authentic witnesses of truth. What for Perizonius was important to recognize were, in fact, the possible *truths* critically established in the light of the ethical and methodical question at the same time as the distinction between the *certain* and the *probable*, far removed from abstract, fantastic conjectures. Thus, in wanting to understand history correctly it is necessary to examine all the circumstances associated with the facts, since this experience does not provide absolute knowledge, nor does it search for truth of *things in themselves*, but for the meaning the events express in the testimonies that narrate them. Based on such premises, reflection had necessarily led to stressing the centrality of two principles in methodological analysis: 1) that historical investigation has the search for *truth* as its aim; 2) that the historian must first of all know and utilize the sources he makes use of correctly. It is dangerous as well as useless to concern oneself with history if a direct and critical knowledge of the sources has not first been acquired. Methodological Perizonian criticism demands that the concrete control of the possibility of an event has not been reached by extrapolating the fact from its source, but by examining it from within and from its degree of certainty. The historian – for the Dutch philologist – is not an unapealla-ble judge who acts by examining the individual fact from outside, but a critic who invites the analysing and classifying of every authority in order to ascertain the truth of the event. He must not, therefore, be concerned with the fact in itself and for itself but with the evidence of the fact in the context of the source that hands it down. The competent critic however, knows not only how to 'measure' the sources utilized, but also how to discover new truth that is guaranteed through his expertise with which the documents are examined, as well as by the principles that govern the reconstruction of the facts. To interpret them critically before accepting them is an exigency prompted by the established uncertainty of the ancient documentation, by the diffidence towards erudite research that appeared shortcoming in its premises, and inconclusive in its findings. For Perizonius proof of the legitimacy of such principles are the unsuccessful attempts of historico-philological criticism regarding the origin of Rome as well as the Romulus legend in particular, to which he dedicates an important *Dissertatio*[26] that of previous exercises on the theme already matured in Leyden in the works of his masters Theodorus Ryckius and Jacobus Gronovius which represents better theoretical-historiographical focusing[27].

Being of an imposing structure, the history of the origins of the Urbs, being a bank of proof for politicians lends itself as a good example for demonstrating how ancient history interprets the *evidence* it possesses, if such a demonstration is dictated by literary sources that are not always contemporary to the facts narrated, and thus inevitably exposed to the reservations of sceptics as the French critics' analyses had efficaciously shown. In responding to this problem, Perizonius judges it appropriate to distinguish between the "desire" and the "reality" of having documents available for the examination of tradition on the theme in question. In fact, also by applying the evaluation criteria of *possibility*, *reality* and *non-inconsistency* of the relative sources to the Romulus legend, he first and foremost made it clear that he had no intention of considering absurdities such as "[...] an Romulus fuerit Martis Filius, an ab Lupa nutritus, et quae sunt

26 PERIZONIUS 1740. For date this work cf. MOMIGLIANO (1957) 1960, pp. 71–72, note, and ERASMUS 1962, pp. 76–78.

27 See RYCKIUS 1684, Chap. 10, pp. 431ff. and GRONOVIUS [JACOBUS] 1684. On this theme see ERASMUS 1962, pp. 79, 102ff. and MOMIGLIANO (1963) 1987, pp. 180–181. For the relationship between Perizonius and Gronovius see MEIJER 1971, pp. 32ff. and 137ff. An important report is already in *ACTA ERUDITORUM* 1703, I, pp. 12–19 and VIII, pp. 366–369.

eius generis plura". And yet the historian's discretion comes to a halt before the documents interpreted and respected for what they in fact testify according to the rules of sound reason and experience that they do not reject *a priori,* but also justify the improbable elements of ancient Roman history "manifestis argumentis". Of the latter Perizonius did in fact furnish an adequate explanation, ascribing their causes on the one hand to the "circumstantiae" introduced to make up for the missing information – according to what is documented about the story of Rea Silvia's illness handed down by Dioniges of Halicarnassus (I, 77) – and on the other for propagandistico-ideological purposes of the same Roman kings, such as the *fable* invented by Romulus on his presumed divine descendancy testifies: "[...] Vel ultro ex verisimili ac decoro, saepe etiam ex postremi temporis moribus"[28]. On identifying the reasons for the presence of *fabulous* places in traditional evidence, the real critic had, instead, to keep to the basic nucleus of the story to the *summa rei* that Perizonius – as earlier in the *Animadversiones Historicae* – does not hesitate to consider *certa historia* lacking all the improbable details and based on real sources accepted by the majority of ancient historians: "Sufficit enim heic nobis, quod vera esse possit, quodque nihil contineat a veri similitudine alienum, aut tale, quod iustis rationibus confutari, ac abiici queat"[29]. Thus the affirmation is re-

28 PERIZONIUS 1740, pp. 683–684, 686, 707, 708, 712.

29 PERIZONIUS 1740, p. 686. Erasmus observes that "The basic outlines of early Roman history, despite criticism on numerous points of detail, are accepted as historical in 1685 and in 1709. The sources for early roman history which he considers reliable in 1685, are still considered sufficiently reliable in 1709 to justify the acceptance as historical of the *summa rei* of the Romulus-legend. As one of the sources on which the ancient historians had based their accounts of early Roman history, Perizonius in 1685 mentions old *carmina*, and in 1709 these *carmina* are again mentioned in a review of the sources for the history of the origins of Rome which had been available to the ancient historians" (ERASMUS 1962, p. 117).

peated in this context that the uncertain character of certain parts of the traditional account cannot authorize invalidating its entire significance and value. Having assigned to every fact the degree of probability or likelihood apertaining thereto, one must avoid accepting everything without discrimination, as well as refusing a *priori* everything only because the love for the fantastic – that has always reigned with equal intensity – has embellished it with alluring fictions. The historical tradition cannot be accepted before demonstrating its reality adequately, nor be rejected without convincing documented reasons. Here basically for him was the weak point of contemporary historiography that was incapable of guaranteeing fixed rules of interpretation: "Imprudentis enim foret et imperiti, res adeo antiquas, nulla nisi unius populi traditione confirmatas, multis asseverationibus contendere fidei et veritatis esse certae. Sed aeque imprudentis est et temerarii, eas confidenter adeo affirmare falsas, nisi manifestis id argumentis probare queat, quod itidem difficile prorsus censeo". It is rather the *consensus Romanorum de sua origine* that is able to legitimise the *probability* of Roman history, of that history *communi consensu vere a Romanis recepta* described by Fabio Pittore, Cato and by other ancient historians down to Livy, Velleius and Florus. In support of such considerations suffice it also to note how differently from La Mothe le Vayer's hypothesis whereby if the Carthaginians had won the Punic wars the circumstances would have been presented differently by the particular *genre* of each writer who would have done everything possible to make the enemy pass to the wrong side, Perizonius reasserts the authenticity of the war between Rome and Carthage, clinging totally to the fidelity of the testimonies and chronology of Polybius who managed to salvage the first treaties stipulated between the two opposing citizen bodies: "Sed et alia superfuisse antiquitatis Historicae monumenta clarissime patet utique vel ex Polybii *lib. 3 cap. 22* etc. ubi ille antiquissima Romanorum foedera cum Carthaginiensibus, eorumque foederum leges, exponens, primum memorat, quod factum sub primis et plane proximis post Reges eiectos consulibus"[30]. The question, moreover, did not fail to pose the problem for the possible use of non-Roman contemporary sources for the early years of life of Rome, such as those going back to Diocles of Pepareto, an obscure Greek writer considered by Plutarch (*Rom.,* III e VIII) as the first to have treated the origins of the Urbs, then followed by Fabio Pittore and by Dioniges of Halicarnassus. In this regard, Perizonius is very cautious regarding the dangerous hypothesis of Cluver, who in support of his sceptical objections had arbitrarily deduced from Livy (VI, 1) the thesis of the non-existence of authentic documents on the origin of Rome, which had been completely destroyed by the Gauls' burning of Rome. For this hypothesis, lacking the necessary documentation the historians following Fabio Pittore modified and even transformed the traditional account, thus making its identification difficult. The history that one reads in Diodorus, Dioniges of Halicarnassus and Livy is thus the outcome of centuries of drafting and redrafting of early testimonies, just as the tradition on the origins of Rome is in fact the account that these three historians of antiquity have given of it. All this was objected to by Perizonius through the consideration of the several sources that have come down to us, including the *Annales Maximi,* the Lintel books, the *cantica vetusta* and the annals of the cities bordering on Rome. In reporting the war, they indirectly demonstrated that they could be considered as *true* sources, and perfectly utilizable for reconstrucing the origins of the Urbs with sufficient *certainty*:

> [...] Varia post illud captae Urbis tempus superfuisse, unde summam rerum antiquarum colligerent Livius, et alii posterioris temporis Scriptores,

30 PERIZONIUS 1740, pp. 686, 688, 697; LA MOTHE LE VAYER (1638) 1756–1769, I, p. 783.

non modo Annales Maximos, seu Commentarios Pontificum, sed et libros linteos, cantica vetusta, et vicinarum Urbium quoque Annales[31].

Cartesianism and Philological Criticism: the Meeting with Le Clerc

With his intervention Perizonius expressed concerns and motives that were most widespread throughout the Republic of Letters of the end of the seventeenth century. Some years before the anti-Pyrrhonistic *Oratio*, amid the polemical climate following the publication of Marten Schoock's small-scale work *De figmento legis regiae Epistola* dated 1661, Ulrik Huber had exposed Pyrrhonism first in his *Disputationes iuris fundamentales* and then in the *Digressiones Justinianeae* (1670, 1688, 1696) as a dangerous obstacle from the critico-philological and historico-political viewpoint for the understanding of the *Corpus Iuris* and the modern *ius civitatis*. This was a well-worn path in the years just before Johann Friedrich Gronow and Gerard Noodt who in dealing with the Roman *lex regia* albeit in highly personal forms and overtones, had reproposed and examined with through critical rigour the theme of *auctoritas* and the *obligatio ex consensu* in the light of contemporary political and religious debate, not without becom-

31 PERIZONIUS 1740, p. 695. "Ego vero neutiquam ex eo sequi autumo, quod Diodes ille Graecus et Fabius Pictor Romanus eodem fere modo originem Urbis Rom. enarrarint, Romanum ergo istam Scriptorem a Graeco suam Historiam necessario hausisse. Potuerunt enim sua ex iisdem habuisse fontibus" (PERIZONIUS 1740, p. 703). On the theme – after ERASMUS 1962, p. 80 – see MAZZARINO 1972², II.1, pp. 65ff. On Fabio Pittore and Diocles in the tradition on the origins of Rome see MOMIGLIANO (1960) 1987, pp. 275–288.

ing fully aware of the dangerous developments of the radically sceptical interpretations of Roman historiography[32].

Although in a completely different cultural setting, Jean Le Clerc too looked for responses to the vexed questions regarding the value of tradition and its moral content. It is precisely from this viewpoint that some motives may be reconstructed that mark his philosophical development that include the gradual refinement of his critico-philological method that was to offer a new interpretation of the old and new testament tradition in the years of the repeal of the Edict of Nantes, on the basis of reconsidered relationships between philosophy and theology, metaphysics and religion in the important polemical writings of 1685 (*Entrétiens sur diverses matières de théologie* composed with the collaboration of Le Cène more especially in the *Sentiments de quelques théologiens de Hollande sur l'Histoire Critique du Vieux Testament, composée par le père Simon de l'Oratoire*).

Abandoning Geneva on account of the severe impositions of triumphant orthodox Calvinism[33], the five years' travelling (1678–1683) through France, England and Germany represents a delicate and decisive moment in Le Clerc's cultural development. First tutor at Grenoble, he was then at Saumur whose Academy, a centre for the diffusion of Irenistic conceptions and tolerant in the religious ambit, demonstrated through its activity the close relationship and the reciprocal influence which was established in the 17th century between Arminianism and French

32 Cf. LOMONACO 1990, Chapp. 1, 2 and LOMONACO 1997.

33 Gregorio Leti, Le Clerc's father-in-law, described the Genevan setting: "Ma in Geneva senza esempio il rigore è passato così oltre, che non si vuole ammettere in quella Chiesa alcun Ministro, che non giuri (come si è detto) di credere, e d'insegnare contro la grazia universale [...]; ma quel che dà tanto più dell'horrore, che questa violenza si è fatta in una città di Geneva, dove giornalmente fu predicata da quei ministri contro l'Inquisitione di Roma, perché violenta la libertà delle conscienze" (LETI 1686, p. 504).

culture, in contrast with the rigid orthodoxy defended by the Academy of Sedan. The interpretration of the Arminian writings, and the scholastic (theological and philosophical) disputes would have convinced the young Geneva scholar of the erroneous use of metaphysics in approaching theological questions. Meditation on arguments of faith should not be based on any metaphysical-type hypothesis or basis: the absolute reference point was and remained the revelation to the faithful, towards the understanding of which the theologians'efforts had to be directed. In letters exchanged more especially with Pierre Allix, Jacques Lenfant and Isaac Papin from 1683 onwards, Le Clerc reached a very high state of theoretical awareness, observing how reasonings about metaphysics, especially if applied to religion, mutually destroy each other, in spite of each continuing to appear equally *evident*: "Jugez par là s'il est sûr d'embrasser une opinion par de simples raisons de Métaphysique. Le moien donc de se débarrasser de ces difficultés qui sont tout à fait insurmontables c'est d'abandonner ces idées abstraites qui ne sont bonnes à rien, et de se renfermer dans de certaines bornes qui comprennent toutes nos [connaissances] et utiles et certaines"[34]. However, in developing this rejection of metaphysics (a rejection that he is to encounter in another regular correspondent of his, namely John Locke) Le Clerc did not fail to revise his orginal critical confrontation with Cartesianism, the methodological claims of which he was prepared to accept, yet rejecting its metaphysical premises and conclusions on philosophical and theological grounds. However, to promoting his conversion to the remonstrating doctrine had been the Arminian theologian Etienne de Courcelles who in 1650 had published a Latin edi-

34 LE CLERC to Papin 1684, p. 276. On the relations with Papin, see HAASE 1952; IOFRIDA 1979; SIMONUTTI 1982 and 1984. For this and the following observations, see SINA 1987, pp. VII–XXVII; LOMONACO 1990b and MANNARINO 2008, pp. 453–477.

tion of the *Discours sur la Méthode* in Amsterdam[35]. Yet he became inclined towards that confrontation more especially by the memory of the Genevan lessons of his old master Jean-Robert Chouet whose missives filled with affectionate comprehension, were not without criticism regarding his pupil's anti-Cartesian developments by revising his ancient teaching even at some considerable distance both in time and place[36].

By now the *Liberii De Sancto Amore Epistulae Theologicae* (1681) of the young Genevan had so provoked the indignation of orthodox theologians as to force him to abandon Saumur first for London[37] and then for Amsterdam. Clear-sighted and prudent, Le Clerc consolidated his education through stimulus

35 DESCARTES 1650.

36 "Voilà, Monsieur, ce me semble quel est vôtre système; il parait beau, et je ne doute point qu'il ne plaise à bien des gens; j'y trouve pourtant diverses difficultés, qu'il faut que vous tachiés de lever. [...] Il me semble [...] que rien n'empêche que nous ne recevions la Règle des Cartésiens, *Tout ce que nous connaissons clairement est vrai*, sans la restriction, que vous luy voulés donner, *dans les choses, pour la connaissance des quelles la Raison nous a été donnée*, c'est à dire, dans les choses utiles; car premièrement cette limitation me parait inutile pour le but, que vous vous proposés. qui est d'empêcher les Métaphysiciens de décider, comme ils font, les Questions dont il s'agit" (CHOUET to Le Clerc 1685, pp. 343, 344–345 and now in SINA 2008, pp. 245, 247). About this theme, besides the classical mograph, DE BUDE 1899, pp. 144–153 (with an important epistolary Appendix), we refer back to the studies of SINA 1984, pp. 3–14 and LOMONACO 1990, pp. 157–168. On Le Clerc, Limborch and Locke about "New Theological Strategies" and "the Collapse of Cartesianism" see ISRAEL 1995, pp. 464ff. and 477ff.

37 He wrote from here on 9 June 1682 to his friend Philippus van Limborch, expressing his wish to settle in Amsterdam, where he hoped to experience liberty of Christian belief: "Rogo te, per amicitiam nostram, ut me commonefacias si quis locus sit apud vos in quo honeste victitare possim. Eum sane propter te et Christianam libertatem quae apud vos viget, omni alii praeferrem. Possem docere humaniores literas Latinas et Graecas, Philosophiam, Geometriam, ut iam linguam Hebraicam et Theologiam omitta" (LE CLERC to van Limborch 1682, p. 45).

for and contact with the Dutch environment during the years of his stay in Amsterdam as Professor of Philosophy at the college that remonstrated through Limborch's intervention, then also as professor of Hebrew and *Humanités,* as well as of Church History on the latter's death in 1712. The scholar painted a very dramatic picture of all the politico-religious contrasts in the city's cultural life, including the Erasmian tradition and the first natural law theory (iusnaturalism), heretical thought and Arminian doctrine, Irenical theology, Nicodemism and tolerance in religious disputes. In a letter dated 10th November 1684 he described to his friend Antoine Vattemare, now exiled in London, the struggles between the Walloon church and the Arminians, the political conflicts between the citizen magistrates and the Prince of Orange who had brought about the supression of sermons in French at the Seminary of the Remonstrators where he worked[38].

Thus with reference to a particular problematical politico-religious situation, the Author of the *Ars Critica* fled from the opposite, yet basically equivalent risk of dogmatic acceptance of all testimonies and the radical Pyrrhonistic rejection of their reliability, theorizing the need to reintroduce the significance of critico-philological research as an indispensable instrument for

38 "Quoy qu'il en soit le peu d'apparence que je vis de demeurer à Londres me fit venir en Hollande, pour y voir quelques uns de mes amis qui tiennent un rang considerable parmi les [Remontrants], avec qui j'avois commerce depuis long-temps. Ces Mrs. Current que mon Ministère pouvoit être en edification parmy eux et que pour me trouver de l'employ il fallout essayer d'établir un exercice françois. Il fut résolu que je prêcherois une fois la semaine dans le temple qu'ils ont à Amsterdam. J'y ai prêché pendant troix mois, mais les différents politiques qui ont été entre les magistrats de cette ville et Mr. Le Prince d'Orange ont été cause qu'on nous a fait dire de les interrompre [...]" (LE CLERC to Vattemare 1684, pp. 261–262). On the cultural and political-religious life in Amsterdam during the seventeenth century, after P. GEYL, E.H. KOSSMANN and P. DIBON, see BURKE 1974 and TOGNON 1987.

arriving at a form of valid *certainty* in the field of chance human events. Hence the search for new *rules* (the criterion of *probability,* the *use* of *common sense* and *reason*) and empirical instruments also to ascertain the eventual factual *evidence*, the outcome of long and tiring investigations aimed at overcoming the bias of modern historians, conditioned by their prejudices, being prisoners of radical ignorance. Yet, all this – in Le Clerc's situation as earlier in Bayle's – did not mean that the exercise of criticism and historico-philological work proved outside the contemporary philosophical debate, since the theoretical contribution to Leclerchian discourse offered by Cartesianism became an essential, albeit "weak" form of Cartesianism essentially reduced to furnishing methodological indications to be used in historical research, with a view to arriving even at factual, and not necessarily at just mathematical, e*vidence.* Precisely the search for a happy medium between absolute scepticism and dogmatico-traditional apologetics might lead to an originalattempt at an opening to the historical world, the understanding of which only apparently seemed to be precluded from Cartesian philosophy[39].

As early as the first tome of the "Bibliothèque Universelle et Historique" (1686) the editor published a *Préface,* containing the guiding criteria of the three-monthly presentation and review of the works published. In unequivocal polemics with the aims and principles that had sustained Bayle in publishing his "Nouvelles de la République des Lettres" which Le Clerc had not hesitated to attack in the 1684 letters[40], the "Bibliothèque" set itself a rig-

39 On cartesianism and history – after HAZARD and LAPORTE, MOMIGLIANO and SESTAN – cf. WATSON 1966; LISSA 1973, espec. Chap. 1, pp. 9–108; RICUPERATI 1982, pp. 275–386 and BORGHERO 1983.

40 "Mr. Desbordes m'a dit que vous seriez bien aise d'apprendre ce que l'on dit de vos Nouvelles; et vous connaissant comme je fais, je croi que vous ne serez pas fâché, si je vous dis ce que j'en ai ouî dire. On dit en général que l'auteur des nouvelles s'étend trop sur des choses qui ne sont pas si nécessaires, et qu'on pourrait aisément réduire les cinq feuilles

orously historico-informative objective, philologically disciplined and far removed from abstract interpretations, and from arbitrary value judgements[41].

The moderate criticism – which Perizonius'philological analyses were based on – claimed against Le Clerc's "philosophical" criticism, albeit within a like cultural context in the light of common interests and analogous methodological objectives, the rights of the erudite professional philologist to reconstruct the normative value of ancient tradition, far removed from the absolute certainty. In the closing section of the third act of the *Ars Critica* (1697), "De iudicio de stylo et charactere scriptoris ferendo", in defending the instruments and rules of *criticism* indicating a more rigorous way towards historical knowledge, susceptible of arriving at results to some extent certain, albeit limited, the Author, had judged it opportune to offer a detailed historico-philological analysis of Quinto Curtius Rufus' work[42]. And it was this that attracted ruthless attacks from the Leyden philologist who, considering analysis as a sort of *philosophical* interference by

---

à troix, ou même à deux" (LE CLERC to Bayle 1684, p. 177). An opinion similar to this is also expressed by LE CLERC to Papin 1684, p. 278.

41 "Comme on se trouve en un païs de liberté, on peut promettre, qu'on ne prendra jamais parti dans les disputes des [Savants], qu'on rapportera fidèlement les raisons de part et d'autre, et qu'on ne dira rien qui puisse prévenir le Lecteur [...]. Afin que cette Bibliothèque puisse porter justement le titre *d'Historique,* on ne dira rien de son chef, et on ne fera simplement que narrer les opinions des Auteurs. Ainsi l'on sera obligé de lire exactement les livres, et cela [pourraît] empêcher que l'extrait de quelques-uns ne parût si tôt" (*BIBLIOTHÈQUE UNIVERSELLE ET HISTORIQUE* 1686, I, pp. 11–12, 14, without page number). On this theme cf. also LENFANT to Le Clerc 1687, p. 477). On this Journal – after BARNES 1938, pp. 116–120 – cf. BOTS et al. 1981, pp. 7ff., 27–28, 67–68ff., 106–107, 124–127ff., 334–339. On journalism in the modern Holland cf. HATIN (1865) 1964 and RICUPERATI 1983.

42 LE CLERC 1697–1700, III, sectio III, pp. 419–552: "De Judicio de Stylo et Charactere Scriptoris ferendo". See LOMONACO 1990, Chap. 3.

incompetent critics, claimed the solution to the complex critical problems associated with the theme under examination for the exclusive competence of philologists. Le Clerc also came to be ranked alongside the masters of historic Pyrrhonism including La Mothe le Vayer and Bayle, and his theses seemed to provide arguments for Pyrrhonist and Libertine radicalism, indirectly contributing to the annihilation of the *fides historica* as well as the respect due to antiquity in deference to a perverse *ratio philosophandi* which, passing beyond its limits, had claimed apodyptic demonstrations where only the authority of the testimonies could be found[43]. Le Clerc's response, inspired by his intention to give a positive reply to the same questions as Perizonius had posed, did not avoid the querelle's main themes that were of a historico-critical character. The pages of the 1704 "Bibliothèque Choisie" relaunched the contrast, and by revealing the significance of his critical interventions in detail, defended their merit from his adversary's reservations of rendering the implications clear at the historico-historiographical reflection level. Perizonius was able to attack some of the examples put forward, yet agreeing indirectly on the basic terms of the question:

> Toute la dispute consiste en quelques exemples particuliers, où il pretend que je me suis trompé. Mais quand je me serois trompé dans ces exemples, ce que je ne croi pas, nous sommes d'accord dans le fonds de la chose; et je [pourrais] toûjours [conclure] que *Quinte-Curse* n'a sû ce que c'étoit qu'Astronomie, que Géographie et que Chronologie; et que par consequent Il a été destitué des secours nécessaires, pour bien écrire l'Histoire d'Alexandre [...]. Enfin j'ai soûtenu qu'il avoit exprimé les choses d'une manière, qui, sentoit plûtôt son Déclamateur que son Historien[44].

43 PERIZONIUS 1703.

44 *BIBLIOTHÈQUE CHOISIE* 1704, III, p. 180. On this theme see BARNES 1938, pp. 148, 152 and on the Journal WIJNGAARDS 1986, pp. 105–106, 115–118, 155–156, 199–200.

However, the Genevan's interest in the Dutch philologist's review was not occasional, being dictated by external editing requirements, by mere exigencies of erudite divulgation, since the analysis of the work in question was coherent with his research and study programme on the antique in the light of a new, rigorous critical method which through Le Clerc's efforts had continued to become ever more refined especially through the interpretation of the sacred texts, and his influential contact with John Locke who had been introduced to him by Van Limborch. Locke, who in Tome VIII of the "Bibliothèque universelle et historique" (1688) had published the *Extract* – translated by Le Clerc himself – of *An Essay concerning Human Understanding* whose integrated edition he would have obtained only after the Author's return to his fatherland. In a letter dated July 1688, reasoning on the rules and restrictions of real "criticism", Le Clerc declared explictly the dependence of the studies – that appeared in Tome X (1688) of the same "Bibliothèque" – on the *Règles de Critique. Pour l'intelligence des Anciens Auteurs* from the "philosophy of language" contained in the 3rd Book of Lock's *Essay*[45]. In the subsequent missive of 14th October 1688, sending the abovementioned tome to the English philosopher, he confirmed such a relationship of dependence and defined its meaning from the methodological viewpoint: "[...] Vous avez examiné les principes les plus abstraits de la science que j'entreprends de traiter. Je suis

45 "Je me persuade que pour être bon critique, il faut avoir considéré les langues d'une manière bien plus philosophique que lui ne [sauraît] faire [...]. Vôtre troisième Livre m'a beaucoup confirmé en diverses pensées que j'avais eues touchant la manière d'expliquer les écrits des Anciens, et m'a ouvert l'esprit pour faire attention [...] des choses où je n'avais pas assez pensé. Vous verrez dans le X Tome de la Bibliothèque, que je dois composer moi seul, si j'ai profit, de vos idées, car il se trouve qu'il y a des livres qui me donnent occasion de m'étendre sur cette matière, ce que je fais volontiers, parce que je vois qu'elle est presque inconnue" (LE CLERC to Locke 1688, p. 494).

obligé de supposer tout ce que vous avez dit dans vôtre troisième livre comme démontré; parce que mon dessein n'est pas tant de donner les principes Métaphysiques de la Critique, que de réduire ces principes en pratique. C'est ce que j'ai tâché de faire dans le petit Discours que vous verrez dans ce volume. Voilà mon dessein [...]"[46]. On the basis of this project – an authentic synthesis of the significance of Le Clerc's method – the Author of the *Ars Critica* compared himself with the results reached by the most inured of historians and philologists on the study of antiquity. It was a lucid and concise comparison which took shape not only among the works written in Latin, full of notes, annotations and quotations, but also in a series of observations published in French, in the tomes of the "Bibliothèques" with a style that had the merit of a discursiveness capable of resolving, in simple and at the same time comprehensive terms, the theoretical, critical and at times extremely complicated thorny issues of the questions faced. Precisely in the pages dedicated to examining the *Règles de Critique. Pour l'intelligence des Anciens Auteurs* erudition and philology on one side, biblical exegesis, remonstrating rationalism and Lockian empiricism on the other, were brought together to provide a most unsatisfactory critical picture of traditional approaches. Le Clerc's *criticism*, albeit incisive and radical, is not meant to be destructive. In demolishing the arbitrary historical reconstructions, he tends, on one side, to elaborate a method of research founded on reliable principles and, on the other, to liberate historical investigation from all dogmatic and prejudicial constraints that impede a correct interpretation of the facts. The radically Pyrrhonistic developments on which the subtle conceptual analyses of certain Cartesian premises were based ended by frustrating the scholar's attempts to give a basis of certainty to historical knowledge, at the same time ascribing to it a less

46 LE CLERC to Locke 1688, p. 500.

abstract, more empirical method, founded on the instruments of criticism and susceptible of achieving results to some extent certain, albeit limited. Abandoning traditional schemes of knowledge never means for Le Clerc denying the very possibility of knowing, but rather it means opening up the way to a correct interpretation of the facts, the outcome of a positive, progressive process of approximation to authentic reality of language, far from the prejudice that distorts and transfigures the datum of fact. Le Clerc's criticism is a historico-philological criticism, and the principles which it adopts are hidden within linguistic research, in direct contact with the realistic history of the words to be analyzed and interpreted: "Les idées, qui sont attachées aux mots et aux phrases, changent si fort selon les occasions où les emploie, et les manières de parler auxquelles on les joint, qu'il n'y a point de dictionnaire qui puisse marquer toutes ces significations et tous les [changements] qui y arrivent [...]". At the same time, "[...] Chaque Auteur a des manières de parler, qui ne sont pas simplement fondées sur les maximes générales de la Langue dont il se sert, mais sur ses opinions, sur ses coûtumes, et qui coulent, pour ainsi dire, de sa manière d'étudier, et d'un certain génie qui le distingue de tous les autres". It is thus advisable to make a careful distinction between the *facts* considered in themselves and the *manner* of recounting them, comparing several historians to see on what they agree and then assuming this what as the *truth* of history. Once the facts have been ascertained, other particular aspects may be judged without running the risk of straying too far from the truth. Through the incontestable facts and the general knowledge of the "interests" and "intentions" of the different *forces* examined, at least the general *motives* that make them *act* can be recognized. A historian is not obliged, in fact, to recount everything or to affirm only that which he is perfectly sure of; he is only required not to recount anything false as though it were true, and not to assert with assurance what is uncertain[47]. The exaltation of the *critique* is translated into implementing a complex of positive procedures aiming at a reliable historical reconstruction, appositely rooted in the *language* which, inasmuch as a privileged way of access to the historical world, exalts the respect for the truth of the fact to be ascertained with a rigorously analytical discipline far removed from all empty, authoritarian superstitions.

With this particular theoretical and methodological project being thus justified, Le Clerc's interest for the themes examined controversially with Perizonius, likewise showing that it went well beyond the boundaries of the personal clash, and was destined, amid responses and counter-responses to occupy the protagonists for more than five years. The fact that this was not simply a matter of a mere personal academic dispute is well documented by contemporary reviews. In its 19th January 1705 issue, the "Journal des Sçavans" published a laudatory extract of Penizonius' *Curtius restitutus et vindicatus,* openly taking up a position against Le Clerc's principles of revision and interpretation of antiquity against which the Dutch philologist's analysis aimed at keeping the value of tradition unaltered, was opposed. Aware

47 LE CLERC 1718, pp. 327, 346, 354–356. In Book III (Chap. 11) of LOCKE (1690) 1975 [1988] we read "of the remedies of the foregoing imperfections and abuses". "For Words, especially of languages already framed, being no man's private possession. but the common measure of commerce and communication. 'tis not for any one, at pleasure, to change the stamp they are current in; nor alter the *Ideas* they are affixed to [...]. Indeed, the necessity of communication by language, brings man to an agreement in the signification of common words, within some tolerable latitude, that may serve for ordinary conversation; and so a man cannot be supposed wholly ignorant of *Ideas,* which are annexed to words by common Use, in a Language familiar to him" (LOCKE [1690], 1975 [reprint in 1988], Book III, Chapp. 10 and 11, pp. 505, 506, 509, 514, 522). Cf. VOELTZEL 1968, pp. 33–52 but espec. CANTELLI 1971, Chap. 2, pp. 31–54; CANTELLI 1972 and SINA 1978, pp. 19–33, 49–67.

of the implications of a historico-philosophical order relating to the problem of the revision of ancient historiography, the reviewer exposed seriously doubt on its pedagogical value from the pages of the *Ars Critica,* observing conclusively that:

> Au reste, M. Perizonius n'est pas de ceux qui croyent que la Critique est un art dangereux; au contraire il prétend qu'il n' y a rien de plus utile dans la République des Lettres, qu'une judicieuse et exacte Critique; mais il veut qu'elle soit faite avec discennement, et par d'habiles gens. Il convient que M. Le Clerc a beaucoup d'habileté, mais il ne [saurait], dit-il, souffrir sa vanité, et l'orgueil qu'il fait [paraître] dans les [jugements] qu'il porte sur les écrits des meilleurs Auteurs, sans épargner même les Pères de l'Eglise[48].

From the Historica "de Singularibus" to the Philosophical History

Through Perizonius' participation, the discussion on the possibilities of knowledge in the historical field took on the form of a *querelle* between opposing positions and experiences, tending now to impair that cultural unity that the European Republic of letters had thitherto demonstrated and vaunted. And yet such a contrast was in fact able to prove schematic. The polemic had, in fact, shown that those involved in the dialogue were nearer than they realised, devoted as they all were to preserving the value of historic knowledge from absolute Pyrrhonism, non-critical and indifferent to the peculiarity of the facts and their evidence. On several accounts Perizonius showed he had received the methodological inheritance of Bayle and Le Clerc's

48 *Journal des Sçavans* , 1705, XXXIII, 58. See also *Acta Eruditorum* 1704, V, pp. 216–221. On this Journals cf. Barnes 1938, p. 194 and Lomonaco 1990, p. 235.

constructive critical work. The correct response to the latter's theses did not in fact leave the question basically unanswered regarding the value to be attributed to the techniques to be employed in historiography and tradition as a source of historical knowledge of the past. For him too the real problem of historiographic investigation is that of the testimonies which history is made of. If reference is continually made to events, it is, however the judgement about the reliability of the sources that allows a legitimate reconstruction of the past that, rather than presenting itself immediately to the historian, is always the result of a process of critical analysis of the relative testimonies. Thus the fact taken in itself is not essential, but rather the *relationship* between the fact and the testimonies that introduce it. The reading and study of traditional historical sources attracted the critical commitment about Roman history, a history incapable of being converted into universal history, precisely because of its continuous self-comparison with facts and documents. The study of antiquity, inasmuch as research and analysis of documents, is not conducive towards constructing an exhalted perfect ideal model, and to a periodization from universal history, but rather to gathering the various testimonies of the *exemplum,* and to pluralizing the same sample examined. Supported by the *fides historica,* that is to say by the confidence of being able to define the conditions of ascertaining *truth* the study of the individual fact obliges the historian to avoid every abstract conceptual superimposition, but to safeguard the rules of the *critique* realistically, by conferring special importance on philological work, operating as an ever more aware component of theoretical-historiographical discourse, as the informant of the relationship between tradition and criticism, between *knowledge* of the past and *science* of history. It was this that was the progressive affirmation of updated critical discourse, aimed at founding a specific *logic* of historical knowledge, to react against the *impasse* brought about by the affirmation of absolute mathematical-type *evidence* and by the consequent sceptical negation of every form of certainty, according to theoretical-historiographical schemes and myths of dogmatic Cartesianism especially of a Malebranchian tone, in which a great part of Dutch culture of the 17th century had taken refuge[49].

With the Perizonius-Le Clerc polemic in Holland, the seventeenth-century *querelle* regarding ancient history and its sources may be said to be over. However, when the learned philologist breaks with the positions of Bayle and the Genevan critic, and shows himself aware of such a rupture at the historico-historiographical organization level, he is in the presence of a more comprehensive awareness that is not wrapped up in a sterile counterposition of theses (certainty and utility of history vs uncertainty and uselessness of history). Perizonius brings to completion earlier critical experiences, summing up in himself the instances, the exigencies of erudition and *historica* through polemical, but not modern, references to historiography and philosophy.

Philology and antiquity studies enjoying considerable authority from the end of the seventeenth century, thanks above all to the work of the Maurini, of the Jansenists and then the erudite Italians (Muratori and Maffei, in particular), had reached a crisis after the early decades of the 18th century, proving to be an expression only of puritanical trends of primitive Christianity, yet neutral and pedantic from every other viewpoint. Erudite research, nurtured prevalently by historico-juridical investigation, was unable of itself to provide an effective basis for the struggle against the subversive action of doubt. The theoretical 'strong' model – though subject to elaborate critical revision – still remained basically the Cartesian one that was neither capable or desirous of providing a *logic* for historical knowledge as an acceptable theoretical solution. Its vaunted indifference towards

49 Cf. LOMONACO 1990, Chap. 1, p. 60 and notes.

philological thoroughness and exalted *impartiality* also responded in many cases to old defence schemes of the ancient Reason of State. Behind such impartiality everything that the scientific revolution had attempted to demolish could be accepted: the idea of considerable immobility of the human condition, respect for and acceptance of the past and present sanctioned by the action of perennial providentialism with the consequent rejection of the *new*[50]. Of the seventeenth century Reason of State it was Pyrrhonism no less that basically revealed the deep crisis as the causal link between facts and their motives, and now being questioned had undermined the necessary traditional correspondence between intuition and events, and had obscured divine intentions themselves, thus re-dimensioning providentialism, the idea, that is to say, of predicted and guided history. The doubt exerted on the link between actions and aims, on the finalistic and providentialistic aspect of acting, was not resolved, therefore, only in a negation of the *fides historica,* since it directly affected the problem of the possible reconstruction of the *sense* of the history of man who returned hence to be responsible from the ethico-religious viewpoint. Under the threat of Pyrrhonism, history ceased to be an interpretation of human escatological destinies and became an *exact* and *certain* narration of facts, enriched by trustworthy testimonies, by sure unquestionable documents. Besides mystifying the historian's language, the wave of polemics was also destined to enhance its theoretical depth by forcing it through methodical doubt to ascertain the complex relationship between *truth* and *certainty*. Seen from such a viewpoint Pyrrhonism and erudition appeared identical, as prisoners of the same limit in their final convergence in a conception of history which deals *de singularibus,*but not basically devoid

50 On this point BERTELLI 1955. For the relationship between Maffei and Brenkman cf. MOMIGLIANO (1962) 1966, I, pp. 179–196 and for the relationship between Perizonio-Brenkman cf. STOLTE 1981, pp. 7–9, 47, 92, 114, 126, 128.

of the characteristics of the *ars* attributed to it by the humanistic school[51].

In the central decades of the eighteenth century subversive criticism of Pyrrhonism was to lose a great part of its incisiveness, since it already dealt with overcoming the converging conclusions of erudition and doubt involved in solving the problem – namely that of the direction and destiny of human history – which was insoluble as much within the ambit of Cartesianism as within that of anti-Cartesianism. To provide a possible solution to this problem, Enlightenment historiography was then obliged to intervene, which first defined the limits of an all-retrospective erudition, thereby incapable of recognising the dynamic action of the *new*, and later levelled an attack against Pyrrhonism the equal and opposite incapacity to that of erudition – of which it was a symbolic expression – of understanding the authentic meaning of the being of modern man in history, in a history that he himself is called on to produce. A new and different synthesis came into being which going beyond the "intrigues", "powers" and "calculations" of the ancient Reason of State, was rooted in action and praxis, accompanied by a completely new trust in the self-governing capacities of man in the world which rather than continue to investigate among insignificant details now needed to change. It was the new *philosophical* orientation of eighteenth-century historiography, from Vico to Montesquieu and Voltaire, from Hume to Robertson, up to Winckelmann and Gibbon, destined to elaborate a new combination between 'philosophical history' and the antiquity method of erudition and philosophy. These historian-philosophers posed problems relating to the present, as well as questions re-

51 This is G. Giarrizzo's interpretation. He rightly stresses the original historiographic synthesis of the eighteenth century. The advance beyond historical Pyrrhonism is dealt with in the magisterial but outdated account given by Hazard (GIARRIZZO 1954, pp. 51ff. and GIARRIZZO [1962] 1981, pp. 9–51).

garding the comprehensive developments of the human race of such proportions that the *exactness* of the details that had been painstakingly achieved and extolled by seventeenth-century erudition might now appear gratuitous or at any rate irrelevant. The idea of *civilisation* became, instead, the main theme, the favourite objective of the task of history, art, religion and customs, thitherto specialised areas of antiquary commitment, now became permeated and dominated by the interests of eighteenth-century historian-philosophers[52]. Thus it came about that Perizonius' analysis of sources as essential vehicles of information and historical knowledge was barely touched upon by the new antiquity studies of the eighteenth century. Other authors as well as other problems rendered the theory developed by the main representative of late-seventeenth-century obsolete Dutch culture, archiving their works away once and for all. It was necessary to await the new cultural climate that opened from the nineteenth century for the complex Perizonian philological criticism to be re-appraised by the rediscovery that Niebuhr's genius had made of it at the beginning of the nineteenth century[53].

52 On the theoretical and methodological change in enlightenment historiography see MOMIGLIANO's classical essays (1950) 1984, pp. 3–45 and (1958) 1984, pp. 86–88; HAY (1977) 1981, espec. Chapp. 7–8, pp. 141–195 with particular attention to the AngloSaxon culture. Above all see SARTORI 1980. R. Ajello's observations provide an interesting account of the themes relating to the cultural situation in Naples and Italy in general during the eighteenth century (AJELLO 1988, pp. 39–60).

53 In 1739 J.A. ERNESTI observed that "Perizonii animadversions [...] harum litterarum studiosis valde necessaries putamus" but his work was published after thirty years (1771) by TH. CH.HARLES: cf. MOMIGLIANO (1957) 1960, pp. 72, 73, notes.

CHAPTER IV

Sovereignty and Roman Law in Gerard Noodt: "Dissertatio" of 1699

Jurist and Historian of Law, Noodt rendered his own picture of theoretical-historiographic references more complicated through his own critical insight by integrating the lesson of modern ius-naturalism therein. In his *Dissertatio de religione ab imperio iure gentium libera* (1706) he examined the "civilis societas" characteristics, by identifying their origin "non [in] religionem et Dei cultum" but through the need for security generated by fear of abuse. "Humanae metus iniuriae" is the mark of the pre-social condition. Just as the ecclesiastical society, so too the state order is not a gift of *natura*, it is not born of man's natural tendency towards society, from his *appetitus societatis*, in keeping with Grotius'well-known formula (*De iure belli ac pacis*, *Prol.*, § 6). Sociability on the contrary, must be traced back to the human desire to avoid the dangerous state of nature, where "nondum inventis legibus, nec constituto civili iure, nulli fas est mortali, sententiam ferre de Deo, deque eius cultu; et contumacem bello, vi, armis, coercere"[1]. In this regard, in the commentary notes to his

1 NOODT (1706) 1999, p. 203. After BURMANNUS 1738, pp. 249–253 and BOELES 1878–1889, II, pp. 279–284 see FRIJHOFF 1981, pp. 107ff., AHSMANN-FEENSTRA 1984, pp. 176ff. and VAN DEN BERG 1998, pp. 229–233. About the "Dutch Legal scholarship between Humanism and Enlightenment" he observes that "Noodt played a crucial role in this development. His address on the freedom of religion (1706) assured him a place in the history of Enlightenment and making of a legal the-

translation (1707) of the *Dissertatio,* Jean Barbeyrac emphasises the closeness of Noodt's theses to Pufendorf's[2] that lead to an indirect comparison with another great maestro of 17th century European culture, Thomas Hobbes. For a scholar of the *scientia iuris* between the 17th and 18th centuries, the work of the English philosopher, which had been banned by the Dutch authorities in 1674 (together with Spinoza's *Tractatus theologico-politicus*), exerted an influence, a constant force of attraction that did not necessitate making them explicit. Pufendorf's *De iure naturae et gentium* had made wide use of Hobbes' thought, re-proposing the theme of the reciprocal fear for the origin of the great lasting societies. The ancient "patresfamilias" rejected natural freedom and founded civil societies. The main reason for this decision was to be referred to the wish to be defended from those evils "quae homini ab homine imminent"[3]. In keeping with Hobbes' text (*De Cive*, I, 2), this consideration developed, however, on the religious-ethical level with somewhat different outcomes from those to be identified in the English philosopher's reflection. In his *De habitu religionis christianae ad vitam civilem* (1687) Pufendorf examined the delicate transition from the state of nature to the civil one in order to define, without hesitation, the character of the religious experience in the State. When the "patresfamilias" rejected natural freedom to give life to the

---

ory of human rights, but up to now it has been seen too much in isolation. A detailed analysis of Noodt's work places it in context and allows for an assessment of his contribution to the development of civil law as well as to Roman law scholarship" (VAN DEN BERG 1998, V).

2 BARBEYRAC 1731, I, p. 155, note.

3 So PUFENDORF (1672) 1759, Book VII, Chap.1, §VII. II, pp. 119, 120–121. "Tra la visione hobbesiana e quella pufendorfiana [...] vi è una convergenza di fondo che va colta al di là della facile ed estrinseca contrapposizione tra un Hobbes che sostiene che lo stato di natura è uno stato di guerra e un Pufendorf che sostiene, al contrario, che lo stato di natura è uno stato di pace" (PALLADINI 1990, p. 148). For an up- to date information cf. LOMONACO 1999, pp. 5 ff. and BURGIO 2001.

States, they did not in the religious setting subject their own will to the sovereign's, to whom they conceded the use of force and property, in order to achieve "genuinum civitatum finem" and to guarantee "securitatem civium"[4].

In Noodt the definition of the state of nature presupposed the rejection of Hobbes' conclusions, that aimed at identifying in the authoritative law of the absolute state the only guarantee for preserving individual life. For the Dutch jurist the generative process of existence in society, set in motion by the *fear*, from the passionate experiences of men, does not produce conflicts but a need for order. The *ordo civilis* is not the negation of natural liberties; it is not born – as it is for Hobbes – with the purpose of neutralizing religious conscience and eliminating the scission between *private opinion* of individuals and the *public* one of the citizens:

> Hunc ob oculos habent qui in civitatem consentiunt [...]; nec dubium; quin, ut habeant, velint, principi licere cuncta sine quibus is omnino obtineri nequeat. Ita quidquid se huc fert, omnibus bonum, quidquid inde recedit, omnibus malum videri debet. Alterum imperat princeps, alterum vetat[5].

In the Holland of Noodt's day, an interesting source of the anti-Hobbesian polemic in function of the re-definition of *conscience* is Jean Le Clerc's reflection. In recommending Willem van der Muelen's *Dissertatio de sanctitate summi imperii civilis* (1689) the reviewer of the "Bibliothèque universelle et historique" contested Hobbes' definition of *conscience*, observing:

> Il n'y a rien de plus absurde, que la doctrine de Hobbes, qui a enseigné que c'est une erreur opposée au bien de la societé, que de croire *que ce qu'un sujet fait contre sa conscience est un peché* [...]. L'homme aiant l'idée des

4 PUFENDORF 1687, p. 17. On this see BUCKLE 1991, pp. 53–124.
5 NOODT (1706) 1999, p. 204. For this work – after HUUSSEN 1989, pp. 122–123 – cf. VAN EIJNATTEN 1999.

> vertus et des vices, et sachant les distinguer, il juge de la justice, et de l'injustice, sans attendre la décision d'un souverain [...]. Il est donc faux qu'on sujet ne peche pas contre sa conscience, lors qu'il obeït à un prince qui lui commande des choses contraires à la droite raison.

Such recognition rested on the awareness of the inevitable differences between liberty of action in civil life and the ethico-religious exigencies, functional to the "salut de l'âme"[6].

Also for Noodt the State does not come into being with the task of eliminating all the traces of the state of nature but proposes to confer stability and security on all its achievements. Thus, the passage from natural to civil life creates new relationships only from the formal point of view. On the other hand it consolidates the validity of the inalienable natural rights that the sovereign does not have the power to suppress. If in the state of nature no individual is attributed the right to judge God and religion, it is not lawful to assign "plus principi civili iure, quam singulis naturae lege concedatur". Released from scholastic theology and ethics, rational natural law justified sovereign power, at the same time limiting its action within a religious setting. Here the *princeps* is equal to all other men, he has the same rights and duties as they have, nor can he claim the power never conferred on him, of being concerned with the saving of the soul. The public *auctoritas* goes beyond the limits of the *mandate*, when it claims it is able to prescribe by law the contents of individual religious sentiment. If a magistrate considers it lawful to impose a religious faith and practice, he extends his own right illegally, annihilating the private life of his subjects like a tyrant:

6 BIBLIOTHÈQUE UNIVERSELLE ET HISTORIQUE 1689, XIII, pp. 149, 150–151, 153. On van der Muelen's *Dissertatio* cf. BLOM 1989 and on natural law, civil society and sovereignty BLOM 1995, pp. 251–260. On van der Muelen Grotius' commentator mentioned by Vico cf. PIRO 2000. For the *Dissertatio* 1689 cf. now CLERICI 2007, pp. 175–196 but also pp. 147ff.

> Sic existimo [...] magnam esse atque excellentem principis in civilibus negotiis auctoritatem; sed in religione non supra caeteros haberi; ac si ei praescribat regulam quam et poenis adversus contumaces sanciat; divini, id est, alieni, rem imperii attingere; nec tantum nihil magnopere praestare, sed ne a tyrannide quidem excusari posse[7].

On the politico-juridical level, the polemic against tyranny had already been advanced by Noodt in his dissertation *De iure summi imperii et Lege Regia*, declaimed in 1699, on occasion of the termination of his first Rectorship of the University of Leyden. Re-published in 1706, the first edition in Latin underwent translations into French (1707, 1714, 1731, 1775), into English (1708, 1781) and into Dutch (1716, 1784)[8]. His presence in the political and cultural debate at the beginning of the 18th century was favoured above all by Jean Barbeyrac's French translation in 1707 and witnessed by the detailed reviews that appeared in the "Journal des Sçavans" and in the "Bibliothèque choisie"[9]. The work documents the level of maturity reached by the juridical and political thought of the author in the 17th–18th century debate on the origin and the competencies of *summa potestas*. Noodt was writing at a particularly dramatic historical moment for Dutch society which, in the years of William III of Orange (1689–1702), had witnessed the outbreak of the War of Spanish Succession and the alliance with England against the monarchical absolutism of the France of Louis XIV. The editors of the "Journal Littéraire" would have made reference to this historico-political situation and to Noodt's *Dissertatio* in 1713 by recognising the author's original and courageous initiative of: "Un pareil

7 NOODT (1706) 1999, pp. 203, 206.

8 NOODT (1699) 1724, I, pp. 623–633. After AHSMANN-FEENSTRA 1984, pp. 436ff. – see VAN DEN BERG 1988, pp. 191–206 and LOMONACO 1990, pp. 28ff.

9 Cf. *JOURNAL DES SÇAVANS* 1701, XXIX, pp. 191–194; *BIBLIOTHÈQUE CHOISIE* 1705, VII, 228–255 (on second édition of 1699 *Dissertatio* published in NOODT 1705).

Discours ne pouvait guéres manquer de déplaire à ce prince [Guillaume III], mais malgré tout cela M. *Noodt* ne voulut pas cacher ni déguiser ses véritables sentiments"[10].

The style of the 1699 *Dissertatio* and the critical slant of the argumentations proposed rule out the idea that the author wishes to follow the classical-style and celebrative scheme of an academic work. Its priority interest is to reflect on the origin and limits of *summa potestas*, denouncing its degeneration into tyranny, into an arbitrary power of the individual who exercises it with force at the expense of his subjects and to satisfy his own ambitions. If in the tyrannical government the obligation does not have any legal foundation, in the *auctoritas* of a good and just prince it is the government of the laws to guarantee the order, peace and security for all his subjects:

> Cum his [principi et tyranno] nihil aeque contrarium sub hominis aestimationem cadere possit. Alter enim volentibus, alter invitis imperat. Alter reipublicae, alter sibi consulit. Alter legibus servit, alter insultat. Alter a cuiusque vita, libertate, bonis, tamquam a rebus sacris, manus, oculos, mentemque abstinet. Alter ea res sui iuris atque arbitrii esse opinatur[11].

In dwelling on the problem of the *princeps*-subjects relationships, with his original critical sensitivity Noodt analysed the themes of *auctoritas* and of *obligatio ex consensu*. In this way he traced back to complex points of classical-humanistic political philosophy of clear Aristotelian ascendancy the themes of the origin and legitimacy of political action, and those related to the techniques of the formation and conservation of sovereign power, mediating them with interpretation modules of Stoic origin, that were well tried and widespread throughout 17th cen-

10 So in *JOURNAL LITTÉRAIRE* 1713, I, II, p. 262 (on NOODT 1713). For this Journal see GORI 1972, pp. 73–74ff. and the important studies in 1986, *Documentatieblad 18e Eeuwm*, 18, pp. 117ff. Cf. also SGARD 1991, II, pp. 759ff.

11 NOODT (1699) 1724, I, p. 623a.

tury Leyden culture[12]. In the first part of the 1699 *Dissertatio*, the theory of political obligation rested on the *auctoritas* of the *lex naturalis*, in keeping with typical positions of modern iusnaturalism. The abstract and hypothetical *state of nature* of the theologians is enriched in Noodt with realistic contents, with possible pacific and integral human relationships, as being founded on the natural law of liberty and equality, binding man as a rational being even prior to his being a citizen. The *lex naturae* is in fact, a rule wished for by God, to whom without exception are subject "magistratus et subditi, servi et domini", categories which "natura [...] ignorat", since "tantum homines fecit, omnes liberos, omnes pari conditione"[13]. If the characteristics and aims of nature refer to God's wise action, the modern formulation of Noodt's iusnaturalism must nevertheless be stressed. Divine right is no longer set in contrast against the natural one since the *ordo naturalis* is the place in which the divine will is manifested; it is the very divine order translated into human forms of rational law. Inevitable and inviolable because wished for by God, the *lex naturalis* is such only for the man who knows it *naturally*, through his rational faculty, as a necessary rule, "quam Dei providentia ad humani generis salutem iussit". Noodt's iusnaturalism does not ask the state power to establish new conditions for life. It only wants those of civil life to be made stable and secure through the institution of an *auctoritas* capable of having natural law and the principles of human reason respected against violence and the will of the tyrannical government that exacerbates the shortcomings of the natural condition. The State is not a reality distinct from the individuals who have instituted it but is founded on the rights of which each man is proprietor by *nature*. Thus, his action, taken by force and conquest, in order to be legitimate must be ruled by *consensus* accorded with the *pactum*:

12 Cf. DIBON 1954, pp. 59–64 and DIBON 1990, espec. pp. 3–311.
13 NOODT (1699) 1724, I, p. 624b.

"Sed homines, cum initio liberi essent nati, ipsique suae iudices utilitatis constituti, demum principem sua voluntate ac pactione invenisse; [...] hunc tamen non publicae decoctorem utilitatis, sed custodem rectoremque constituisse". Consensual agreement ratifies the participation of the individuals contracting in the social life, the voluntary subordination of their actions to the natural law, the assumption and purpose of the *pact.* The choice of guaranteeing through consensus a juridical foundation on the origin of the sovereignty and the life of the subjects imposes revoking every form of divine legitimization of civil authority. It thus obliges abandoning the traditional definition of the State as *Dei praeceptum*, and reacting to the myth of the absolutism of divine right, that appeared as consecration of the personal and arbitrary wish of the sovereign[14]. Thus, Noodt's 1699 and 1706 *Dissertationes* will be judged as "deux Discours séditieux" by the compilers of the "Mémoires pour l'Histoire des Sciences et des Beaux Arts", Trévoux's well-known periodical that came into being at the beginning of the eighteenth century as response of the Jesuits'cultural policy towards the Jansenistic offensive and modern rationalism. The anonymous signalling of the French edition of the *Dissertationes*, edited by Barbeyrac in 1707, condemned the "faux raisonnements du Sieur Noodt" on the origin and limits of sovereignty, since "il y a contradiction à ce que la puissance souveraine ne soit pas souveraine, mais restreinte et

14 NOODT (1699) 1724, I, pp. 626b, 625b. "[...] Reges, aut Principes, aut quocumque tandem titulo summi honos Magistratus eminet, primo de coelo demissos esse; non hominum placito et consensu electos? An non res loquitur, unam esse naturalem rationem, illam veram ac divinam, quae prima hominem homini conjunxit, atque eam societatem, quia sine legibus et imperiis haberi nequit, legibus atque imperiis firmari iussit? Quid ni igitur a Deo constitui aut mutari dicantur imperia quae ad hominibus ad tuendam societatem ratione, id est, divina voluntate, aut constituuntur aut abrogantur" (NOODT [1699] 1724, I, pp. 624a–b). On Noodt's natural law see DONAHUE 1985, pp. 609–629.

bornée". Starting out from this observation, the reviewer did not hesitate, then, to define "esprits orgueilleux et inquiets" all those disposed towards legitimising the right to subvert the constituted sovereign power. The wise man who listens to reason and believes in God remains subject of the State, because he understands "que chaque particulier en entrant dans la societé civile dépose sa propre volonté, et que toute autorité legitime vient d'en haut". If Noodt's definition of sovereignty rested on the "consentement des hommes", the Jesuit-reviewer undertook to demonstrate its inconsistency. The argumentation of the Dutch jurist risked extending the confines of human nature, by indirectly confirming the temporal power of the Church and the legitimate divine right of the *princeps*, the correct, *natural* dependence of *summa potestas* by the will of God: "Le pouvoir souverain, soit qu'il reside en la personne d'un prince ou dans un Sénat, est fondé sur la loi naturelle, qui émane de Dieu, et par-là il vient originairement du ciel"[15].

In the 1699 *Dissertatio* the reference to the history of the law proved functional to the need to investigate contemporary civil life and, in particular, the characteristics of sovereign power. In keeping with the political debate of his time, Noodt dialogued above all with Grotius, favoured by the common cultural matrix and by a direct knowledge of the writings of the jurist of Delft. The premises of Noodt's reflection had found a secure point of reference in the pages of the *De iure belli ac pacis*. At the theoretical and historiographical level however the work aroused considerable perplexity for the application of the definition of *summa potestas* to the problem posed with urgency by modern iusnaturalism: whether in fact absolute power encounters a limit in natural law and in the subjects' will. A theme, this latter one, of great currency in the Holland from the latter half of the 17th

15 *MÉMOIRES POUR L'HISTOIRE DES SCIENCES ET DES BEAUX ARTS* 1709, pp. 778, 779, 780. On this Journal cf. SGARD 1991, II, pp. 805–816.

century, since, the assassination in 1672 of the Gran Pensionnaire, Jon de Witt, favoured the ascendancy of William III of Orange. The new policy of the Statolderat would also have influenced Noodt's native town. In the province of Gelderland, to which Nijmegen belonged, the *regeringsreglement*, imposed in 1675, had been contested by father Peter and by those who denounced Orangist absolutism. The ordinance in fact, made the election of the magistrates dependent on the will of the *princeps*, thereby annihilating the republican liberties and the entire democratic life of the city[16].

Sensitive to the motives dominating the juridical and political debate of his times, in Book I of his *De iure* Grotius had defined sovereign power (*summa potestas*) as that whose acts are independent of every other power and such as not to be able to be annulled "voluntatis humanae arbitrio". He had also distinguished its *subiectum* into *commune* (the *civitas*, *coetus perfectus*) and into *proprium* which is one or more persons, according to the laws and customs of every action: in a word, the Sovereign. From these definitions of principle there derived consequences relevant for the solution of the *obligatio ex consensu* and the detection of the conditions of the sovereign *potestas*. To the problem whether it is lawful for a people to alienate its own liberty from the *princeps* the jurist from Delft had replied in the affirmative, rejecting the *opinion* of one who claims that the *summa potestas* belongs "ubique et sine exceptione" to the people, considered in possession of the illegal king's right to "coercere et punire" the *imperium*. The *pactum subiectionis* rendered absolute the transfer of *auctoritas* to the sovereign who acquired it "iure pleno proprieta-

16 See HARTOG 1976–1977 and – with regard to the political contrasts in Nijmegen during the years of the Republic of Regents (1702–1747) – ISRAEL 1995, pp. 959ff., 962–963. This latter mentions Noodt's work *Diocletianus et Maximianus* (1704), his criticism of Willelm III and his methods, which had caused the degeneration of criminality: on 1706 *Dissertatio* cf. 674. In general see also SCHILLING 1984.

tis", administering it freely as his own patrimony. In documenting his theses, he then made reference to the ancient law to observe that, "ut et ex lege hebraea et romana apparet", every man could choose to remain "in privatam servitutem". Thus, also a free people decided – "sui iuris" – to subject itself to one or two persons, transferring to them the right to govern, without reserving any prerogative for itself. And among the reasons that induced to alienate the sovereignty, were emphasised those dictated by the "periculum vitae", by the impossibility of finding other means for the conservation, "aut quia inopia pressus aliter habere non potest copiam unde se sustentet". The voluntary loss of a part of natural liberty does not alter the *pactum subiectionis* that can have any kind of content whatsoever, and conserve its validity and obligatoriness. And all that, in virtue of Grotius' well-known maxim "iuris naturae est stare pactis" that excludes any possible discussion of the conditions of the contract's validity. The value of the *pactum* cannot depend on the conditions fixed in the contract nor influence the function of the *summa potestas* that has in itself a juridical title of absolute value. Also in the hypothesis of the total loss of liberty (by consensus or also by way of penalty, "ex publico delicto"), the servitude of a people would prove "per se perpetua", despite the succession of generations: "Populi servitus per se perpetua est, quia successio partium non impedit quo minus unus sit populus". Isolated and conditioned by the rule of the *princeps*, the conscience of the *subditus* is obliged to become annulled. Albeit accepting the apostolic rule ("oboedire oportet Deo magis quam hominibus") to reaffirm that a command contrary to "naturali iuri aut divinis praeceptis" is illegal, Grotius, however, had immediately specified that in any case it is not lawful to resist public authority. The eventual *iniuriae* must be tolerated, because it is impossible to claim the *ius naturale* also when the latter has been broken by the positive law[17].

In referring to the current political situation, Noodt put forward reservations that were in no way rhetorical against the outcomes of Grotius' reflection, that was disposed to justifying absolutism for its "natural" origin and the alienation of individual liberty that belongs to the sphere of civil rights bound to *summa potestas*. With explicit reference to the quotations indicated in the *De iure*, the disciple of Johann Schulting and Johann Georg Graeve stated that the power of a man could not be unlimited. Also at the origin of the relationship between a master and his slave there is a consensual relationship, a *pact* founded on the respect for reciprocal usefulness and trust: "Quod si non vi, sed fide, constat servitus, [...] non ad solius domini utilitatem spectat servitus, etiam servo prodest; quia, quod pacti proprium est, uterque se respexit, cum in pactionem consensit"[18].

To the value of individual religious conscience, claimed in the 1706 *Dissertatio*, there corresponds, in the politico-juridical ambit, the affirmation of the free existence of the citizens reflected in the modern theory of the *pactum societatis*. The latter being understood as the regulating principle and exigency of human reason, Noodt undertook to redefine the contents and conditions for the existence of sovereignty. If the juridical foundation of the State is in *consensus*, the *summa potestas* ceases to be a private possession of the sovereign. It appears instead as a power to be exercised to guarantee the pacific existence and common good to all those contracting the *pactum*. Unlike tyr-

17 GROTIUS 1680, Book I, Chap. 3, pp. 50ff., 59, 60, 68; Book II, Chap. 5, p. 186; Book I, Chap. 4, pp. 88–103. On the theme – after DEL VECCHIO 1957, pp. 18–22 – see TODESCAN 1991, pp. 90–100 for the "ideological and methodological variations". Cf. also DE SANCTIS (1994) 1996, pp. 27–53.

18 NOODT (1699) 1724, I, p. 627b.

anny, civil power acquires legitimacy from the *pactum societatis* that creates rights and duties both for the rulers as well as for the ruled. Whoever has turned a man into his own slave, in transgressing the natural law of liberty and equality acts as a tyrant moved by the will of his violence, far removed from reason and from the right of the peoples: "Non hoc ratio appellet aut servitutis, aut dominii ius, magis insaniam dixerit, quam hominum arrogantia fecit, ius gentium quo ea comparata sunt, ignorat". Without consensus, the power of a prince who inflicts "ad totius populi, aut maioris partis laesionem" is a despotic, *ipso facto* illegitimate power "humani generis hostem". He institutes relationships of war, authorizing the active "resistance" of the subjects not indulging "belli metu, et otii dulcedine"[19]. The aim was to denounce the *auctoritas* of sovereign power as *iniuria* if not supported by the consensus of the people and if exonerated from the observance of the laws, the guarantee of stability and certainty of sovereign right. The conferring of *summa potestas* could occur on certain conditions, those required by the natural right that the future sovereign will have to respect in order not to be dismissed. From the juridical viewpoint, the form of transmission of the *potestas* took shape, in fact, as a *concessio imperii*, revocable whenever the appointed *princeps* had eluded the limits agreed upon. For Noodt this is an act of faith in the *potestas* of the law that in the 1699 *Dissertatio* rests on the authority of ancient Roman law, the authentic expression of the Dutch jurist's cultural formation. Traversed by a fundamentally humanistic inspiration, Noodt's thought is nurtured on a prevalent interest for the law which is born from the study of Roman Classical culture[20]. To *scientia iuris* he united a profound knowledge of an-

19 NOODT (1699) 1724, I, pp. 627a, 633a.

20 Van den Bergh observes in Noodt and in his 1699 *Dissertatio* a "combined critical potential of humanistic philology and natural law rationalism" (VAN DEN BERGH 1988, pp. 132, 191–206). Veen has expressed his reservations about the far too generic and generalised analysis, which

cient literature and history, deserving the nickname of the "Cuiacio of Holland" for his pledge to bring back within the limits of an equilibrated historical-critical analysis the excesses of *Emblemata Triboniana* research. It was an undertaking which, without ever obstructing his ordinary activities, would be translated into a patient and careful study of the *Corpus Iuris*[21] (repeatedly broken off and taken up again over many years). To this activity he was in fact, to dedicate his mature philological-juridical work, winning fame and prestige in the *république des lettres*. But Noodt's interest in ancient law proved extraneous to any and every erudite or antiquarian purpose, aimed at learning juridical facts "non auctoritatem, sed rationem"[22]. In his 1699 *Dissertatio* the Roman model is not referred to in order to be imitated or re-proposed according to the schemes of traditional rhetoric. The history of Roman law is judged as a collection of experiences and facts to be subjected to the reflection of the jurist-historian. To him Ancient Rome offers the certain and exemplary image of a State founded on the virtue of laws verifiable in a concrete historical situation. Expert connoisseur of codes and pandects, the historian of law is, at the same time, the jurist who investigates into man and his laws that regulate actions in civil life. He is the genial interpreter who through his critical skill and ability of synthesis renders his historico-philological education

are contained in the review published in "Rechtsgeleerd Magazijn Themis", 1989, pp. 365–366. Noodt has been associated to " 'Elegant' or 'Antiquarian' School of Roman Law" by FEENSTRA-WAAL 1975, p. 11. Cf. also VAN DEN BERGH 2002, pp. 6ff., 13ff., 37ff., 46ff., 52–55ff., 66ff., 83ff., 101ff., 111ff., 123ff., 133ff., 141ff.

21 See PALAZZINI FINETTI 1953, pp. 333–335 but also pp. 241–242, 301, 350, 380, 390, 440.

22 NOODT (1699) 1724, I, p. 628a. "Cum enim de iure Imperii disputamus, non lex huius minoris civitatis quaestioni est; sed illius maioris quae cum sole fines metitur. Si tamen cui placet, ad civile ius provocare, etsi initio nolui, etiam huc me demittam, neque enim puto, hoc egisse Ulpianum [...]" (NOODT [1699] 1724, I, p. 628a).

of humanistic matrix sensitive to the political experiences of the present, to the values of modern *iurisprudentia* and legislation. Thus in Noodt, the admiration for the ancient model was translated into the examination of a privileged epoch and of a briefer time span: that imperial post-Augustan one of more marked analogies with the current politico-cultural context. To the historical reflection of juridical interest an interesting anti-dogmatic force could be guaranteed by the use of modern *non-literary evidence*. Thus, the guiding thread of Noodt's 1699 *Dissertatio*, rendered explicit by its very title, was the anti-absolutist interpretation of the Roman *Lex Regia de imperio Vespasiani*[23]. With Grotius' interpretation of *summa potestas* under discussion, Noodt showed the outcomes of the polemic at the juridical and historiographical level[24]. He referred to ancient Roman law, examining the *lex* in question through a detailed consultation of ancient documents and modern erudition. More especially he activated a comparison with the more significant achievements of modern juridical philology, from Jean Coras to François Connan, from Denis Godefroy to Iohannes Fredericus Gronovius, "vir summus, quem honoris causa appello [...], et huius Academiae, et totius literati orbis ingens atque immortale decus". The reference was to Gronovius'*Oratio de lege regia* (1671), eulogised for opportunely defending the historicity of the *lex*[25]. But Noodt's reflection took its origin from the theses of Jacques Cujas who

23 Regarding the presence of these themes in the Dutch historical-juridical culture at the end of the seventeenth century see *supra*, Chapp. 1, 3 and LOMONACO 1990.

24 GROTIUS 1680, Book I, Chap. 3, p. 63.

25 NOODT (1699) 1724, I, p. 629a. "Unum tantum addam, neque a Clarissimo illo Viro, neque ab aliis traditum, quod qualecumque fuerit Senatusconsultum, quod Augustum legibus solvit; non illo delatum ei imperium fuit" (NOODT [1699] 1724, I, p. 629a–b). In Leyden Noodt was able to hear Gronovius' public lessons from 1669 onwards (see VAN DEN BERGH 1988, p. 23). On Gronovius'*Oratio* cf. *supra*, Chap. 1 and LOMONACO 1988.

in the *Observationum et emendationum libri XXVIII* (1556–1558) had contested the value of a general principle of the Ulpian formula (*D.*,1, 3, 31): "Princeps legibus solutus est; Augusta autem licet legibus soluta non est, princeps tamen eadem illi privilegia tribuunt quae ipsi habent"[26]. To establish whether the *princeps* is *legibus solutus*, means investigating the basis and legitimacy of *summa potestas*. Far from recognizing the justification of an absolute power in the Ulpian maxim, Noodt tried to define its contents and limits. Inspired by the ancient source, his anti-absolutism found strong support in the *restrictiva legibus* interpretation of the *potestas* of the *princeps*. The application of the Ulpian maxim referred only to certain special provisions of private law, established by the *Lex Iulia et Papia Poppaea*, two laws emanated by Augustus in 18 and in 9 B.C. to regulate testamentary successions. In all the other cases, the *princeps* was held to respect the limits and laws observed by the people who, before the concession of the *imperium*, possessed only a limited power, and therefore would not have been able to transmit a different one[27]. In neglecting the original historical context of that maxim, the interpreters and, above all, the artificers of the Justinian compilation, attributed a general significance to a particular and limited affirmation, in order to accord an absolute power to the first emperors and thus to ensure a more ancient tradition to Byzantine despotism. In anticipating reflections matured in the 1706

26 CUIACIUS I. (1556–1558) 1836, pp. 703–704. See REBUFFA 1972, pp. 113–117.

27 NOODT (1699) 1724, I, p. 630b. "Exposui, AA [Auditores], quae ad Ulpiani interpretationem pertineant. Sentio, unum restare quod offendat; nisi et ei remedium ponam. Nempe, non ait Ulpianus, Principem lege solutum esse; sed esse le gibus solutum. Videtur igitur indicare, eum non una, sed pluribus, vel omnibus, le gibus solutum esse. Atque ea molesta vobis locutio est; fuisse et Dioni Cassio gravem, supra suspicatus sum" (NOODT [1699] 1724, I, p. 630b).

Observationes[28], the theses of the 1699 *Dissertatio* rested on an important passage of the *Institutiones* (1, 2, 6), as well as on that almost identical one of the *Digesto* (1,4,1 *pr. Ulpianus, l. 1 Institutionum*): "Quod principi placuit, legis habet vigorem; utpote cum lege regia, quae de imperio eius lata est, populus ei et in eum omne suum imperium et potestatem conferat". Retracing the Ulpian text to its classical version, Noodt verified its sense and value in the light of the ancient juridical reality, emphasising the wish of the jurisconsult to identify the power of the *princeps* not with personal interest but with the "iuris potestas", "sub lege illa prima et optima quae communi omnium saluti prospexit"[29].

To witness the correct interpretation of the Ulpian formula a contribution was made by the analysis of the fragment of the *Lex Regia* – relating to Vespasian's rule – to which is dedicated the last part of Noodt's 1699 *Dissertatio.* The clauses of the *Lex* that attest the definitive transfer of powers from the Roman people to the prince, must not be taken literally. The *Lex Vespasiani* is a *lex de imperio*, a general and periodical law, reproposed for the election of every emperor with the purpose of attributing openly to him and once only (through a *senatusconsultus*) those titles and competencies that the first emperors had obtained in juridical forms and at differentiated times. Noodt's reconstruction historicizes Roman late-Republican events, recalling in the interpretation of the *Lex Regia* the specificity of the ancient document and the particular historico-juridical circumstances. With the specific indication of the *potestates* conceded by the Roman people, the *lex* attributed juridical significance to the *princeps'* activities, tacitly subjecting his *imperium* to the authority

28 Here Noodt dwelt upon Ulpiano's formulation in *Digestum* (1, 4, 1) and examined the expression "ei et in eum" from a linguistic point of view; he affirmed that this was unable to demonstrate the absolute alienation of *summa potestas* from people to *princes.* See NOODT (1706) 1724, I, pp. 298–299.

29 NOODT (1699) 1724, I, p. 631a.

of the law, which is the expression in man of the *recta ratio* and source of juridical obligation. Approaching the traditional literary sources (above all Dio Cassio's *Historia Augusta* and *Historiae Romanae*) those taken from Gronovius' work, Noodt dwelt on Augustus' *potestates*. He stressed that the proclamation of the *solutus legibus*, referred erroneously by Cassius Dio to Augustus, did not render his *auctoritas* absolute and independent of all the laws but only subtracted it from those indicated by the Senate, case by case:

> Legibus solutum fuisse Augustum, non omnibus, sed quibus Senatus eum nominatim solvit [...]. Praeterquam quod his in principatus ingressu uno concessa sunt senatusconsulto aut lege, quae Augustus non uno tempore, nec una lege, aut senatusconsulto, sed diversis temporibus, et legibus, aut senatusconsultis accepit[30].

The complexity of the historico-philological argumentation does not prevent accepting theunitary and political character that sustains Noodt's reflection on Roman history. The interpretation of the *Lex Regia* and of Roman law between *respublica* and principate shows that a stance of theoretical conscience is strongly rooted in him aimed towards testing the limits of modern absolutism. It is, more particularly, an interpretation of the *princeps-populus* relationship that upsets Hobbes' theses, that was well known to the Dutch debate at the end of the 17th century. In the "Bibliothèque universelle et historique" of 1689, Le Clerc, in signalling the referred-to *Dissertatio* of Willem van der Muelen, denounced the "erreur de Hobbes" which judged the limit set on the *princeps* contrary "à la nature de l'empire souverain". Instituted by the *will* and the "consentement du peuple", *summa potestas* cannot contrast, as in Hobbes, with the principles of the law that "mettent le prince en droit de disposer de ses sujets et de leur bien, comme il le croit nécessaire et utile pour leur bon-

30 Noodt (1699) 1724, I, p. 630a.

heur". The English philosopher, therefore was accused of annulling the differences between civil government and despotic power, "entre la domination juste, et la tyrannie, entre un gouvernement légitime, et un empire usurpé". If the wish of the people is subjected to the fundamental laws of associated life, then all the more so "l'empire y doit être sujet, et être renfermé dans les mêmes limites". To such limits as these is also subjected the action of the prince as a special individual, living in a condition equal to that of the other members of the social community, "puis qu'il reçoit l'empire et les conditions du gouvernement comme particulier, n'étant prince qu'après qu'il les a reçues"[31]. In this context Jean Barbeyrac, in 1707, in the notes to the French translation of the *Dissertationes*, emphasised the many points of contact between Noodt's thought and John Locke's texts, published and already often translated in the Holland at the end of the 17th century[32]. In 1690 the *Two Treatises of Government* had appeared anonymously and at the end of 1691 an anonymous text, "traduit de l'anglois", *Du gouvernement civil*, was published in Amsterdam announced by Le Clerc in the "Bibliothèque universelle et historique" (1691). The Huguenots had circulated it who found in that writing the justification of the opposition to the sovereign-tyrant[33]. A trace of the Noodt-Locke relationships is, however, to be had in Lock's epistolary correspondence. It dates back to the 29th August 1700, when Benjamin Furly wrote from Rotterdam to the author of the *Epistola de tolerantia*, announcing to him the despatch of the *Dissertatio de iure summi imperii*, as "a free oration of his last year". The re-

31 Bibliothèque Universelle Et Historique, 1689, XIII, pp. 161, 162, 163.

32 See Barbeyrac 1731, I, pp. 146–147, 152–153, 70–171, 175, 198, 204, 214–215.

33 Bibliothèque Universelle Et Historique 1691, XX, pp. 263–265. The content of *Du gouvernement civil [...]* has been compared with that of the 1699 *Dissertatio* by Mastellone 1988, XII.

quest had been made by "Professor Noodt of Leyden [...], a hearty man and lover of liberty"[34]. It is very difficult, however, to claim that Noodt's theses may be assimilated *tout court* to those of the English philosopher. It has appeared more correct to a recent and acute interpreter to refer the verifiable thematic analogies to the common iusnaturalism[35]. Whether or not he had the writings of the English philosopher directly in front of him, Noodt could certainly not forget that the criticism against the Hobbesian mode of despotic power had been one of the more qualifying outcomes of Lock's reflection. In the *Second Treatise* was in fact claimed the consensual origin of the power founded on the prerogatives of natural law, to go so far as to prove the incompatibility of the monarchy absolute with civil society. The theoretical objective was that of showing the incapacity of the *summa potestas* to overcome the "inconveniencies of the State of Nature". The natural condition is destined to persist in the relationships between sovereign and subject when an "Appeal" is not given to the latter and he is denied the "liberty to judge of his Right, and according to the best of his Power, to maintain it"[36]. This latter theme was destined to return in the final pages of the 1699 *Dissertatio*. In them, the definition of *summa potestas* is reached through the assimilation of the *princeps-populus* relationship to that of private law between mandate holder and mandant, documented by Roman law (*D.*17, tit. I, "Mandati, vel contra", l. 60, 4): "Quid hic populus? [...] Quo consilio? Non alio,

34 FURLY to Locke 1700 (1982), vol. VII, p. 127.

35 Here there is a reference to van den Bergh opinion, who thinks that even if Locke and Noodt had friends and sources in common, it is impossible for Locke to have been able to influence the Dutch jurist directly: see VAN DEN BERGH 1988, pp. 198–200, 227–228.

36 LOCKE 1690 (1970), pp. 344, 345. On this work cf. LE CLERC in *BIBLIOTHÈQUE UNIVERSELLE ET HISTORIQUE* 1690, XIX, pp. 559–573. On Toleration in seventeenth century Dutch and English Thought see ISRAEL 1994, p. 28 with a reference to 1706 *Dissertatio*.

quam quo suo quisque procuratori liberam rerum administrationem mandat [...]. Hoc in privato procuratore et ius et ratio definit. Atque idem in publico, id est, principe, populus agit"[37].

The people is the real proprietor of sovereignty also when the exercise of this has been alienated by mandate. The action of the *princeps* takes place in representation of the people being valid and legitimate only in the ambit of the mandate received. Particular interesting is the comparison with Ulrik Huber's theses. Noodt's predecessor at Franeker, Huber was a jurist who was placed by van den Bergh alongside the philologist Jacobus Perizionius, "in the humanistic intellectual circles to which Noodt belonged"[38]. Their theses express the alternative theories about the origin and duty of sovereignty as elaborated by the Dutch historical-political culture of the 17th century. In the second (1682) and the third (1694) editions of *De iure civitatis* Huber included an extensive treatment of this subject, which was the result of his political experiences in the Frisian Supreme Court between 1679 and 1682. It was a consequence of the political contrasts developed in Dutch civil life after the Peace of Nijmegen (1678), which was stipulated to stem Louis 14th's threats of invasion. This work emphasized the constitutional events of Antiquity as a detailed study of the principles of sovereign legitimacy, which was defined as the supreme and absolute power of the State[39]. Absolute power does not mean abuse, but is the lawful juridical right of its holder to act within the positive limits of the legal system. To govern his State the sovereign has to respect the interests of his sovereignty. This is attested by the real meaning of *lex regia,* which after the decline of the Roman Empire had become a theoretical principle of public law. Sovereignty is not subject to anyone, but is the absolute power in the

37 NOODT (1699) 1724, I, p. 631b.

38 So VAN DEN BERGH 1988, p. 193.

39 HUBERUS (1672) 1708, pp. 64, 329, 69, 93. See *The Peace of Nijmegen 1676–1678/9* 1979.

State. From this thesis developed the traditional prejudice whereby the people had, without exception, a greater power than the sovereign's, and so they were not obliged to tolerate his abuses. The theses of Johannes Althusius (the famous theorist of "popular sovereignty") were the reference point for these theories. In the first Book of *De iure civitatis* (section 2, ch. 3) Huber rejected the most important theories expressed in *Politica* (1603). In the commentary on an observation concerning *iura maiestatis* contained in the *Preface* he criticized the thesis whereby the people could not alienate the supreme power: "Et quia populus, imperio ad unum hominem vel concilium delato, *desiit esse unum quid*, desiit esse corpus, nec personam amplius repraesentat, sed nihil quam singuli, et dissoluta est multitudo. Unde nec ullum ius, *quod est qualitas personae competens*, populo post imperium translatum tribui possit"[40]. A forerunner of the modern "iusnaturalistic constitutionalism", as he was defined by Otto von Gierke, a supporter of the absolutism *tout court,* according to van den Bergh[41], Huber strove to elaborate a new doctrine of "authority", theorizing a compromise between the popular sovereignty model derived from Althusius, and that of *summa potestas*, re-elaborated by Hobbes. Huber had criticized Althusius' *maiestas populi* principle, but had agreed with him in rejecting Hobbes' theses about the constitution of the State. It is impossible for the subjects to have given up all their rights in favour of the sovereign because they are an *unum quid.* Sovereignty is

40 HUBERUS (1672) 1708, pp. 56–57 and Book I, section 2, Chap. 3, p. 40: "De fundamento et efficacia imperii, quae primum e natura status democratici indagatur". Huber criticized the theory of popular sovereignty in Book I, section 2, Chap. 6, pp. 53–54: "Quo rationes contra summam potestatem examinantur". About Huber and Althusius see VEEN 1976, pp. 14, 19, 75, 107, 156–157, 219–221, 361. For the relationship between Huber and Noodt cf. VAN DEN BERGH 1988, pp. 204–205.

41 VON GIERKE (1880) 1943 [1974], pp. 222–223 and VAN DEN BERGH 1988, pp. 204–205.

not, as Hobbes held, an expression of a contract of submission drawn up by the people, which rids its holder of any obligation. On the contrary, the relationship between governor and governed is regulated by a contract, in fact on transferring the sovereignty, the people retain the *ius personae*[42]. This statement – which shows a strong Althusian influence (used at a new theoretico-political level) – was not in contrast with the theory whereby alienation from power had to be absolute. According to Huber, it was possible, in virtue of natural law, to set inviolable juridical limits on the *tacit* clauses of contracts. These contracts imposed a "natural obligation" on the sovereign to safeguard the right of personal status, the right of ownership, the right of freedom of thought as well as the right of obedience to the divine order. These are inviolable rights that each man possesses by nature. Also the "expressed fundamental laws" have the same binding power; they set the sovereign power limits just when they express its basis. Indeed those laws represent the condition necessary for sovereignty. Thus it is possible to affirm that, although it is ratified by the clauses of the civil law contract, the relationship between subjects and sovereign has always maintained its validity from the viewpoint of natural law. So the contractual clauses ensured the validity and implementation of the pact, making the existence of sovereign power possible. According to Huber this power could not be given by the people through a *mandate*, because even in democracy it represented an absolute and indivisible authority[43]. Thus, the third edition of *De iure civitatis* (1694) contained in a *sectio* "exhibens dissertationem

42 HUBERUS (1672) 1708, pp. 40, 88. On the theme see GOUGH (1936) 1986, pp. 205–206. The thesis has been accepted and re-elaborated by KOSSMANN et al. 1960, pp. 108–109 and KOSSMANN 1960, pp. 82–103. Regarding the Huber-Hobbes opposition see VEEN 1976, pp. 160–201. About "Thomas Hobbes and Holland" see SCHONEVELD 1983, pp. 29–62.

43 HUBERUS (1672) 1708, pp. 85, 86, 45, 2, 41.

de imperio, sine vi, a populo sui iuris constituto", a sharp criticism of Perizonius[44]. These theories were based on an original analysis of the state of nature that was very different from Huber's conception of human nature and from his radical pessimism, which was the anthropological and historical presupposition of the idea of a strong and non-democratic State whose aim was to dominate human *passions*. In contrast, Perizonius started out from an optimistic conception of man and his history. The contract did not impose one to give up the natural law or to transfer it to the *princeps*, as Hobbes and Huber thought, but to combine the individual powers into a "ius commune". Consequently it was not a "pactum subiectionis", but a "pactum societatis" which permitted man to become subject only of himself and maintain his original freedom[45]. These theses would have fomented the political debate at the end of the 18th century on the various models of sovereignty. In a Dutch edition (1784) of the 1699 *Dissertatio*, the anonymous translator reported on the *back* of the frontespiece a quotation taken from the constitution of Pennsylvania. In the relative *Preface* he associated the question of *summa potestas* with contemporary political reflection, exalting Noodt as theoretician of *popular sovereignty*. To this, moreover, referred the legitimate right of active *resistance* against the rulers and the Statolder who had violated the natural law and the constitution[46]. The concluding reflections of the 1699 *Dissertatio* contain a decisive defence of the right to resistance against the arbitrary power of the tyrant who opposes personal interest in the "ius naturae" and in the common good: "Sed ut iidem

44 HUBERUS (1672) 1708, Book I, section 10, p. 346.

45 PERIZONIUS (1689) 1746, p. 62. For Perizonius' nomination at Franeker et Leyden Universities see MEIJER 1971, pp. 49f. and 84f. Noodt was summoned from the Franeker University in 1679 to replace Huber. On this theme and regarding the relationship with Perizonius see – after VAN DEN BERGH 1988, pp. 44–45, 119–120 – here, *supra*, Chap. 3.

46 See VAN DEN BERGH 1988, pp. 205–206.

remedia, si quae in mundo sint, non adspernamur naturae iure; sic quo minus populus suas vires, si quas habeat, adversus tyrannum intendat, ratio non impedit"[47]. The use of violence upsets the legal order and demolishes the basis of its foundation. It destroys the security granted by the law of reason, and it provokes war; all this is due to the *princeps* abuses and not to the people, who have "to be offended" and to "suffer the consequences of civil war". The *princeps'* opposition to the tyrant, who is an enemy of the "human race", was based on the recognition of the meeting between "divine will" and "natural law"[48] which are necessary for asserting lawful civil authority.

The exercise of violence upsets the legal order, mortifying the very reasons for which that their institution has been requested. It annihilates the security that the law of reasons guarantees, causing the fall into a state of war, imputable to the unjust *princeps* and not to the people forced to undergo "scelera atque iniurias", as well as "civilis belli mala"[49]. Having reached a definition of *summa potestas* alternative to that of the *De iure belli ac pacis*, that had impeded Grotius' iusnaturalism from fully recognising the right to resistance against the tyrant[50], Noodt proposed a moderate exercise of such a right. The reasons were dictated by the necessity of conjugating the need for liberty with that of a legal order, of excluding an autonomous right of resistance as that theorized by Johannes Althusius who, in the popular will, expressed by the *contractus*, had identified the origin of the State and the justification of the *rebellion*, the limit-measure of sovereign power. Not by chance, Noodt paid special attention to the definition of the conditions and the limits with which to subject anti-tyrannical reaction. When the breakdown of the

47 NOODT (1699) 1724, I, p. 633b.
48 NOODT (1699) 1724, I, p. 633a.
49 NOODT (1699) 1724, I, p. 633b.
50 Cf. GROTIUS 1680, Book I, Chap. 3, pp. 66–67 and Chap. 4, pp. 89–90, 103–106. On the theme cf. ZARKA 1995.

relationship of trust between people and sovereign involves only a few individuals it is well that they, although preserving the right of defending themselves against the abuse of sovereign power, do not undertake an uneven and harmful struggle. The condition of "humanae infirmitatis" forces the people to support something illegal and not to disturb the public peace and tranquillity, proving "magis utile (est) quiescere, quam inani ultionis studio maius sibi malum arcessere"[51]. In such a reflection, the lesson of a classical source of ordinary consultation assumed special importance, such as Tacitus (whose expressions, "rara temporum felicitate, ubi sentire quae velis, et quae sentias dicere licet", taken from *Historiae*, I, 1, introduced to the *Dissertatio* of 1699). Its utilization was not, however, aimed at showing the principles of the Machiavellian *Reason of State*, according to an interpretation scheme adopted by almost all the politicians and historians of the latter half of the 16th century (from Jacopo Sertino to Traiano Boccalini, from Giusto Lipsio to Pietro Andrea Canonieri). Noodt's Tacitus, a most diffused classic in the humanistic culture of Leyden, after the rebirth favoured by Lipsius and Scaligero, is a Tacitus aware of the fatal decline of the republican institutions and of the negative effects of despotism. He is a sharp observer of the tyrant's psychology, warned by the intrigues characterizing the traditional *arcanum imperii*, even disposed not only to denounce them with lucidity but also to trace them back with prudence into the order of history, free from the opportuneness of Livy's narrations[52]. Le Clerc also referred to the ancient historian's authority, and in 1705, in conclusion of signalling Noodt's 1699 *Dissertatio*, did not to fail to eulogise its opportune intention of limiting the exercise of the right to resis-

51 NOODT (1699) 1724, I, p. 633a.

52 On this point see the learned study of BUGTER 1980, pp. 85ff., 175–200. On Tacitus in Holland from Geldenhauer to Grotius see SCHÖFFER (1968) 1975, pp. 78–101.

tance[53]. In the quoted review of 1689 to van der Muelen the Genevan recommended particular moderation and caution before depriving the sovereigns of *auctoritas*. He thus was in agreement with the judges of the recommended author who had reported an important suggestion of Tacitus (*Hist.*, IV, 74)[54], the same source utilized by Noodt to claim that "neque enim semper convelli illa moles in tantis fortunae viribus potuit; et ideo tolerare scelera quibus resisti non posset, prudentiae fuit. Sicut imbrem, et frigus, et alia naturae incommoda, ferimus, ubi non licet aliter". And yet that did not imply that the subject was deprived of the right-duty to react "principis atrocitati", especially when, "consumpta omni patientia", he decided to contrast "extrema [...] crudelitatis aut superbiae exempla", without waiting until "de coelo descendat Deus". The opposition of the just *princeps* against the tyrant, enemy "humani generis", rested on the recognition of the convergence of "naturae lex" and "divina voluntas", essential requisites for the affirmation of a legitimate civil *auctoritas*[55].

53 "La matière dont il s'agit, est de si grande importance, qu'il est bon que tout le monde en soit bien instruit, et qu'il l'examine avec soin, pour ne tomber, ni dans l'anarchie tumultueuse d'un Etat purement populaire, ou dans l'extrémité opposée d'une autorité arbitraire et sans bornes" (*Bibliothèque Choisie* 1705, VII, p. 254).

54 *Bibliothèque Universelle Et Historique* 1689, XIII, pp. 167–168.

55 Noodt (1699) 1724, I, pp. 632b, 633a. "Si, quod eius fidei convenit, omnium quietem illius vigilia custodiat; omnium fortunas, vitam, libertatem illius iustitia, ac fortitudo tueatur; omnium periculis illius prudentia occurrat; omnium mala atque infortunia illius benignitas soletur; Quid multa? Si se non Tyrannum, sed civem, non dominum, sed patrem praster, postremo si si hominem se, et hominibus praeesse, arbitretur. [...] Quamquam, si estrema patiatur crudelitatis aut superbiae exempla, quis culpet eum qui consumata omni patientia, non ea ignavia sit; ut exspectandum sibi putet, donec de coelo descendat Deus, in umani generis hostem sua missurus fulmina? Imo quis non eum laudet, quod aliquando se circumspiciat, et a Deo reprimi putet, qui Naturae lege, id est, divina voluntate coërcetur? Praestat tamen, aliquam esse rempublicam, quam

In modern *iusnaturalism* the *ius naturae* appeared as a right of men to be respected in their individuality. An important turning-point developed in the juridical-political reflection. Space could no longer be found by the traditional references to the *arcana imperii.* Having achieved its purpose – namely, that of indicating the instruments for gaining and conserving forms of personal power – was now able to leave the scene. Their obscure and esoteric style was continually replaced by the tone of all clarity and rationality of the *natural right* ordered *geometrically*. The objective became the content of the new reflection on the right of the State and on *public right*. The responses ensured by the conventional precepts to the problems of the origin and limits of sovereign power now appeared inadequate and surpassed. The modern juridical theories searched once again for more satisfactory questions posed by a *scientia iuris* renewed in its contents and methods. Ruled by the norms of the universal human and divine right, this *science* was able to stand comparison with the *new science*, and set itself at the basis of the modern State, supported by the consensus of the citizens and administered in function of the usefulness for the people, aware of its legitimate right to resist against the prince-tyrant:

> Summum magistratum – observed Noodt in concluding the 1699 *Dissertatio* and summarising its contents – qualiscumque sit in republica, non de coelo demitti, sed communi civium consensu imponi; ac, si se principem aut magistratum praebere velit, non legibus solutum, sed alligatum profiteri oportere; nec suam potestatem sua libidine, sed populi utilitate metiri; caeterum non principem aut magistratum agere, sed tyrannum; atque a suis civibus omni iure, et divino et humano coerceri posse[56].

---

nullam; praestat, pacem esse, quam bellum. Quasi respublica sit in qua leges nomen sunt, sudicia iacent, omnia vi aut faccione, nihil ratione, nihil aequo iure decernitur" (NOODT [1699] 1724, I, pp. 632b–633a).

56 NOODT (1699) 1724, I, p. 633b.

Chapter V

Right, Conscience and "Summa Potestas" in Jean Barbeyrac

Natural Right and Freedom of Conscience

With Pufendorf and Locke Jean Barbeyrac shares the demand of an ethic founded upon certain laws, which can be demonstrated deductively like physical laws. The *modus* of existence of the human *conscience*, the same value of the moral tie are guaranteed from the ability of legal obligation. From this point of view, the criterion of rational *evidence* – theorized by Bayle as autonomous source of value – cannot be sufficient. The result of the practical reason in Bayle – which deep from the point of view of the individual conscience the absolute validity of the ethical principles – is the legitimation of the *atheism*. By denying God, the atheists deny, for Barbeyrac as for Locke, the same idea of natural right and the principle of freedom of conscience that comes down from it. Atheism and its libertine effects risk invalidating the ethical finalities of the society, the trust in the moral character of the human association: "[...] Mais épurez tant qu'il vous plaira l'athéisme; jamais vous n'en tirerez que des conséquences pernicieuses, qui ménent tout droit au plus grand libertinage". In his commentary to Book II of Pufendorf's *De iure naturae et gentium* (1734), the translator opposed to Bayle's theses the limits that also Grotius had set to his own hypothesis. The author of the *De iure belli ac pacis*, specifying that the *rules* of the natural right "*auraient lieu* en quelque manière", underlined the chief relationship that the "idées de convenance ou disconvenance", founded upon the human *nature*, have with God's *will* [367]. For all of this, Barbeyrac, apart from Bayle's unacceptable deductions, set out to define the basis of moral obligation and the relative natural law through the appeal to the right of a *Superior* legislator. In this context it is interesting to notice the critical use in Barbeyrac's translation of the admired Pufendorf. In a footnote to the French version of the *De officio hominis et civis* (1707), he stressed the weakness of Pufendorf's *iustae causae*, justifing the right to impose an obligation: "Cette variation et cette confusion est déjà un préjugé désavantageux pour la justesse de ses idées; mais si on examine toutes les raisons qu'il établit pour fondement du droit dont il est question, on verra aisément, qu'il n'y en a aucune qui par elle-même ait assez de force". Assuring an unitary and certain dimension to the law, the *vis* of divine superior legislation implicates a real obligation of human conscience. It valorizes, that is, the ethical character of the legal tie that imposes the respect of the *duties*. Therefore, Barbeyrac can share the interpretation which seems sometimes to stick to Pufendorf himself of asserting, for instance, the inadequacy of the factor "generation" to sanction the power over the children. If the parents are "des instruments aveugles" and "des causes, pour ainsi dire, occasionelles" of human life, their authority derives from an another strength, from the "source" divine, creative of the soul and of the human body. To all the faculties God is able, therefore, to prescribe the limits that he judges opportune and to condition even the use that the men will make of it. This *consensus*, that is the basis of the "just" power of the laws and every legitimate *auctoritas* among men, draws all of its strength by the

367 PUFENDORF 1734, Book II, Chap. 3, § XIX, t. I, pp. 232, 230. See PALLADINI 1988. On the theme and, in general, on the matters here examined, see LOMONACO 1999b, pp. 67ff. A basic work on Barbeyrac is that of MEYLAN 1937 (with *Bibliography*, pp. 245–248).

divine will to make to respect the promises and the arranged appointments: "Voilà le grand et premier fondement de tout Devoir et de toute Obligation"[368].

Barbeyrac's choice to make the necessary criterions to the action and knowledge of natural right depend on divine obligation avowedly leaned on a voluntaristic reading of Pufendorf's natural law doctrine. Commenting and correcting the definition of law in the *De officio,* the translator annotated: "Cette définition de la *loi*, prise dans son idée la plus générale, n'est pas assez pleine ni assez exacte". The law is, instead, in his opinion, the Superior's will manifested in the world. It directs the actions of the subjects or all or at least those of a certain type, in such way to be imposed the necessity to act or not to act in a determined way, leaving, nevertheless, to the men "*la liberté d'agir ou de ne point agir, comme ils le jugeront à propos*". For to avoid introducing into ethics an arbitrary principle, Barbeyrac had to prefer the concept of divine, "Superior" legislator to that of human legislator, as author and basis of the relationship between norm and sanction. Only God has, in fact, the power to direct all in all of their actions unlike every other superior who, intervening only on *actions* of a "certain type", can never go beyond his limited power[369]. The same natural laws depend ("originairement de l'*institution divine*") from the God's *will*, because founded upon Supreme Good's wisdom and goodness, which cannot contradict and cannot want to destin man to a goal without forcing him, at the same time, to adjust the actions to the anticipated purpose[370]. The order of the universe created by God is not a datum of fact, since it asks to be realized by human reason. It imposes him to the point by forcing him in conscience; it exists,

368 PUFENDORF 1735, Book I, Chap. 2, § V, t. I, pp. 41–43. Cf. PALLADINI 1990, pp. 49–67 and note 20.
369 PUFENDORF 1735, Book I, Chap. 2, § II, t. I, pp. 36–38.
370 PUFENDORF 1734, Book I, Chap. 1, § IV, t. I, p. 5. See ZURBUCHEN 1991, pp. 125–139.

that is, as a demand of his rational nature. Men have to discipline their actions on the ground of the laws which their reason is able to discover as divine *obligations.* Barbeyrac's reason-conscience – as that of Locke – is, therefore, that all practical principles conform to divine law.

But Barbeyrac's idea-God, last basis of the natural law, is not the traditional one of positive religions. Also from this point of view, the French jurist's discourse is planned on authentic premises of natural law doctrine that don't undermine the theorized separation between reason and faith, law and theology. Therefore, the reference to human conscience-reason leads the risky implications which were known in previous religious literature. With the affirmation of divine obligation the supremacy of *conscience* doesn't justify the exaltation of one further "revelation" in such degree as to promote by faith behaviours harmful to the civil society. This divine obligation doesn't estrange right from reality, because it is set in operation of human reason, disciplining the its activities in terrestrial life. The approval of right in terms of obligation is finalized to essentially increase human phenomena and to strengthen *conscious* actions from the inside. The voluntaristic perspective, privileged by Barbeyrac in his commentary on Pufendorf, admits God but it excludes faith. It abandons, that is, dogmatic theology and assigns instead to this theory of obligation the task of guaranteeing universal ethical values of *conscience.*

All of this involves a secularization and rationalization of the ethics to which Pufendorf's commentator attempted to defend him against Leibniz's circumstantial criticism espoused in the *Monita quaedam ad principia pufendorfiani operis De officio hominis et civis* (1709), translated and published in appendix to the French version of the *De officio* in 1718. In the corresponding *Réflexions* Barbeyrac criticised the German philosopher's arguments for not having linked the rules of human actions and the nature of the Just with divine will. The principle of natural right must be looked for not in God's *will* but in his *intellect*, not so much in his *auctoritas* as in the benign *sapientia*. Justice, in the *Monita*, was inspired by the rules of "equity" and "proportion", which are exclusively founded in the immutable "nature of things" and in divine intellect's ideas[371]. To confirm the critical judgment on Pufendorf Leibniz had introduced a comparison with the praised Grotius. This last, for Leibniz, had justly connected "doctrinam scholasticorum de lege Dei aeterna cum principio socialitatis", eliminating from such *lex* transcendence and making to coincide it with *ius naturale*. Having elevated social reason to the constitutive principle (*principium essendi*) of right, Grotius had favoured its definitive separation from the theology. An impracticable separation for Pufendorf who, instead, had maintained *ratio* in the opposite condition of *principium cognoscendi*[372]. Then Barbeyrac's defensive line consists in underlining the insufficiency of "rules of justice" to impose ties, taking back and revaluing, on the subject, Pufendorf's thought:

> [...] Mais il soutient, qu'avec tout cela, la raison propre et directe pourquoi les hommes sont *obligés* de suivre les règles de la justice, ce qui leur impose la *nécessité* morale de s'y conformer, c'est la volonté de Dieu, qui en qualité de leur maître souverain, a plein droit de gêner leur liberté naturelle, comme il le juge à propos.

The theoretical implication of this passage was the necessity to maintain the distinction between law and theology, God's justice and human justice, which are different in origin and exten-

371 Composed in 1706, Leibniz's intervention appeared in Appendix to BOEHMER 1709, then in PUFENDORF 1735, pp. 379–435: cf. 411. The Italian translation is in LEIBNIZ 1951, pp. 247–260. On the fortune of the *Monita* and on the meaning of the polemic with Pufendorf see – also for the understanding of Barbeyrac's position – BOBBIO (1947) 1965, pp. 129–145. See also SÈVE 1989, pp. 59–67.

372 LEIBNIZ to Bierling (1711), 1978, vol. VII, pp. 498, 488. See DROETTO 1968, pp. 297–298.

sion. In men the *iustitia* is a quality that they must and can acquire only through the *obligation* imposed by an external principle namely God's *will* [373]. The polemic was not of low profile nor was it destined to stay without echo, as testified by the punctual criticism to the *De officio*'s translation in the "Bibliothèque ancienne et moderne" (1718). Here Le Clerc, concentrated attention on the issue of the definition of *efficient cause* of the law, shared by the voluntaristic interpretation, this exalting the historical-critical value of Pufendorf's natural law doctrine: "On n'a qu'à lire Mr. *Barbeyrac*, et l'on conviendra que Mr. de *Pufendorf* ne pouvait pas être censuré"[374].

But in his intervention Barbeyrac doesn't limit himself to oppose Leibniz's reasons for a secularized natural law doctrine. He also seeks to defend his master Pufendorf from the accusation of legitimating the Hobbesian model through the appeal to the Superior legislator. The acceptance of voluntarism so go the accusations, alters the basis of natural right which risks being enacted by the *imperium* of a coercive power. To recognize such sanctions means to admit that duties come true only when a Superior imposes them. If divine obligation is enough to create law, it is able, at the same time, to justify a tyrannical government as that sustained by Trasymachus in Plato's *Republic*. To Leibniz's critique of Pufendorf Barbeyrac, his follower, opposed the intimate relationship between law and morality. All the juridical norms attest a binding value from the moral point of view. The *obligatio*, that implicates an *internal* responsibility, distinguishes itself from any immediate and exterior *coercion*. Not by

373 LEIBNIZ in PUFENDORF 1735, pp. 413, 405–406. On Barbeyrac and the contradictions among the "rationalism" of his theory of the conscience and the defence of Pufendorf's "voluntarism" see HOCHSTRASSER 1995, p. 46.

374 See *BIBLIOTHÈQUE ANCIENNE ET MODERNE* 1718, IX, pp. 457, 459. On this Journal and with regard to *Histoire des Provinces Unies des Pays Bas* see DONI GARFAGNINI 2004, pp. 103–142.

chance the French translator argues strongly to show that the "volonté de Dieu" is never arbitrary. It always reveals itself in a relationship with the human nature, founded upon its *duties*, opposite to the criterion of the *utility* of clear Hobbesian matrix: "L'anonyme [Leibniz] [...] confond visiblement l'*honnête*, avec l'*utile*; et cela paraît d'ailleurs par l'exemple qu'il allégue d'une *société de brigands* [...]. Mais [...] il ne s'agit point ici d'*utilité*, il s'agit de *devoir* et d'*obligation* ". The lesson of the much admired Pufendorf, rigorously interpreted to the light of anti-Hobbesian "voluntarism", could favour the individualization of possible places of convergence among *motivation* and *obligation*. The point of departure remained, however, the acquired awareness of their modern conflict, in opposition to the traditional finalism of the Aristotelian and scholastic theories. The basis of natural law must be individualized in the obligation imposed by the divine legislator's will, the absolute guarantee of the validity and autonomy of individual conscience. The liberty of man, which springs from the foundation of his nature, doesn't find in external reality anything that has the force of obligatory strength. The same relationships of "convenience", "order", "beauty" and "honesty", to which the definition of the just one leads, remain only abstract, speculative ideas, teach that we don't recognize in God the author of the "nature of things" and of reason. He reveals them to men and approves them and he wants that men adjust their external and inside actions: "Là commence le *devoir*; la volonté de l'être souverainement parfait est la règle de la nôtre, et celui qui nous a fait tout ce que nous sommes, peut sans doute exiger que nous ne fassions pas tout ce dont il pourrait nous prendre envie"[375].

The looked out upon approach to Hobbesian theses was how much riskier they could appear to Barbeyrac himself a theoretician of the individual and inalienable right to the "liberté

375 LEIBNIZ in PUFENDORF 1735, pp. 415, 416, 430–431.

de conscience". This last was expunged by Hobbe's theory, worried about guaranteeing the survival of one only "public conscience", coincident with the law of the sovereign power, with the authority and the rationality of the State theorized in the *Leviathan*[376]. After all, Pufendorf's interpretation – that Barbeyrac contributed to accredit – was anti-Hobbes in its coherent formulation. He attributed, in fact, to the much admired jurist solutions, which often conflicted with the finalities of his natural law doctrine, as far as sustaining that "la nuit et le jour ne sont pas plus opposés, que les systèmes de Machiavel et d'Hobbes, d'un côté; et ceux de Grotius et de Pufendorf, de l'autre"[377]. Among the formulated critical judgments in the commentary on *De iure naturae et gentium*, it is interesting to signal what indicates the precariousness, in Pufendorf, of the foundation of the right of the superiority of God over the men. To sustain – as did the German jurist – that we can be demanded from others (in virtue of an *ius perfectum*) only what is arranged, runs the risk of assigning with Hobbes an essential role to strengthen in the constitution of that law. This is a dangerous and unacceptable consequence in Barbeyrac's opinion who warned, therefore, of the need to correct his author. Strength doesn't re-enter in what constitutes the right to impose some *obligation.* It serves only to make valid that *ius,* that never fades away, even when the Superior is deprived of the necessary *strengths* to make use of it[378]. Duty exists, therefore, in all of its power and extension independently from any possible sanctions. Besides, to sustain that divine action effects itself on a human nature already bound to obedience of the absolute command, means to introduce the divine will as some-

376 HOBBES (1651) 1992, part II, Chap. 29, pp. 264–265. For Barbeyrac's critique to Hobbesian Pufendorf and on the Leibniz's *Jugement* is always profit MORI 1986, pp. 16–29.

377 GROTIUS 1759, *Préface du traducteur,* XXXII. See PALLADINI 1990, pp. 277–278.

378 PUFENDORF 1735, Book I, Chap. 2, § V, t. I, p. 40.

thing of accessory and to reduce it to that of a *princeps*, father, master or of another wordly superior. If God proposes his *will* instead as a model to imitate, then it remains to be demonstrated that he doesn't demand from the men anything that he himself doesn't own, as his *sovereign perfections* require or allow; and not to reveal himself, therefore, as a *severe master*[379].

To the central theme of obligation on the theoretical plan corresponds, on the historical-juridical, the demand to deepen the relationships between the power of the civil *auctoritas* and the prerogatives of the *conscience*. All efforts to guarantee a juridical and rational basis to absolutism collided with the complicated attempt to reconcile the two theoretical demands of *obedience* and *liberty*, of *auctoritas* and *conscience*. The assignment that Barbeyrac intended to fulfil against Hobbes was to conjugate individual liberty in the civil life with recognition of a real and responsible political authority. From such a point of view, a guide could be recognized in John Locke's theoretical and political thought. Confirmed from the English philosopher, the premises of natural law doctrine, never abandoned, they prepared him to refuse not absolutism *tout court* but its harmful transformation in *despotism*. Althought he recognized the right of freedom of *conscience*, Barbeyrac expanded on the definition of the assignments of *summa potestas*. The intention was to establish possible structures of reference, made worthy as necessary *measures* in the choices of conscience. In confirmation of such a thesis and in opposition to Hobbesian definition of an unique and indivisible *summa potestas*, Barbeyrac argued for the separation of the powers in the *imperium*. The drawbacks of this choice are, in his opinion, always preferable to the risks of a despotic power. Commenting on the Pufendorf's *De officio,* prone to welcome the dangerous Hobbesian theses, he could observe: "Mais comme l'expérience fait voir qu'on abuse facilement d'une puissance étendue, les incon-

379 LEIBNIZ in PUFENDORF 1735, p. 419.

venients qui naissent du partage de quelques-uns des droits de la souveraineté, seront toûjours beaucoup moindres, que ceux auxquels on est exposé par la régularité dont parle notre auteur, laquelle n'est bonne qu'en idée"[380]. In his notes to the *De iure naturae et gentium* he judged the definition of sovereignty to be a simple and indivisible institution as an opinion that seems founded upon a false hypothesis. The *summa potestas* is, instead, the mass in unity of different rights and powers, attributed for a goal: the good of the society. Therefore, nothing prevents that they are practiced by separate subjects. It is enough, however, that they are in the State's *body* without being subdued to the will of a foreign power[381]. But for Barbeyrac, Pufendorf and Locke's disciple, the people don't confer *summa potestas* without reserving to itself the right to take it back again, when the *princeps* abuses his *auctoritas*, thus opposing the authentic finality to it:

> Mais il ne s'ensuit [...], qu'on l'ait [le pouvoir] conféré d'une manière à ne se réserver en aucun cas le droit de le reprendre. Cette *réserve* est quelquefois *expresse*; et il y en a toûjours une *tacite*, dont l'effet se déploie, lors que celui à qui on a conféré le pouvoir, en abuse d'une manière directement et notablement contraire à la fin pour laquelle il lui a été[382].

The individual and *summa potestas* coexist without confusing or hindering themselves and practicing clearly diversified rights and duties. Barbeyrac's problem of legislation imposed the de-

380 PUFENDORF 1735, Book II, Chap. 7, § IX, t. II, p. 307.
381 PUFENDORF 1734, Book VII, Chap. 4, § I, t. II, p. 317.
382 GROTIUS 1759, Book I, Chap. 3, § VIII, p. 121. The "right of resisting" in Barbeyrac, what theoretical and political "place" of meeting among Pufendorf and Locke's motives, has been investigated with acuteness by ZURBUCHEN 1995, pp. 166–167. On the subject is penetrating also HOCHSTRASSER 1995, pp. 15–16, who in French translator's work has recognized a conciliation between Pufendorf's "voluntarism" – base of the moral obligation – and Locke's "contractualism", sets to base of the political obligation (see also pp. 41f. with reference to relative critical literature).

mand to distinguish legality from morality, the legal relation from the ethical-religious, the rights to freedom of conscience from the prerogatives of civil life. Tracing this distinction, Barbeyrac submits to revision the relationship between civil and natural law in tune with the matrix of his natural law doctrine. The positive law of the judge derives from the obligation of the *lex naturalis*. It is in virtue of this that civil law imposes itself to *conscience*. *Ius gentium* and positive law are a projection, an extension of the law of nature. The latter remains the condition of validity of the civil order and constitutes its true *measure*. of it. To make up for the separation between human *nature* and *lex*, the political institutions must restore and reproduce the *natural* norms, implied by their existence. The attribution of the *imperium* happens with the *pactum subiectionis* in determined conditions: those required by the inviolable natural rights that the sovereign will have to respect, punishment being his immediate dismissal. Tyrannical government founds itself upon an arbitrary and not political rule, because it promotes an explicit violation of the *ius naturale*. Natural rights represent the guaranteed limits within which positive law can operate, the legal conditions under which the duty of the obedience of subjects ends. Based on upon the respect of natural law, the theory of the political obligation involves the rejection of the divine right of *princeps*. Therefore, civil society holds on to the *natural order*. The *conventions* draw, in fact, entire their value from the principles of the *lex naturalis*, thus made worthy in the State from a formal and material point of view. The *strength* of the sanctions doesn't alter the sense of this native truth: "Pour ce qui est des loix naturelles qui prescrivent ou qui défendent quelque chose, le droit civil les confirme, ou doit les confirmer par son autorité, autant que le permet ou le demande le bien public". If for its effective realization the *natural law* is imposed with the *auctoritas* of the civil laws, these must recognize in the *lex naturalis* the condition of their applicability. The observance of that *lex* becomes not only the sufficient but necessary premise for human liberty in the civil life. The concentration of power in the *summa potestas* doesn't involve the mortification or cancellation of the subjective rights. It contributes, instead, to form the space for individual conscience, setting the juridical conditions of existence. The obligation of obedience to the *external* civil law doesn't interfere with *internal* human liberty. The rights of *conscience* represent a limit to the exercise of sovereignty, the necessary condition to be protected from possible abuses of the *princeps.* The defence of the *ius naturale* is submitted to the right to apply, in extreme cases, the final judgement of *conscience.* The subject cannot be, however, satisfied with only internal "resistance", because he is able to openly manifest his dissent. From the affirmation of the individual right of freedom of conscience derives the recognition of the *ius resistendi* against a sovereign who governs as tyrant imposing with strength his own affairs, much so annulling the universal principles of natural right and morality: "On ne doit jamais obéir à ses supérieurs, au préjudice de son devoir. Bien loin de là, et à moins que d'être dans une entière impuissance de leur resister, il faut montrer un noble courage à empêcher de toutes ses forces qu'ils n'oppriment l'innocent"[383]. By violating the natural law, despotic governments threaten the existence of the civil virtues, causing the purposes for which they have been founded to fail. Strictly speaking, the tyrants don't belong to the human community anymore and not only can they be dismissed but also destroyed his strength. From this point of view, the right to resist appears as a necessary action of defence in the partnership life, authorized to protect its own affairs. And, nevertheless, the reference to Pufendorf's lesson matures to the light of Locke's influence which in using of the right to resist, had recommended prudence and moderation. Of the English philosopher Barbeyrac, in his commentary on *De iure naturae et gentium*, quoted the

383 PUFENDORF 1734, Book III, Chap. 1, § § I, VI, t. II, pp. 430, 441.

famous *Second Treatise of Government* (1698, XVIII, §§ 208–210), in opposing the scurvy *populace*, to the undifferentiated one, the small group of righteous to the healthiest part of the subjects, the only part fit to define itself *people* and to promote the action of legitimate rebellion against the tyranny:

> Quand on parle d'un tyran, qui peut légitimement être déposé par le peuple, on n'entend pas par le mot de *peuple* la vile populace ou la canaille du pays, ni une cabale d'un petit nombre de séditieux; mais la plus grande et la plus saine partie des sujets [...]. De plus, il faut que la tyrannie soit notoire et de la dernière évidence, en sorte que personne n'en puisse plus douter[384].

This is a moderate position, modelled on the ideals of the modern merchant classes, on the values of liberty and conscience, in opposition so to the theological dogmatism as to the monarchic absolutism and the new-feudal structures which in such form of government had found a valid support. At the same time, the corrections and the integrations to Pufendorf's model, through the critical use of Locke's lesson, bring us back to the matters of religious and civil ethics that inspire Barbeyrac's biographical story as an exiled Huguenot. In fact he always foresees justification, in religious terms, that the *ius resistendi* had

384 PUFENDORF 1734, Book VII, Chap. 8, § VI, t. II, p. 404. Locke's influences on the right of resisting in Barbeyrac has been put in rilief with critical vigor by DERATHÉ 1974², p. 91 and note. This reading is prepared, nevertheless, to confirm Barbeyrac's traditional image (few effective on the theoretical and political plan) as "eclectic" thinker, supporting of the alternative two theories of the popular sovereignty and the absolutism. On Barbeyrac "en politique [...] disciple de Locke" and critic of Pufendorf's absolutism has treated EHRARD 1963, t. I, p. 344 (but see also t. II, p. 486 and note, p. 491 and note, p. 500 and note, p. 527). For an up-to-date information see SCOTT 1994, pp. 115–132. On the "right of resisting" see the contributions in SPITZ et al. 1995, espec. pp. 557–574. For a interesting reconstruction see also LABRIOLA 2003 (with Bibliography, pp. 697ff.).

given first in the monarchomach theories and, then, in the Huguenots, recalling to themselves the rights of *conscience* of the subjects against the privileges of a despotic and intolerant sovereignty. Yet, from the leaders of the Huguenot party – as Jean Claude and Pierre Jurieu – the intention got him to re-examine further the problem of the "liberté de conscience" in the light of the natural law. Connected to the *ius naturae*, the notion of *conscience* looses the justification of religious character, of private place of divine action to which Jurieu's pages had made reference, treating *Des Droits des deux souverains en matière de religion, la conscience et le prince* (1687)[385]. The definition of the right to resist conducts the theorist of the modern natural law to question traditional dogmatic theology. Already in his *Préface* to Pufendorf, a violent denouncement of the "Ministres publics de la religion", "des Pères de l'*Église*" and "des ecclésiastiques et théologiens protestants", which were all responsible for having subjected moral science to the power of an intolerant ethical-religious model, appeared. To this last Barbeyrac contrasted the positive work of the modern natural law doctrine, emancipated from the guardianship of theological dogmatism in the evolution of juridical knowledge and in an autonomous and systematic *science*. On this subject, he assembled his praise on Grotius who had broken the ice and started a methodical study of law, offering, for the first time, a systematic *ius naturale* as well as Pufendorf for having abandoned the language and the hairsplitting of the scholastics, from which Grotius had purged his work. Pufendorf succeeded, in fact, in undermining the tyrannical yoke "d'une si pernicieuse coûtume" and in following with courage the tracks of his great predecessor, conquering "une réputation immortelle". Taking the negative response of the Roman inquisition and of Swedish and German Protestant theologians towards the writings of the two masters into consideration, Barbeyrac con-

385 See TURCHETTI 1991, pp. 317–319 and now MINERBI BELGRADO 2008.

cluded with the warning that "la morale ainsi négligée et presque bannie du monde par les ministres publics de la religion, s'est réfugiée chez les laïques". After all, the same *Préface* to the *De iure naturae et gentium* shows that the purpose of the translation was not only technical-professional, serving the juridical education of young people destined for employment in church and government. The objective priority remained, in fact, that starting with the principles of ethics, of jurisprudence and politics "les gens sans lettres, ou les gens du commun", of which they were ignorant to the point that the expression *natural right* was "aussi inconnu, que les terres australes"[386]. For such awareness Barbeyrac declared himself able to share the theses of his friend Le Clerc which he quoted and commented on, making explicit reference to the *Parrhasiana* (t. II, 1701) and, particularly, to the *Pensées sur la nécessité et sur la manière d'étudier, pour les personnes qui ne font pas profession de lettres.* Grotius's and Pufendorf' translator shared trust in the human capacity of education which appears in the context of the principles of the ethics, politics and theology, established in a Lockean way through *experience* and *reflection*[387]. The privileged source is, naturally, *The Second Treatise* (IV, 23), quoted in one note to Pufendorf's *De iure* and in the *Traité de la morale des Pères* (1728), to confirm that a man can never confer to others an arbitrary power over his life, of which he is not himself master[388].

386 PUFENDORF 1734, *Préface du traducteur*, § § VI, IX, XI, XXIX, XXX, XII, XXXII, T. I, pp. XXII–XXV, XXVII–XXXVII, LIII–LVI, CIV, CVI–CVII, LVI, CXII, CXIII: cf. also the *Avertissement* to this *Préface* in Appendix to GUIDA 1981, pp. 159–165.

387 PARRHASE [LE CLERC] 1701, t. II, pp. 91, 94.

388 BARBEYRAC 1728, Chap. 12, § XXIX, p. 180. See PUFENDORF 1734, Book VII, Chap. 8, § VI, t. II, p. 406. On Barbeyrac and Locke with regard to this *Traité,* see the useful information offered by MASTELLONE 1988, pp. XIII–XIV.

All that confirms that Barbeyrac's point of view, the prevalent orientation of his reflection are of a juridical character and not a theological one. The aim, set out in greater detail in the *Traité* of 1728, is that of emancipating *jurisprudence* from *faith*, of stimulating, that is to say, the process of secularisation in the political authority and, in general, in civil life. Unlike traditional concept of freedom of religion that of *conscience* makes more choices possible. It helps to identify the position and duties of man in *this* world, to establish herein the range of action which God and rational norm have destined for him. The safeguarding of the right to *freedom of conscience* is completely removed from ecclesiastical jurisdiction. The idea of this *freedom* appears in political-juridical life as a problem of civil coexistence, secularized in its functions and opposed to temporal and spiritual tyranny.

Noodt and Barbeyrac in the confrontation with Bayle

At the beginning of the eighteenth century, while interpreting the Cartesian *criterium veritatis* for himself, Noodt, approached somewhat originally the complex question of truth or falsehood that had been formulated in the modern debate on religious freedom. His 1706 *Dissertatio* stated that God did not want to transmit a religious formula identical for all humanity, nor had attributed to religion the same level of evidence as that granted to arithmetic: "Sed o immensa, o admirabilis, Dei sapientia! [...] Quam certo ea revereri debemus, etiam cum causam ignoramus! Aliud tibi in numeris, aliud in religione, placuit"[389]. With regard to religion it was necessary, therefore, to respect everyone's free

389 NOODT (1706) 1999b, p. 200. For the republication of this text and, above all, for full bibliographical information cf. LOMONACO 1999b, pp. 195–221.

will by reforming the perspective of orthodox Cartesianism of a Malebranchian matrix from within, through recognizing the validity and autonomy of moral certainties, which may be traced back in sacred and profane history. Hence the search for an intermediary solution between Cartesian mathematical reductionism and libertine scepticism. It was basically the choice of a conjectural method of a probabilistic type, which closely recalls Carneadean academic probabilism, praised by the Baylian *Dictionnaire* for its practical cognitive character[390], far from the apodeictic demonstrations of the *ratio philosophandi*. The field of action of probabilism may be extended from the juridical sphere to the religious one and proposed as an alternative to scholastic ontology, and to its apodeictic demonstrations, utilized by the ecclesiastic *auctoritas* for imposing religious truth. For Noodt, it was not a question of defending the latter from scepticism or of denying its existence, but rather of showing the relationship of authenticity to conscience. Adherence to a religious credo does not imply control or theological dogmatism. It remains as a private fact of the individual's conscience, considering that only God has the power to judge "de puniendo animi atque intellectus vitio, errore, labe". Hence the intention to set the sense of diversity and plurality against the dogmatic approach of gomarism. If intolerance assumes the unilaterality of truth, then religious freedom implies the positive value of plurality, together with the awareness of the relativity of what is true: "Ita sit una salutis via; tamen cum de una ambigitur, et multae ostenduntur ex quibus suam quisque commendat diligentissime; quod dubium est, utrum oporteat me, iudicii mei, an alieni, fidem sequi; cum interim, ut salvus sim, magis mea, quam alterius, intersit?". To abandon every dogmatic perspective in juridical and religious discourse meant jeopardising the basis of the ancient

390 BAYLE (1697–1698) 1740, pp. 58–59. See PAGANINI 1980, pp. 325–326 and 2008, pp. 353ff.

political and social order, which is to say that it meant going beyond the *arcana iuris* of the ancient regime and the traditional concept of *truth*, which not even Grozian natural law theory had succeeded in removing completely. In religion too, human reason recognises the fact that absolute certainties do not exist, which are founded metaphysically in God's goodness and truth. The search for truth is, in fact, a continuous process open to the control of appearance and of the relative, to the possibility of doubt and error, which cannot be overcome by instruments of coercion: "Quid, si recte sentiat quem tu errare opinaris? Quoties enim evenit, ut in eo quod vero proximum habetur, falsum, aut in hoc quod falsum videtur, verum contineatur? [...] Tam difficilis, tam obscura, tam lubrica, est veri contemplatio"[391]. Here the conviction develops that the meaning of religious experience includes the recognition of the right to error, subjectively experienced in an authentic way. The aim is to legitimise the principle of freedom, attributing to human conscience a dignity, which, in its search for truth it still merits, even if it has fallen into error. In religion such error is not generated by a predisposition towards moral evil, but rather by the radical *weakness* of human reason which "non enim suo vitio errat, sed infirmitate". Thus, man knows he is able to do without false assurances and that he must accept the risk of error, rooted in the conscience of those who do not have the faith or fortune to recognise the only true and certain salvation: "Nobis quos coelestis iuvat et circumstat doctrina, una occurrit, vera, et certa, ad salutem via. Sed quae est nostra, non est aliorum quibus non aeque favet Deus, aut spes aut fortuna". If there is no absolute guarantee of religious experience, error is not only always possible on account of

391 NOODT (1706) 1999b, pp. 209, 207. A critical analysis of juridical "probabilism" in Noodt is in *BIBLIOTHÈQUE CHOISIE* 1705, VII, 225 and 1713, XXVI, pp. 258–259. On the theme and, in general, on Noodt's historical-juridical thought, see VAN DEN BERGH 1988, pp. 138ff.

the limitations of human faculties, but is also in a moral sense to be considered not ascribable to the will, nor punishable by law. Lack of faith is not a fault, since God himself has so willed it, and one certainly cannot know "quod eum scire noluit Deus". It is, in this view, a direct attack on the violence exercised by theological dogmatism, which had imposed on human conscience the assumed evidence of essential truths for eternal salvation from outside. The reference was, in fact, to the well-known Augustinian doctrine which, on ascribing the error of faith to individual and voluntary motivations, all rooted in the original moral guilt, had supported the legitimacy of having recourse to coercion in religious questions. There was some confusion at this point – observed the Dutch jurist – "legis et religionis officia [...] quae ratio distinguit"[392]. The Augustinian interpretation of the evangelical precept *compelle intrare* (*Luke*, XIV, 23), called on in support of modern intolerance toward heretics, must have sounded alien to Noodt and to his *forma mentis* which was in tune with the opinions of the Dutch debate, converging also in the *Conversations sur diverses matières de religion* which Charles Le Cène and Jean Le Clerc published in 1687: an *annus mirabilis* – as Antonio Rotondò has rightly defined it – in the history of relationships between tolerance and freedom of conscience; a year marked by the publication of Noël Aubert de Versé's *Traité de la liberté de conscience* and Pierre Jurieu's virulent response to Bayle's *Commentaire philosophique* (1686)[393]. Although it never proves easy to reconstruct the picture of the sources of the *Dissertatio*, it is still interesting to compare, with due critical caution, the Noodtian approach to the problem of truth and error in religion with Bayle's relative reflection and the theses indirectly put forward by him for seventeenth-eighteenth century European culture.

392 NOODT (1706) 1999b, pp. 210, 206–207, 209, 213.

393 So ROTONDÒ 1992, pp. 46, 83 (with Bibliography). See also SIMONUTTI 1996.

From the theoretician of *tolérance civile*, as a guarantee of religious pluralism as opposed to ecclesiastic intolerance, Noodt could have borrowed the theory of relative knowledge. It had been applied, as is known, in religion right from the *Nouvelles lettres de l'auteur de la Critique générale de l'histoire du calvinisme* (1685), to support the right of the "respective" truth as well as of *error* to bind the individual conscience, as against the model of absolute truth imposed by traditional theology[394]. The two scholars agreed on this thesis, being only too aware of painful personal experiences and the attacks of Calvinistic orthodoxy, still sharply felt in the closing years of the 17th century. In order not to prove outdated and still conditioned by having recourse to the traditional principle of tolerance, the use of the term *conscience* had, especially in religion, to direct one's attention towards the modern idea of *freedom*. Against the intolerant approach that justified the use of force to coerce the "wanderer" to assent and to combat his stubbornness Noodt, like Bayle, objected to the fact that the state of coercion excluded the possibility of a serene and free examination. All too often *constancy* and sound *convictions* were taken as straightforward *stubbornness*: "Mollienda tamen dolore et metu est pertinacia et inflexibilis obstinatio. Scilicet, tu obstinatum vocas quem ratione vincere non potes. Quid, si idem convicium faciat tibi? Stat pro sua quisque sententia fortiter"[395]. In this regard, the Dutch jurist reacted against the ancient custom

394 BAYLE (1685) 1727 [1965–1982], II, pp. 219a–222a, 228a.

395 NOODT (1706) 1999b, p. 211. The passage is to compare with *Commentaire philosophique*, part II: "On n'use point de violence afin de gêner la conscience, mais pour réveiller ceux qui refusent d'examiner la vérité. Illusion de cette pensée. Examen de ce qu'on appelle opiniatreté" (BAYLE [1686] 1713, part II, Chap.1, in BAYLE 1727 [1965–1982], II, pp. 393–397). See now VAN EIJNATTEN 1999. In the boundless bibliography about Bayle and the tolerance a critical-historical orientation offers MORI 1996, pp. 41ff. and 205–208. See also MORI 1999, espec. Chap. 6: "Conscience et tolerance", pp. 273–320.

of identifying the religion of a people with the *vetus religio* and of judging every novelty with diffidence, authorizing its annihilation with force. Against the integrity of civil life and that of the State no harm could ensue from the presence of new religions which were respectful of public morality and of public order: "Quaeso, quod periculum principi aut reipublicae ab opinione, ac secta, etsi nova; dum neque aliena sit a bonis moribus; et serviat venerationi summi imperii? Nam si perdendae sit reipublicae; non quia nova est prohiberi debet, sed quia noxia"[396].

And yet the many passages of themes shared in common with the Noodtian *Dissertatio* and with Bayle's thought cannot ignore the interesting reasons for divergence nor confuse the tracts, which are characteristic of different theoretical and methodological commitment. If reference to religious freedom in Noodt rests on its right as an essential principle for the correct conduct of life, in Bayle's recourse to law is translated into the individual's subjective intentions. The *lex*, that is to say, appears as though a fact of *conscience* which conserves the twofold meaning of moral law and inner feeling, which is morally neutral in accordance with Malebranchian's meaning. From this point of view, subjectivism comes to mean the awareness that conscience is exclusively identified with "le sentiment intérieur" of truth. And it is this for every individual "la règle de ce qu'il doit croire et faire", to the point that fidelity to their "instincts de sa conscience" renders an evil action more tolerable and not punishable by law. The appeal to the conscience, which tolerates and justifies the "wanderer", does not presuppose the existence of an innate and universal morality. Rather it bears wit-

396 NOODT (1706) 1999b, p. 215. It is interesting to compare this judgement with Bayle's observations on the "équivoque du terrible mot de nouveauté", incapable to reveal the heretical character of a doctrine "en matière de religion, où se mettra en bon train, mais ce sera sur un océan immense dont les tempêtes sont bien à craindre" (see *NOUVELLES DE LA RÉPUBLIQUE DES LETTRES* 1685,V, pp. 1005, 1006).

ness to the impossibility of identifying conscience and ethical law, also giving grounds for adherence to absolutism on the political plane[397]. To that end, however Noodt remained alien, defining religious freedom a right as a function of an ethical-rational choice and in respect of essential civil virtues. They would moreover have certainly recognised the "Nouvelles de la république des lettres". In May of 1706 (under the guidance of Jacques Bernard) they offered European readers a summary of the *Dissertatio* which appeared at the beginning of the year. The eulogy on the author's direct effective style preceded a judgement on the notion of religious freedom which, deriving from the theoretical viewpoint drawn from the conditioning of traditional theology, was traced back to the authentic ethical and religious values of man, to the historic-empirical effective conditions in which "les mouvements de sa conscience" were practised[398]. This was the patrimony, which Noodt passed on to his century, making a perfect contribution to the modern process of secularisation of culture and politics, to the "positive" and reformatory aspirations of a fully matured European Enlightenment. And it is here that the reflection on religious *freedom* was to meet with exceptional success in terms of criticism, thanks above all to the work of interpretation and divulgation carried out by Jean Barbeyrac.

The translator of Noodt's *Dissertatio de religione* and of Samuel Pufendorf's *De iure naturae et gentium* raised incisive objections against modern scepticism, which was accused of refusing to recognise certainty to moral conscience and of drawing unjustified conclusions from the differences of opinions encoun-

397 BAYLE [1686] 1713 in BAYLE 1727 [1965–1982], pp. 440b, 432a. See TARANTO 1994, Chap. 7, pp. 173–200. On the paradox see LAURSEN 2001, pp. 211–228.

398 NOUVELLES DE LA RÉPUBLIQUE DES LETTRES 1706, XXXVIII, pp. 586, 585. On the themes here examined see BOTS 1977.

tered "au sujet des vertus et des vices"[399]. In keeping with such a judgement Bayle's writings were also perused, being defined in 1706 as "plus dangereux [...] que les livres de *Hobbes*, et de *Spinoza*"[400]. In the same year, the *Dictionnaire historique et critique* were denounced to Pierre Des Maizeaux, together with the theses reproposed therein of the precursors of seventeenth century scepticism, all to be refuted for their damaging influences on moral life[401]. In Barbeyrac's eyes, the Baylian claim of individual *conscience*, as sole principle of ethical action, and the elevation of reason to an absolute moral value brought about negative consequences at an ethical-juridical level. The risk was that of transforming moral life into a scheme of pure formal relationships, incapable, on account of their universal and absolute value, of guaranteeing *certainty* in action. The content of the action risked passing to a second level: it was the direction of the *subjective conscience* that was to impose sufficient ethical and religious value and to become the only intermediary between man and God. Thus Bayle's negative solution was rejected, being attributed to the problem of *truth* and *certainty*. The conclusions of historical Pyrrhonism could not be shared, being unacceptable also from the political viewpoint:

> Mais quoi qu'en dise ce fameux philosophe [Bayle] [...], si l'on examine bien la bonne politique, l'on trouvera que la plupart de ses principes et de ses maximes ont une certitude, qui a approche fort de la démonstration; et que dans les choses mêmes le plus problématiques, l'obscurité vient plutôt de la difficulté de l'application, de l'ignorance des circonstances, ou du peu d'attention qu'on y fait, que de l'impossibilité absolue d'établir là-dessus aucune règle un peu sûre[402].

399 PUFENDORF 1734, *Préface du traducteur*, § IV, t. I, pp. XVII, XIX.
400 BARBEYRAC to Le Clerc 1706, III, p. 14. Cf. KORKMAN 1999–2000.
401 BARBEYRAC to Des Maizeaux 1706, p. 21r.
402 PUFENDORF 1734, Book I, Chap. 2, § IV, t. I, pp. 26–27.

The judgement assumed tones of a *querelle* between opposing positions and experiences, and tended to upset that cultural unity which the European Republic of Letters had thitherto vaunted. The "Pyrrhonist" philosopher, according to Barbeyrac, is to be confuted, because the theorized invalidity of the moral and historic world, heedless of all precaution, risks compromising the relationship between knowledge and action, and between theory and practice. This was a topic – despite his being aware of their different sensitivities and standpoints – which brought Barbeyrac close to the theses of Jean Pierre de Crousaz, Professor of Philosophy at Lausanne (and Rector of the Academy until 1737) who had initially adhered to theoretical positions of Cartesian matrix, but then later accepted Locke's teaching, thanks especially to Le Clerc's direct influences. It is not by chance, in fact, that Barbeyrac offers in the "Bibliothèque raisonnée", a detailed analysis of the *Examen du pyrrhonisme ancien et moderne* (1733), sharing the author's reservations and pointing out that "l'esprit de pyrrhonisme [est] le caractère de celui de l'auteur, et qu'il [a] eû un dessein fixe et soutenu d'inspirer les mêmes dispositions à ses lecteurs"[403]. Of Baylian pyrrhonism he was unable to accept, more than anything else, the fideistic conclusions. The distinction that was lacking in the areas of application of reason and faith had led to the uncertainty of moral life and necessitated accepting only the truths of religion revealed as sole criterion of human action: "Il s'attache surtout à mettre en opposition avec la raison, la morale de l'*Evangile*; quoique, dès qu'on reconnaît la divinité de l'Ecriture Sainte, on ne puisse que regarder ses préceptes moraux comme

403 *Bibliothèque raisonnée des ouvrages des savants de l'Europe* (1733, XI), pp. 56, 57. On this Journal see ROTONDÒ 1998. For the polemic against Bayle in Barbeyrac, see HOCHSTRASSER 1993 and 1995, pp. 15–51. More inclined to accentuate the critical distance of the French jurist from Crousaz is LAGARRIGUE 1993, p. 219.

parfaitement conformes aux lumières naturelles"[404]. The latter represented judgements already supported in the *Préface* to Pufendorf's *De iure*. Here too, recognising the true principles of morality which are founded on the "idées générales" of religion, the translator had not hesitated to denounce the weak expedient of the Pyrrhonists. After working intensively to weaken the "lumières de la raison", they referred to those of faith to solve our doubts as if the "*lumières de la foi*" did not presuppose those of reason, and the proofs of truth of the facts – on which revelation is based – were "plus évidentes" than the maxims of "droite raison au sujet de nos devoirs, et de leurs vrais fondements". Revelation has not been conceded to men to communicate definitively all that they need know. On the contrary, it assumes some knowledge possessed or acquired, and the faculty of drawing conclusions from the principles known "ou par les lumières seules de la raison, ou par l'Ecriture Sainte"[405]. The thesis in 1709, took its cue from the contemporary polemic on the morality of *play*. In Chapter III of the *Traité du jeu*, to the question whether it is contrary to the spirit of the Gospel, Barbeyrac replied with documented references to the sacred text, observing that play, not explicitly condemned by Christian morality, is permitted and is compatible with the principles of modern natural law theory. Bayle's limits also emerged, in this interpretative perspective, which in order to support the opposite thesis had attributed (in the quoted *Continuation des Pensées diverses*) an exclusive character to Christian religion and morality, comprehensible only to the chosen few:

> Dans cette supposition [...] Jésus-Christ n'a point proposé sa religion comme une chose qui pût convenir à toutes sortes de personnes, mais seulement à un petit nombre de sages; étrange imagination, où l'on ne

404 *BIBLIOTHÈQUE RAISONNÉE DES OUVRAGES DES SAVANTS DE L'EUROPE* (1733, XI), p. 69. See LOMONACO 1999, pp. 253–267.
405 PUFENDORF 1734, *Préface du traducteur*, § XXXII, t. I, pp. CXIV, CXIII.

serait jamais tombé, si l'on avait lû le Nouveau Testament avec tant soit peu d'attention et avec un esprit désintéressé[406].

Barbeyrac's aim was, in contrast, to acknowledge for the Christian religion the significance of a universal experience, favouring at the same time, a "middle road" in the area of the *science des moeurs* and natural right. Also in these contexts it is a question of rejecting not only the objections of the sceptics and the pyrrhonists who want "douter purement et simplement pour douter", but also the critical reservations of those who adopt abstract and almost unintelligible principles to explain the "*origine des idées innées*". They are not happy with proof that may be identified in the *truth* of religion and morality. Between the *pyrrhonism* of the former and the dogmatic *innatism* of the latter, it is expedient to single out an theoretical intermediary space which adapts man's choices to the functions of his *ratio*[407]. In 1706 the thesis was reasserted to his friend Pierre Des Maizeaux, confirming that a "middle road" could be identified between traditional dogmatism and Baylian pyrrhonism[408]. Indeed the search for a compromise between absolute scepticism and dogmatic apologetics might have favoured an original redefinition of experience and the moral world. To get to know the *general ideas* of natural law and the true origins of human *duties* only required "l'expérience la plus commune de la vie, et un peu de réflexion sur soi-même et sur les objets qui nous envi-

406 BARBEYRAC 1737², t. I, p. 39. In the critique to the second French edition of Noodts' s *Dissertationes* (1714) Jean Le Clerc, in reference to the theses in *Traité du sort* (published in Appendix to the edition reviewed in 1714), declared himself "du sentiment de Mr. Barbeyrac, touchant le sort" (see BIBLIOTHÈQUE ANCIENNE ET MODERNE 1714, I, II, pp. 456–457).

407 PUFENDORF 1734, *Préface du traducteur*, § § III, IV, t. I, pp. XIV, XVIII, XVI.

408 BARBEYRAC to Des Maizeaux 1706, 20v–21r.

ronnent de toutes parts"[409]. The reference to experience implies the rejection of ancient and modern metaphysics which risks invalidating problems of morality. It seeks, above all, to free knowledge of the law of nature from traditional claims, so as to be able to attribute its constitution in man to the action of the conscience-reason. No truth imposed from outside can set itself up as a model of practical rule, since authentic freedom lies in the respect of one's own conscience. This, the expression in man of his very own existence, is not, however, absolutely certain, being written in the natural order, yet it is the outcome of a complex construction of normative value. It is the faculty of establishing connections on empirical basis, taken from the conditioning of a single absolute criterion of truth. In this context it is not difficult to identify one of the sources of Barbeyrac's thought. The appeal to *experience* and *reason*, indispensable guides for reflection on morality *(science des moeurs)* and on natural right represents a very interesting point of convergence of the teachings of Pufendorf and of the other great master, John Locke. In his *Préface* to the *De iure naturae et gentium*, the French editor of the work had recourse to the authority of the *Essay concerning Human Understanding* (1690) in order to defend his theses. With Pufendorf and Locke, Barbeyrac shares the exigency of a morality founded on fixed laws, deductively demonstrable like those of physics. The *modus* of existence for the human *conscience* and the value itself of the moral bond are guaranteed by the obligation capacity of the law. From this viewpoint the criterion of rational *evidence* theorized by Bayle can no longer suffice as an autonomous source of value. The outcome of Baylianan practical reason – which lays the foundations for the absolute validity of ethical principles from the point of view of the individual conscience – is the legitimisation of *atheism.* In denying God, both for Barbeyrac and Locke, the atheists deny the idea of

409 PUFENDORF 1734, *Préface du traducteur*, § I, t. I, pp. III, IV.

natural right itself, together with the principle of the freedom of conscience, which derives therefrom. Atheism and its libertinism outcomes risk invalidating the ethical aims of society, the trust in the moral character of human association: "[...] Mais épurez tant qu'il vous plaira l'athéisme; jamais vous n'en tirerez que des conséquences pernicieuses, qui ménent tout droit au plus grand libertinage". In the comment to Book II of Pufendorf's *De iure*, the translator applied to the well-known theses of the philosopher of Rotterdam the same limits which Grotius had set on his own hypothesis. The author of the *De iure belli ac pacis*, in stating that the rules of natural right "*auraient lieu* en quelque manière", emphasised the centrality of the relationship which the "idées de convenance ou disconvenance", founded on human nature, have with the "volonté de Dieu"[410]. In this context Barbeyrac identified yet again the main sources of his reflection in Locke and in Noodt. From the ethical-political viewpoint the common exigency was that of rejecting both religious intransigence of the French absolute monarchy of Catho-

410 PUFENDORF 1734, Book II, Chap. 3, § XIX, t. I, pp. 232, 230. See PALLADINI 1988, pp. 401–402 and notes. On PUFENDORF 1734, Book II, see Le Clerc's critique in *BIBLIOTHÈQUE CHOISIE* 1706. He recalled the attention, above all, on Barbeyrac's polemic against Bayle that the reviewer opportunely judged as engaged to "une énumeration des désordres affreux, qui arriveraient dans une république d'athées. Il continue la même matière sur le liv.II ch.III, 19 et ch. IV, 3 et réfute très-bien la pensée de Mr. *Bayle*, qui prétend qu'une république d'athées aurait été aussi bien réglée, que les républiques païennes". The conclusion was in a critical judgement of Le Clerc on the limits to establish "en quelque part une république d'athées, pour voir ce qui en serait; (qu') une république, selon les idées de Platon; et désormais les raisonnements de Mr. *Bayle* ne feront pas grand mal au monde" (see *BIBLIOTHÈQUE CHOISIE* 1706, IX, pp. 403, 404). The "apologetical" value of the connexion between Grotius and Pufendorf in Barbeyrac against Hobbes has been recalled by PALLADINI 1990, pp. 277–278. About the contradictions in Barbeyrac among the *rationalism* and *voluntarism*, see HOCHSTRASSER 1995, p. 46. On Barbeyrac and Pufendorf see LOMONACO 2000, pp. 197–207.

lic faith, as well as the authoritarianism of Genevan Calvinism, by reasserting the reasons for *freedom* and *conscience* of modern man. And in 1731, in a note to Noodt's *Dissertatio de religione*, commenting on the investigation into the powers and limits of sovereignty in the ethical-religious field, the translator referred to the content of his *Discours sur la permission des loix* and *Sur le benefice des loix*. A quotation fell also on Chapter 12 of the *Traité de la morale des Pères de l'Eglise* (1728) which attributed a definite educational function to the sovereign, able to support the part "d'honnête-homme et de chrétien", to operate with instruments destined for *education* and for *persuasion*, thus without exercising "aucune contrainte"[411]. The thesis had been amply shared and furthered by Noodt. In a note to the *Dissertatio* Barbeyrac even referred to the authority of the *Commentaire philosophique* (part III, art. III and ff.) of the criticised Bayle, agreeing on the illegitimacy of the persecution of the *wandering conscience*. In this regard he also referred to Chapters 12 and 16 of the *Traité*, where very bitter criticism was made with regard to the "crasse ignorance" of the Church Fathers and their disseminators "en fait de droit naturel et de morale, aussi bien qu'en matière de critique", as reported in the review devoted to the work by the same author in the "Bibliothèque raisonnée" of 1728[412].

411 NOODT (1699) 1724 in BARBEYRAC 1731, t. I, p. 159, note and p. 160, note. The reference is to BARBEYRAC 1728, Chap. 12, §§ LIII, XXXVIII, pp. 194, 184. See PUAUX 1881, pp. 161–169. On Noodt and Barbeyrac, with regard to the distinction among "Christian and civil Tolerance", see VAN EIJNATTEN 1993, pp. 122, 339 and note (but see, above all, Chap. 3, pp. 99–126 and pp. 408–457 for Bibliography). On the fortune of Noodt's and Barbeyrac's ideas at the end of the eighteenth century it is to signal VAN EIJNATTEN 1999(b), pp. 41–51.

412 NOODT (1699) 1724 in BARBEYRAC 1731, t. I, p. 182, note 2 and *BIBLIOTHÈQUE RAISONNÉE DES OUVRAGES DES SAVANTS DE L'EUROPE* (1728, I,II), p. 318. On this critique see LAGARRIGUE 1993, pp. 55–56. To that "Bibliothèque", with regard to the defense of tolerance against the religious orthodoxy, see BOTS 1996, pp. 557–559.

In the first decades of the eighteenth century, in an age of rediscovered political *equilibrium* – as that in which Barbeyrac lived – different religions and political orders co-existed peacefully. One witnesses in fact the discussions from every perspective about intolerant despotic power and universal monarchy. This latter argument, proposed in France by Louis XIV, had been invalidated at the beginning of the "enlightened" century by the claim of the *rights* of *conscience*, destined to mark the new concept of *tolerance*. This becomes a limit imposed on the intrusive state action and on the dogmatic-ecclesiastic organization to support their reciprocal independence. In denouncing the dogmatic character of every judgement which claims to bind the *conscience*, the reflections of the translator of Noodt and Pufendorf are symbolically differentiated by the contents of the seventeenth-century debate on *tolerance*. The epoch of religious struggles has ended. The old order of dogmas and politico-confessional formulas has collapsed and the age of modern *reason*, of the *lay* spirit and of *freedom* has come to fruition. Considerable merit is due to Barbeyrac for sensing and, in his limited capacities of speculation, for theorizing the passage from the idea of *libera religio* to that of *libertas conscientiae*, thereby epitomizing the transition from rationality of natural law theory to enlightenment.

Afterword

The two full-bodied introductions that Fabrizio Lomonaco has attached as preface to the English publication of his essays devoted to the questions arising from the huge problem of the *Lex Regia* provide the access key to these studies. Such introductions intrinsically represent a central chapter in his research which has transformed Fabrizio into a recognized and highly thought of expert in Neapolitan, Italian, and European historical /philosophical culture between Gravina and Vico during their projection into Europe. There would be nothing else to say, except to express the gratification of one who – as Fabrizio also on this occasion generously acknowledges – got him started on these studies, at a time when he on his own part was already interested in fathoming the historicity of Law as well as its philosophy. In pursuing a line of research of his own initiative Fabrizio soon found his own space as is attested, amongst other things, by the reactions of authoritative researchers, Italian and Dutch alike, involved in the same discipline area. And yet the temptation is difficult to resist, as Fabrizio affectionately but firmly reiterates, to underline the precise historiographic option already made, when setting out from the school of research he wished to pursue, and herein confirmed, while reflecting on the work, already achieved which is now at a phase of condensation that allows it to be recognized and classified, as it were, within the "history of studies".

Following a historicist interpretation of the history of philosophy, of ideas, and of culture as *historical histories*, *epochal and non-categorical histories*, Fabrizio reasons the meaning of the "philosophy-historiography" relationship, translating it into the latter relationship of "philosophy-philology" (which the former examines in depth). It is not only the resumption of the Vichian topos *philosophia et philologia geminae ortae*, but is something more. It is shown by the precise direct and indirect interpretation proposals made by the classical interlocutors of the *Lex Regia*, leaving aside its ideological and methodological dimensions. On one side, it deals with the identity of Platonic Vico's "modernity", that is not hesitant but seen as an interlocutor of the great themes of the "New Science", the "New History", and of the "New Politics", using his erudition, which is outmoded if you like, but nevertheless sound on account of its intelligent originality, as to provide new responses to his restless questioning of the "endless antiquities" while wading through boring, difficult, unusual and antiquated texts. And all this was – as the shrewder Vichian historiography, with Fabrizio included among their number, have already shown – a lesson in historical method, namely that the past hides nothing from him, nor is he denied anything, exchanging the new with the avant-garde trend of arrogant petulant intellectuals, he is persistently questioning himself in order to give meaning to the dimensions of historical constructions, which are not impromptu fadings away of bright improvisations, but transformations, also radical ones, of reasoned innovation, that have the ability to communicate and execute, when they are consolidated according to a process of linguistic, categorical and cultural "changes" that are able to connect – but without distorting – the inventiveness of the creative subjects (liberty) and the social objectification of the already known (necessity).

On another front, which is the documentation of Vico's non-provincial European modernity, in his cosmopolitan Naples at the "confines of the empire", Fabrizio takes up the precious suggestion of Giuseppe Giarrizzo, when he emphasized the conclusive importance of the phase of Vichian reflection that pivots around the *De Uno* and the *De Constantia* (1720-1723). Fabrizio associates this with the other important teaching of Pietro Piovani and of the others who have harvested his inheritance, which is namely to examine scrupulously through the work of the critical edition of Vico's works, its precise historical scanning, within its context, of the development of Vico's thoughts. It was this that was the starting point of a new, renewed interpretation of Vico, not as a philosopher obsessed with the upward tension from the *De Antiquissima* (when not before) to the third *Scienza Nuova* (1744), but rather as a tireless investigator of new ideas, between continuity and interruptions, amid confirmations and aware criticality, of a "political", "non-monastic", philosophy that can be understood only if every work and every phase of reflection is outlined in its own specificity and autonomy. And not in order to give into a hack whim of inventing a Vico One, a Vico Two and a Vico Three, with the risk of finding yourself – with a sceptical and cynical Pirandello-like Search for an Author, – facing a Vico One, No One and a Hundred Thousand. Or rather a transformed Vico (it seems a historiographical curse) from a lingering "loner", confined within provincial Naples, the "precursor", the "anticipator", the "pioneer" of everything and all, who finds pinned on himself the badly-sewn identity of a "Mr Nobody" all within a hotchpotch history. Setting out from this point, and fully aware of knowing how to use the non-superimposable suggestions at times in conflict with each other made by two different teachers, namely Arnaldo Momigliano and Santo Mazzarino, Fabrizio Lomonaco sets Vico at the origins of modern historiography, between Antiquarianism and Pyrrhonism, making thereof a document of philological history (that history also of the Grotian Dutch and not Grotian readers of the *Lex Regia*), which combines Ancient History and Modern Historiography and opens up the way to the Historiography and the Philosophy of its Historicism, not in the sense of different and always unfounded anticipations, but rather in that of the identification of a precise tradition or movement of ideas. The traditions that are able and must be given of philosophies and of historiographies able to metabolize ignorant methodologism of history and philosophy, inasmuch as example of the most useless and loquacious of the sciences (alas how recently widespread in our studies too). Piovani has said that "the history either is philological or it is not".

It seems to me that this is the trademark of the work of Fabrizio Lomonaco, who, without arrogance, always with a low and humble declaration of his own debts, knows how to bring, and in fact has brought remarkable innovations to the fields of study he has cultivated and still cultivates with untiring hard work. This declaration of mine is not a conventional concession to the forms of the literary civilization, which is moreover seasoned with affection: rather it is a judgment, pronounced with a convinced strict assumption of scientific responsibility. And however, if I may close on a personal note, on a point that perforce at all costs must be uttered. It is gratifying to have seen a young boy grow up, intelligent, hard-working, and ambitious, that I met thirty five years ago and who has become a master, and as master knows how not to lose the duty of fidelity, which is not only and simply the duty of gratitude, but is awareness of self. It is the honest examination of self that is the highest form of liberty, full of one who proudly claims his own role, without surrendering to false exploitations, to deceptive submissiveness to cover up the frustrations of repressed rebelliousness and unbridled social climbing Hence the presentation of the works of a pupil, who has become a colleague, cannot and has no wish to conclude in any other way than to repeat to Fabrizio and with Fabrizio, the words of Giuseppe Capograssi, that were dear to Piovani, Capograssi's pupil, and are dear to me, Piovani's pupil. "What is the master if not he who put aloft the sign, ever higher than the normal stature of a normal man, whom in fact he invites to climb, to look around, and in keeping with Rosmini's ever-living words, to think big?"

Naples, 3 May 2010

Fulvio Tessitore

Bibliography

AARSLEFF H. 1981, *Vico and Berlin*, in "London Review of Books", 5–18 november, 6–7.

ABEL G. 1978, *Stoizismus und Frühe Neuzeit*, Berlin-New York: de Gruyter.

ACTA ERUDITORUM 1687, 1691, 1703, 1704, 1714, Lipsiae: apud J. Grossium et J. F. Gleditschium.

AELIANUS CL. 1701, *Varia historia [...]*, cum versione Justi Vulteji [...] et perpetuo commentario Jacobi Perizonii, Lugduni in Batavis: apud J. du Vivie, I. Severinum.

AHSMANN M.- FEENSTRA R. 1984, *Bibliografie van hoogleraren in de rechten aan de Leidse Uuniversiteit tot 1811,* Amsterdam-Oxford-New York: B.V. Noord-Hollandsche Uitgevers Maatschappij.

AJELLO R. (1968) 1976, *Legislazione e crisi del diritto comune nel Regno di Napoli. Il tentativo di codificazione carolina*, in AJELLO R. 1976, *Arcana iuris. Diritto e politica nel Settecento italiano*, Naples: Jovene.

AJELLO R. 1976, *Arcana iuris. Diritto e politica nel Settecento italiano*, Naples: Jovene.

AJELLO R. 1985, *Continuità e trasformazione dei valori giuridici; dal probabilismo al problematicismo*, in "Rivista storica italiana", 97, pp. 884–931.

AJELLO R. 1988, *Ercolano tra Antiquari e Filosofi*, in *Le Antichità di Ercolano*, Naples: Banco di Napoli.

ALBERTARIO E. (1910) 1953, *Nota su alcuni tribonianismi rilevati nelle "Praelectiones iuris civilis" di Ulrico Huber*, in ALBERTARIO E. 1953, *Studi di diritto romano. VI. Saggi critici e studi varii*, Milan: Giuffrè.

Album amicorum. ΦΙΛΟΜΝΗΜΩΝ *seu memoriae faventium Johanni Frederico Gronovio hammaburgensi*, Groningae, XXIII Kal. April. Juli, anno Christi MDCXXXIV.

Album studiosorum Academiae Lugduno-Batavae, 1875–1925, ed. Kroon J.E., Leiden: Sijthoff.

Allix P. to Le Clerc J. 10 January 1685, in Le Clerc J. 1987, *Epistolario*, ed. Sina M., Florence: Olschki.

Alpers S. 1984, *The Art of Describing. Dutch Art in the Seventeenth Century* (1983), Italian translation by Cuniberto F., Turin: Boringhieri.

Althusius J. (1586) 1592, *Iurisprudentiae Romanae methodice digestae libri duo […]*, Herbornae: ex officina Ch. Corvini.

Amaya F. de 1667, *Antiquariensis observationum iuris*, in Amaya F. de 1667, *Opera iuridica, seu Commentarii in tres posteriores libros Codicis imp. Iustiniani [...]*, Lugduni: sumptibus Ph. Borde, L. Arnaud et P. Borde.

Amodio P. 1998, *Scepsi e critica storica*, in La Mothe Le Vayer F., Introduction to La Mothe Le Vayer F., *Della poca certezza che c'è nella storia*, Italian translation by Amodio P., Soveria Mannelli: Rubbettino.

Amodio P. 2005, *Luoghi del bonheur. Elementi per un'antropologia tra libertinismi e mondo dei lumi*, Naples: Giannini.

Aprosio A. 1641, *L'occhiale stritolato di Scipio Glareano* [pseud. di A. Aprosio], per risposta al Signor Cavalier Tommaso Stigliani, in 1642, *Il buratto*; replica di Carlo Galistoni al molino del Signor Carlo Stigliani [...], in Venetia: nella stamparia Sarziniana, appresso T. Pavoni.

Aprosio A. 1673, *La Biblioteca aprosiana.* Passatempo autunnale di Cornelio Aspasio Antivigilmi trà vagabondi di Tabbia detto l'aggirato [...] In Bologna: per li Manolessi.

Archi G.G. 1986, *Sanctissimum templurn iustitiae*, in *Le Pandette di Giustiniano. Storia e fortuna di un codice illustre*, Florence: Olschki.

ARIENZO A. and BORRELLI G. 2000–2001, *Bibliografia saggistica sulla letteratura della ragion di Stato*, 1995–2000, in "Archivio della Ragion di Stato",7–8, pp. 161–182.

ARMINIUS JACOBUS et al. 1684, *Praestantium ac eruditorum virorum Epistolae ecclesiasticae et theologicae quarum longe maior pars scripta est a Jac. Arminio, Joan. Uytenbogardo, Conr. Vorstio, Ger. Joan. Vossio, Hug. Grotio, Sim. Episcopio, Casp. Barlaeo,* Editio secunda [...], Amstelaedami: apud H. Wetstenium.

ARNAULD A. - NICOLE P. 1662, *La logique ou l'art de penser [...]*, Paris: J. de Launay.

ASOR ROSA A. 1961, *Aprosio Angelico*, in *Dizionario biografico degli italiani*, vol. III, Rome: Istituto della Enciclopedia italiana.

ASTON T. ed. (1965) 1968, *Crisis in Europe (1560–1660)*, intr. of Ch. HILL, Italian translation by INCARNATO G., Naples: Giannini.

BADALONI N. 1961, *Introduzione a G.B. Vico*. Milan: Feltrinelli.

BALDUINUS F. (1545) 1728, *Iustinianus, sive De iure novo commentariorum libri quatuor [...]*, Halae et Lipsiae: ex officina crugina.

BARBEYRAC J. to Des Maizeaux P., Berlin, 22 December 1706, London, British Library, Add. ms. 4281.

BARBEYRAC J. to Le Clerc J., 10 April 1706, then in LE CLERC J. 1994, *Epistolario*, eds. SINA M. G. and SINA M., Florence: Olschki.

BARBEYRAC J. 1720, in GROTIUS H. *De iure belli ac pacis [...]. Cum annotatis auctoris [...]; nec non Joann. Fried. Gronovii [...] notis in totum opus [...]. Notulas denique addidit Joannes barbeyrac [...]*, Amstelaedami: apud Janssonio-Waesbergios.

BARBEYRAC J. 1724, *Le droit de la guerre et de la paix par Hugues Grotius*, Nouvelle translation par BARBEYRAC J. [...], Amsterdam: chez P. De Coup.

BARBEYRAC J. 1728, *Traité de la morale des Pères de l'Eglise: où en défendant un article de la Préface sur Pufendorf, contre l'Apologie de la morale des Pères du P. Ceillier, religieux bénédictin de la Congrégation de St. Vanne et de St. Hydulphe, on fait diverses réflexions sur plusieurs matières importantes, par Jean Barbeyrac […]*, Amsterdam: chez P. de Coup.

BARBEYRAC J. 1731, *Recueil de discours sur diverses matières importantes […]*, par BARBEYRAC J., Amsterdam: Humbert.

BARBEYRAC J. 1737², *Traité du jeu, où l'on examine les principales questions de droit naturel et de morale qui ont du rapport à cette matière par Jean Barbeyrac […]*, Amsterdam: chez P. Humbert.

BARBIERI G. 1957, *Lex de imperio Vespasiani*, in *Dizionario Epigrafico di Antichità Romane*, ed. DE RUGGIERO E., vol. IV, Rome: L. Pasqualucci.

BARFOOT C.C. et al. 1992, *The Great Emporium. The Low Countries as a cultural crossroads in the Renaissance and the eighteenth century*, ed. by BARFOOT C.C. and TODD R. Amsterdam-Atlanta: Rodopi.

BARNES A. 1938, *Jean Le Clerc (1657–1736) et la République des Lettres*, Paris: Droz.

BATES E. S. 1911, *Touring in 1600: a Study in the Development of Travel as a Means of Education,* New York: B. Franklin.

BAYLE P. (1682) 1727–1731 [1965–1982], *Critique Générale de l'Histoire du Calvinisme*, in 1727–1731, *Oeuvres diverses*, La Haye: chez Husson P. [et al.; reprint, Hildesheim-New York, Olms G., 1965–1982].

BAYLE P. (1685) 1727 [1965-1982], *Nouvelles lettres de l'auteur de la Critique générale de l'histoire du calvinisme* [1685], in 1727, *Oeuvres diverses*, La Haye: chez Husson P. [et al., reprint, Hildesheim-New York, Olms G., 1965–1982].

BAYLE P. [1686] 1713, *Commentaire philosophique sur ces paroles de Jésus-Christ, Contrain-les d'entrer […]*, Canterbury: chez Litwel Th. and Rotterdam: Fritsch et Bohm.

BAYLE P. (1697–1698) 1740, *Dictionnaire historique et critique […]* (1697–1698), V ed., Amsterdam-Leide-La Haye-Utrecht: chez Brunel P. [et autres].

BAYLE P. 1727–1731 (1965–1982), *Oeuvres diverses*, La Haye: chez Husson P. [et al., reprint, Hildesheim-New York: Olms G., 1965–1982].

BERGH VAN DEN G.C.J.J. 1988, *The Life and Work of Gerard Noodt (1647–1725). Dutch Legal Scholarship between Humanism and Enlightenment*, Oxford: Clarendon Press.

BERGH VAN DEN G.C.J.J. 2002, *Die holländische elegante Schule. Ein Beitrag zur geschichte von Humanismus und Rechtswissenschaft in den Niederlanden 1500–1800*, Frankfurt am Main: V. Klostermann.

BERKEL VAN K. & DE GOEI L. et al. 2010, *The International Relevance of Dutch History,* in "BMGN-The Low Countries Historical Review", 125, 2-3, pp. 1-365.

BERLIN I. 1976, *Vico and Herder. Two Studies in the History of Ideas*, London: The Hogarth Press.

BERLIN I. 1981, *Isaiah Berlin Responds to the Foregoing Criticism of His Work*, in "London Review of Books", 5–18 november, pp. 7–8.

BERTELLI S. 1955, *La crisi dello scetticismo e il rapporto erudizione-scienza agl'inizi del secolo XVIII*, in "Società", 11, pp. 435–456.

BERTELLI S. 1962, *Erudizione e crisi religiosa nella coscienza europea avanti l'opera muratoriana*, in "Atti e Memorie della Deputazione di storia patria per le antiche province modenesi", II, pp. 151–181.

BERTELLI S. 1973, *Ribelli, libertini e ortodossi nella storiografia barocca*, Florence: La Nuova Italia.

BERTELLI S. et al. 1986, *La Storia. I grandi problemi dal Medioevo all'Età Contemporanea,* eds. TRANFAGLIA N. and FIRPO M., Turin: Utet.

BERTI S. 1988, *Autobiografia, storicismo e verità storica in Arnaldo Somigliano*, in "Rivista Storica Italiana", 100, pp. 297–312.

BETTI E. 1957, *I principi di Scienza nuova di G.B. Vico e la teoria della interpretazione storica*, in "Nuova Rivista di Diritto Commerciale, Diritto dell'Economia, Diritto Sociale", 10, pp. 48–59.

BIANCHI L. 1987, *Bayle, i dizionari e la storia*, in BAYLE P., *Progetto di un Dizionario critico,* ed. BIANCHI L., Naples: Liguori, pp. 11–156.

BIANCHI L. 1988, *Tradizione libertina e critica storica. Da Naudé a Bayle*, Milan: F. Angeli.

BIBLIOTHEQUE ANCIENNE ET MODERNE 1714, 1718, 1720, Amsterdam: D. Mortier et R. et G. Wetstein, reprinted in 1968, Genève: Slatkine.

BIBLIOTHEQUE CHOISIE 1705, 1713, Amsterdam: H. Scelte, reprinted in 1968, Genève: Slatkine.

BIBLIOTHEQUE RAISONNEE DES OUVRAGES DES SAVANTS DE L'EUROPE 1728, 1733, Amsterdam: Wetstein & Smith.

BIBLIOTHEQUE UNIVERSELLE ET HISTORIQUE 1687, 1689-1691, 1693, 1699, 1717, Amsterdam: Wolfgang, reprinted in 1968, Genève: Slatkine.

BIONDI B. 1911, *I Tribonianismi avvertiti da J.J. Wissenbach ed H. Eckhard*, Palermo: Gaipa.

BLOM H. W. 1989, *A Dutch context to late 17th century republican thought. Gulielmus van der Muelen's dissertation on sovereignty*, in "Il pensiero politico", 22, pp. 66–73.

BLOM H. W. 1995, *Morality and Causality in Politics. The Rise of Naturalism in Dutch Seventeenth-Century Political Thought*, Utrecht: Proefschrift ter verkrijging van de graad van doctor aan de Universiteit.

BOBBIO N. (1947) 1965, *Leibniz e Pufendorf*, in BOBBIO N. 1965, *Da Hobbes a Marx*, Naples: Morano.

BOBBIO N. et al. 1979 (1984), *Società e Stato nella filosofia politica moderna*, Milan: il Saggiatore.

BOCHART S. (1663, 1668–1681, 1674) 1692, *Lettre à Mr. de Segrais ou dissertation sur la question, si Enée a jamais été en Italie*, in 1668–1681, *L'Eneide de Virgile*, ed. REGNAULD DE SEGRAIS J., Paris: chez Thierry D. and in Appendix to BO-

CHART S. (1674) 1681, *Geographia sacra* [...], Francofurti ad Moenum: impensis Zunneri J. D., typis Christophori B.

BODIN J. (1576) 1593 [1986], *Les six livres de La République [...]*. Texte revu par FREMONT CH., COUZINET M.-D., ROCHAIS H., Paris: Fayard.

BOEHMER I. CH. 1709, *Programma disputationibus XII pufendorfianis ab Io. Christoph. Leonhard Gera-Varisco respondente in iis perpetuo publice instituendis praemissum* herausgegeben. Accedit *Epistola viri excellentissimi ad amicum qua monita quaedam ad principia Pufendorfiani operis De officio hominis et civis continentur.* Helmstadii: ex officina hammiana.

BOELES W.B.S. 1864, *Levenschetsen der Groninger Hoogleeraren*, in Appendix to JONCKBLOET W.J.A., *Gedenkboek der Hoogeschool te Groningen ter gelegenheid van haar vijfde halve eeuwfeest op last van den Akademischen Senaat [...]*, Groningen: J.B. Wolters.

BOELES W.B.S. 1878–1889, *Frieslands Hoogeschool en het Rijks Athenaeum te Franeker*, Leeuwarden: H. Kuipers

BŒUF E. 2007, *La Bibliothèque parisienne de Gabriel Naudé en 1630. Les lectures d'un libertin érudit*, Genève: Droz.

BONFATTI E. 1983, *Magistratura e tragedia. Il "De Constantia" di Justus Lipsius e il servo fedele di Grillparzer*, in "Intersezioni", III, pp. 265–284.

BOOT I.C.G. 1883, *Hugo Grotius et Cornelius Tacitus*, Amstelaedami: apud Io. Mullerum.

BORGHERO C. 1983, *La certezza e la storia. Cartesianesimo, pirronismo e conoscenza storica*, Milan: F. Angeli.

BOSSUET J.B. (1693) 1862–1866, *Traité de la concupiscence*, in 1862–1866, *Oeuvres complètes publiées [...]* par LACHAT F., Paris: L. Vivès.

BOTS H. 1977, *L'esprit de la République des Lettres et la tolérance dans les trois premiers périodiques savants hollandais*, in "XVIIe siècle", 116, pp. 45–47.

BOTS H. et al. 1981, *De "Bibliothèque universelle et historique" (1686–1693). Een periodiek als trefpunt van geleerd Europa,* Amsterdam: APA-Holland Universiteits Pers.

BOTS H. 1994, *Hugo Grotius et André Rivet : deux lumières opposées, deux vocations contradictoires*, in *Hugo Grotius Theologian. Essays in Honour of G.H.M. Posthumus Meyjes*, edited by Nellen H.J.M. and Rabbie E., Leiden-New York-Köln: E.J. Brill, pp. 145–155.

BOTS H. 1996, *Le plaidoyer des journalistes de Hollande pour la tolérance (1684–1750)*, in *De l'Humanisme aux Lumières, Bayle et le protestantisme.* Mélanges en l'honneur d'Elisabeth Labrousse, eds. MAGDELAINE M., PITASSI C., WHELAN R. and MCKENNA A., Paris-Oxford: Universitas-Voltaire Foundation.

BOTS H. - WAQUET F. (1997) 2005, *La République des Lettres*, Italian translation by FERRARA R., Bologna: il Mulino.

BROEUS F. 1622, *Expositiones in imperatoris Iustiniani Institutionum libros quatuor. In tres partes distinctae [...]*, Lutetiae Parisiorum: apud S. Cramoisy, via Iacobaea sub Ciconijs.

BUCKLE S. 1991, *Natural Law and the Theory of Property. Grotius to Hume*, Oxford: Clarendon Press.

BUDE E. DE 1899, *Vie de Jean-Robert Chouet, professeur et magistrat genevois (1642–1731)*, Genève: M. Reymond et C.

BUGTER S.E.W. 1980, *J.F. Gronovius en de Annales van Tacitus*, Leiden: Proefschrift Rijksuniversiteit.

BURGIO S. 2001, *La via media del diritto. Tolleranza e libertà di coscienza*, in "Giornale critico della filosofia italiana", 80, pp. 360–366.

BURKE P. (1947) 1988, *Venice and Amsterdam. A Study of Seventeenth-Century Elites*, Italian translation by MIRETTI M., Ancon-Bologna: Transeuropa.

BURMANNUS C. 1738, *Traiectum Eruditorum, Virorum doctrina inlustrium [...]*,Traiecti ad Rhenum: apud Jurianum a Paddenburg.

BUZAS L. 1972, *Geschichte der Universitätsbibliothek München*, Wiesbaden: L. Reichert Verlag.

CALASSO F. 1949, *Gli ordinamenti giuridici del rinascimento medievale*, Milan: Giuffrè.

CALASSO F. (1951) 1970, *Introduzione al diritto comune*, Milan: Giuffrè.

CALASSO F. 1954, *Medio evo del diritto. Le fonti*, Milan: Giuffrè.

CALASSO F. 1957, *I glossatori e la teoria delta sovranità. Studio di diritto comune pubblico*, Milan: Giuffrè.

CANTELLI G. 1971, *Vico e Bayle: premesse per un confronto*, Naples: Guida.

CANTELLI G. 1972, *Mito e storia in Leclerc, Tournemine e Fontanelle*, in "Rivista critica di storia della filosofia", 27, pp. 269–286, 385–400.

CANTIMORI D. (1966) 1971, *Storia e storiografia in Benedetto Croce*, in CANTIMORI D. 1971, *Storici e storia. Metodo, caratteristiche e significato del lavoro storiografico*, Turin: Einaudi.

CAPPELLINI P. et al. 1987, *Materiali per un lessico politico europeo: "Prudenza"*, in "Filosofia politica", I, pp. 229–402.

CARCOPINO J. 1937, *Les prétendues "Lois Royales"*, in "Mélanges d'Archéologie et d'Histoire", 54, pp. 344–376.

CASAUBONUS I. 1638, *Epistolae, quotquot reperiri potuerunt, nunc primum iunctim editae [...]*, Hagae-Comitis: ex officina T. Maire.

CHOUET J. R. to Le Clerc J., Geneva, 16 June 1685, in LE CLERC J. 1987, *Epistolario*, ed. SINA M., Florence: Olschki.

CICOGNA E. A. 1847, *Saggio di bibliografia veneziana*, Venice: dalla tipografia di G.B. Merlo.

CINELLI CALVOLI G. 1734–1747, *Biblioteca volante di Gio: Cinelli Calvoli continuata dal dottor Dionigi Andrea Sancassani*, Venezia: presso G. Albrizzi Q. Girolamo.

CLAPMARIUS A. (1605) 1624, *De arcanis rerumpublicarum libri sex [...]*, Francofurti: typis I. F. Weissij, sumptibus I. Berneri.

CLERICI A. 2007, *Monarcomachi e giusnaturalisti nella Utrecht del Seicento. Willem van der Muelen e la legittimazione olandese della Gloriosus Revolution*, Milan: F. Angeli.

CLUVERIUS P. 1624, *Italia antiqua [...]*, Lugduni Batavorum: ex officina Elseviriana.

COHEN G. 1921, *Ecrivains français en Hollande dans la première moitié du XVIIe siècle*, The Hague-Paris: Nijhoff-Champion.

COMPARATO V. I. 1980, *Il pensiero politico dei libertini*, in *Storia delle idee politiche, economiche e sociali,* ed. FIRPO L., Turin: Utet.

CONNANUS F. 1553, *Commentariorum iuris civilis libri 10 [...].* Tomus prior, quinque libros complectens [...], Basileae: apud N. Episcopium iuniorem.

CONTI V. 1983, *Le leggi di una rivoluzione. I bandi della repubblica napoletana dall'ottobre 1647 all'aprile 1648*, Naples: Jovene.

CONTI V. 1984, *La rivoluzione repubblicana a Napoli e le strutture rappresentative (1647–1648)*, Florence: Centro 2P.

CONTI V. 1987, *Il modello politico olandese in Italia durante la prima metà del Seicento*, in *Modelli nella storia del pensiero politico*, ed. COMPARATO V. I., Florence: Olschki.

CONTI V. 1997, *Consociatio civitatum. Le repubbliche nei testi elzeviriani (1625–1649),* Florence: Centro Editoriale Toscano.

CORASIUS J. 1598, *Miscellaneorum iuris civilis llbri septem [...]*, Coloniae Agrippinae: apud viduam I. Gymnicum, sub Monocerote.

CORNELISSEN J. D. M. 1938, *Hooft en Tacitus. Bijdrage tot de kennis van de vaderlandsche geschiedenis in de eerste helft der 17e eeuw*, Nijmegen-Utrecht: Dekker et van De Veget.

CORTESE E. (1966) 1982, *Il problema della sovranità nel pensiero giuridico medievale*, Rome: Bulzoni.

COSTA G. 1977, *Le antichità germaniche nella cultura italiana da Machiavelli a Vico*, Naples: Bibliopolis.

COSTA G. 1984, *Appunti sulla fortuna dello pseudo-Longino nel Seicento: Alessandro Tassoni e Paganino Gaudenzio*, in "Studi Secenteschi", 25, pp. 123–143.

CRIFÒ G. 1984, *Ulpiano e Vico. Diritto umano e ragion di Stato*, in *Sodalitas, Scritti in onore di Antonio Guarino*, Naples: Giuffrè.

CUIACIUS I. 1556, *Ad libros quatuor. Institutionum Iustiniani notae [...]*, Coloniae Agrippinae: apud I. Gymnicum, sub Monocerote.

CUIACIUS I. (1556–1558) 1836, *Observationum et emendationum libri XXVIII* (Book XV, chap. 30, "Ad l. Princeps. 31. D. de 1egib.", in CUIACII I. 1836, *Opera ad parisiensem fabrotianam editionem diligentissirne exacta in tomos XIII. distributa auctiora atque emendatiora. Pars prima. Tomus primis*, Prati: ex officina fratr. Giachetti.

D'ADDIO M. 1962, *Il pensiero politico di Gaspare Scioppio e il machiavellismo del Seicento*, Milan: Giuffrè.

D'ANGERS J. E. 1976, *Recherches sur le stoïcisme au XVIe et XVIIe siècles*, ed. par ANTOINE L., Hildesheim-New York: G. Olms.

DE FRANCISCI P. 1925, *L'antitribonianismo di G.B. Vico*, in "Rivista internazionale di filosofia del diritto", V, pp. 428–436.

DEL VECCHIO G. (1946) 1959, *La giustizia*, Rome: Studium.

DEL VECCHIO G. 1957², *Due note su Alberico Gentili e su Ugo Grozio*, Rome: Società italiana di filosofia del diritto.

DE MATTEI R. (1951) 1982–1984, *Sapienza e Prudenza nel pensiero politico italiano dall'Umanesimo al sec. XVII*, then in DE MATTEI R. 1982–1984, *Il pensiero politico italiano nell'età della Controriforma*, Milan-Naples: Ricciardi.

DE MICHELIS PINTACUDA F. 1967, *Le origini storiche e culturali del pensiero di Ugo Grozio*, Milan: F. Angeli.

DEN BOER W. 1979, *The Dutch Republic and Antiquity*, in "Bijdragen en Mededelingen betreffende de Geschiedenis der Nederlanden", 94, pp. 419–436.

DERATHE R. 1974², *Jean-Jacques Rousseau et la science politique de son temps*, Paris: J. Vrin.

DE SANCTIS F. (1994) 1996, *Grozio: diritto naturale e diritto civile. Note introduttive al 'De jure belli ac pacis'* in 1996, *Problemi e figure della filosofia giuridica e politica*, Rome: Bulzoni.

DESCARTES R. to Mersenne M., Amsterdam, 27 Mai 1630, in 1969, *Oeuvres de Descartes,* ed. ADAM C. and TANNEY P., Paris: J. Vrin.

DESCARTES R. 1650, *Specimina philosophiae: seu, Dissertatio de methodo recte regendae rationis et veritatis in scientiis investigandae: Dioptrice, et Meteora.* Ex gallico, translata, et ab auctore perlecta, variisque in locis emendata, Amstelodami: apud L. Elsevirium.

DE SETA C. 1982, *L'Italia nello specchio del "Grand Tour"*, in *Storia d'Italia,* Annali. V, ed. DE SETA C., Turin: Einaudi.

DIAZ F. 1976, Il *Granducato di Toscana. I Medici*, in *Storia d'Italia*, ed. GALASSO G., Turin: Utet.

DIAZ F. 1988, *Momigliano e la riflessione sulla storia*, in "Rivista Storica Italiana", 100, pp. 334–347.

DIBON P. 1954, *La philosophie néerlandaise au siècle d'or. Tome I : L'enseignement philosophique dans les universités à l'époque précartésienne (1575–1650)*, Paris-Amsterdam-Londres-New York: Elsevier Publishing Company.

DIBON P. 1964, *Le voyage en France des étudiants néerlandais an XVIIème siècle*, The Hague: Nijhoff.

DIBON P. et al. 1974. *Inventaire de la correspondence de Johannes Fredericus Gronovius (1631–1671)*, The Hague: Nijhoff.

DIBON P. 1975, *L'Université de Leyde et la République des Lettres au 17e siècle*, in "Quaerendo", V, pp. 5–38.

DIBON P. 1976, *Les échanges épistolaires dans l'Europe savante du XVII siècle*, in "Revue de synthèse", 81–82, pp. 31–50.

DIBON P. 1978, *Communication in the Respublica literaria of the 17th century*, in "Res publica litterarum. Studies in the Classical Tradition", I, pp. 43–55.

DIBON P. 1981, *Les avatars d'une édition de correspondance: les Epistolae I. Casauboni de 1638*, in "Nouvelles de la République des Lettres", 2, pp. 25–65.

DIBON P. and WAQUET F. 1984, *Johannes Fredericus Gronovius, pèlerin de la République des Lettres. Recherches sur le voyage savant an XVIIe siècle*, Genève: Droz.

DIBON P. 1986, *Communication epistolaire et mouvement des idées au XVIIème siècle*, in *Le edizioni dei testi filosofici e scientifici del '500 e del '600. Problemi di metodo e prospettive di ricerca*, ed. CANZIANI G. and PAGANINI G., Milan: F. Angeli.

DIBON P. (1990), *Regards sur la Hollande du siècle d'or*, Naples: Vivarium.

DILTHEY W. (1891–1904) 1927, *Weltanschaunng und Analyse des Menschen seit Renaissance und Reformation*, in 1927, *Gesammelte Schriften*, ed. MISCH. G., II, Italian translation by SANNA G., Venice: La Nuova Italia.

DINI V. 1983, *La prudenza da virtù a regola di comportamento: tra ricerca del fondamento razionale ed osservazione empirica*, in DINI V.-STABILE G., *Saggezza e prudenza. Studi per Ia ricostruzione di un'antropologia in prima età moderna,* Naples: Liguori.

DIONISOTTI C. 1989, *Ricordo di Arnaldo Momigliano*, Bologna: il Mulino.

DODWELL H. 1701, *De veteribus Graecorum Romanorumque cyclis [...]*, Oxonii: e Theatro Sheldoniano, prostant apud B. Tooke.

DONAHUE Ch. 1985, *Noodt, Titius, and the natural law school : the occupation of wild animals and the intersection of property and tort*, in *Satura Roberto Feenstra oblate*, Fribourg: Editions Universitaires.

DONELLUS H. (1589–1596) 1762, *Commentariorurn de iure civili,* in DONELLI H. 1762, *Opera omnia [...],* Tomus primus cum notis Osualdi Hilligeri. Accedunt Summaria, et Castigationes theologicae, Lucae: typis J. Riccomini.

DONI GARFAGNINI M. 2004, *Jean Le Clerc e gli spazi della ragione. Percorsi di critica e di storia*, Rome: Edizioni di Storia e Letteratura.

DROETTO A. (1950) 1968, *Il Tacitismo nella storiografia groziana*, in DROETTO A. 1968, *Studi groziani*, Turin: Giappichelli.

DROETTO A. 1958, *Introduction* to B. Spinoza, in *Trattato politico,* ed. DROETTO A., Turin: Ramella.

DROETTO A. 1968, *Studi groziani*, ed. BOBBIO N., Turin: Giappichelli.

DURAND Y. 1973, *Les Républiques au temps des Monarchies*, Paris: P.U.F.

EHRARD J. 1963, *L'idée de nature en France dans la première moitié du XVIIIe siècle*, Paris: S.E.V.P.E.N.

EIJNATTEN VAN J. 1993, *God, Nederland en Oranje. Dutch Calvinism and the Search for the Social Centre*, Amsterdam: Vrije Universiteit.

EIJNATTEN VAN J. 1999, *Gerard Noodt's Standing in the Eighteenth-Century Dutch Debates on Religious Freedom*, in "Dutch Review of Church History", 79, pp. 74–98.

EIJNATTEN VAN J. 1999(b), *Mutua Christianorum Tolerantia. Irenicism and Toleration in the Nederlands The Stinstra Affair, 1740–1745*, Florence: Olschki.

ERASMUS H.J. 1962, *The Origins of Rome in Historiography from Petrach to Perizonius*, Assen: van Gorcum & Comp. N.V.-Dr. H. J. & H.M.G. Prakke.

ESTIENNE H. 1600, *Musa monitrix*, in BARCLAY W., De *regno et regali potestate* adversus Buchananum, Brutum, Boucherium, et reliquos monarchomachos, libri sex [...], Parisiis: apud G. Chaudière, via Iacobaea.

ETTER E.L. 1966, *Tacitus in der Geistesgeschichte des 16. und 17. Jahrhunderts*, Basel-Stuttgart: Helbing & Lichtenhahn.

EYSINGA VAN W. J. M. 1942–1947, *Quelques observations sur Grotius et le droit romain*, in "Grotiana", 10, pp. 18–28.

FABRICIUS J. A. 1728, *Bibliotheca latina, sive Notitia auctorum veterum latinorum [...]*, Venetiis: apud S. Coleti.

FABRONI A. 1791–1795 [1971], *Historia Academiae Pisanae*, Pisis: excudebat C. Magnainius [repr. Bologna: Forni].

FASSÒ G. 1971, *Vico e Grozio*, Naples: Guida.

FAUCCI D. 1968, *Vico e Grozio "Giureconsulti del genere umano"*, in "Filosofia", 19, pp. 501–550.

FEENSTRA R. (1958) 1962, *Zur Rezeption in den Niederlanden*, in KOSCHAKER P. (1958) 1962, *Europa und das römische Recht*, Italian translation by BISCARDI A., Florence: Sansoni.

FEENSTRA R. and WAAL C. J. D. 1975, *Seventeenth-Century Leyden Law Professors and Their Influence on the Development of the Civil Law. A Study of Bronchorst, Vinnius and Voet*, Amsterdam-Oxford: North-Holland Publishing Company.

FEENSTRA R. 1979, *Les romanistes de l'Université de Leyde du XVIIe siècle et leur influence sur le droit privé européen*, in *Le nuove frontiere del diritto e il problema dell'unificazione*, Milan: Giuffrè.

FEENSTRA R. et al. 1985, *De Franeker juridische faculteit in nationaal en internationaal perspectief. Inleidende beschouwingen gevolgd door een studie over juridische onderwijsliteratuur sinds het midden van de zeventiende eeuw*, in JENSMA G. TH. et al., *Universiteit te Franeker 1585–1811. Bijdragen tot de geschiedenis van de Friese hogeschool*, Leeuwarden: Fryske Akademy.

FIRPO L. ed. 1976, *La Ragion di Stato*,Turin: Bottega d'Erasmo.

FOCKEMA ANDREAE S. J. et al. 1968, *Album studiosorum Academiae Franekerensis (1585–1811, 1816–1844)*, Franeker: T. Wever.

FRIJHOFF W. 1981, *La société néerlandaise et ses gradués, 1575–1814. Une recherche sérielle sur le statut des intellectuels à partir des registres universitaires*, Amsterdam: Apa-Holland University Press.

FURLY B. to Locke J., Rotterdam 29 August 1700, in 1982, *The Correspondence of John Locke*, by BEER E. S., Oxford: Clarendon Press.

GABBA E. 1955, *Sulla Storia Romana di Cassio Dione*, in "Rivista storica italiana", 67, pp. 289–333.

GABBA E. 1995, *Ricordo di Arnaldo Momigliano storico del mondo antico*, in *Cultura classica e storiografia moderna*, Bologna: il Mulino.

GALASSO G. 1982–1983, *Il Vico di Giarrizzo e un itinerario alternativo*, in "Bollettino del Centro di Studi Vichiani", 12–13, pp. 199–235.

GARIN E. 1966, *Leggi, diritto e storia nelle discussioni dei secoli XV e XVI*, in *La storia del diritto nel quadro delle scienze storiche*, Florence: Olschki.

GARIN E. 1981, *Le citazioni di Vico*, in "Giornale Critico della Filosofia Italiana", 62, pp. 380–386.

GASSENDI P. (1658) 1964, *Syntagma philosophicum*, in 1964, *Opera omnia* in sex tomos divisa [...], Stuttgart-Bad Cannstatt: F. Fronmann.

GAUDEMET J. 1982, *La contribution des romanistes et des canonistes médiéval à la théorie moderne de l'Etat*, in *Diritto e potere nella storia europea*, Florence: Olschki.

GEER L. DE to Gronovius J.F., Amsterdam, 4 December 1640, in 1984, *Johannes Fredericus Gronovius, pèlerin de la République des Lettres. Recherches sur le voyage savant an XVIIe siècle*, Genève: Droz.

GENTILI S. (1600), *De lege regia, de imperio principis*, in GENTILI S. 1763–1769, *Opera omnia in plures tomos distributa [...]*, Neapoli: sumptibus J. Gravier et Nepotis.

GERRETZEN J.G. 1940, *Schola Hemsterhusiana. De Herleving der Grieksche Studien aan de Nederlandsche Universiteiten in de achttiende eeuw van Perizonius tot en met Valckenaer*, Nijmegen-Utrecht: Dekker.

GIARRIZZO G. 1954, *Edward Gibbon e La cultura europea del Settecento*, Naples: Istituto italiano per gli studi storici.

GIARRIZZO G. (1956) 1981, *Cultura illuministica e mondo settecentesco*, in GIARRIZZO G. 1981, *Vico, la politica e la storia*, Naples: Guida.

GIARRIZZO G. (1962) 1981, *Alle origini della medievistica moderna (Vico, Giannone, Muratori)*, in GIARRIZZO G. 1981, *Vico, la politica e la storia*, Naples: Guida.

GIARRIZZO G. 1968, *La politica di Vico*, in GIARRIZZO G. 1981, *Vico, la politica e la storia*, Naples: Guida.

GIARRIZZO G. (1977) 1981, *'Aequitas' e 'Prudentia': storia di un topos vichiano*, in GIARRIZZO G. 1981, *Vico, La politica e la storia*, Naples: Guida.

GIARRIZZO G. (1992) 1995, *Santo Mazzarino. Un maestro*, in *Per una storia della storiografia europea. Gli storici, la storia*, Acireale, Bonanno.

GIARRIZZO G. 2002, *Lo storicismo degli storici nel secondo Novecento*, in *I percorsi dello storicismo italiano nel secondo Novecento*, eds. MARTIRANO M. and MASSIMILLA E., Naples: Liguori.

GIBBON E. (1776–1788) 1967, *History of the Decline and Fall of the Roman Empire*, Italian translation by FRIZZI G., with an Essay of MOMIGLIANO A., Turin: Einaudi.

GIDDEY E. 1960, *Les conditions matérielles et spirituelles du voyage d'Italie à la fin du XVIe et au début du XVIIe siècle*, in "Etudes de lettres", III, pp. 173–195.

GIERKE O. F. von (1880) 1943 [repr.1974], *Johannes Althusius und die Entwicklung der naturrechtlichen Staatstheorien*, Italian translation by GIOLITTI A., Turin: Einaudi.

GIERKE O. F. von. (1913) 1960, *Das deutsche Genossenschatsrecht* [*Natural Law and the Theory of Society 1500 to 1800,* with a Lecture on Natural Law and Humanity by TROELTSCH E., Translated with an Introduction by BARKER E., Cambridge: University Press].

GIPHANIUS H. 1611, *In quatuor libros Institutionum iuris civilis Iustiniani principis commentarius absolutissimus.* Secunda hac editione [...], Argentorati: sumptibus L. Zetzneri bibliopolae.

GIUFFRE V. ed. 1977, *Les Lois des Romains,* VII édition par un groupe de romanistes des "Textes de droit romain", Naples: Jovene.

Le glorie degli Incogniti o vero gli huomini illustri dell'Accademia de' Signori Incogniti di Venetia, in Venetia: appresso F. Valvasense 1647.

Godefroy J. 1653, *Fontes quatuor iuris civilis in unum collecti […]*, Genevae: sumptibus I.A. et S. De Tournes.

Gori G. 1972, *La fondazione dell'esperienza in Gravesande*, Florence: La Nuova Italia.

Gough J.W. (1936) 1986, *The Social Contract. A Critical study of its Developments*, Italian translation by CASADEI R., Bologna: il Mulino.

Graevius J.G. to Le Clerc J., 1687, in LE CLERC J. 1987, *Epistolario*, ed. SINA M., Florence: Olschki.

Gravina G. (1708) 1756, *Originum iuris civilis*, in Gravina G., *Opera, seu Originum iuris civilis libri tres […],* recensuit, et adnotationibus auxit Gotfridus Mascovius […], Neapoli, publica auctoritate excudebat I. Raymundus sumptibus A. Cervone.

Gregory T. 1979, *Theophrastus redivivus. Erudizione e ateismo nel Seicento*, Naples: Morano.

Gronovius Jacob to Magliabechi A., Deventer, 14 Juin 1678, in 1981, *Lettere e carte Magtiabechi. Regesto,* ed. Doni Garfagnini M., Rome: Istituto storico italiano per l'età moderna e contemporanea.

Gronovius Jacob 1683, *Exercitationes academicae de pernicie et casu Judae […]*, Lugduni Batavorum: apud D. a Gaesbeeck.

Gronovius Jacob 1684, *Dissertatio de origine Romuli […]*, Lugduni Batavorum: apud J. Luchtmans.

Gronovii J. 1712, *Honoraria dissertatio de lege regia,* habita die et loco solito quum Magnifici Rectoris insigna denuo deponeret, Lugduni in Batavis: ex officina Luchtmanniana.

Gronovius J. F. 1637, *In P. Papinii Siatii Silvanum libros V. Diatribe ad Th. Graswinckelium equitem et IC.*, Hagae-Comitis: ex officina Th. Maire.

GRONOVIUS J.F. to Heinsius N., The Hague, 16 March 1637, in BURMANNUS P. 1727, *Sylloges epistolarum a viris illustrantibus scriptarum tomi quinque […]*, Leidae : apud S. Luchtmans.

GRONOVIUS J.F. to Grotius H., The Hague, 2 November 1638, in BRANDT J. 1702, *Clarorum virorum Epistolae centum ineditae de vario eruditionis genere […]*, Amstelaedami: apud Seb. Petroldum.

GRONOVIUS J.F. to Rivet A., London, 25 May 1639, in 1984. *Johannes Fredericus Gronovius, pèlerin de la République des Lettres. Recherches sur le voyage savant an XVIIe siècle*, Genève: Droz.

GRONOVIUS J. F. (1639) 1662, *Observationum libri III […]*, Lugduni Batavorum: ex officina D. et A. a Gaasbeeck.

GRONOVIUS J.F. to Doni G., Genève, 7 August 1641, in 1984. *Johannes Fredericus Gronovius, pèlerin de la République des Lettres. Recherches sur le voyage savant an XVIIe siècle*, Genève: Droz.

GRONOVIUS J.F. to Dupuy J., Lione, 10 september 1641, in 1984, *Johannes Fredericus Gronovius, pèlerin de la République des Lettres. Recherches sur le voyage savant an XVIIe siècle*, Genève: Droz.

GRONOVIUS J.F. to Gaudenzio P., Genève, 8 August 1641, in 1984, *Johannes Fredericus Gronovius, pèlerin de la République des Lettres. Recherches sur le voyage savant an XVIIe siècle*, Genève: Droz.

GRONOVIUS J.F. to Heinsius N., Venice 14 April 1641, in 1984, *Johannes Fredericus Gronovius, pèlerin de la République des Lettres. Recherches sur le voyage savant an XVIIe siècle*, Genève: Droz.

GRONOVIUS J.F. to Loredano G.F., Vienna, 30 July 1641, in 1984, *Johannes Fredericus Gronovius, pèlerin de la République des Lettres. Recherches sur le voyage savant an XVIIe siècle*, Genève: Droz.

GRONOVIUS J.F. to Naudé G., 1641. Bologna, 3 April 1641, in 1984. *Johannes Fredericus Gronovius, pèlerin de la République des Lettres. Recherches sur le voyage savant an XVIIe siècle*, Genève: Droz.

GRONOVIUS J.F. to Naudé G., Venice, 28 April 1641, in 1984. *Johannes Fredericus Gronovius, pèlerin de la République des Lettres. Recherches sur le voyage savant an XVIIe siècle*, Genève: Droz.

GRONOVIUS J.F. to Rhodius J., Venice, 30 April 1641, in 1984. *Johannes Fredericus Gronovius, pèlerin de la République des Lettres. Recherches sur le voyage savant an XVIIe siècle*, Genève: Droz.

GRONOVIUS J.F. to Rivet A., Venice, 8 April 1641, in 1984. *Johannes Fredericus Gronovius, pèlerin de la République des Lettres. Recherches sur le voyage savant an XVIIe siècle*, Genève: Droz.

GRONOVIUS J.F. to Rivet A., Genève, 30 July 1641, in 1984. *Johannes Fredericus Gronovius, pèlerin de la République des Lettres. Recherches sur le voyage savant an XVIIe siècle*, Genève: Droz.

GRONOVIUS J.F. to Heinsius N., Haarlem, 8 August 1642, in 1984, *Johannes Fredericus Gronovius, pèlerin de la République des Lettres. Recherches sur le voyage savant an XVIIe siècle*, Genève: Droz.

GRONOVIUS J. F. (1643) 1656, *Liber de sestertiis [...]*, Amstelodami: apud L. et D. Elzevirium.

GRONOVIUS J.F. to Heinsius N., s.l., 6 December 1645, in BURMANNUS P. 1727, *Sylloges epistolarum a viris illustrantibus scriptarum tomi quinque [...]*, Leidae: apud S. Luchtmans.

GRONOVIUS J.F. to Clément A., Hambourg, 29 August 1656, in GRONOVIUS J.F. 1691, *De sestertiis, seu subsecivorum pecuniae veteris graecae et romanae libri IV [...]*, Lugduni Batavorum: ex officina J. Du Vivié.

GRONOVIUS J. F. 1658–1659, *L. Annaei Senecae Opera omnia* ex ult. I. Lipsii et I. F. Gronovii emendat. et M. Annaei Senecae rhetoris quae exstant [...]. Tomus primus; tomus secundus in quo *Epistolae, et Quaestiones naturales* [...], Amstelodami: apud Elzevirios.

GRONOVIUS J. F. 1661, *L. Annaei Senecae Tragoediae* I. F. Gronovii recensuit [...], Lugduni Batavorum: ex officina Elzeviriana.

GRONOVIUS J. F. (1661) 1664, *De centesimis usuris, et foenore unciario [...]*, Lugduni Batavorum: ex officina D. et A. a Gaasbeeck.

[GRONOVIUS J.F.] 1668, *Allocutio ad serenissimum principem Cosmum, magnum Etruriae principem.* Cum academiam visitaret, facta publice per Iohannem Fredericum Gronovium [...], Lugduni Batavorum: apud viduam et haeredes J. Elsevirii, academiae typographos.

GRONOVIUS J.F. (1672) 1703, *Notae in C. Svetonium Tranquillum a Joh. Georg. Graevio [...]*, Traiecti ad Rhenum: apud A. Schouten, bibliopolam.

GRONOVIUS J.F. 1678, *Oratio de lege regia. Pro concione, quum Fàsces Academicos secundum deponeret, recitata die solemni VIII, febr. 1671,* Lugduni in Batavis: ex officina H. Severini.

GRONOVIUS J.F.1680. [GROTIUS H. 1680]. *De iure belli ac pacis. Libri tres, in quibus ius naturae et gentium, item iuris publici praecipua explicantur [...]. Nec non Ioann. Frid. Gronovii V.C. notae in totum opus [...]*, Hagae Comitis: apud Leers.

GRONOVIUS J.F. 1703, *Phaedri Augusti Liberti* Fabularum Aesopiarum libri V. *Cum notis perpetuis Joan. Fred. Gronovii P., et Jac. Gronovii, F. Accedunt Nic. Dispontinii in Phaedrum collectanea [...],* Amstelaedami: apud Janssonio-Waesbergios.

[GRONOVIUS J.F. - LE CLERC J. 1710] 1735, *T. Livii Patavini Historiarum libri qui supersunt ex editione et cum notis I. Clerici adiecta est diversitas lectionis Gronoviae cum praefatione Io. M. Gesneri [...]*, Lipsiae: in officina Weidmanniana.

GRONOVIUS J.F. 1876–1877, *Johanni Frederici Gronovii ad Albertum Rubenium Epistolae X. E codice leidensi edidit et praefatus est Johannes Cornelius Gerardus Boot*, in "Atti della R. Accademia dei Lincei. Memorie della classe di Scienze morali, storiche e filologiche", 274, pp. 3–24.

GROTIUS H. to Gronovius J.F., Paris, 25 April 1639, n 1976, *Briefwisseling van Hugo Grotius*, eds. MOLHUYSEN P. C. and MEULENBROEK B. L., The Hague: Nijhoff.

GROTIUS H. 1680, *De iure belli ac pacis. Libri tres, in quibus ius naturae et gentium, item iuris publici praecipua explicantur [...]. Nec non Ioann. Frid. Gronovii V.C.*, Hagae Comitis: apud A. Leers.

GROTIUS H. 1759, *Le droit de la guerre et de la paix* par Hugues Grotius. Nouvelle translation, par BARBEYRAC J. [...], Leide: aux dépens de la Compagnie.

GUEZ DE BALZAC J. L. to Gronovius J.F., s.l. 30 October 1641, in GUEZ DE BALZAC J. L. (1647) 1658, *Lettres choisie de S.r de Balzac*, Paris: chez A. Courbé.

GUIDA F. 1981, *Jus naturale e jus gentium nell'opera di Jean Barbeyrac (1674–1744). Contributo alla storia delle origini della dottrina del diritto internazionale*, Naples: D'Agostino.

HAASE E. 195, *I. Papin à l'époque de la Révocation (trois lettres inédites)*, in "Bulletin de la Société de l'Histoire du Protestantisme français", 99, pp. 94–122.

HACKMANN W.D. (1975) 1979, *Lo sviluppo della scienza nei Paesi Bassi tra Seicento e primo Settecento*, in 1979, *The Emergence of Science in Western Europe*, ed. CROSLAND M. P., Italian translation by BINI B. and PETRUCCIOLI S., Bologna: il Mulino.

HAITSMA MULIER E.O.G. 1980, *The Myth of Venice and Dutch Republican Thought in the Seventeenth Century,* translation by MORAN G. T., Assen: van Gorcum.

HAITSMA MULIER E.O.G. 1986, *La società delle Sette Province Unite nel Seicento*, Italian translation by MARTENS M. A., in 1986, *La Storia. I grandi problemi dal Medioevo all'Età Contemporanea,* eds. TRANFAGLIA N. and FIRPO M., Turin: Utet.

HALL F. W. 1913, *A Companion to Classical Texts*, Oxford: Clarendon Press.

HARTOG M. W. 1976–1977, *Prins Willem III en de hertogshoed van Gelderland*, 1673–5, in "Gelre", 69, pp. 125–155.

HATIN L. E. (1865) 1964, *Les Gazettes de Hollande et la presse clandestine aux XVIIe et XVIIIe siècles*, Genève: Slatkine.

HAY D. (1977) 1981, *Annalists and Historians. Western Historiography from the Eighth to the Eighteenth Centuries*, Italian translation by BALDAZZI A. and PUCA C. C., Rome-Bari: Laterza.

HAZARD P. (1935) 1968 [2007], *La crise de la conscience européenne (1680–1715)*, ed. SERINI P., Milan: il Saggiatore [now with intr. of RICUPERATI G., Turin: Utet, 2007].

HEINECCIUS J.G. (1726) 1744, *Antiquitatum romanarum iurisprudentiam illustrantium syntagma secundum ordinem Institutionum Iustiniani digestum [...]*,Venetiis: ex typographia Balleoniana.

HEINECCIUS J. G. (1735) 1771, *Schediasma de recta Tribonianomastigum*, in 1771, *Variorum opuscula ad cultiorem iurisprudentiam adsequendam pertinentia. Tom. VII*, Pisis: ex typographia A. Pizzorno.

HEINSIUS N. to Dupuy J., Rome, 7 December 1646, in BOTS H. 1971, *Correspondance de Jacques Dupuy et de Nicolaas Heinsius (1646–1656)*, The Hague: Nijhoff.

HEINSIUS N. to Gronovius J.F., Naples, 4 May 1647, in BURMANNUS P. 1727, *Sylloges epistolarum a viris illustrantibus scriptarum tomi quinque [...]*, Leidae: apud S. Luchtmans.

HISTORIAE AUGUSTAE SCRIPTORES 1671, VI, *Aelius Spartianus, Vulc. Gallicanus, Iulius Capitolinus, Trebell. Pollio, Aelius Lampridius, Flavius Vopiscus.* Cum integris notis Isaaci Casauboni, Cl. Salmasii et Jani Gruteri. Cum indicibus locupletissimis rerum ac verborum [...], Ludguni Batavorum: ex officina Hackiana.

HOBBES TH. (1651) 1992², *Leviathan*, Italian translation by PACCHI A. with the collaboration of LUPOLI A., Rome-Bari: Laterza.

HOBBES TH. (1666) 1960, *A Dialogue between a Philosopher and a Student of the Common Laws of England*, ed. ASCARELLI T., Milan: Giuffrè.

HOCHSTRASSER T.J. 1993, *Conscience and Reason: the Natural Law Theory of Jean Barbeyrac*, in "The Historical Journal", 36, pp. 288–308.

HOCHSTRASSER T.J. 1995, *The Claims of Conscience: Natural Law Theory, Obligation, and Resistance in the Huguenot Diaspora*, in *New Essays on the Political Thought of the Huguenots of the Refuge*, ed. LAURSEN J. Ch., Leiden-New York-Köln: Brill.

HOLSTENIUS L. to Gronovius J.F., Rome, 17 March 1641, in DIBON P. et al. 1974, *Inventaire de la correspondence de Johannes Fredericus Gronovius (1631–1671)*, The Hague: Nijhoff.

HOTMAN F. 1567, *Commentarius in quatuor libros Institutionum iuris civilis*, Secunda editio ad auctore recognita [...], Lugduni Batavorum: apud A. Gryphium.

HOTMAN F. 1599–1600, *Antiquitatum romanarum liber I. Pars prior [...]*, in *Operum [...]*, Genevae: excudebant haeredes E. Vignon et I. Stoer.

HUBERUS U. (1665) 1746, *Oratio inauguralis* habita Franekerae, cum ex ordinaria Eloquentiae et Historiarum Cathedra solenniter in Iuridicam deduceretur: Exhibens historiam Iuris Romani, et ex eius argumento continuam probationem, literas humaniores cum iurisprudentia esse coniugendas. A.D. XIII.Kal.VIIIbr. M. DC. LXV, in HUBERUS U. 1746, *Opera minora et rariora, iuris publici et privati [...]*, Traiecti ad Rhenum: sumptibus J. H. Vonk van Lynden.

HUBERUS U. (1670) 1688, *Digressiones iustinianeae [...]*, Franequerae: apud H. Amama et Z. Taedama.

HUBERUS U. (1672) 1708, *De iure civitatis, libri tres [...]*, Francofurti et Lipsiae: apud J.F. Zeitlerum.

HUBERUS U. (1678–1690) 1735, *Praelectionum iunis civilis tomi III secundum Institutiones et Digcsta Iustiniani [...]*, Lipsiae: sumptibus J.F. Gleditschii B. filii.

HUBERUS U. 1684, *De ratione iuris docendi et discendi Dialogus*, Franequerae: ex officina J. Gyselaar.

HUBERUS U. 1687, *De concursu rationis et Sacrae Scripturae liber* ad reverendos viros D.D. Johannem van der Waeyen et Hermannum Alexandrum Röell, Franequerae: apud J. Gyselaar.

HUBERUS U. 1688, *Disputationes iuris fundamentales secundum duos priores Institutionum iuris libros*, Franequerae: apud J. Gyselaar.

HUBERUS U. 1688b, *Dissertationes Theologicae VII [...]*, Franequerae: apud H. Amama et Z. Taedama.

HUBERUS U. (1689) 1746, *De iure popularis, optimatium, et regalis imperii, sine vi, et a sui iuris populo, constituti, ad regenda hominum circa res maximas iudicia*, contra periculosissimos errores, *Dissertatio*, in HUBERUS U., *Opera minora et rariora, iuris publici et privati [...]*, Traiecti ad Rhenum: sumptibus J. H. Vonk van Lynden.

HUBERUS U. 1693, *De calumnia centum et viginti errorum Jacobi Perizonii [...], Specimen Epistolicum [...]*, Franequerae: apud H. Amama et Z. Taedama.

HUBERUS U. 1700, *Eunomia romana sive Censura censurae iuris iustinianaei [...]*, Franequerae: apud L. Strickium.

HUBERUS U. et al. 1793, *Variorum opuscula ad culttiorem iurisprudentiam adsequendam pertinentia*, Pisis: apud A. Pizzorno.

HULSHOFF POL E. 1961, *Brievencollectie Gronovius voor U.B. Leiden verfilmd*, in "Bibliotheekleven", XLVI, pp. 383–385.

HUUSSEN A.H. jr. 1989, *De joden in Nederland en het probleem van de tolerantie*, in *Een schijn van verdraagzaamheid. Afwijking en tolerantie in Nederland van de zestiende eeuw tot heden*, by GIJSWIJT-HOFSTRA M., Hilversun: Verloren.

ILARI V. 1981, *L'interpretazione storica del diritto di guerra romano fra tradizione romanistica e giusnaturalismo*, Milan: Giuffrè.

IOFRIDA M. 1979, *Note sul pensiero teologico e filosofico di Jean Leclerc*, in "Annali della Scuola Normale Superiore di Pisa", 9, pp. 1497–1524.

ISRAEL J. 1994, *Toleration in Seventeenth-Century Dutch and English Thought*, in *The Exchange of Ideas. Religion, Scholarship and Art in Anglo-Dutch Relations in the Seventeenth Century*, by GROENVELD S. and WINTLE M., Zutphen: Uitgeversmaat schappij Walburg Pers.

ISRAEL J. 1995, *The Dutch Republic. Its Rise, Greatness, and Fall 1477–1806*, Oxford: Clarendon Press.

ISRAEL J. 2001, *Radical Enlightenment. Philosophy and the Making of Modernity 1650–1750*, Oxford-New York: Oxford University Press.

JENSMA G. TH. et al. 1985, *Universiteit te Franeker 1585–1811. Bijdragen tot de geschiedenis van de Friese Hogeschool*, Leeuwarden: Fryske Akademy.

JOURNAL DES SÇAVANS 1701, 1705, Amsterdam: chez les Janssons à Waesberge.

JOURNAL LITTERAIRE 1713, 1714, La Haye, chez J. van Duren.

KENNEY E. J. 1974, *The Classical Text. Aspects of editing in the Age of the Printed Book*, Berkeley-Los Angeles-London: University of California Press.

KOESTERMAN K. 1960, *Codex Leidensis B.P.L. 16 B. ein vom Mediceus II unabhängiger Textzeuge des Tacitus*, in "Philologus", 104, pp. 92–115.

KORKMAN P. 1999–2000, *Barbeyrac on Scepticism and on Grotian Modernity*, in "Grotiana", 20–21, pp. 77–106.

KOSCHAKER P. (1958) 1962, *Europa und das römische Recht*, Italian translation by BISCARDI A., Florence: Sansoni.

KOSSMANN E. H. 1960, *Politieke theorie in het zeventiende-eeuwse Nederland*, Amsterdam: North-Hollandse Uitgevers Maatschappij.

KOSSMANN E. H. et al. 1960, *The Development of Dutch Political Theory in the Seventeenth Century*, in *Britain and the Netherlands*, by BOROMLEY J. S. and KOSSMANN E. H., London: Chatto & Windus.

KOSSMANN E. H. 1971, *De Dissertationes Politicae van Ulric Huber*, in *European Context Studies in the History and Literature of the Netherlands Presented to Theodoor Weevers*, Cambridge: Publications of the Modern Humanities Research Association.

KOSSMANN E. H. 1975, *Some Late 17th Century Dutch Writings on Raison d'Etat*, in *Staatsräson. Studien zur Geschichte eines politi-*

schen Begriffs, ed. SCHNUR R., Berlin: Duncker & Humblot.

KOSSMANN E. H. 1985, *Dutch Republicanism,* in *L'età dei lumi. Studi storici sul Settecento europeo in onore di Franco Venturi*, Naples: Jovene.

KRAMER G. 1828, *Elogium Jacobi Perizonii*, Berlin: Inaugural Dissertation.

LABRIOLA G. M. 2003, *Barbeyrac interprete di Pufendorf e Grozio. Dalla costruzione della sovranità alla teoria della resistenza*, Naples: Editoriale Scientifica.

LACOSTE E. 1929, *Bayle nouvelliste et critique littéraire [...]*, Paris: Picard.

LAEVEN A.H. 1986, *De "Acta Eruditorum" onder redactie van Otto Mencke. De Geschiedenis van een internationaal Geleerdenperiodiek Tussen 1682 en 1707*, Amsterdam & Maarssen: Apa-Holland Universiteits Pers.

LAGARRIGUE B. 1993, *Un temple de la culture européenne (1728–1753). L'histoire externe de la Bibliothèque raisonnée des ouvrages des savants de l'Europe*, Nijmegen: Katholieke Universiteit.

LA MOTHE LE VAYER F. (1638) 1756–1769, *Discours de histoire*, in LA MOTHE LE VAYER F. 1756–1769, *Œuvres,* Nouvelle édition revue et augmentée, précedée de l'abrégé de la vie de La Mothe le Vayer, Dresde: M. Groell [reprint Genève: Slatkine, 1970].

LA MOTHE LE VAYER F. (1668) 1756–1769, *Du peu de certitude qu'il y a dans l'histoire*, in LA MOTHE LE VAYER F. 1756–1769, *Œuvres,* Nouvelle édition revue et augmentée, précedée de l'abrégé de la vie de La Mothe le Vayer, Dresde: M. Groell [reprint Genève: Slatkine, 1970].

LANDUCCI S. 1972, *I filosofi e i selvaggi: 1580–1780*, Bari: Laterza.

LAURSEN J.Ch. 2001, *The necessity of conscience and the conscientious persecutor : the paradox of liberty and necessity in Bayle's theory of toleration*, in *Dal necessario al possibile. Determinismo e libertà nel pensiero anglo-olandese del XVII secolo*, ed. SIMONUTTI L., Milan: F. Angeli.

LE CLERC J. to Bayle P., Amsterdam, 3 June 1684, in LE CLERC J. 1987, *Epistolario*, ed. SINA M., Florence: Olschki.

LE CLERC J. to Vattemare A., Amsterdam, 10 November 1684, in LE CLERC J. 1987, *Epistolario*, ed. SINA M., Florence: Olschki.

LE CLERC J. to Papin I., Amsterdam, 18 December 1684, in LE CLERC J. 1987, *Epistolario*, ed. SINA M., Florence: Olschki.

LE CLERC J. to Locke J., Amsterdam, 23 July 1688, in LE CLERC J. 1987, *Epistolario*, ed. SINA M., Florence: Olschki.

LE CLERC J. to Locke J., Amsterdam, 14 October 1688, in LE CLERC J. 1987, *Epistolario*, ed. Sina M., Florence: Olschki.

LE CLERC J. 1697–1700, *Ars Critica [...]*, Editio secunda auctior et emendatior. Volumen secundum, Amstelaedami: apud G. Gallet.

LEIBNIZ G.W. 1709, *Monita quaedam ad principia pufendorfiani operis De officio hominis et civis*, in BOEHMER I. Ch. 1709 and PUFENDORF S. 1735.

LEIBNIZ G. W. to Bierling F. W., Hanoverae, 7 July 1711, in LEIBNIZ G.W. 1978, *Die philosophischen Schriften*, hrsg. von GERHARDT C. I., Hildesheim-New York: G. Olms Verlag.

LEIBNIZ G. W. 1951, *Scritti politici e di diritto naturale,* ed. MATHIEU V., Turin: Utet.

LENFANT J. to Le Clerc J., Heidelberg 20 Mai 1687, in LE CLERC J. 1987, *Epistolario*, ed. SINA M., Florence: Olschki.

LESUISSE L. 1961, *Tacite et la 'Lex de Imperio des premiers empereurs romains*, in "Les études classiques", 29, pp. 157–165.

LETI G. 1686, *Historia genevrina o sia Historia della città e republica di Geneva. Cominciando dalla sua prima fondattione sino al presente*, Amsterdam: per P. & A. van Someren.

LIPSIUS I. 1589, *Politicorum sive Civilis doctrinae libri sex [...]*, Lugduni Batavorum: ex officina Plautiniana apud F. Raphelengium.

LISSA G. 1973, *Fontenelle tra scetticismo e nuova critica*, Naples: Morano.

LOCKE J. 1690 (1970), *The second Treatise of Government. An Essay concerning the True Original, Extent, and End of Civil Government,* in 1970, *Locke's Two Treatise of Government.* A critical edition with introduction and notes by LASLETT P., Cambridge: at the University Press.

LOCKE J. (1690) 1975 [1988], *An Essay concerning Human Understanding*, ed. NIDDITCH P. H., Oxford: Clarendon Press [repr. ivi 1988].

LOMONACO F. 1984–1985, *Reviews*, in "Bollettino del Centro di Studi Vichiani", 14–15, pp. 395, 408–409.

LOMONACO F. 1987, *Il viaggio in Italia di Iohannes Fredericus Gronovius negli anni 1640–1641* (con tre lettere inedite), in "Giornale Critico della Filosofia Italiana", 66, pp. 499–533.

LOMONACO F. 1987–1988, *Reviews*, in "Bollettino del Centro di Studi Vichiani", 17–18, pp. 371–372.

LOMONACO F. 1988, *L' Oratio de lege regia di Johannes Fredericus Gronovius. Il mito di Roma tra antiquaria e storia nella culura olandese del secondo Seicento*, in "Archivio di storia della cultura", I, pp. 305–362.

LOMONACO F. 1990, *Lex Regia. Diritto, filologia e fides historica nella cultura politico-filosofica dell'Olanda di fine Seicento*, Naples: Guida.

LOMONACO F. 1990b, *Tra erudizione e critica storica: note sull'epistolario Le Clerc (1679–1689)*, in "Bollettino del Centro di Studi Vichiani", 20, pp. 157–168.

LOMONACO F. 1992–1993, *Vico tra diritto, politica e storia: note sulle prospettive attuali della ricerca in Italia (1980–1986)*, in "Bollettino del Centro di Studi Vichiani", 22–23, pp. 401–424.

LOMONACO F. 1995, *Huguenot critical theory and "ius maiestatis" in Huber and Althusius*, with two appendices, the Latin and English versions of the Preface to the 1610 edition of Johannes Althusius's *Politica Methodice digesta atque exemplis sac-*

ris et profanes Illustrata, in *New Essays on the Political Thought of the Huguenots of the Refuge*, ed. LAURSEN J. Ch., Leiden-New York-Köln: Brill.

LOMONACO F. 1997, *Readers of Locke. Cartesianism and historical criticism from Perizonius to Le Clerc*, in "Geschiedenis van de Wijsbegeerte in Nederland", 8, pp. 103–111.

LOMONACO F. 1999, *Barbeyrac et le 'Pyrrhonisme historique' dans la 'Bibliothèque raisonnée des ouvrages des savants de* l'Europe', in *La vie intellectuelle aux refuges protestants.* Actes de la Table ronde de Münster du 25 juillet 1995, ed. HÄSELER J. and MCKENNA A., Paris: Champion.

LOMONACO F. 1999b, *Tolleranza e libertà di coscienza. Filosofia, diritto e storia tra Leida e Napoli nel secolo XVIII.* Préface by VAN DEN BERGH G. C. J. J., Naples: Liguori.

LOMONACO F. 2000, *Jean Barbeyrac als Ausleger Pufendorfs. Natürliches Recht und Gewissensfreiheit*, in *Die Hermeneutik im Zeitalter der Aufklärung.* Proceedings of the Congress (13–15 October 1996), eds. BEETZ M. and CACCIATORE G., Köln-Weimar-Wien: Böhlau Verlag.

LOMONACO F. 2004, *Introduction* to GRAVINA G. 1713, *Originum juris civilis libri tres* (Naples, F. Mosca), eds. LOMONACO F. and TESSITORE F., Naples: Liguori; then in LOMONACO F. 2006, *Filosofia, diritto e storia in Gianvincenzo Gravina*, presentation of ROSSI P., Rome: Edizioni di Storia e Letteratura.

LOMONACO F. 2005, *Tracce di Vico nella polemica sulle origini delle Pandette e delle XII Tavole nel Settecento italiano*, presentation of CACCIATORE G., Naples: Liguori.

LORAUX N. 1998, *Note sur Santo Mazzarino, la stasis et la révolution*, in *Atti del Convegno per Santo Mazzarino* (Rome, 9–11 May 1991), Rome: "L'Erma" di Bretschneider.

LOREDANO G.F. to Gronovius J.F., Venice [...]1648, in 1685, *Delle lettere del Signor Gio: Francesco Loredano nobile veneto.* Divise in cinquantadue capi; e raccolte da Henrico Giblet cavalier [pseud. di G.E. Loredano], In Venetia: appresso A. Tivani.

LUCREZI F. 1982, *Leges super principem. La 'monarchia costituzionale di Vespasiano*, Naples: Jovene.

LUNSINGH SCHEURLEER Th. H. and POSTHUMUS MEYJES G.H.M. 1975, *Leiden University in the Seventeenth Centuty. An Exchange of Learning*, Leiden: Brill.

MACHIAVELLI N. (1513–1521), *Discorsi sopra la prima Deca di Tito Livio*, in 1938, *Opere*, ed. PANELLA A., Milan-Rome: Rizzoli.

MAFFEI D. (1956) 1972, Gli *inizi dell'umanesimo giuridico*, Milan: Giuffrè.

MAGLIABECHI A. to Panciatichi L. [sine anno], in 1730–1735, *Prose fiorentine raccolte dallo Smarrito accademico della Crusca* [pseud. di Carlo Dati] [...], in Venezia: presso D. Occhi.

MANACORDA G. 1901–1902 and 1902–1903, *Dai carteggi allacciani. Note bibliografiche*, in "La Bibliofilia", III, 7–8, pp. 213–231; 9–10, pp. 298–300; 11–12, pp. 382–387; IV.1–2, pp. 37–42, 5–6, pp. 157–167; 7–8, pp. 242–249.

MANNARINO L. 2008, *Storie e profezie. Le regole del racconto sacro in Jean Le Clerc*, in "Giornale Critico della Filosofia Italiana", 87, pp. 453–477.

MANUTIUS P. 1557, *Antiquitatum romanarum [...]. Liber de legibus [...]*, Parisiis: apud B. Turrisanum.

MASTELLONE S. 1963, *Il libertinismo erudito a Napoli nella seconda metà del Seicento*, in "Critica Storica", 11, pp. 451–463.

MASTELLONE S. 1975, *Antonio Magliabechi: un libertino fiorentino?*, in "Il pensiero politico", 8, pp. 33–53.

MASTELLONE S. 1983, *Holland as a Political Model in Italy in the Seventeenth Century*, in "Bijdragen en mededelingen betreffende de geschiedenis der Nederlanden", 4, pp. 568–582.

MASTELLONE S. 1985, *I repubblicani del Seicento ed il modello politico olandese*, in "Il pensiero politico", 18, pp. 145–163.

MASTELLONE S. 1988, *Introduction* to Locke J., *Du gouvernement civil, traduit de l'anglois*, Florence: Centro editoriale Toscano.

MAUGAIN G. 1909, *Etude sur l' évolution intellectuelle de l'Italie de 1657 à 1750 environ [...]*, Paris: Librairie Hachette.

MAYLENDER M. (1926–1930) 1976, *Storia delle Accademie d'Italia*, Sala Bolognese: A. Forni.

MAZZACANE A. 1968–1969, *Umanesimo e sistematiche giuridiche in Germania alla fine del Cinquecento: "equità" e "giurisprudenza" nelle opere di Hermann Vultejus*, in "Annali di storia del diritto", 12–13, pp. 257–319.

MAZZARINO S. [1945], *Dalla monarchia allo stato repubblicano. Ricerche di storia romana arcaica*, Catania, G. Agnini.

MAZZARINO S. 1951, *Aspetti sociali del IV secolo. Ricerche di storia tardo-romana*, Rome: "L'Erma" di Bretschneider.

MAZZARINO S. (1953–1954) 1961, *Gli studi romani dal Rinascirnento alla "Storia dei Romani" del De Sanctis*, in *Guida allo studio della civiltà romana antica*, ed. USSANI V. and ARNALDI F., Naples: Istituto editoriale del Mezzogiorno.

MAZZARINO S. 1954, *Storia romana e storiografia moderna*, Naples-Rome-Catania-Palermo-Pescara-Turin: Conte.

MAZZARINO S. (1959) 1988, *La fine di Roma nell'interpretazione dell'umanesimo*, in MAZZARINO S., *La fine del mondo antico*, Milan: Rusconi.

MAZZARINO S. 1960, *Croce, i Greci e l'idea di storicismo*, in "Cultura e Società", I, pp. 393–400.

MAZZARINO S. 1964, *Qu'est-ce-que l'histoire*, in "De Homine", 9/10, pp. 61–88.

MAZZARINO S. 1966, *Storia e diritto nello studio delle società classiche*, in *La storia del diritto nel quadro delle scienze storiche*. Atti del primo Congresso internazionale della Società italiana di storia del diritto, Florence: Olschki.

MAZZARINO S. 1971, *Vico, l'annalistica e ii diritto*, Naples: Guida.

MAZZARINO S. 1972, *Il pensiero storico classico*, II. 2, Bari: Laterza.

MAZZARINO S. 1975, *L'umanesimo romano come problema di storiografia giuridica (A proposito di CIL, IV 1899 e altri testi)*, in *La filosofia greca e il diritto romano. Colloquio italo-francese* [Rome, 14–17 April 1973], Rome: Accademia Nazionale dei Lincei.

MAZZARINO S. 1979, *Vico, Holland and Modern Conceptions of History*, in "Quaderni catanesi di studi classici e medievali", 1, pp. 355–372.

MCILWAIN CH. H. (1940) 1956, *Constitutionalism: Ancient and Modern*, Italian translation by DE CAPRARIIS V., Venice: Neri Pozza.

MEIJER Th. J. 1971, *Kritiek als herwaardering. Het levenswerk van Jacob Perizonius (1651–1 715)*, Leiden: University Press.

MEIJER Th. J. 1973, *Album promotorum Academiae Franekerensis (1591–1811)*, Franeker: Wever.

MEINECKE F. (1924) 1970, *Die Idee der Staatsrdson in der neueren Geschichte*, italian translation by SCOLARI D., Florence: Sansoni.

MEMOIRES POUR SERVIR A L'HISTOIRE DES SCIENCES ET DES BEAUX ARTS [...] 1709, Trévoux: De l'Imprimerie de S.A.S.

MENDELL C. W. 1957, *Tacitus. The Man and his Work*, Yale: University Press.

MEYLAN Ph. 1937, *Jean Barbeyrac (1674–1744) et les débuts de l'enseignement du droit dans l'ancienne Académie de Lausanne. Contribution à l'histoire du droit naturel*, Lausanne: F. Rouge & C. S.A.

MINERBI BELGRADO A. 2008, *Sulla crisi della teologia filosofica nel Seicento. Pierre Jurieu e dintorni*, Milan: F. Angeli.

MIRTO A. 1994, *Stampatori, editori, librai nella seconda metà del Seicento.* Parte II: *I grandi fornitori di Antonio Magliabechi e della corte medicea,* Florence: Centro Editoriale Toscano.

MIRTO A. 1999, *Lucas Holstenius e la corte medicea. Carteggio (1629–1660)*, Florence: Olschki.

MOLHUYSEN P. C. 1913–1924, *Bronnen tot de Geschiedenis der Leidsche Universiteit*, La Haye: Rijks geschiedkundige Publicatiën.

MOLLERUS J. 1759, *Cimbria literata, sive scriptorum ducatus utriusque slesvicensis et holsatici, quibus et alii vicini quidam accensentur, historia literaria tripartita [...]*, Hauniae: sumptibus et typis orphanotrophii regii.

MOMIGLIANO A. (1936) 1984, *La formazione della moderna storiografia sull'impero romano*, in MOMIGLIANO A. 1984, *Sui fondamenti della storia antica*, Turin: Einaudi.

MOMIGLIANO A. [1948] 1969, *Review* to MAZZARINO S. 1947, *Fra Oriente e Occidente. Ricerche di storia greca arcaica*, in MOMIGLIANO A. 1969, *Quarto contributo alla storia degli studi classici e del mondo antico*, Rome: Edizioni di Storia e Letteratura.

MOMIGLIANO A. (1950) 1955, *Ancient History and the Antiquarian*, in MOMIGLIANO A. 1955, *Contributo alla storia degli studi classici*, Rome: Edizioni di Storia e Letteratura, Italian translation by CODINO F., in MOMIGLIANO A. 1984, *Sui fondamenti della storia antica*, Turin: Einaudi.

MOMIGLIANO A. (1954) 1966, *An Unsolved Problem of Historical Forgery: The Scriptores Historiae Augustae*, in MOMIGLIANO A. 1966, *Studies in Historiography*, London-New York: Harper and Row.

MOMIGLIANO A. [1955] 1960, *Il linguaggio e la tecnica dello storico*, in MOMIGLIANO A. 1960, *Secondo contributo alla storia degli studi classici*, Rome: Edizioni di Storia e Letteratura.

MOMIGLIANO, A. (1957) 1960, *Perizonius, Niebuhr and the Character of Early Roman Tradition*, in MOMIGLIANO A. 1960, *Secondo contributo alla storia degli studi classici*, Rome: Edizioni di Storia e Letteratura; Italian translation by CODINO F., in MOMIGLIANO A. 1984, *Sui fondamenti della storia antica*, Turin: Einaudi.

MOMIGLIANO A. (1958) 1984, *L'eredità della filologia antica e il metodo storico*, in MOMIGLIANO A. 1984, *Sui fondamenti della storia antica*, Turin: Einaudi.

MOMIGLIANO A. (1960) 1987, *Linee per una valutazione di Fabio Pittore*, in MOMIGLIANO A. 1987, *Storia e storiografia antica*, Bologna: il Mulino.

MOMIGLIANO A. (1961–1962) 1975, *Storiografia su tradizione scritta e storiografia su tradizione orale*, in MOMIGLIANO A. 1975, *Erodoto, Tucidide, Senofonte: letture critiche*. ed. CANFORA L., Milan: Mursia.

MOMIGLIANO, A. (1962) 1966, *Scipione Maffei e Hendrik Brenkman: due progetti di collaborazione intellettuale italo-olandese nel Settecento*, in MOMIGLIANO A. 1966, *Terzo contributo alla storia degli studi classici*, Rome: Edizioni di Storia e Letteratura.

MOMIGLIANO A. (1963) 1987, *An Interim Report on the Origins of Rome*, Italian translation by BARONI A., in MOMIGLIANO A. 1987, *Storia e storiografia antica*, Bologna: il Mulino.

MOMIGLIANO A. (1964) 1984, *Le conseguenze del rinnovamento della storia dei diritti antichi*, in MOMIGLIANO A. 1984, *Sui fondamenti della storia antica*, Turin: Einaudi.

MOMIGLIANO A. (1965) 1980, *La nuova storia romana di G.B. Vico*, in MOMIGLIANO A. 1980, *Sesto contributo alla storia degli studi classici e del mondo antico*, Rome: Edizioni di Storia e Letteratura.

MOMIGLIANO A. 1966 (1984), *Vico's Scienza Nuova: Roman "Bestioni" and Roman "Eroi"*, Italian translation by TAVONI M, in MOMIGLIANO A. 1984, *Sui fondamenti della storia antica*, Turin: Einaudi.

MOMIGLIANO A. (1967) 1969, *Santo Mazzarino e il pensiero storico classico* I–II, I [1966, 2 voll.], in MOMIGLIANO A. 1969, *Quarto contributo alla storia degli studi classici e del mondo antico*, Rome: Edizioni di Storia e Letteratura.

MOMIGLIANO A. (1968) 1969, *Praetor Maximus e questioni affini*, in MOMIGLIANO A. 1969, *Quarto contributo alla storia degli studi classici e del mondo antico*, Rome: Edizioni di Storia e Letteratura.

MOMIGLIANO A. (1969) 1975, *The Origins of the Roman Republic*, Italian translation by PIANCIOLA D., in MOMIGLIANO A. 1975, *Quinto contributo alla storia degli studi classici e del mondo antico*, Rome: Edizioni di Storia e Letteratura.

MOMIGLIANO A. (1974) 1984, *Historicism revisited*, Italian translation by TAVONI M., in MOMIGLIANO A. 1984, *Sui fondamenti della storia antica.* Turin: Einaudi.

MOMIGLIANO A. (1974) 1984, *Le regole del gioco nello studio della storia antica*, in MOMIGLIANO A. 1984, *Sui fondamenti della storia antica*, Turin: Einaudi.

MOMIGLIANO A. 1978, *The Historians of the Classical World and Their Audiences: Some Suggestions*, in MOMIGLIANO A., *Sesto contributo alla storia degli studi classici e del mondo antico*, Rome: Edizioni di Storia e Letteratura.

MOMIGLIANO A. 1984, *Sui fondamenti della storia antica*, Turin: Einaudi.

MOMIGLIANO A. 1987, *Preface* to *Storia e storiografia antica*, ed. GABBA E., Bologna: il Mulino.

MOREL H. 1970, *La place de la 'Lex Regia' dans l'histoire des idées politiques*, in *Etudes offertes à Jean Macqueron*, Aix-en-Provence: Faculté de Droit et des Sciences Èconomiques.

MORI M. 1986, *Giusnaturalismo e crisi dell'ordine naturale*, in "Rivista di filosofia", 77, pp. 16–29.

MORI G. 1996, *Introduzione a Bayle*, Rome-Bari: Laterza.

MORI G. 1999, *Bayle philosophe*, Paris: Champion.

MURETUS M.A. 1744, *D. N. Iustiniani […] Institutionum, sive Elementorurn per Tribunianum, virum magnificum, magistrum et ex quaestore sacri palatii, et Theophilum, et Dorotheum, viros illustres, et antecessores, libri quatuor [...].* Accedunt huic editioni annotationes et notae THEODORI MARCILII IC. et MARCI ANTONII MURETI IC. [...], Lugduni Batavorum: apud S. Luchtmans.

MUSTI D. 1960, *Allacci Leone*, in *Dizionario biografico degli italiani*, vol. II, Rome: Istituto della Enciclopedia italiana.

NAUDE G. (1639) 1958, *Science des Princes ou Considérations politiques sur les coups d'Etat [...]*, Italian translation by BERTOLUCCI P., Turin: Boringhieri.

NAUDE G. to Gronovius J. F., 13 April 1641, in DIBON P. et al. 1974, *Inventaire de la correspondence de Johannes Fredericus Gronovius (1631*–1671), The Hague: Nijhoff.

NOODT G. (1699) 1724, *Dissertatio de iure summi imperii et lege regia*, habita in Academia Lugduno-Batava a. d. V. Id. Febr. A. MDCXCIX. Cum Magnifici Rectoris munere abiret, Lugduni Batavorum: apud A. Elzevier, in NOODT G. 1724, *Opera omnia*, ab ipso recognita, aucta, emendata, multis in locis, atque in duos tomos distributa [...], Lugduni Batavorum: apud J. van der Linden, iuniorem.

NOODT G. 1705, *Opera omnia [...]*, Lugduni Batavorum: apud F. Haaring.

NOODT G. (1706) 1724, *Observationum liber primis* in NOODT G. 1724, *Opera omnia*, ab ipso recognita, aucta, emendata, multis in locis, atque in duos tomos distributa [...], Lugduni Batavorum: apud J. van der Linden, iuniorem.

NOODT G. (1706) 1999, *Dissertatio de religione ab imperio iure gentium libera,* habita in Academia Lugduno-Batava a.d. VI. Id. Febr. A. MDCCVI. Cum abiret Magnifici Rectoris munere, Lugduni Batavorum: apud F. Haaring 1706, in LOMONACO F. 1999, *Tolleranza e libertà di coscienza. Filosofia, diritto e storia tra Leida e Napoli nel secolo XVIII*, Préface by VAN DEN BERGH G.C.J.J., Naples: Liguori.

NOODT G. 1713, *Opera omnia, cum ante edita, tum adhuc inedita [...]*, Lugduni Batavorum: apud J. van der Linden, iuniorem.

NOUVELLES DE LA REPUBLIQUE DE LETTRES 1685, 1706, 1707, Amsterdam: H. Desbordes, reprinted in 1966, Genève: Slatkine.

NUZZO E. 1982, *Vico e il mito veneziano*, in *Vico e Venezia*, eds. DE MICHELIS C. and PIZZAMIGLIO G., Florence: Olschki.

NUZZO E. 1984–1985, *Vico e l'Aristotele pratico: la meditazione sulle forme "civili" nelle "Pratiche" della Scienza Nuova Prima*, in "Bollettino del Centro di Studi Vichiani", 14–15, pp. 63–129.

NUZZO E. (1985) 1987–1988, *Il diniego della "Sagesse": Vico e i moralisti moderni*, in "Bollettino del Centro di Studi Vichiani", 17–18, pp. 25–114.

NUZZO E. 1986, *I percorsi della "quiete". Aspetti della trattatistica politica meridionale del primo Seicento nella crisi dell' "aristotelismo politico"*, in "Bollettino del Centro di Studi Vichiani", 16, pp. 7–93.

OESTREICH G. 1969, *Geist und Gestalt des frühmodernen Staates. Ausgewählte Aufsätze*, Berlin: Duncker & Humblot.

OESTREICH, G. 1982, *Neostoicism and the Early Modem State,* ed. OESTREICH B. and KOENIGSBERGER H. G., translation by MCLINTOCK D., Cambridge-New York: Cambridge University Press.

OGG D. (1932) 1938, *Europe in the Seventeenth Century*, London: A. and Ch. Black.

ORESTANO R. (1953) 1987, *Introduzione allo studio del diritto romano*, Bologna: il Mulino.

OVEN J. C. VAN 1934–1935, *Le droit romain aux Pays-Bas*, in *Atti del Congresso internazionale di diritto romano*, Pavia: Tip. Fusi.

OVEN J.C. VAN 1954, *Hugo de Groot's "Inleiding" als Lehrbuch des römischen Rechts*, in *L'Europa e il diritto romano. Studi in memoria di P. Koschaker*, Milan: Giuffrè.

PAGANINI G. 1980, *Analisi della fede e critica della ragione nella filosofia di Pierre Bayle*, Florence: La Nuova Italia.

PAGANINI G. 2008, *Skepsis. Le débat des modernes sur le scepticisme. Montaigne-Le Vayer-Campanella-Hobbes-Descartes-Bayle*, Paris: J. Vrin.

PALAZZINI FINETTI L. 1953, *Storia della ricerca delle interpolazioni nel Corpus iuris giustinianeo*, Milan: Giuffrè.

PALLADINI F. 1988, *Volontarismo e "laicità" del diritto naturale. La critica di S. Pufendorf a Grozio. De iure belli ac pacis, Prol. 11 e I, 1, 10*, in *Reason in Law*, Proceedings of the Conference Held in Bologna (12–15 December 1984), Milan: Giuffrè.

PALLADINI F. 1990, *Samuel Pufendorf discepolo di Hobbes. Per una reinterpretazione del giusnaturalismo moderno*, Bologna: il Mulino.

PAQUOT J. N. 1768, *Mémoires pour servir a l'histoire littéraire des dix-sept provinces des Pays-Bas, de La principauté de Liège et de quelques contrées voisines*, Louvain: De l'Imprimerie Academique.

PARRHASE [LE CLERC] Th. 1701, *Parrhasiana ou Pensées diverses sur des matières de critique, d'histoire, de morale et de politique par Theodore Parrhase*, Amsterdam: chez H. Schelte.

PATIN G. 1846, *Lettres*, cit. by COHEN G. 1921, *Ecrivains français en Hollande dans la première moitié du XVIIe siècle*, The Hague-Paris: Nijhoff-Champion.

THE PEACE OF NIJMEGEN 1676–1678/9 1979, Amsterdam and Maarssen: Apa-Holland University Press.

PEIRESC N.-CL. F. DE to Barberini F., s.l., 5 Juny 1636, in *Biblioteca Inguimbertine di Carpentras*, ms. n. 1872, 1. 179, then in RIZZA C. 1965, *Peiresc e l'Italia*, Turin: Giappichelli.

PERIZONIUS J. (1683) 1740, *Oratio funebris de vita et morte Cl. Abrah. Gravii*, in PERIZONIUS J. 1740, *Orationes XII.* Varii et praestantioris argumenti in gratiam cultorum elegantiorum litterarum collectae, Lugduni Batavorum: apud J. A. Langerak.

PERIZONIUS J. to Rijckius Th., Franeker, 19 September 1684, in MEIJER Th. J. 1971, *Kritiek als herwaardering. Het levenswerk van Jacob Perizonius (1651–1715)*, Leiden: University Press.

PERIZONIUS J. 1685, *Animadversiones historicae [...]*, Amstelaedami: ex officina Henrici et Viduae Th. Boom.

PERIZONIUS J. (1689) 1746, *Oratio de origine et natura imperii, in primis regii, a libero et sui iuris populo simpliciter delati*, dicta Kalendis iuniis, MDCLXXXIX, in HUBERUS U. 1746, *Opera minora et rariora, iuris publici et privati [...]*, Traiecti ad Rhenum: sumptibus J.H. Vonk van Leyden.

PERIZONIUS J. 1690, *Cum Viro Amplissimo Ulrico Hubero Disquisitio de Praetorio. Cum alibi, tum rnaxime in Urbe Roma, eiusque Praet. Praefecto, ac vero sensu verborum Pauli, Phil. I. 13 [...]*, Franequerae: apud J. Gyselaar.

PERIZONIUS J. 1690, *Dissertatio philologica de origine*, significatione et usu vocum Praetoris et Praetorii, veroque sensu loci ad Philipp. I. 13. Defendente Joanne Sibranda Frisio, in PERIZONIUS J. 1690, *Cum Viro Amplissimo Ulrico Hubero Disquisitio de Praetorio.* Cum alibi, tum rnaxime in Urbe Roma, eiusque Praet. Praefecto, ac vero sensu verborum Pauli, Phil. I. 13 [...], Franequerae: apud J. Gyselaar.

PERIZONIUS J. 1693, *Specimen errorum supra centum et viginti ex uno et primo tomo Historiae civilis V.A. Ulr. Huberi, in usum Academicae iuventutis collectum [...]*, Franequerae: apud J. Gyselaar.

PERIZONIUS J. 1702 (1992), *Oratio de fide historiarum contra Pyrrhonismum Historicum.* Dicta postrid. Nonas Febr. M DCC II. Quum historiam quoque Foederatae Belgicae ex illustriss. curatorum et consulum decreto suscepisset profitendam. Lugduni Batavorum: apud J. Verbessel, then in Appendix to LOMONACO F., *Pirronismo e metodo storico: l'Oratio de fide historiarum di Jacobus Perizonius*, in "Rivista di Storia della Storiografia moderna", 13, pp. 103–127.

PERIZONIUS J. 1703, *Q. Curtius Rufus restitutus in integrum et vindicatus per modum speciminis a variis accusationibus et immodica atque acerba nimis crisi viri celeberrimi Johannis Clerici*, Lugduni in Batavis: H. Teering.

PERIZONIUS J. 1711, *Origines babylonicae et aegyptiacae*, Lugduni Batavorum: J. van der Linden.

PERIZONIUS J. 1740, *Orationes XII.* Varii et praestantioris argumenti in gratiam cultorum elegantiorum litterarum collectae, Lugduni Batavorum: apud J.A. Langerak.

PERIZONIUS J. 1771, *Animadversiones historicae [...]*, curavit HARLES TH. CHR., Altenburgi: ex officina Richteria.

PIANO MORTARI V. 1976, *Dogmatica e interpretazione. I giuristi medievali*, Naples: Jovene.

PIANO MORTARI V. 1977, *La formazione storica del diritto moderno francese. Dottrina e giurisprudenza del secolo XVI*, in *La formazione storica del diritto moderno in Europa*, Florence: Olschki.

PIANO MORTARI V. 1978, *Diritto logica metodo nel secolo XVI*, Naples: Jovene.

PINTARD R. (1943) 1983, *Le libertinage érudit dans la première moitié du XVIIe siècle*, Genève-Paris: Slatkine.

PIOVANI P. 1966, *Un esame di coscienza storiografica*, in PIOVANI P., *Conoscenza storica e coscienza morale*, Naples: Morano.

PIOVANI P. 1969 [1990], *Per gli studi vichiani*, in *Campanella e Vico*, ed. CASTELLI E., Rome: Archivio di Filosofia [then in PIOVANI P. 1990, *La filosofia nuova di Vico*, ed. TESSITORE F., Naples: Morano].

PIRO F. 2000, *I presupposti teologici del giusnaturalismo moderno nella percezione di Vico*, in "Bollettino del Centro di Studi Vichiani", 30, pp. 125–149.

POPKIN R.H. (1979) 2008, *The History of Scepticism from Erasmus to Spinoza*, Italian translation by RINI R., Milan: Mondadori.

POPKIN R.H. 2003, *The History of Scepticism from Savonarola to Bayle*, Oxford-New York: Oxford University Press.

PUAUX F. 1881, *Les précurseurs français de la tolérance au XVIIe siècle*, Paris: G. Fischbacher.

PUFENDORF S. (1672) 1759 [1967], *De iure naturae et gentium [...]*, recensuit et animadversionibus illustravit Gottfridus Mascovius, Francofurti et Lipsiae: ex officina Knochio-Eslingeriana [reprint Frankfurt a. M.: Minerva G.M.B.H., 1967].

PUFENDORF S. (1687) 1972, *De habitu religionis christianae ad vitam civilem, liber singularis [...]*, Bremae: apud A.G. Schvverdfegerum [repr. Stuttgart-Bad Cannstatt, F. Frommann Verlag].

PUFENDORF S. 1734, *Le droit de la nature et des gens, ou Système général des principes les plus importants de la morale, de la jurisprudence, et de la politique*, par le Baron de PUFENDORF, traduit du latin par BARBEYRAC J. […], V ed. Amsterdam: chez la veuve de Coup.

PUFENDORF S. 1735, *Les devoirs de l'homme et du citoien, tels qu'ils lui sont prescrits par la loi naturelle*, traduits du latin du Baron de PUFENDORF, par BARBEYRAC J. […], V ed. Amsterdam: chez la veuve de P. de Coup, & G. Kuyper

RANUM O. 1980, *Artisans of Glory. Writers and Historical Thought in Seventeenth-Century in France*, Chapel Hill: University of North Carolina.

REBUFFA G. 1972, *Jean Bodin e Il 'princeps legibus solutus'*, in "Materiali per una storia della cultura giuridica", 2, pp. 89–123.

RICHTER G. to Gronovius J.F., Norimberg 14 May 1642, in RICHTERIUS G. 1662, *Epistolae selectiores […]*, Norimbergae: typis et sumptibus M. Endteri.

RICUPERATI G. 1982, *Alle origini della storiografia illuministica: storia sacra e storia profana nell'età della crisi della coscienza europea*, in *Il ruolo della storia e degli storici nella civiltà*, ed. BUTTÀ G., Messina: Società degli storici italiani [Tip. La grafica].

RICUPERATI G. 1983, *Le parole di Clio e l'illuminismo. I. Linguaggio e mestiere dello storico nel primo Settecento*, in "Studi storici", 24:, pp. 7–36.

RIVET A. to Gronovius J.F., The Hague 21 April 1639, in 1984, *Johannes Fredericus Gronovius, pèlerin de la République des Lettres. Recherches sur le voyage savant an XVIIe siècle*, Genève: Droz.

ROBINSON H. 1931, *Bayle, the Sceptic*, New York: Columbia University Press.

RÖD W. 1970, *Geometrischer Geist und Naturrecht: Methodengeschichtliche Untersuchungen zur Staatsphilosophie im 17. und 18. Jahrhundert*, München: C. H. Beck.

ROTONDÒ A. (1973) 1982, *La censura ecclesiastica e la cultura*, in 1982, *Storia d'Italia*, Turin: Einaudi.

ROTONDO A. 1992, *Europe et Pays-Bas. Evolution, réélaboration et diffusion de la tolérance aux XVIIe et XVIIIe siècles. Lignes d' un programme de recherches*, Florence: Università degli Studi-Dipartimento di Storia.

ROTONDÒ A. 1998, *Stampa periodica olandese e opinione pubblica europea nel Settecento. La "Bibliothèque raisonnée" (1728–1753)*, in "Rivista Storica Italiana", 110, pp. 166–221.

ROSSI P. 1981, *Chi sono i contemporanei di Vico?*, in "Rivista di filosofia", 72, pp. 51–82.

ROSSI P. 1999, *Le sterminate antichità e nuovi saggi vichiani*, Florence: La Nuova Italia.

RUYSSCHAERT J. 1949, *Juste Lipse et les Annales de Tacite: une méthode de critique textuelle au XVIe siècle*, Louvain: Bibliothèque de l'Université.

RYCKIUS Th. 1684, *Dissertatio de primis Italiae colonis et Aeneae adventu*, in Appendix to HOLSTENIUS L. 1684, *Notae et Castigationes posthumae in Stephani Byzantini ΕΘΝΙΚΑ [...]*, Lugduni Batavorum: apud J. Hackium A. C.

SABBADINI R. 1971, *Storia e critica di testi latini*, Padova: Antenore.

SALMASIUS Cl. to Gronovius J.F., Leiden 1 July 1637, in SALMASIUS Cl. 1656, *Epistolarum*. Liber primus accurante CLEMENTIO A., Lugduni Batavorum: ex typographia A. Wyngaerden.

SANCTIUS F. 1687, *Minerva, sive de causis latinae linguae commentarius*, cui accedunt animadversiones et notae Gasperis Scioppii, et longe uberiores Jacobi Perizonii [...], Franequerae: apud L. Strickium.

SANDYS J.E. 1903–1908, *A History of Classical Scholarship*, Cambridge: University Press.

SARRAU C. to Rivet A., Paris 20 December 1641, in BOTS H. and LEROY P. 1978, *Correspondance intégrale d'André Rivet et de Claude Serrau*, Amsterdam: University Press.

SARTORI M. 1980, *Una fonte di storia imperiale: l'Historia Augusta, la storiografia cartesiana e gli illuministi*, in "Clio", 16, pp. 313–344.

SARTORI M. 1980, *L' "Incertitude" dei primi secoli di Roma ed il metodo storico nella prima metà del Settecento*, in "Clio", 18, pp. 7–35.
SASSO G. 1985, *Il "contributo" di Arnaldo Momigliano*, in SASSO G, *Il guardiano della storiografia. Profilo di Federico Chabod e altri saggi*, Naples: Guida.
SAUMASIUS Cl. to Dupuy J., Paris, 7 April 1638, Bibliothèque National de Paris, collection Dupuy, DCCCXCVIII.
SCATTOLA M. 2002–2003, *L'ordine del sapere. La bibliografia politica tedesca del Seicento*, in "Archivio della Ragion di Stato", 10–11, pp. 5–467.
SCHAMA S. (1987) 1988, *The Embarrassment of Riches*, Italian translation by SPERTI V., Milan: il Saggiatore.
SCHILLING H. 1984, *Der libertär-radikale Republikanismus der holländischen Regenten. Ein Beitrag zur Geschichte des politischen Radikalismus in der frühen Neuzeit*, in "Geschichte und Gesellschaft", 10, pp. 498–533.
SCHNUR R. (1963) 1979, *Individualismus und Absolutismus. Zur politischen Theorie von Thomas Hobbes (1600–1640)*, Italian translation by CASTRUCCI E., Milan: Giuffrè.
SCHÖFFER I. (1968) 1975, *The Batavian Myth during the Sixteenth and Seventeenth Centuries*, in *Britain and the Netherlands in Europa and Asia*, ed. BROMLEY J.S. and KOSSMANN E.H., vol. V, London: Mcmillan (also in 1987, *Veelvormig verleden. Zeventie Studies in de vaderlandse Geschiedenis*, Amsterdam: De Bataafsche Leeuw).
SCHONEVELD C.W. 1983, *Intertraffic of the Mind. Studies in Seventeenth-Century Anglo-Dutch Translation with a Checklist of Books Translated from English into Dutch, 1600–1700*, Leiden: E.J. Brill-Leiden University Press.
SCHOOCKIUS M. 1643, *Admiranda methodus novae philosophiae Renati Des Cartes [...]*, Ultraiecti: ex officina J. van Waesberge.
SCHOOCKIUS M. 1652, *De Scepticismo.* Pars prior, sive libri quatuor [...], Groningae: ex officina H. Lussinck.

SCHOOCKIUS M. 1661, *De figmento legis regiae Epistola [...]*, Groningae: typis J. Cölleni.

SCHOOCKIUS M. 1668, *Tractatus de quadruplici lege regia [...]*, Francofurti ad Oderam: impensis haeredum J. Wilhelmi.

SCHOTEL G.D.J. 1875, *De Academie te Leiden in de 16e, 17e en 18e eeuw*, Haarlem: Kruseman & Tjeenk Willink.

SCOTT J. 1994, *The Law of War: Grotius, Sidney, Locke, and the Political Theory of Rebellion*, in *The Exchange of Ideas. Religion, Scholarship and Art in Anglo-Dutch Relations in the Seventeenth Century*, eds. GROENVELD S. and WINTLE M., Zutphen: Uitgeversmaatschappij Walburg Pers.

SERRURIER C. 1930. *Descartes, Leer en Leven*, s' Gravenhage: M. Nijhoff.

SÉVE R.1989, *Leibniz et l'école moderne du droit naturel*, Paris: P.U.F.

SGARD J. 1991, *Dictionnaire des journaux (1600–1789)*, sous la direction de J. Sgard, Paris: Universitas.

SIEDSCHLAG K. 1978, *Der Einfluss der niederländisch-neustoischen Ethik in der politischen Theorie zur Zeit Sullys und Richelieus*, Berlin: Duncker & Humblot.

SIEGENBEEK M. 1829–1832, *Geschiedenis der Leidsche Hoogeschool, van hare oprigting in den jare 1575, tot het jaar 1825*, Leiden: S. en J. Luchtmans.

SIMONUTTI L. 1982, *Questioni di filosofia nel carteggio di due teologi protestanti: Jean Leclerc e Isaac Papin*, in "Annali della Scuola Normale Superiore di Pisa", 12, pp. 269–358.

SIMONUTTI L. 1984, *Arminianesimo e tolleranza nel Seicento olandese. Il carteggio Ph. van Limborch-J. Le Clerc*, Florence: Olschki.

SIMONUTTI L., 1996, *Between Political Loyalty and Religious Liberty: Political Theory and Toleration in Huguenot Thought in the Epoch of Bayle*, in "History of Political Thought", 17, pp. 523–554.

SINA M. 1978, *Vico e Le Clerc: tra filosofia e filologia*, Naples: Guida.

SINA M. 1984, *Con Jean Le Clerc alla scuola cartesiana*, in "Rivista di filosofia neoscolastica", 76, pp. 3–14.

SINA M. 1987, *Introduction* to LE CLERC J., *Epistolario*, ed. SINA M., Florence: Olschki.

SINA M. 2008, *La corrispondenza di Jean-Robert Chouet professore di filosofia a Saumur e a Ginevra.* Con documenti inediti relativi al suo insegnamento filosofico, Florence: Olschki.

SINI A. 1969, *Arminianesimo olandese e 'Jura circa Sacra'*, Padova: Cedam.

SLEE J.C. VAN 1916, *De Illustre School te Deventer, 1630–1878. Hare geschiedenis, hoogleeraren en studenten, met bijvoeging van Album studiosorum*, The Hague: Nijhoff, 121–125.

SOLARI G. (1930) 1974, *La politica religiosa di Spinoza e la sua dottrina del "ius sacrum"*, in *La filosofia politica,* ed. FIRPO L., Rome-Bari: Laterza.

SOLARI G. (1931) 1974, *Il "ius circa sacra" nell'età e nella dottrina di Ugone Grozio*, in SOLARI G. 1974, *La filosofia politica,* ed. FIRPO L., Rome-Bari: Laterza.

SMITSKAMP H. 1953, *Perizonius en de Crisis der Geschiedswetenschap in de 17e eeuw (het historisch Pyrrhonisme)*, in "Verslag van de Algemene Vergadering van het historisch Genootschap te Utrecht", 68, pp. 47–68.

SPANNEUT M. 1973, *Permanence du Stoïcisme de Zenon à Malraux*, Gembloux: J. Duculot.

SPINI G. (1950) 1983, *Ricerca dei libertini. La teoria dell'impostura delle religioni nel Seicento italiano*, Florence: La Nuova Italia.

SPINI G. et al. 1980, *Il libertinismo in Europa*, Milan-Naples: Ricciardi.

SPITZ J.F. 1995, *Locke e i monarcomachi. Problemi storiografici sul diritto di resistenza*, in "Rivista di storia della filosofia", 50, pp. 557–574.

STOLLEIS M. 1980, *Arcana Imperii und Ratio Status.* Bemerkungen zur politischen Theorie des frühen 17. Jahrhunderts, Göttingen: Vanderhoeck und Ruprecht.

STOLLEIS M. 1981, *Säkularisation und Staaträson in Deutschland um 1600*, in *Cristianesimo, secolarizzazione e diritto moderno*, ed.

LOMBARDI VALLAURI L. and DILCHER G., Baden-Baden, Milan: Nomos Verlagsgerelschaft-Giuffrè.

STOLLEIS M. (1990) 1998, *Staat und Staaträson in der frühen Neuzeit: Studien zur Geschichte des öffentlichen Rechts*, Italian translation by IOVINO S. and SCHULTZ Ch., Bologna: il Mulino.

STOLTE B. H. jr. 1981, *Henrik Brenkman (1681–1736). Jurist and Classicist. A Chapter from the History of Roman Law as Part of the Classical Tradition*, Groningen: Bouma's Boekhuis.

STONE L. (1965) 1972², *The Crisis of the Aristocracy 1558–1641*, Italian translation by SERAFINI A., Turin: Einaudi.

SUAREZ F. 1614, *Defensio fidei catholicae et apostolicae adversus anglicanae sectae errores [...]*, Coloniae Agrippinae: in officina Birckmannica, sumptibus H. Mylii.

TARANTO D. 1987, *Sullo scetticismo politico di La Mothe le Vayer*, in "Il pensiero politico", 20, pp. 179–199.

TARANTO D. 1988, *Introduction* to LA MOTHE LE VAYER F., *Petit traicté sceptique sur cette commune façon de parler. N'avoir pas le sans-commun*, Naples: Liguori.

TARANTO D. 1994, *Pirronismo ed assolutismo nella Francia del '600. Studi sul pensiero politico dello scetticismo da Montaigne a Bayle (1580–1697)*, Milan: F. Angeli.

TER MEULEN J. et al. 1950, *Bibliographie des écrits imprimés de Hugo Grotius*, The Hague: Nijhoff.

TESSITORE F. 1983, *Gli studi vichiani di Giuseppe Giarrizzo*, in "Giornale Critico della Filosofia Italiana", 62, pp. 108–117.

TESSITORE F. 1985, *Filosofia e storiografia*, Naples: Morano.

TESSITORE F. (1987) 1988, *Tra storicismi e storicità*, in 1988, *La mia prospettiva filosofica*, Padua: Gregoriana Libreria editrice.

TESSITORE F. (1996) 1997, *La questione dello storicismo, oggi* [then in vol. 1997 Soveria Mannelli, Rubbettino].

TESSITORE F. 1999, *Presentation* of GIARRIZZO G., *La scienza della storia. Interpreti e problemi,* ed. TESSITORE F., Naples: Liguori.

TESSITORE F. (1990) 2000, *Sul Vico di Santo Mazzarino*, in TESSITORE F. 2000, *Contributi alla storia e alla teoria dello storicismo*, vol. V., Rome: Edizioni di Storia e Letteratura; then also in TESSITORE F. 2003, *Mazzarino e lo storicismo degli storici*, Catania: Università degli Studi-Facoltà di Lettere e Filosofia.

THIJSSEN-SCHOUTE C. L. 1950, *Le cartésianisme aux Pays-Bas*, in *Descartes et le cartésianisme hollandais,* ed. DIJKSTERHUIS E.J., SERRURIER C., DIBON P., POS H. J., ORCIBAL J., THIJSSEN-SCHOUTE C. L., LEWIS G., Paris-Amsterdam: P.U.F.-Editions françaises d'Amsterdam.

THIJSSEN-SCHOUTE C. L. 1954, *Nederlands Cartesianisme* (avec sommaire et table des matières en français) [...], Amsterdam: N.V. Noord-Hollandsche Uitgevers Maatschappij.

THUAU É. (1966) 2000, *Raison d'Etat et pensée politique a l'époque de Richelieu*, postface de G. Mairet, Paris: A. Michel Colin.

TODESCAN F. 1983, *Le radici teologiche del giusnaturalismo laico. Il problema della secolarizzazione nel pensiero giuridico di Ugo* Grozio, Milan: Giappichelli.

TODESCAN F. 1991, *Itinerari critici dell'esperienza giuridica*, Turin: Giappichelli.

TOFFANIN G. (1933) 1954, *Storia dell'umanesimo.* III: *La fine del Logos*, Bologna: Zanichelli.

TOFFANIN G. 1972², *Machiavelli e il Tacitismo. La Politica storica al tempo della Controriforma*, Naples: Guida.

TOGNON G. 1987, *'Universalisti' e 'integrati' nella République des lettres. L'edizione critica dell'epistolario di Jean Le Clerc*, in "Giornale Critico della Filosofia Italiana", 66, pp. 586–592.

TOTARO P. 1999, *Libri e circolazione libraria nelle lettere di Antonio Magliabechi a corrispondenti olandesi*, in "Lexicon Philosophiqum", 10, pp. 173–195.

TROELTSCH E. (1923) 1960, *Die Soziallehren der christlichen Kirchen und Gruppen*, Italian translation by SANNA G., Florence: La Nuova Italia.

TURCHETTI M. 1991, *La liberté de conscience et l'autorité du magistrat au lendemain de la Révocation.* Aperçus du débat touchant la théologie morale et la philosophie politique des réformés:

Pierre Bayle, Noël Aubert de Vers, Pierre Jurieu, Jacques Philipot et Elie Saurin, in *La liberté de conscience (XVIe–XVIIe siècles)*, eds. GUGGISBERG H. R., LESTRINGANT F. and MARGOLIN J.-C., Genève: Droz.

ULVIONI P. 1975, *Stampa e censura a Venezia nel Seicento*, in "Archivio Veneto", 104, pp. 45–93.

VALLETTA N. to Magliabechi A., Naples, 26 August 1681, in 1978, *Lettere dal Regno ad Antonio Magliabechi,* ed. QUONDAM A. and RAK M., Naples: Guida.

VALLETTA N. to Magliabechi A., Naples, 28 July 1682, in 1978, *Lettere dal Regno ad Antonio Magliabechi,* ed. QUONDAM A. and RAK M., Naples: Guida.

VEEN Th. J. 1967, *Een professorenruzie in Franeker*, in "Gronings juridisch Studentenblad", I, pp. 10–19, 2–7, 9–17.

VEEN Th. J. 1973, *De beste staat: een quaestio politica bij Huber en Spinoza*, in "Bijdragen en Mededelingen betreffende de Geschiedenis der Nederlanden", 88, pp. 38–51.

VEEN Th. J. 1976, *Recht en nut. Studiën over en naar aanleiding van Ulrik Huber (1636–1694)*, Zwolle: Tjeenk Willink.

VEEN Th. J. 1982, *De legitimatie van de souvereiniteit der Staten bij Huber en Kluit*, in "Bijdragen en Mededelingen betreffende de Geschiedenis der Nederlanden", 97, pp. 185–215.

VEEN Th. J. 1984, *Ratio Status en Arcana Imperii*, in "Tijdschrift voor Rechtsgeschiedenis", 52, pp. 151–159.

VEEN Th. J. 1985, *Interpretations of Inst. 1, 2, 6, D. 1, 4, 1 and D. 1, 3, 31: Huber's Historical, Juridical and Political-Theoretical Reflections on the 'Lex Regia'*, in "Tijdschrift voor Rechtsgeschiedenis", 53, pp. 357–377.

VEEN Th. J. 1987, *Quod principi placuit, legis habet vigorem*, in *Brocardica in honorem G.C.J.J. van den Bergh.* 22 Studies over oude Rechtsspreuken onder redactie van J.E. Spruit en M. van de Vrugt, Deventer: Kluwer.

VEEN Th. J. 1989, *Review* to VAN DEN BERGH G. C. J. J. 1988, *The Life and Work of Gerard Noodt (1647–1725). Dutch Legal*

Scholarship between Humanism and Enlightenment [...], in "Rechtsgeleerd Magazijn Themis", 7, pp. 365–366.

VENEZIANI M. 1982, *Il tema del consensus gentium nei giusnaturalisti del secolo XVII*, in "Recherches sur le XVIIème siècle", 5, pp. 123–129.

VENTURI F. 1970, *Utopia e riforma nell'Illuminismo*, Turin: Einaudi.

VERBEEK Th. 1988, *La querelle d'Utrecht. René Descartes et Martin Schoock*, préface de J.-L. Marion, Paris: Les Impressions Nouvelles.

VERBEEK Th. 1992, *Descartes and the Dutch. Early Reactions to Cartesian Philosophy*, Southern Illinois U.P.: Carbondale and Edwardsville.

VICO G. (1725) [1979] 1990, *Principj di una Scienza Nuova intorno alla natura delle nazioni per la quale si ritruovano i Principj di altro sistema del diritto naturale delle genti. All'Eminentiss. Principe Lorenzo Corsini Amplissimo Cardinale dedicati*, Napoli: per Felice Mosca [repr. ed. GREGORY T. 1979, Rome: Edizioni dell'Ateneo & Bizzarri; then in VICO G. 1990, *Opere*, ed. BATTISTINI A., Milan: Mondadori].

VICO G. (1725–1728) 1990, *Vita di Giambattista Vico scritta da se medesimo*, in VICO G. 1990, *Opere*, ed. BATTISTINI A., Milan: Mondadori.

VICO G. (1730–1731) 2004, *Ragionamento primo. D'intorno alla Legge delle XII. Tavole venuta da fuori in Roma*; then in VICO G. 2004, *La Scienza Nuova 1730*, ed. CRISTOFOLINI P., with the collaboration of SANNA M., Naples: Guida.

VICO G. to Concina N., Naples, 16 September 1736, in National Library Naples, *Carte Villarosa*, XIX 42, III, 46, cc.2; then in VICO G. 1992, *Epistole con aggiunte le Epistole dei suoi corrispondenti,* ed. SANNA M., in *Opere di Giambattista Vico*, Naples: Morano.

VICO G. (1744) 1990, *Principj di Scienza Nuova di Giambattista Vico d'intorno alla comune natura delle Nazioni in questa terza Impressione dal medesimo Autore in un gran numero di luoghi corretta, schiarita, e notabilmente accresciuta*, Napoli: nella stamperia Muziana, a spese di Gaetano, e Stefano Elia; then in VICO G. 1990, *Opere*, ed. BATTISTINI A., Milan: Mondadori [repr. ed. VENEZIANI M. 1994, Florence: Olschki].

VISENTIN S. 1998, *Assolutismo e libertà. L'orizzonte repubblicano nel pensiero politico olandese del XVII secolo*, in "Filosofia politica", XII, pp. 67–85.

VLUGT W. VAN DER 1916, *Twee Nederlandsche meesters in de rechtsgeleerdheid [Huber and Noodt]*, Leiden: Brill.

VOELTZEL R. 1968, *Jean Le Clerc et la critique biblique*, in *Religion, érudition et critique à la fin du XVIIe siècle et au début du XVIIIe*, Paris: P.U.F.

VOET G. 1663–1676, *Politicae ecclesiasticae partis primae [...]*, Amstelaedami: ex officina J. a Waesberge.

WATERBOLK E. H. 1960, *Reacties op het historisch Pyrrhonisme*, in "Bijdragen voor de Geschiedenis der Nederlanden", 15, pp. 81–102.

WATSON R. A., 1966, *The Downfall of Cartesianism (1673–1712). A Study of the Epistemological Issues in the late XVIIth Century Cartesianism*, The Hague: M. Nijhoff.

WICKENDEN N. 1993, *G.J. Vossius and the Humanist Concept of History*, Assen, The Netherlands: van Gorcum.

WIJNGAARDS G.N.M. 1986, *De "Bibliothèque Choisie" van Jean Le Clerc (1657–1736). Een Amsterdams Geleerdentijdschrift uit de Jaren 1703 tot 1713,* Amsterdam & Maarssen: Apa-Holland Universiteits Pers.

WILSON Ch. 1968, *The Dutch Republic and the Civilisation of the Seventeenth Century*, Italian translation by LUPPIS L., Milan: il Saggiatore.

WISSENBACH J. J. (1633) 1642, *Emblemata Triboniani sive Leges a Triboniano interpolatae, et ad novi iuris rationem inflexae [...]*, Franequerae: typis I. Alberti, impensis J. F. Deüring.

WYDUCKEL D. 1979, *Princeps legibus solutus. Eine Untersuchung zur frühmodernen Rechts-und Staatslehre*, Berlin: Duncker & Humblot.

ZARKA Y.-Ch. 1995, *La mutazione del diritto di resistenza in Grozio e in Hobbes. Dal diritto collettivo del popolo al diritto dell'individuo*, in "Rivista di storia della filosofia", 50, pp. 543–556.

ZOLI S. 1989, *Europa libertina tra Controriforma e illuminismo. L' "O-riente" dei libertini e le origini dell'Illuminismo. Studi e ricerche*, Bologna: Cappelli.

ZURBUCHEN S. 1991, *Naturrecht und natürliche Religion. Zur Geschichte des Toleranzproblems von Samuel Pufendorf bis Jean-Jacques Rousseau*, Würzburg: Königshausen & Neumann.

ZURBUCHEN S. 1995, *Jaucourt, Republicanism, and Toleration*, in *New Essays on the Political Thought of the Huguenots of the Refuge*, ed. LAURSEN J. Ch., Leiden-New York-Köln: Brill.

Index of Names

I thank Dr. Edvige Di Ronza for the preparation of this *Index*, further proof of his intelligent and patient collaboration.

Studies in Early Modern European Culture
Studi sulla cultura europea della prima età moderna

The scholarly series *Studies in Early Modern European Culture/Studi sulla cultura europea della prima età moderna* aims at publishing scholarly works in the areas of Venetian studies, early modern and modern history, and cultural studies. The series includes monographs and interdisciplinary works in English, Italian, German, and French, as well as editions of texts and manuscripts belonging to the early modern era, ca. 1400-1800.

La collana *Studies in Early Modern European Culture/Studi sulla cultura europea della prima età moderna* comprende monografie, raccolte di saggi ed edizioni di testi nell'area degli studi veneziani e veneti, di storia delle idee della prima età moderna, e nell'area, sempre relativa alla prima età moderna, degli studi culturali. La collana pubblica testi, in particolare opere di carattere interdisciplinare, in italiano, inglese, tedesco e francese, ed edizioni di manoscritti e opere della prima età moderna, 1400-1800.

Vol. 1 Giulio Bodon
Veneranda Antiquitas. Studi sull'eredità dell'antico nella Rinascenza veneta.
359 p. 2005. ISBN 3-03910-477-2.

Vol. 2 Francesco Sberlati
Castissima donzella. Figure di donna tra letteratura e norma sociale (secoli XV-XVII). A cura di Laura Orsi.
251 p. 2007. ISBN 978-3-03910-959-3.

Vol. 3 Diego Lucci
Scripture and Deism. The Biblical Criticism of the Eighteenth-Century British Deists.
256 p. 2008. ISBN 978-3-03911-254-8

Vol. 4 Johanna Fassl
Sacred Eloquence. Giambattista Tiepolo and the Rhetoric of the Altarpiece.
391 p. 2010. ISBN 978-3-0343-0035-3

Vol. 5 Lomonaco, Fabrizio
New Studies on Lex Regia. Right, Philology and Fides Historica in Holland Between the 17th and 18th Centuries.
351 p. 2011. ISBN 978-3-0343-0543-3